TORTURE AND EUCHARIST

Theology, Politics, and the Body of Christ

William T. Cavanaugh

BLACKWELL
Publishers

First published 1998

Reprinted 2000

Blackwell Publishers Ltd
108 Cowley Road
Oxford OX4 1JF
UK

Blackwell Publishers Inc.
350 Main Street
Malden, Massachusetts 02148
USA

British Library Cataloguing in Publication Data

A CIP catalogue record for this book is available from the British Library.

Library of Congress Cataloging-in-Publication Data

Cavanaugh, William T.
Torture and the Eucharist: theology, politics, and the body of
Christ / William T. Cavanaugh.
p. cm. – (Challenges in contemporary theology)
Originally presented as the author's thesis (doctoral) – Duke University.
Includes index.
ISBN 0–631–21119–5 (hdbk: alk. paper). – ISBN 0–631–21199–3 (pbk. : alk. paper)
1. Lord's Supper–Catholic Church. 2. Torture–Religious aspects–
Christianity. 3. Persecution–History. 4. Persecution–Chile–
History–20th century. 5. Catholic Church–Chile–History–20th
century. 6. Chile–Church history–20th century. I. Title. II. Series.
BX2215.2.C38 1998
234'.163 – DC21
98–7113
CIP

Typeset in 10½ on 12½ pt Bembo by Ace Filmsetting Ltd, Frome, Somerset
Printed in Great Britain by T.J. International, Padstow, Cornwall

This book is printed on acid-free paper

For Tracy

CONTENTS

ACKNOWLEDGEMENTS

A great many great people have had a hand in making this book. I can only hope that the finished product is worthy of them.

I must give thanks first to my Chilean friends from Peñalolén and Colegio Andacollo who allowed me to share their lives and taught me much about the gospel: Manuel Pacheco and Margarita Barrientos, Hugo Alvarez and Elsa, Rosa Gutiérrez, Hugo Valdivia and Ana, Luis Flores, Felipe Vargas, Teresa Mondaca, Humberto Vilches, and many others. Their openness and generosity made me feel the reality of the Body of Christ which unites us across national boundaries. Thanks are also due to the Holy Cross priests and brothers in Chile, and my fellow Holy Cross Associates: Kevin Moser, Mary Jo Oeschlin, Sylvia Elixavide, Margy Pfiel, Anne Attea, and Corey Timpson. I would also like to express my gratitude to the late Fr. William Lewers, CSC, for hiring me upon return from Chile to work on the archives of the Vicariate of Solidarity at the University of Notre Dame Law School.

In conducting research upon my return to Chile in 1993, I incurred many debts which I am happy to acknowledge here. The following people gave their time for often lengthy interviews: Fr José Aldunate, SJ, Bishop Fernando Ariztía, Roberto Arroyo, Fr Alfonso Baeza, Fr Roberto Bolton, Bishop Carlos Camus, Fernando Castillo, Fr Sergio Concha, CSC, Bishop Sergio Contreras, Fr Fermín Donoso, CSC, Isabel Donoso, Bishop Carlos González, Bishop Tomás González, Mary Gunn, Rosa Gutiérrez, Bishop Jorge Hourton, Bishop Alejandro Jiménez, Elizabeth Lira, Fr Tony Mifsud, SJ, Archbishop Antonio Moreno, Fr Ronaldo Muñoz, SSCC, Claudio Orrego, Bishop Bernardino Piñera, Eduardo Rojas, Fr Ricardo Tong, Hugo Valdivia, and Bishop Manuel Camilo Vial. I owe a debt of gratitude to Miguel Espinosa and Norma Diaz of the Office of Communications for the Archdiocese of Santiago for very graciously assisting me in setting up interviews with members of the episcopate throughout the country. Encarnación Moll, Fr

Fermín Donoso, and Fr Andrés Guljas helped prepare my stay in Chile. Special thanks go to Br Donald Kuchenmeister and the staff and children of the Hogar Santa Cruz for taking me in for a two-month stay and making me feel at home.

This book is based on my doctoral dissertation at Duke University, completed under the direction of Stanley Hauerwas. When I was an undergraduate at Notre Dame, Stanley saved me from being a lawyer by convincing me that theology did not have to be dull. At Duke I had the advantage of his keen insights and his unfailing generosity. I have been privileged to call him not just teacher but friend (reports of his ferocity being greatly exaggerated). Others at Duke – especially Teresa Berger, Romand Coles, Thomas Spragens, Kenneth Surin, and Geoffrey Wainwright – likewise generously taught me, encouraged me, and prodded me toward greater understanding.

I have been blessed with wonderful friends and conversation partners. I owe a special debt to those who have read and commented on various chapters of this book: Fritz Bauerschmidt, Mike Baxter CSC, Dan Bell, John Berkman, Jim Buckley, David Cunningham, Michael Dauphinais, Jim Fodor, Steve Fowl, Mike Hollerich, Araminta Johnston, Greg Jones, Steve Long, Mike Naughton, Terry Nichols, and Paul Wojda. Many other colleagues at Duke and St Thomas have helped shape my thinking, especially Don Briel, Gail Hamner, David Hunter, David Oli Jenkins, Lucas LaMadrid, David McCarthy, Cory Patton, and Chris Thompson. My friendship with Rev. David Oli Jenkins and the yearly journeys we made to Honduras continue to challenge me to assess my work in light of the poor. Special thanks go to Mike Baxter and Fritz Bauerschmidt, with whom I have discussed, debated, argued, commiserated, gossiped, prayed, laughed, and "wasted" untold hours. Their friendship and faithfulness have made me both a better theologian and a better person.

Thanks is also due to an extraordinary woman I never met. Sister Gay Redmond, CSJ, was researching Chile's Sebastián Acevedo Movement for her doctoral dissertation at Drew University when she succumbed to cancer. Her congregation, the Sisters of Saint Joseph of Medaille in New Orleans, kindly lent me the material she had gathered, some of which is incorporated in chapter 6 of this book. My thanks go to Sister Janet Franklin and Sister Barbara Hughes for gathering her materials and for telling me stories of Gay Redmond, a scholar/activist of great spirit. Thanks are also due to Sister Anne Meridier. I am pleased and honored that at least some of her research will see the light of day through the present work.

My work on this project was supported by a Julian Price Graduate Research

Fellowship and a Harry Frank Guggenheim Foundation Dissertation Award. I would like to acknowledge the support provided respectively by the Joseph and Kathleen Bryan Foundation and the Harry Frank Guggenheim Foundation for these fellowships.

I would like to thank the following for permission to reproduce material used in this book: "Hope," "His Eye is on the Sparrow," from Last Waltz in Santiago by Ariel Dorfman. Copyright © 1988 by Ariel Dorfman and Edith Grossman. Used by permission of Viking Penguin, a division of Penguin Books USA Inc. Thanks also to Bob Koerpel and Mike Olson for their help on the index.

My family, especially my parents Marian and William Cavanaugh, have been a constant source of support and encouragement. Thanks, too, to my editors, Alex Wright and Lewis Ayres.

This book is dedicated to my wife Tracy Rowan. She is a constant source of love, patience, and joy. She brings home to me the original meaning of the word "Eucharist," the daily imperative to "give thanks."

INTRODUCTION

Lord, you who are everywhere,
have you been
in
Villa Grimaldi
too?

Ariel Dorfman,
"His Eye is on the Sparrow"

The most notorious of Chile's clandestine torture centers, Villa Grimaldi, was a short walk up José Arrieta Avenue from the house where I lived in Santiago. By the time I lived there in the 1980s, the buildings had been leveled and the grounds had been abandoned by the secret police. On walks up to Villa Grimaldi, friends taught me to pull a chunk of dirt out of the crumbling adobe wall surrounding the complex, a symbolic gesture of defiance. Today the grounds have been converted into a Peace Park, a monument to the unspeakable suffering inflicted there.

The park is part of the ongoing battle for the memory of the Pinochet years in Chile. For the Christian, I believe the battle comes down to the question that Ariel Dorfman asks: "Lord . . . have you been in Villa Grimaldi?"[1] Like so many brought to Villa Grimaldi, Jesus was tortured to death. *But Lord, have you been in Villa Grimaldi? How can your tortured Body be redemptive for those who suffered there?*

In attempting to answer these questions, my argument will open up into broader questions of Christian ecclesiology, theology of the political, and sacramental theology. Torture is one instance of a larger confrontation of

[1] Ariel Dorfman, "His Eye is on the Sparrow," in *Last Waltz in Santiago*, trans. Edith Grossman (New York: Viking Press, 1988), 11.

powers over bodies, not just individual bodies but social bodies as well. I argue that a Christian practice of the political is embodied in the Eucharist, the remembering of Jesus' own torture at the hands of the powers of this world. The Eucharist is the church's response to torture, and the hope for Christian resistance to the violent disciplines of the world.

This study focuses on the experience of Chile, and the Catholic church there, before and during the military dictatorship of General Augusto Pinochet Ugarte, 1973-90. I present torture in the Pinochet regime as a social strategy, the effect of which is to discipline the citizenry into a complex performance scripted by the state. That performance atomizes the citizenry through fear, thereby dismantling other *social* bodies which would rival the state's authority over *individual* bodies. I describe this not only as the violation of individual rights but as the very creation of individuals. Unfortunately, the ecclesiology of the Catholic church in Chile initially debilitated the church's ability to resist the regime's strategy. In a well-intentioned effort to extricate itself from coercive politics, the church had embraced "social Catholicism," an attempt to confine the church's activities to a putative "social" sphere while vacating the "political" sphere. This attempt to stake a position as the "soul" of civil society amounted to a handing over of bodies to the state. Under the regime, nevertheless, parts of the church were able to break out of this ecclesiological bind and draw on the resources of the Eucharist to resist the regime. I present these practices as embedded in Christian sacramental theology, especially the theology of the body of Christ.

By way of introduction, I will situate this argument within three wider discussions in the English-speaking world in the fields of (1) social ethics and human rights, (2) ecclesiology and the state, and (3) sacramental theology and ethics. I will not attempt to survey the vast literature in each of these areas, but will try instead to characterize in general terms the problematics that this book seeks to address.

1 Social Ethics and Human Rights

Much of what is written from an ethical point of view about torture can be summed up in the sentence "Torture is very bad." What more can an ethicist say about torture than to denounce it as a grave moral evil and demand that it stop? It is generally considered helpful to declare that a person should not be tortured because each person has a *right* not to be tortured. Each person, for example, has a right to "personal integrity" because each person is a child of God, made in God's image. Or perhaps, if mention of God is not sufficiently universal, a Christian theorist – without abandoning her own convictions about God – will seek a more general essence of human nature upon which all humans *qua* humans can agree in prohibiting its violation. Whether or not rights are grounded in universal rationality or are more culturally specific, torture is usually treated as a violation of individual integrity, and the prevention of torture tends to rely on the proper formulation of *why* exactly torture is wrong, so as to convince potential torturers that they ought not do it.

Rights language is notoriously malleable and may be useful under some circumstances; for an indigenous Chilean woman to learn that she has an inherent dignity and an inherent "right" not to be treated as a beast of burden by the *patrón* may be a moment of revelation for her. To tell her that she has a "right" not to be tortured, however, is likely to add little to her realization that the torture she has suffered at the hands of the secret police is gravely wrong. More to the point, the secret police are unlikely to respond to the language of human rights, since they do not think of a Mapuche woman as "human" in the same way that they are.

Beyond the question of whether or not universal human rights exist as such, I argue that what accounts for the failure of human rights language to stop acts of torture is a misunderstanding of the nature of torture as primarily an attack on individual bodies. While certainly individual bodies suffer grievously, the state's primary targets in using torture are social bodies. Torture is not merely an attack on, but the creation of, individuals. In this aspect, torture is homologous with the modern state's project of usurping powers and respon-sibilities which formerly resided in the diffuse local bodies of medieval society and establishing a direct relationship between the state and the individual. The realization of a single, unquestioned political center was intended to make equivalent each individual before the law, thereby freeing the individual from the claims of any social group inferior to the state. As Robert Nisbet sums up this process, "The real conflict in modern political history has not been, as is so often stated, between State and individual, but between State and social group."[2] In medieval society, the notion of right was embedded in an overlapping network of privileges and duties corresponding to social groups. In modernity, however, "it was the sheer impact of State upon medieval custom and tradition, with the consequent atomizing and liberating effects, that, more than anything else, precipitated the modern concern with positive individual rights."[3]

---

[2] Robert Nisbet, *The Quest for Community* (Oxford: Oxford University Press, 1953), 109.
[3] Ibid., 107.

One of the reasons that rights language can be ineffectual, therefore, is that it is founded in the same atomization of the body politic from which the state derives its power. Rights as they have developed in the West transfer power from particular social groups to the universal state and build a protective wall around the individual. Torture aims likewise at the destruction of social bodies and the construction of walls around the individual – though the walls have ceased to be protective. This is not to imply that rights are somehow equivalent to torture, only that rights are little help in resisting the individualizing pathology of state terror. By absorbing powers from local bodies, the state is left as the *de jure* and *de facto* guarantor of rights. As in the case of Chile, denunciations of torture and abuses of rights are channelled into the very state that is responsible for the torture. But if this is the case, then true resistance to torture depends on the reappearance of social bodies capable of countering the atomizing performance of the state. In the context of Pinochet's Chile, I examine the theology and practice of the church's eventual reappearance as the body of Christ in opposition to the social strategy of torture.

2 Ecclesiology and the State

In the chapters that follow I criticize the key modern distinction between the political and the social, or the state and civil society. I explore this distinction in the case of Chile under the influence of Pius XI and Jacques Maritain, but the distinction is one of great importance in much of Western thinking on the relation of religion and politics. The first related assumption – with which I wholeheartedly concur – is that the removal of the church from the taint of coercive power is a positive development. The second is more problematic; it assumes that the sovereign state's monopoly on coercive power promotes peace as a proper consequence of the separation of two essences that had become confused – religion and politics. Religion, in this conception, is not necessarily privatized, hidden from the public view, but the church takes its rightful place in civil society, and occupies itself directly with the social, and only indirectly with the political, which pertains to the state.

The genealogy of these and corollary distinctions often begins with the so-called "Wars of Religion" in the Western Europe of the sixteenth and seventeenth centuries. As the story is told, the separation of religion and politics was necessitated by the violence between Catholics and Protestants following the Reformation. Religious passion and coercive power is a dangerous mixture. Their differentiation with the creation of the modern state would be the only way to secure peace.

I argue in greater detail elsewhere that this tale is historically and theologically false.[4] Protestants and Catholics often fought on the same sides of the battles, for what was at stake in these wars was not mere doctrinal zealotry but the dominance of the rapidly centralizing sovereign state over the local privileges and customs of the decaying medieval order. In other words, the wars were the effect of the rise of the centralized modern state and its need to create an autonomous political sphere from which would be excluded its greatest rival, the church. To call these "wars of religion" is anachronistic, for what was at stake in these wars was the very creation of "religion" as a universal impulse essentially separate from an activity called "politics." The resulting appearance of the plural "religions" is said to make the secular state necessary, but in fact there is nothing inherently violent in religious pluralism and theological politics *unless* one assumes that politics means the totalizing practice of the state.

The distinction between politics and religion was not discovered but invented. Before the seventeenth century, politics was associated with the commonweal in a broad sense, a political and moral order which included what we would call state and society. The distinction of ecclesial and civil powers in the medieval period was a distinction not of spatial jurisdictions, nor of means, but of ends; the temporal power served the temporary ends of the *civitas terrena*, which was passing away. "It was only in the seventeenth century that politics was first linked to the idea of an abstract, impersonal, sovereign state distinct from other parts of society (church, economy, civil associations)."[5] The modern state, in Weber's famous diagnosis, is defined not in terms of its ends — for it has no ostensible ends, other than its own self-preservation — but by its means, which is coercion. A state, according to Weber, "is a human community that (successfully) claims the *monopoly of the legitimate use of physical force* within a given territory."[6] Of course, what makes violence "legitimate" is simply its sanction by the state.

The state's monopoly on legitimate violence is meant to produce peace by resolving the conflicts in what has become known as "civil society," that is,

[4] William T. Cavanaugh, " 'A Fire Strong Enough to Consume the House': The Wars of Religion and the Rise of the State," *Modern Theology* 11:4 (Oct. 1995), 397–420.

[5] Bob Jessop, *State Theory: Putting Capitalist States in their Place* (University Park, Pa.: The Pennsylvania State University Press, 1990), 350.

[6] Max Weber, "Politics as a Vocation," in *From Max Weber: Essays in Sociology*, trans. and ed. H. H. Gerth and C. Wright Mills (New York: Oxford University Press, 1946), 78.

the social organizations which stand "outside" the state by virtue of their lack of access to the means of coercion. Even those who are keen to limit the state's power still rely on the myth of the state as peacemaker, as the place where the conflicts of civil society are taken up and resolved. Civil society, after all, is said to be necessarily a place of conflict, between workers and managers, retirees and taxpayers, members of one religion and members of another. It is the state's responsibility to oversee and absorb these conflicts through its political mechanisms. Many variations on the concept of social contract exist, but all agree that peace depends at the very minimum on individuals surrendering the right to use violence to the state, the impersonal center of sovereignty. Peace, therefore, depends on the differentiation of the universal state from all particular associations beneath the state, and the limiting of the power of coercion to the state. This differentiation is usually depicted in spatial terms; religion especially must be "removed" from the "sphere" of the state in order to assure peace.

From Hegel comes the first important theoretical elaboration of the relationship of civil society to the state. In Hegel's thought the contrast between civil society and the state of nature found in early modern thinkers such as Hobbes and Rousseau is superseded by a three-phase conception of natural–civil–political.[7] The three phases follow a progressive integration, from the unorganized natural realm of self-interested need to the universalizing project of the state. Between the natural and the political, we pass through the educative project of civil society, composed of "corporations" or associations intermediary between the individual and the state. Civil society remains a realm of "unorganized atoms,"[8] however, because each association is only composed of like-minded individuals set to pursue the self-interest of the group. Civil society is especially the realm of labor, which must be tamed and subsumed to the universal interest through the pedagogy of the state, which is the "actuality of the ethical Idea."[9] As such, the state does not simply coordinate the natural and the civil, but reveals itself as the "true ground" of those phases. Thus, "that show of mediation is now cancelled and the state has become directly present before us. Actually, therefore, the state as such is not

---

[7] G.W.F. Hegel, *The Philosophy of Right*, trans. T.M. Knox (Oxford: Clarendon Press, 1952), §256, 154–5. Much of my discussion of Hegel is informed by Michael Hardt, "The Withering of Civil Society," *Social Text* 45, 14:4 (Winter 1995), 27–34. See also Michael Hardt and Antonio Negri, *Labor of Dionysius: A Critique of the State-Form* (Minneapolis: University of Minnesota Press, 1994), 257–61.

[8] Hegel, *Philosophy of Right*, §255, 154.

[9] Ibid., §257, 155.

so much the result as the beginning."[10] The relationship between the individual and the state is in fact unmediated, and the person only gains "objectivity, genuine individuality, and an ethical life" as a member of the state.[11]

Much of contemporary Christian thinking on church and state is intent on limiting the power of the state, but in fact adopts Hegel's soteriology of the state as peacemaker for the conflicts inherent in civil society. However, rather than acknowledge the subsumption of civil society into the state, most contemporary Christian thought seeks to limit the state by maintaining a sharp theoretical distinction of state and civil society, making civil society the origin and ground of the state.

An influential example of such an inversion of Hegel among Christian theorists of religion and politics is John Courtney Murray, to whom most Catholic "public theologians" continue to bow. For Murray, maintaining the division between state and civil society is absolutely central to a democratic and Christian view of politics; the alternative is espousal of a totalitarian government.[12] Murray believes that the virtue of the American constitutional tradition is its limiting of the state to just one functional part of the society as a whole, specifically that part which attends to public order, not the entirety of the common good. Included in public order are three goods: public peace ("the highest political good"), public morality (as determined by common consensus), and justice. "These functions are defined by constitutional law, in accord with the consent of the people. In general, 'society' signifies an area of freedom, personal and corporate, whereas 'state' signifies the area in which the public powers may legitimately apply their coercive powers."[13] Rather than see the state as the realm of freedom, as does Hegel, Murray sees the state as the strictly limited realm of coercion. Notice that Murray's theory of the small state pares the state down to its *essence*, which is coercion. But this coercion is exercised above all in the name of public peace. The first two articles of the First Amendment are therefore "articles of peace"[14] which perform the state's

---

[10] Ibid., §256, 155.

[11] Ibid., §257, 156.

[12] John Courtney Murray, SJ, "The Problem of Religious Freedom," in *Religious Liberty: Catholic Struggles with Pluralism*, ed. J. Leon Hooper, SJ (Louisville: Westminster/John Knox Press, 1993), 145.

[13] Ibid., 144-5.

[14] John Courtney Murray, SJ, "Civil Unity and Religious Integrity: The Articles of Peace," in *We Hold These Truths: Catholic Reflections on the American Proposition* (Kansas City: Sheed and Ward, 1960), 45–78.

role of subsumption of conflict by excluding religious difference from the political sphere.

In theory Murray refused the privatization of religion by limiting the state and assigning religion to the public role in civil society of shaping common discourse. The constitutional ordering is silent about God, thus promoting peace among adherents of different beliefs and nonbeliefs. Under this arrangement, however, silence about God assumes an official public status. To break the silence is to deviate from it, and so to act in the capacity of private citizen.[15] In the same vein, a contemporary Murrayite such as Richard John Neuhaus wants the church to play a public role, but insists it cannot do so on the basis of doctrine or revelatory claims, which he *defines* as "essentially private."[16]

From the Protestant side, Reinhold Niebuhr has been extremely influential on the agenda of English-speaking theologians in their reflections on state and society. The social as the realm of conflict is one of Niebuhr's most persistent themes. The democratic state is the best possible form of governance in a fallen world not because it achieves the good (which is impossible short of the eschaton) but because it achieves the best approximation of peace and justice as a balance among the conflicting self-interests of civil society.[17] Because the social is the realm of conflict and compromise, the purity of the Gospel must remain a possibility only for the individual. The Gospel is allowed an inchoate motivational influence on history through the actions of private individuals; the church is a collection of such individuals, and not in any sense a communal enactment of an alternative "politics" within history.[18]

One of the purposes of this book is to call into question the church's acquiescence in this imagination of a prior conflict from which the state saves us. Chile under Pinochet is obviously an extreme case of this imagination in practice, but I would ask the reader simply to note the common appearance of this imagination in many different modern construals of the relationship of church and state. My suspicion is that the establishment of a political realm

---

[15] David Schindler makes this point in his "Religious Freedom, Truth, and Anglo-American Liberalism: Another Look at John Courtney Murray," in *Heart of the World, Center of the Church: Communio Ecclesiology, Liberalism, and Liberation* (Grand Rapids, Mich.: Wm. B. Eerdmans, 1996), 68-9.

[16] Richard John Neuhaus, *The Naked Public Square* (Grand Rapids, Mich.: Wm. B. Eerdmans, 1984), 36.

[17] This thesis is put forward in Niebuhr's classic *The Children of Light and the Children of Darkness* (New York: Charles Scribner's Sons, 1944).

[18] Reinhold Niebuhr, *An Interpretation of Christian Ethics* (New York: Seabury Press, 1979), 62–136.

which fundamentally excludes the body of Christ as a body does not so much *solve* conflict as *enact* it. The rise of the modern centralized state is predicated, as we have seen above, on the transfer of authority from particular associations to the state, and the establishment of a direct relationship between the state and the individual. We encounter one another in the center, where politics is defined as the realm of coercion, and we are taught in practice to deal with one another through the mechanism of contract. Despite good intentions to limit the state in theory, in fact state and society are inseparable, and the state becomes pedagogue once it is given a monopoly on coercive power. Hegel was closer to the truth descriptively when he acknowledged that the state is at the origin of civil society, and not vice-versa.

As some contemporary state theory has emphasized,[19] it is not necessary to imagine the state as a conscious entity directing some grand conspiracy; state and society are rather two moments of a wider imagination of how bodies are organized. In modernity, we have been scripted into a drama in which state coercion is seen as necessary to subdue a prior violence already inherent internally in civil society and externally in the form of other nation-states. Given that the state arises in conjunction with the atomization of civil society and the creation of national borders, however, it can be said that the state defends us from threats which it itself creates.[20] The church buys into this performance by acknowledging the state's monopoly on coercion, handing over the bodies of Christians to the armed forces, and agreeing to stay out of the fabricated realm of the "political." Acquiescence to this drama saps the church's ability to resist where and when states become violent.

This drama has affinities with the social practice that St Augustine critiques in *The City of God*, critiques which have been taken up recently by Rowan Williams, John Milbank, and others in an effort to provide a Christian reimagining of the political.[21] Augustine sees that the *Pax Romana* is based on the myth of violent conquest of a prior disorder. Virtue, for the Romans, is

---

[19] E.g. Hardt, "The Withering of Civil Society," 34–40; Kenneth Surin, "Marxism(s) and 'The Withering Away of the State,' " *Social Text* no. 27 (1990), 42–6; Jessop, *State Theory*, 278–306; and Antonio Negri, *The Politics of Subversion: A Manifesto for the Twenty-First Century* (Cambridge: Polity Press, 1989), 169–99.

[20] See Charles Tilly, "War Making and State Making as Organized Crime," in *Bringing the State Back In*, ed. Peter B. Evans, Dietrich Rueschemeyer, and Theda Skocpol (Cambridge: Cambridge University Press, 1985), 169–91.

[21] Rowan Williams, "Politics and the Soul: A Reading of the City of God," *Milltown Studies*, no. 19/20: 55–72; and John Milbank, *Theology and Social Theory* (Oxford: Basil Blackwell, 1990), 380–438.

always won through the defeat of something else.[22] The highest civic virtue is the desire for glory, the *libido dominandi*, by which other lusts are controlled. Glory, however, is by its nature individualizing, since it is won in competition with others. The secular order is atomistic in its foundations, because it excludes true worship of God from the political, and replaces it with the worship of the false gods of self-interest and *dominium*, which become ends in themselves.[23] In such an atomized polity, social integration and peace is secured by the conquest of enemies. The domination of some classes of society over others is assumed, and the worst effects of such conflict are merely stayed by the state's pursuit of violent conquest over external enemies in war. According to Augustine, the second Punic War temporarily held back the internal conflict and oppression endemic in Roman society in the third century BC.[24] After the destruction of Carthage in 146 BC, however, the "wholesome fear" that Scipio had seen as a "fit guardian for the citizens" was eliminated, and the citizens of Rome once again turned on each other.[25]

What Augustine helps us to do is to question the modern distinction of religion and politics which has sapped the church's ability to resist the violence of states. The church is certainly *not* called to reimplicate itself in the use of coercive power – to move from "civil society" to "state" – but rather to call those very distinctions into question as fraudulent inventions. As Williams puts it, Augustine "is engaged in a *redefinition* of the public itself, designed to show that it is life outside the Christian community which fails to be truly public, authentically political."[26] Of course, what is "outside" the Christian community can only become fully apparent eschatologically. But what is crucial for a true politics, Augustine argues, is that a commonwealth must be based on justice, and justice depends on giving each his or her due, but this is impossible where God is not given God's due in sacrifice. A true social order is based on sacrifice to God, for only when God is loved can there be love of

---

[22] St Augustine, *The City of God*, trans. Marcus Dods (New York: Modern Library, 1950), 452-6 [XIV. 9]; Milbank, *Theology and Social Theory*, 390–1.

[23] Augustine, *The City of God*, 698-701 [XIX. 20-2]; Williams, "Politics and the Soul," 58–62. See XIV. 28: "Two cities have been formed by two loves: the earthly by the love of self, even to the contempt of God; the heavenly by the love of God, even to the contempt of self . . . In the one, the princes and the nations it subdues are ruled by the love of ruling; in the other, the princes and the subjects serve one another in love, the latter obeying, while the former take thought for all."

[24] Augustine, *The City of God*, 162 [V. 12].

[25] Ibid., 35 [I. 30].

[26] Williams, "Politics and the Soul," 58, italics in original.

others, and the common acknowledgement of right.[27] The true story of the world as revealed in the Scriptures is not one of the restraint of a primordial violence, but of a peaceful creation fallen and restored in Christ's self-sacrifice. A true social order is based not on defeat of enemies but on identification with victims through participation in Christ's reconciling sacrifice. According to Augustine, then, the true sacrifice on which a true politics is based is the Eucharist:

> This is the sacrifice of Christians: we, being many, are one body in Christ. And this also is the sacrifice which the Church continually celebrates in the sacrament of the altar, known to the faithful, in which she teaches that she herself is offered in the offering she makes to God.[28]

3 Sacramental Theology and Ethics

The conjunction of Eucharist and politics might indicate that this book is an exercise in "liturgy and ethics" or "sacramental theology and ethics." I want to resist those categories insofar as they indicate the joining of two fields which are essentially distinct. Attempts to relate liturgy and politics, or some similar combination, are often admirable but fail to overcome the kind of dichotomies they seek to bridge.

A fatal flaw in many such attempts is to see sacrament as a sign or symbol of something in the "real world." For example, the introduction to the *Concilium* volume on *Politics and Liturgy* sets up the problem in this way: "Since politics is the control of power in society, the ways in which liturgy uses symbols of power has much to say in forming images and concepts of power which Christian peoples bring to bear on political questions."[29] Liturgical symbols give Christians new ways to imagine power, and perhaps motivate them to commit to making the world a better place. Nevertheless, the problem with this view is that to enter the political is to leave the liturgical.

When the liturgy must be "applied" or "made relevant" to the political, the fundamental modern separation of religion and politics remains intact. Theme liturgies – world hunger, the war in Bosnia – are necessary to rescue the Eucharist from practical irrelevance. Issues and principles applicable to political

---

[27] Augustine, *The City of God*, 699–706 [XIX. 21–3].
[28] Ibid., 310 [X. 6]; also 705–6 [XIX. 23].
[29] David Power and Herman Schmidt, "Editorial," in *Politics and Liturgy*, ed. Herman Schmidt and David Power (New York: Herder and Herder, 1974), 9.

action are symbolized in the liturgy in the hope that Christians will read their meanings and internalize them, then return to the political processes of the world and apply those meanings "out there" with renewed conviction. Unfortunately, this gnostic internalization of the Eucharist as "meaning" misses what is essential to the Eucharist as *liturgy*. As Orthodox theologian Alexander Schmemann writes, the original sense of *leitourgia* was "an action by which a group of people become something corporately which they had not been as a mere collection of individuals."[30] The emphasis here is on the *externality* of the liturgy to individual bodies, the way it incorporates individuals into the body of Christ. But to participate in a communal and public discipline of bodies is already to be engaged in a direct confrontation with the politics of the world.

For this reason I argue conversely that torture is a kind of perverted liturgy, a ritual act which organizes bodies in the society into a collective performance, not of true community, but of an atomized aggregate of mutually suspicious individuals. Just as liturgy is not a merely "spiritual" formation which then must be applied to the physical world, torture is not a merely physical assault on bodies but a formation of a social imagination. To speak of the imagination does not imply unreal fantasy. As I use the term, the "social imagination" of a group is that vision which organizes the members into a set of coherent performances, and which is constantly reconstructed by those performances.

Blurring the lines between liturgy and politics can take two forms, one helpful and one detrimental. Some brief comments on the detrimental form will help me be clear about what I am *not* saying. Columbian theologian Rafael Avila's book *Worship and Politics* schematizes the relationship of liturgy to the world this way:

If . . .	Church	=	Sign
	World (or History)		Content
Then . . .	Latin American Eucharist	=	Sign
	Latin American History		Content[31]

Many Latin American theologians have taken the Vatican II statements on grace to indicate the breakdown of barriers between the sacred and the secular.

---

[30] Alexander Schmemann, *For the Life of the World* (Crestwood, NY: St Vladimir's Seminary Press, 1988), 25.

[31] Rafael Avila, *Worship and Politics*, trans. Alan Neely (Maryknoll, NY: Orbis Books, 1981), 87.

All the world is "graced," and therefore the content of the Christian witness can be located by sustained social scientific analysis of temporal processes. The church is not a separate sanctuary, but is part and parcel of the politics and economics of the world. Every Eucharist is therefore a sign which points to the political process, which is autonomous from the church, yet imbued, as all the world, with God's presence.

However, if the Eucharist is only a sign and has no content of its own, then the divide between liturgy and politics is only exacerbated. The Eucharist can embody no "politics" of its own but can only point to something other, and other signs might do the pointing just as well. In Leonardo Boff's book on the sacraments, one finds chapters entitled "Our Family Mug as Sacrament" and "My Father's Cigarette Butt as Sacrament."[32] Although Boff considers the Eucharist to be one of the "special" sacraments, he contends that anything on earth can be a sacrament for a particular individual, provided she look through the object itself and see the presence of God. God is always present in everything, he argues, but the person of faith must learn to read the deeper meaning behind the signs. This attempt to re-enchant the secular world, however, only leaves the world more bereft of God. If God always stands "behind" signs, then signs become interchangeable, and God never truly saturates any particular sign. This approach easily flip-flops into the modern post-Kantian suspicion of all representation as unable to reveal the transcendent.

Of course, it is entirely true to see creation as an epiphany of God, for all creation is renewed and fulfilled in Christ. Nevertheless, it is this world (that part of creation in rebellion against God) which rejected Christ and put him to death, and this world which is consequently passing away. In the Eucharist we commemorate not only the incarnation but its completion in the death and resurrection of Christ. In the Eucharist, as I show in chapters five and six, we are lifted up from this world and are given a foretaste of the heavenly Kingdom. As Schmemann says, though, "this is not an 'other' world, different from the one God has created and given to us. It is our same world, *already* perfected in Christ, but *not yet* in us."[33] A Eucharistic counter-politics is not otherworldly or "sectarian" – it cannot help but be deeply involved in the sufferings of this world – but it is in sharp discontinuity with the politics of the

---

[32] Leonardo Boff, *Sacraments of Life, Life of the Sacraments*, trans. John Drury (Washington: The Pastoral Press, 1987). Boff reports with no apparent irony that the sacramental cigarette in question was the last one (of many) his father smoked before dying of a coronary thrombosis; ibid., 16, 19.

[33] Schmemann, *For the Life of the World*, 42. See also 119–26.

world which killed its savior. The point is not to politicize the Eucharist, but to "Eucharistize" the world.

The Eucharist is not a mere sign which points to some more concrete political reality. Christ's Eucharistic body is both *res et sacramentum*, sign and reality. Christ does not lie behind the Eucharistic sign but saturates it. Christians do not simply read the sign but perform it. We become Christ's body in the Eucharist. The Eucharist is the true "politics," as Augustine saw, because it is the public performance of the true eschatological City of God in the midst of another City which is passing away.

In this book I try to display a kind of Eucharistic counter-politics which forms the church into a body capable of resisting oppression. This type of ecclesial performance by no means assumes a heroic or perfectionist ethic; the church is always constituted by foolish and sinful people. As I will show in the final chapter, the body of Christ is enacted in both grand and mundane gestures, some as prosaic as peeling potatoes for a soup kitchen. My analysis of the church is also far from a nostalgia for Constantinianism, some absurd clarion call for the church to take up the sword once again. This analysis is tendered in the hope that the church might offer to the world an alternative to violence, to remember the victims and transform some into martyrs. By narrating the experience of the church in Chile, I wish to suggest ways that the church at large – Orthodox, Protestant, and Catholic – can unimagine the inevitability of violent disciplines, not for the church's own sake, but for the sake of all who suffer violence.

Although the implications of this analysis are of general interest, focusing on Pinochet's Chile will allow us to see, lived out, a particular example of the conflict of church and state, without having to rely simply on broad generalizations about "the state" as such. This book concentrates on one type of modern state power – the Latin American model of militarized bureaucratic authoritarianism in the 1970s and 1980s – and the church's ability and inability to resist that power. The danger in this approach is the temptation to dismiss any attempt at generalization, any analogy with other places and times. Chile in the 1970s and 1980s is sufficiently exotic to North Atlantic readers that moral indignation can easily give way to thanks that it does not happen here. However, while it is problematic to make generalizations about all modern states, it would be equally unhelpful to confine this analysis of state pathologies to Pinochet's Chile alone. Amnesty International estimates that half of the world's countries torture today, and – as Pentagon admissions of its use of torture manuals at the Army School of the Americas attest – the practice is not limited to the "less advanced" nation-states of the Third World.[34] Moreover, even where torture is absent the power of modern states is often predicated on the same control of bodies and individualization of the citizenry at which torture aims. Although it is beyond the scope of this book to explore the atomizing pathologies of all the different types of modern states, I will not discourage the reader from drawing analogies from Pinochet's Chile to other contexts where such analogies are warranted.

This book has two basic movements, scattering and gathering. I display how torture was used as a social discipline to atomize and scatter all social bodies which stand between the individual and the state. I then show how the church attempted to resist this strategy by gathering a body capable of opposing the military regime. The primary context for my discussion of the church is the Catholic church in Chile, but the more general referent of the term "church" as such is the one Christian church of the one Christ into which all Christians – Catholic, Orthodox, and Protestant – are baptized. My argument will have greater resonance perhaps in communions more explicitly oriented toward the liturgy, but I would assume that the issues outlined above would be of general concern to all Christians.

This book is divided into six chapters. In the first chapter, I display torture as an attempt to "disappear" the church and other bodies which would rival the state. Through an examination of the effects of torture on individual bodies and social bodies, I show how torture works to discipline an entire society into an aggregate of fearful and mutually distrustful individuals. From the church's point of view, I narrate this as an attempt not merely to attack the church but to render it invisible. It does so by making bodies disappear and by torturing without leaving any visible effect on the bodies of its victims. The

[34] Legal scholar Edward Peters traces the direct correlation between the spread of torture and the tremendous growth of state power in the nineteenth and twentieth centuries; Edward Peters, *Torture* (New York: Basil Blackwell, 1985), 103–40. This correlation suggests – and the practices of France in Algeria, England in Northern Ireland, and the United States in Latin America affirm – that torture is not alien to the pathology of the modern liberal state. Peters writes "The discovery of Algeria completed a lesson that finally had to be learned by the world of the late twentieth century: torture had not died with the Enlightenment legislative and judicial reforms and their optimistic view of human nature. Nor was it exclusively the eccentric practice of deranged and psychotic governments. It was no longer likely to turn up only in the fragile circumstances of Marxist revolutions, and it was not an importation from barbarous non-European peoples. It was practiced by Europeans upon Europeans and non-Europeans alike, in spite of legislation forbidding it and reformers intent on exposing it"; ibid., 140.

torture project learned how to attack the church without creating martyrs, who are the seed of future resistance, and who make the church visible as the body of Christ. Therefore I conclude this chapter with a discussion of the significance of martyrs and martyrs' bodies for the visibility of the church.

The second chapter undertakes a brief narration of the Catholic church's experience under the Pinochet regime. Based on my own interviews with bishops, residents of slums, and others, I show that, although the Chilean bishops have a not undeserved reputation for standing up to the regime, they only began to do so after the initial years of the regime – the years of the worst violence – had passed. I argue that this was the result of the need to unlearn an inherited ecclesiology which viewed church and state as the twin trustees of the Chilean nation. Official ecclesiology operated within the imagination of the nation-state, such that "Chile" was the main reference of the bishops' discourse. It was assumed that Chile was an organic whole; the state was responsible for Chilean bodies, the church for Chilean souls. The church, in other words, had already handed the bodies of its members over to the state. When the state began to torture those bodies, the church was at a loss, having already for so long neglected its true ecclesial character, construing itself more as "soul of society" than as the true body of Christ. In chapter 2 I also show how the church hierarchy gradually began to unlearn this ecclesiology and to begin to reconstitute the church as body.

The theoretical elaboration of the Chilean bishops' inherited ecclesiology is the subject of chapters 3 and 4. I trace its sources to Catholic Action, Jacques Maritain, and the general attempt of the Catholic church since Pope Pius XI to abandon "political" space in favor of a "social" presence. By a close examination of Catholic Action, Jacques Maritain, and their influence in Chile, I show how this "social Catholicism" in fact resulted in the church's abandonment of social space to the state. The church construed itself not as a real body but as a "mystical body," hovering over the divisions of the "temporal plane," uniting all in soul, if not in body. The church was therefore initially ill-equipped to counter the military regime's strategy of disappearance and isolation, since the church had effectively already "disappeared" itself through its own ecclesiological practice.

In the fifth chapter, I undertake the search for the church as the true body of Christ capable of enacting a counter-practice to that of the state. I begin by providing a genealogy of the designation of the church as mystical body, *corpus mysticum*, as opposed to the true body of Christ, *corpus verum*. Next I show how the resources for the church's enacting the true body of Christ, and thus for resisting the social strategy of torture, are found in the Eucharist, the "imagination of the church." Finally, in the sixth chapter, I narrate three practices of the church in Chile which illustrate what a true Eucharistic ecclesiology would look like: excommunication of torturers, the Vicariate of Solidarity, and the Sebastián Acevedo Movement against Torture. These practices gather the church into the true body of Christ, and thus constitute the scripting of bodies into an economy of pain and the body which stands directly counter to that of torture.

"Body" is a crucial image for the purposes of this book, for several reasons: bodies are the obvious object of torture, "body" is a crucial metaphor for political and social analysis, and most importantly the body of Christ is central to Christian theology of the Eucharist and the church. The contest I will describe in these pages is over bodies, both individual and communal. As anthropologist Mary Douglas points out, these two types of bodies are in constant interaction in any society. "The social body constrains the way the physical body is perceived. The physical experience of the body, always modified by the social categories through which it is known, sustains a particular view of society. There is a continual exchange of meanings between the two kinds of bodily experience so that each reinforces the categories of the other."[35] For my purposes in this book, the generic term "body" will refer to these two terms, used in the following ways. First, there are individual, physical human bodies, which are never "just physical," but are always already invested in certain social performances or practices. Second, there are social bodies, which are more than just groups of individual bodies; rather, they are "bodies" in the sense that they – like individual human bodies – involve the coordination of many different members into certain coherent shared activities or performances. In other words, the investing of individual bodies into certain public and visible performances constitutes what Douglas calls a social body. The church is "social" in this sense, as opposed to individual (yet, as the body of Christ, is a social body *sui generis*). The church, I argue, is *not* called to be "social" as opposed to "political."

Finding the proper voice for this narrative has not been an easy task. I deal with the experience of the church in Chile, but I am not Chilean. I lived in a poor area of Santiago and worked with a cooperative building project there for slightly over two years during the Pinochet dictatorship. I can hardly claim, on the basis of such a brief experience, to speak *for*, or even *to*, Chileans who lived and suffered in their own flesh the full brunt of the Pinochet years. Despite sharing in the life of my friends and neighbors in Peñalolén, I remained and remain a *gringuito*. And yet, I will never forget, at my first Mass

---

[35] Mary Douglas, *Natural Symbols: Explorations in Cosmology* (New York: Vintage Books, 1973), 93.

in Chile, the feeling that I was home, that amidst the displacement of finding myself hanging upside down on the bottom of the earth, I knew what to do at Mass. If the argument of this book is correct, and the Eucharist produces a communion stronger than that of any nation-state, then my identity as a member of the body of Christ is ultimately more important than my country of birth. I can hope at least to speak *about* the experience of the church in Chile as a Catholic, and draw on the common practices and beliefs which unite Christians, transgressing national boundaries.

A more difficult question is that of finding and relaying the voice of the tortured. It is a task that must be assumed, since taking away their voice is the torturers' goal. Nevertheless, it is a task fraught with ambiguity. As an observer, I stand in the position not of the tortured but the torturer. The observer can easily become *voyeur*, the one who sees but is not seen, the occupant of the surveillance tower of the panopticon. A certain detachment is necessary for the study of torture, yet detachment risks constructing the tortured as experimental object, made to emit signs for the investigator's purposes. I have found that there is no simple answer to this problem. I have tried, whenever possible, to let victims speak in their own words. As for my interpretation of their experiences, I can only hope and pray that their words continue to reverberate, however faintly, through mine, and that these words might perhaps remove one more piece from the wall.

Part One

TORTURE

Chapter One

TORTURE AND DISAPPEARANCE AS AN ECCLESIOLOGICAL PROBLEM

When the people of Graciela Pérez's neighborhood on the outskirts of Santiago are lucky enough to have steady work, they usually find it washing the clothes and tending the gardens of Chile's elite, who live a 45-minute bus ride away in another world. Santiago is a city of more outskirts than inskirts, ringed by a dense swath of dusty *poblaciones* where millions live the precarious life of poverty. "Outskirts" refers more to a geography of power than of place; the inhabitants of the *poblaciones* under the Pinochet dictatorship were located at the periphery of relations of power by a pervasive disciplining apparatus. "They speak of people who have been tortured," says Graciela Pérez; "I believe they have tortured all of us equally. They have done it in different ways, but it has been torture for everyone. We have endured so much misery!"[1]

It would be easy for us to dismiss a comment such as this as a case of understandable hyperbole; the many hungers of poverty are indeed terrible, but cannot be likened to the agonies suffered by the victims of General Pinochet's torture chambers. As Edward Peters's study of torture argues, the use of the term "torture" to designate any kind of suffering, physical or mental, threatens to thin out the term to meaninglessness. Peters traces this problem to the Enlightenment shift of the grounds for the condemnation of torture from the strictly legal to the moral. Torture was condemned as incompatible

---

[1] Graciela Pérez, interview by Patricia Politzer, *Miedo en Chile* (Santiago: CESOC, 1985), 195. All translations are mine where the title is not listed in English.

with the new idea of human dignity. In the nineteenth century, the language
of torture became identified with the extreme of moral outrage, such that
torture no longer implied a specific type of action but rather an intensity of
action. Torture became any particularly grave assault on human dignity;
husbands tortured their wives, capitalists tortured their workers. But of course,
if everything is torture, then nothing is.[2]

I have no quarrel with this point, for I have no intention of identifying, for
example, material deprivation with torture. The torture which is the subject
of this chapter and this book is that condemned by the United Nations in 1975,
namely,

> any act by which severe pain or suffering, whether physical or mental, is
> intentionally inflicted by or at the instigation of a public official on a person for
> such purposes as obtaining from him or a third person information or
> confession, punishing him for an act he has committed, or intimidating him or
> other persons.[3]

Nevertheless, Graciela Pérez is right; the effects of torture radiate beyond the
solitary circle of the victim abandoned to the torturer's instruments. Torture
is not meant alone, or even primarily, for individuals but for whole societies.
Just as we misunderstand torture if we spread its meaning too thin, we
misunderstand it as well if we see it as an act of cruelty perpetrated on, or by,
a relatively few unfortunate individuals.

Torture is much more than an assault on the bodies of individuals;
it is rather an assault on social bodies. I will display torture as a central
rite in the liturgy by which the Chilean state manifested its power. The burden
of this chapter will be to show how torture was used by the Chilean military
regime to fragment and disarticulate all social bodies which would rival its
power, especially the church. I will argue that the church's resistance to the
regime of torture therefore depends on its ability to constitute itself as a
disciplined social body capable of countering the discipline of the state.

This chapter has four sections. First, I will emphasize the "productive"
nature of modern torture, and display it as an organized mode of governance
which realizes "liturgically" the state's claim to omnipotence over its citizens.
Second, I will show how this strategy translates into the isolation and
fragmentation of social bodies which rival the state. Third, I will highlight the

[2] Edward Peters, *Torture* (New York: Basil Blackwell, 1985), 148–55.
[3] General Assembly of the United Nations, "Declaration against Torture," December
9, 1975, quoted in Peters, *Torture*, 2.

importance of the invisibility of power in this type of regime. Fourth and finally, I will use the theology of martyrdom to display the contest between the church and the state over discipline of bodies, in order to read torture and disappearance properly as an ecclesiological problem.

1 Torture as Liturgy

There is no way to ease into the subject of torture. I will begin abruptly, like the secret policeman's nocturnal knock at the door. The following testimony is from an Argentinian woman.

> They tie my ankles and wrists and start to apply an electric prod to me, especially on my breasts, genitals, armpits, and mouth. They alternate the prod with groping, masturbation, all the time insulting me and uttering the most repugnant vulgarities. They try to destroy me, telling me that my husband has died, that I had been "cuckolded," that he was a homosexual and had abandoned his children, that he hadn't thought about my parents and things of this nature. The torturer insisted that I insult him and he provoked me saying that surely I was thinking that he was a sadist and that I would call what he was doing "groping," but that I was wrong: he was a scientist, which is why he accompanied all his actions with explanations about my physical makeup, my resistance, the foundations of the different methods.[4]

Our first reactions to an account such as this are to recoil in horror, to decry the senseless cruelty of it, to invoke the inviolability of the human person, to see torture as a throwback to some unenlightened age of barbarism which intrudes awkwardly in the twentieth century. But we must take another look, for the torturer in this account did not lie: he *is* a scientist, a practitioner of a carefully refined tool of state used in half of the world's countries today, and encouraged, taught, and funded by still other "more civilized" nations.[5] If we

---

[4] Quoted in Ricardo Rodríguez Molas, *Historia de la tortura y el orden represivo en la Argentina* (Buenos Aires: Editorial Universitaria de Buenos Aires, 1984), 149. Although most of my examples will be drawn from Chilean sources, I will also use illustrations from Argentina and Uruguay, given the close collaboration between the security apparatuses of these countries during their military dictatorships and the similarities of the methods used. For a summary of this collaboration see the *Report of the Chilean National Commission on Truth and Reconciliation*, trans. Phillip E. Berryman (Notre Dame, Ind.: University of Notre Dame Press, 1993), 476–8, hereafter cited as the *Rettig Report*.

are to understand modern torture, we will have to understand its place in a systematic state repressive apparatus which actually *discourages* mere sadism in its operatives.[6] To begin to fathom torture we must see it as a "mode of governance,"[7] a commonly used extension of the state's normal functions of social control in many parts of the world. We must resist the urge to maintain the unfamiliarity of torture, to consign it to the past, or to a world of monsters. It is very much a part of our world, and we must make the mental effort, however uncomfortable, to put the ideas of "governance" and "torture" together.

In the months following the military coup of September 11, 1973, reprisals

---

[5] After years of denials, the Pentagon was forced on Sept. 20, 1996 to admit officially that Army intelligence manuals used at the School of the Americas to train Latin American military officers contained instructions on torture techniques; see "Pentagon admits use of torture manuals," *National Catholic Reporter*, October 4, 1996. The case of Brazil provides well-documented evidence that the United States has been instrumental in introducing the science of torture into its client states. An American official named Dan Mitrione was one of the first to provide systematic instruction on torture methods to the military regime in Brazil. Mitrione provided classes for the police in Belo Horizonte, using beggars taken off the streets as his subjects. Mitrione was later killed by guerrillas after being transferred to Uruguay, but the Brazilian military continued to conduct classes in torture using live subjects; see *Torture in Brazil: A Report by the Archdiocese of São Paulo*, trans. Jaime Wright, ed. Joan Dassin (New York: Vintage Books, 1986), 13–15. Following the 1973 coup in Chile, Brazilian security agents provided instruction in torture methods to the incipient Chilean intelligence apparatus; see Lawrence Weschler, *A Miracle, A Universe: Settling Accounts with Torturers* (New York: Pantheon Books, 1990), 62–3.

[6] One of the few manuals for torturers that has come to light, the "interrogator's manual" from the Tuol Sleng complex in Kampuchea, makes this point clear to its trainees: "[Torture is] not something we do for fun . . . It's not something that's done out of individual anger, or for self-satisfaction. So we beat them to make them afraid, but absolutely not to kill them. When torturing, it is necessary to examine their state of health first, and then whip. Don't be so bloodthirsty that you cause their death quickly"; David Hawk, "Tuol Sleng Extermination Centre," *Index on Censorship* 15, no.1 (January 1986), 27. An Argentinian prisoner received from a captor a torturer's prayer, which asked the Lord to make the torturer's hand "accurate so that the shot will hit its mark and put charity in my heart so that I fire without hatred"; quoted in Jean Franco, "Gender, Death, and Resistance: Facing the Ethical Vacuum," in *Fear at the Edge: State Terror and Resistance in Latin America*, ed. Juan E. Corradi, Patricia Weiss Fagen, and Manuel Antonio Garretón (Berkeley: University of California Press, 1992), 107.

[7] The phrase belongs to Edward Herman in his *The Real Terror Network* (Boston: South End Press, 1982), 113.

against sympathizers of the defeated government came quickly and furiously, spreading fear like a disease throughout Chile. Summary executions were common, but "disappearances" of the bodies were due to attempts to avoid responsibility for murder and did not yet form part of the regime's coordinated strategy of terror. That strategy began to congeal in November of 1973 with the unofficial formation of the *Dirección de Inteligencia Nacional*, or DINA, a centralized agency which took members from all branches of the armed forces. Now that the regime had consolidated its power, the purpose of the new organization was to coordinate the disciplining of the population, a task previously undertaken haphazardly by the Army, Navy, Air Force, and *Carabineros* (national police) and their respective intelligence services. Although an unfriendly rivalry would persist among the various intelligence groups, the DINA quickly swelled into a large bureaucracy employing thousands, which in coordinating terror would not only help the government but would itself help govern Chile.[8]

By the time the DINA was officially created by Decree Law 521 in June 1974, it had already set the sinister pattern by which it became known. It was chartered as a "military body of a technical and professional nature" whose purpose was "gathering all information from around the nation and from different fields of activity in order to produce the intelligence needed for policy formulation and planning and the adoption of those measures required for the protection of national security and the development of the country."[9] In practice the DINA went far beyond intelligence gathering. The organization included departments of government services, telecommunications, finance, propaganda, counter-intelligence, and economic research.[10] The DINA was most infamous for its operational groups, the secret squadrons with unlimited power to arrest, torture, and kill, and an extensive network of clandestine detention centers in which to ply their trade. The following account from a victim of the DINA is typical.

> I was arrested at about midnight on the 26th of December, 1975. Around 8 civilians arrived at my house, all armed with machine guns and small arms; after searching the house . . . they handcuffed me together with my wife, put tape over our eyes and dark glasses over that. The whole operation was carried out without them identifying themselves at any moment, nor did they show any arrest or search warrant.

---

[8] The origins of the DINA are detailed in the *Rettig Report*, 469–75.
[9] Decree Law 521, quoted in the *Rettig Report*, 472.
[10] *Rettig Report*, 474.

We were put into a private car, that is, one without any distinctive marks, and taken to the Villa Grimaldi. They took us out of the car and immediately I was taken to the torture chamber. There they made me undress and with my hands and feet tied to the metal frame of the lower part of a bunkbed they began to apply electric current to me. This is the 'grill.' During the rest of the night they had me, applying electricity over my whole body, accompanied by blows with sticks, because of which I came out with several fractured ribs. While they applied electricity they threw water on my whole body.

It was already dawn when I was taken off the grill and thrown, with my feet and hands chained, on the patio of the Villa. During the day on several opportunities I was again taken to 'interrogation,' where I was beaten by various men with kicks, fists, and sticks . . . Until the 31st of December I was taken to 'interrogation' every day and every night.[11]

Behind this account stand thousands of similar stories, shocking in their brutality, yet numbing in their bureaucratic precision and repetitiveness. Once the DINA began operation, the modalities were the same: "disappearance," arrest at night under cover of curfew with as few witnesses as possible; unidentified agents dressed in civilian clothes; blindfolding, taking to a clandestine prison; immediate interrogation accompanied by extreme physical pain; long terror-filled waiting, punctuated by periods of torture at any time of day or night. The victim quoted above was released and lived to tell of his torture; several thousand others were not so lucky, and now fill the rolls of the permanently disappeared in Chile.[12]

Firsthand accounts of Villa Grimaldi, one of the DINA's main detention centers on the east side of Santiago, paint a surrealistic portrait of a large administrative apparatus juxtaposed with unspeakable brutality, of people strapped to the "grill" with typists at their sides banging out confession forms in triplicate. Villa Grimaldi was a converted estate, with several adjoining buildings on a large piece of land. Besides torture chambers, the Villa also housed the administrative and logistical headquarters of the BIM, the *Brigada de Inteligencia Metropolitana*, the Santiago branch of the DINA.[13] "It was like

---

[11] Case D.O. 178–1176, archives of the Vicaría de la Solidaridad, Santiago. In order to protect the identity of victims, I will cite case numbers instead of names for those cases which have not been previously published.

[12] I will use the term "disappearance" to cover all those arrests undertaken by agents of the government in which the arrests were not officially recognized and the victims were held in clandestine locations. "The disappeared" refers only to those victims who were never released.

[13] *Rettig Report*, 487.

a palace, with marble stairways and an indoor swimming pool," recounts Humberto Vergara, a peasant union official. "They put four of us inside a container no bigger than a table. In the dark, we could hear screams all day and sobbing all night. It was how I imagined hell would be . . . The guards would splash in the pool and pass by the cells, saying they were going to kill this one or castrate that one."[14]

Who were the victims of the secret police apparatus? They were sympathizers with the defeated government of Salvador Allende, all those who had participated in or supported the restructuring of Chile under the Popular Unity coalition. They were members of leftist parties banned by the military government. They were union organizers, church activists, or people involved in grassroots organizations, which often operated under the aegis of the church. In the decade of the 1980s the CNI – the *Central Nacional de Informaciones* which replaced the DINA in 1977 – increasingly pursued those involved in public protests which shook Chile after 1983. Finally, they were people who were associated with, or could possibly be associated with, any of the above classes of people.[15] Repression came to cast a wide net in Pinochet's Chile. Of those who were killed or remain permanently disappeared, 46 percent were not known to be politically active.[16]

What could the secret police want from these people? The names of the organizations, the *Dirección de Inteligencia Nacional* and the *Central Nacional de Informaciones*, would indicate that what they were after was information, knowledge so inaccessible and needed so desperately that they would torture to obtain it. Certainly the form of the act of torture would lead us to believe that this was the case, for pain was invariably accompanied by interrogation

---

[14] Humberto Vergara, quoted in Pamela Constable and Arturo Valenzuela, *A Nation of Enemies: Chile under Pinochet* (New York: W.W. Norton & Co., 1991), 95.

[15] These general classifications of people are gathered from my work with the microfilmed archives of the Vicaría de la Solidaridad, the Chilean Catholic church's human rights office, from January to July 1990 at the Center for Civil and Human Rights at the Notre Dame Law School. The most important sources of information on torture among the archives are the *Denuncias ante organismos internacionales*, in which victims give detailed accounts of their arrests and torture. Only occasional *denuncias*, however, include information on the victim's activities, political or otherwise, so no complete statistical breakdown of possible motives for arrest is available.

[16] *Rettig Report*, 902. This statistic is based only on those cases in which the Chilean National Commission on Truth and Reconciliation was able to reach a conviction that a human rights violation by government agents was responsible for death or disappearance after arrest.

in Chile's torture chambers. Historically as well, torture has been associated with the search for truth;[17] in French legal terminology the term *la question* was synonymous with *la torture* until torture was abolished.[18] Medieval legal practice used torture when the truth of a case was difficult to discover.[19] We might be tempted to assume that the modern torture apparatus is a throwback to the medieval practice of truth extraction, an anachronistic, unenlightened shortcut to the truth which passes right through and tramples the rights modernity has fought so hard to attain. When we examine Chilean torture more carefully, however, we discover that it is not truth that the regime was after, and far from being medieval, this torture has a peculiarly modern smell about it.

> Meanwhile, they submitted my mother-in-law and my wife to an interrogation also on the grounds of the Talcahuano Naval Base, which began at 10 a.m. and ended at 10 p.m. Of course this interrogation was accompanied at all times by physical aggression of different tones, from slaps in the face to sharp blows on the face and body. Obviously in this type of treatment are included threats and intense psychological pressure, for example: "If you don't sign this declaration we will kill your husband or relatives; anyway they're almost dead but you can save them by signing this declaration that we made."[20]

The last two words of this passage are extremely puzzling, for it is difficult to fathom why the security agents would expend so much energy to coerce the victims into signing a declaration which the agents themselves had fabricated. But in fact in most cases the victim cannot tell the agents anything they do not already know, and certainly nothing that could be of even minimal importance to the regime. This was affirmed by Elizabeth Lira Kornfeld, director of Santiago's *Instituto Latinoamericano de Salud Mental y Derechos Humanos*, a psychologist who has specialized in work with torture victims: "Contrary to what people believe, rarely is torture intended to extract information."[21] Lira tells of many cases in which a prisoner who has resisted giving a piece of information through the most brutal treatment finally gives in, only to be told by the torturer, "We already knew." At the

---

[17] See Page duBois, *Torture and Truth* (New York: Routledge, 1991) for a discussion of the ancient Greek practice of using torture as a touchstone for truth.
[18] Peters, *Torture*, 28.
[19] Ibid., 57.
[20] Case D.O. 46-0775, archives of the Vicaría de la Solidaridad.
[21] Elizabeth Lira Kornfeld, interview by author, July 12, 1993, Santiago, tape recording.

same time, the accounts of torture in Chile are replete with confessions given which both tortured and torturer knew to be false. As one Argentinian prisoner testifies, "The idea was to leave the victim without any kind of psychological resistance, until he was at the mercy of the interrogator, and thus obtain any answer the latter wanted, however absurd. If they wanted you to reply that you had seen San Martín on horseback the previous day they succeeded."[22]

And yet, no matter how seemingly senseless, in modern torture interrogation virtually always accompanies the inflicting of pain, and the questions are delivered with an urgency which lends itself to, and in part produces, the atmosphere of sick drama in the torture room. Questions are never simply asked; they are shouted, hurled in a frenzy of threats and blows. Answers are sought in a gamut which runs from imperious demands to pleading with the victims. A woman taken by the DINA in 1975 describes her first interrogation:

> I was awakened by some tremendous screams and I heard someone kicking the door like a crazy person. It was a demoniac who shouted obscenities and suddenly came flying in and landed on top of me. . . . The guy grabbed me by my braid and started dragging me around the cell, while he continued screaming at me. Finally, he let me go and told me to sign a declaration recognizing that my husband and I were both communists. . . . After a while I began to hear them torturing other people; you could hear the moans and threats: "You so and so, I'm going to hang you upside down so you tell the truth!"[23]

The feigned urgency of the questions has the effect, as Elaine Scarry puts it, of turning the "moral reality of torture upside down,"[24] for by making the seeking of important answers seem like the motive for the torture, the torturer seems able to justify his brutality. No one would think of defending the sheer physical act of torture, the merciless inflicting of pain on a helpless victim. However, once we consider the verbal aspect, the question and answer which seems of such great urgency, the moral contours of torture seem less clear, and

---

[22] Daniel Eduardo Fernández, quoted in *Nunca Más: A Report by Argentina's National Commission on Disappeared People* (London: Faber and Faber, 1986), 43. The reference is to José de San Martín, nineteenth-century hero of Argentina's war for independence from Spain.

[23] "Raquel," interview by Politzer, *Miedo en Chile*, 123.

[24] Elaine Scarry, *The Body in Pain: The Making and Unmaking of the World* (New York: Oxford University Press, 1985), 35.

utilitarian justifications of torture become thinkable, provided the motive for the questions is of sufficient importance.[25]

It is clear from studying firsthand accounts of torture that the questions do not stand apart from torture as the motive but are in fact themselves part of the enacted drama of torture. It is the form of the answer, or the fact of answering, that is of prime importance: "We know you are a communist, but we will hang you until you tell us in your own words." The medieval ordeal used pain to seek truth; the crucial distinction here, in contrast, is not between lies and truth, but between those answers which conform to the torturers' reality and those which deviate.[26] The victims are made to speak the words of the regime, to replace their own reality with that of the state, to double the voice of the state. The state's omnipotence becomes manifest in the horrifying production of power, what Scarry calls a "grotesque piece of compensatory drama."[27] Torture may be considered a kind of perverse *liturgy*, for in torture the body of the victim is the ritual site where the state's power is manifested in its most awesome form. Torture is liturgy – or, perhaps better said, "anti-liturgy" – because it involves bodies and bodily movements in an enacted drama which both makes real the power of the state and constitutes an act of worship of that mysterious power. It is essential to this ritual enactment that it not be public, for reasons that we will explore later in this chapter. The liturgy of the torture room is a *disciplina arcani*, a discipline of the secret, which is yet part of a larger state project which continues outside the torture chamber itself.

The victim of torture is not made simply to take on the voice of the regime in imitation of its discourses. The victim serves a particular function in the drama, that of *enemy*. As Michel de Certeau remarks, "The goal of torture, in

---

[25] The classic case is that of the terrorist who will only under torture tell how to defuse the bomb on the airplane full of innocents. For utilitarian arguments in favor of torture, see Brian Crozier, *A Theory of Conflict* (New York: Charles Scribner's Sons, 1975), 156–61, and Michael Levin, "The Case for Torture," *Newsweek*, June 7, 1982.

[26] See Michel de Certeau, "Corps torturés, paroles capturées", chap. in *Michel de Certeau*, ed. Luce Giard (Paris: Centre Georges Pompidou, 1987); also Scarry, *The Body in Pain*, 29. In some cases one of the motives for torture was to locate another person sought by the regime. As Scarry points out, however, even in these cases "That the information elicited . . . sometimes, in fact, determines the sequence of arrests and torture may only mean that governments sometimes depend on their opponents to provide an arbitrary structure for their brutality"; 329 n. 7.

[27] Scarry, *The Body in Pain*, 28.

effect, is to produce acceptance of a State discourse, through the confession of putrescence."[28] The omnipotence of the state depends on the manifestation of its other – the revolutionary, the subversive – as filth. The victim does not take on the glorious voice of the regime but rather its opposite, the voice of corruption. Torturers do not demand the victim's acknowledgement of the value of the regime's project, for here the victim would never entertain any real doubt, even were he to say the words. Instead of the regime's project, the torturers put the victim himself in question, under conditions guaranteed to produce the degradation of the victim to his required place in the drama.[29] Torturers humiliate the victim, exploit his human weakness through the mechanism of pain, until he does take on the role of filth, confessing his lowliness and betraying cause, comrades, family, and friends. Such filth assumes an important role in the mythos of the regime; witness one of the members of the Chilean Junta, Admiral Merino, publicly justifying repression by referring to the status of Marxists as "*humanoids.*"[30]

As the work of anthropologist Mary Douglas suggests, communities and the religious and political powers which control them often define their identity and legitimate the contours of their power through the ritual expulsion of that which pollutes and defiles.[31] We misunderstand modern torture, however, if we fail to see that enemies of the regime are not so much *punished* as *produced* in the torture chamber. Torture does not uncover and penalize a certain type of discourse, but rather creates a discourse of its own and uses it to realize the state's claims to power over the bodies of its citizens. Torture plays out the dream of a certain kind of state, the production of a type of power/knowledge which I will call the *imagination* of the state. To speak of imagination is not, of course, to imply that state power is "merely imaginary," a disembodied thought. The imagination of the state has a tremendous power to discipline bodies, to habituate them and script them into a drama of its own making. The Chilean torture apparatus, therefore, should not be seen simply as a response to a particular type of threat against the state. Torture is rather both the production of that threat and the response to it, and thus the ritual site at which the state produces the reality in which its pretensions to omnipotence consist.

---

[28] Michel de Certeau, "The Institution of Rot," chap. in *Heterologies: Discourse on the Other*, trans. Brian Massumi (Minneapolis: University of Minnesota Press, 1986), 40–1.

[29] Ibid., 42.

[30] *El Mercurio*, August 31, 1988, C4.

[31] Mary Douglas, *Purity and Danger: An Analysis of the Concepts of Pollution and Taboo* (London: Routledge, 1966).

For a regime such as that of General Pinochet, violence has the crucial function of justifying itself. The story of an infamous helicopter trip will make this clearer. When the coup took place on September 11, 1973, it overthrew Latin America's most longstanding and stable democracy, with a proud tradition of military subordination to civil power. Resistance among center and left parties was minimal, such that between the coup and the end of the year the military and police had lost only twenty-five people, with fifteen of those casualties coming on the day of the coup.[32] The few pockets of armed resistance had been snuffed out decisively. Most expected a swift and relatively peaceful return to democracy. Much of what is written on the human rights record of the Pinochet regime is occupied with puzzling over how so much brutality could have taken place in Chile, given the long constitutional obedience of the military and the lack of armed opposition to the coup.[33]

What many fail to see is that lack of resistance was a *problem* for the Pinochet regime, one which was solved by means of increased brutality. In October 1973 the Junta dispatched General Sergio Arellano Stark on a helicopter tour of military installations where prisoners were being held. The official purpose for the trip was to review sentences for supporters of the Allende government and "to make uniform the criteria for the administration of justice."[34] What in fact happened was somewhat less benign. Everywhere the "Helicóptero de la Muerte" touched down, prisoners were taken out and shot: 19 in La Serena, 13 in Copiapó, 14 in Antofagasta, dozens more in other cities. Most of those shot were still awaiting trial or serving light sentences. They were killed precisely because they posed only a slight threat. Upon General Arellano's arrival in Talca, he asked Colonel Efraím Jaña how many casualties his troops had sustained in subduing the area. When the Colonel replied that the region had been secured peacefully, the General grew furious. "Later I understood," Jaña explained, that "[my attitude] did not square with the superior plans, which called for exacerbat-

---

[32] *Rettig Report*, 147.

[33] See e.g. Alain Rouquié, *The Military and the State in Latin America*, trans. Paul E. Sigmund (Berkeley: University of California Press, 1987), 224–33; and Mary Helen Spooner, *Soldiers in a Narrow Land: The Pinochet Regime in Chile* (Berkeley: University of California Press, 1994), 2–3.

[34] General Joaquín Lagos Osorio, quoted in Eugenio Ahumada and Rodrigo Atria, *Chile: la memoria prohibida* (Santiago: Pehuén Editores, 1989), 1. 350. A book-length account of Arellano's helicopter trip is Patricia Verdugo, *Los Zarpazos del Puma* (Santiago: CESOC, 1989).

ing military fury against the left."[35] The purpose of Arellano's trip was not merely to *stimulate*, but rather to *simulate*, the atmosphere of internal war that the regime needed to justify its policies. Violence was used not as a response to threats to the state, but rather to create the threats from which the only possible protection was the state itself. This type of terror is a mode of governance which is self-justifying. At issue is not "repression" as such, since there was little to repress, but rather *production* of chaos and the scripting of bodies into a drama of fear.

Within the liturgies of fear, the state thus shows itself as both menace and protector; to be truly omnipotent the state must be both the taker and the giver of life. Torture victims speak not only of the pain they endure but of the pervasive sense of powerlessness they are made to feel at the hands of their tormentors. Details seemingly insignificant in comparison to the physical abuse – irregularity of schedules, constant background music, blindfolding, frequent change of cell or location – are calculated to reduce the prisoner to a condition of powerlessness over even the most trivial aspects of his or her daily existence. This impotence is reinforced with verbal abuse. "They would say: 'You're dirt.' 'Since we "disappeared" you, you're nothing. Anyway nobody remembers you.' 'You don't exist.'. . . . 'We are everything for you.' 'We are justice.' 'We are God.' "[36] At the same time, the jailers often exercise the obverse of their power, and prove their omnipotence to alter the prisoner's world for the better. Argentinian journalist Jacobo Timerman gives this account of a torturer's offer of coffee and a blanket after he has been sitting blindfolded, tied to a chair in the cold rain for several hours.

---

[35] Efraím Jaña, quoted in Constable and Valenzuela, *A Nation of Enemies*, 37–8. Jaña was imprisoned for three years for his lack of rigor. During this period other officers were killed or imprisoned and tortured for being too "soft" on political prisoners; see ibid., 54–5 and Ahumada and Atria, *Chile: la memoria prohibida*, 1.369 n.39. General Arellano's son, Sergio Arellano Iturriaga, wrote a book entitled *Más Allá del Abismo* in which he defended his father's actions, claiming, among other things, that in El Loa, the region surrounding Calama, the atmosphere was extremely tense because of an extremist plot to blow up the explosives plant. Eugenio Rivera, military governor of the region in 1973, replied to Arellano Iturriaga's book in a 1985 magazine article: "The department of El Loa maintained itself in complete normality from the first shift of the Chuquicamata mine on September 12, 1973, as did the La Exótica mine, the plant of the National Explosives Company, all the public services, banks, educational establishments, etc. What's more, for reasons of the operation of Chuquicamata, there was no curfew established, only at a later date, when it was ordered established in the whole country"; Eugenio Rivera, quoted in Ahumada and Atria, *Chile: la memoria prohibida*, 1.369 n.35.
[36] Dr Norberto Liwsky, quoted in *Nunca Más*, 25.

Everything about him transmits generosity, a desire to protect me. He asks me if I'd like to lie down a while on the bed. I tell him no. He tells me there are some female prisoners on the grounds, if I'd care to go to bed with one of them. I tell him no. This gets him angry because he wants to help me and, by not allowing him to, I upset his plan, his aim. In some way he needs to demonstrate to me and to himself his capacity to grant things, to alter my world, my situation. To demonstrate to me that I need things that are inaccessible to me and which only he can provide. I've noticed this mechanism repeated countless times.[37]

Here the torturer stands in as the vicar of the state, the presider at the manifestation of the state's awesome power. Torture is an efficacious sign by which the state enacts its power over its subjects' bodies in purest form.

2 Torture and Fragmentation

State power is enacted in the liturgy of torture, but it would be a mistake to envision the state that tortures as active agent and the victims as mere passive recipients of its discipline. State discipline is a larger imaginative project, a grand drama in which victims of torture play important roles. In this section I will describe how torture breaks down and reconstitutes the subjectivities of citizens, adapting them to the state project. The key to this project is individualization. Torture breaks down collective links and makes of its victims isolated monads. Victims then reproduce the same dynamic in society itself, with the net result that all social bodies which would rival the state are disintegrated and disappeared.

The work of Elaine Scarry on pain provides us a window for understanding the connection between physical torment and the atomization of society. Those who study pain, Scarry shows, are struck by its inexpressibility and its incommunicability. Those in great pain are reduced to inarticulate screams and moans, or words which convey little of the actual experience of pain ("throbbing," "stabbing," "burning"). Pain does not merely resist language but actively destroys it, in extreme cases reducing the sufferer to the sounds he used before he learned to speak.[38] Jacobo Timerman:

---

[37] Jacobo Timerman, *Prisoner without a Name, Cell without a Number,* trans. Tony Talbot (New York: Vintage Books, 1988), 40–1.

[38] Scarry, *The Body in Pain,* 3–5. Pain's inexpressibility can in part be explained, Scarry thinks, by the fact that pain has no object. All our other interior states – love, hatred, hunger, longing – take an object: we long or hunger *for* something, we love *somebody,* and so on. Pain is simply pain, and so may resist objectification in language; ibid., 5.

In the long months of confinement, I often thought of how to transmit the pain that a tortured person undergoes. And always I concluded that it was impossible. . . . What does a man feel? The only thing that comes to mind is: they're ripping apart my flesh. But they didn't rip apart my flesh. Yes, I know that now. They didn't even leave marks. . . . When electric shocks are applied, all that a man feels is that they are ripping apart his flesh. And he howls.[39]

For the suffering person, pain is grasped effortlessly; it intrudes on the person like a pestering child, demands attention, destroys consciousness of things other than itself. For another person, although she be in the same room with the sufferer, what is effortless is *not* to grasp the pain. It is possible for the second person to remain unaware of the pain or even to have doubt about it. At best, if the pain of another is grasped, it is only a pale hint of what the sufferer experiences. "[T]o have great pain is to have certainty; to hear that another person has pain is to have doubt."[40]

It is the difficulty of expressing pain, its occult nature buried deep in the body of the sufferer, that lends pain to misdescription and manipulation for political purposes. Verbal signs which lift the reality of pain out of the body and into the world of communication are crucial to pain's alleviation. But at the same time the language of pain is so unstable that it can be used not to display pain but to disguise it, to bury it further into invisibility. If the felt attributes of pain are verbally objectified and attached to their proper referent, the sentience of the suffering body, then pain can become knowable to another person. But as Scarry shows, because of the inherent doubtfulness and instability of the language of pain, it is also possible to take those characteristics of pain − "its incontestable reality, its totality, its ability to eclipse all else, its power of dramatic alteration and world dissolution"[41] − and assign them to another referent, such as a particular governing regime. Scarry's fascinating book *The Body in Pain* is dedicated to showing how, in times of crisis, instability, and war, regimes of power often borrow the "sheer material factualness" of the human body to give an aura of reality to certain cultural constructs.[42]

In torture the state borrows the voice of the victim to double its own voice. Through his terrifying and desperate insistence on confession, the torturer pulls pain from the suffering body of the victim, objectifies it and gives it voice.

---

[39] Timerman, *Prisoner without a Name, Cell without a Number*, 32–3.
[40] Scarry, *The Body in Pain*, 7.
[41] Ibid., 56.
[42] Ibid., 12–14.

The prisoner is made to identify the motive of the suffering, but rather than a true identification, which would elicit normal human sympathy and help, the motive is falsified and the existence of the prisoner's pain and need for aid is denied. The victim's status as a human being in need is discredited and replaced by the regime's need for security.[43] Furthermore, through confession the victim is made to be the active agent of her own annihilation, the cause of her own undoing through her opposition to the regime. Pain is thus pulled out of the body and given voice, but the voice is expropriated by the regime and turned back against the sufferer of the pain. This reversal of the path of pain is a crucial element in the use of the pain of the prisoner to magnify the power of the regime. It can be displayed clearly in the techniques used by the Chilean secret police in training their agents. Covert operatives in Chile's "dirty war" understood themselves as sacrificing not only their own physical safety and ease but also their *moral integrity* so that others might enjoy the benefits of integrity, both physical and moral, in a world free of subversion.[44] By focusing on their own pain and sacrifice, no matter how disproportionate to the pain of torture, torturers deny the reality of the other and confer reality on the concerns of the regime alone. As Scarry puts it,

> Every weapon has two ends. In converting the other person's pain into his own power, the torturer experiences the entire occurrence exclusively from the nonvulnerable end of the weapon. If his attention begins to slip down the weapon toward the vulnerable end, if the severed attributes of pain begin to slip back to their origin in the prisoner's sentience, their backward fall can be stopped, they can be lifted out once more by the presence of the motive. If the guard's awareness begins to follow the path of the bullet, that path itself can be bent so that he himself rather than the prisoner is the bullet's destination.[45]

Thus in torture does the regime's world swell to enormous proportions and occupy reality itself, while the world of the victim dissolves into nothing. If pain destroys language, so too it destroys the world of the prisoner, for it is through language that a person's world is constructed. From the time a child begins to make sounds and words, language is a means of self-expansion, the way in which a person moves beyond the confines of her body. In language a person learns to name the world, to become part of a larger world, to gain

---

[43] Ibid., 36–8.

[44] *Rettig Report*, 61, 497. The private motto of the DINA was "We will fight in the shadows so that our children can live in the sunlight"; Constable and Valenzuela, *A Nation of Enemies*, 90.

[45] Scarry, *The Body in Pain*, 59.

a larger self. For a person in pain, the process is reversed. The immediacy of pain, its monopoly of attention and its incommunicability, reduces the world of the sufferer down again to the limits of the body itself. In older people, bodily frailty often brings the world down to within a few feet of their physical bodies. Their world becomes a ceaseless preoccupation with sitting comfortably, the room temperature, their aches and pains. In torture this phenomenon takes an extreme form. The immediacy of the pain shrinks the world down to the contours of the body itself; the enormity of the agony is the sufferer's only reality.[46] Pain is often called "blinding" because it eliminates all but itself from the field of vision.

The elimination of the victim's world has a temporal dimension as well. Past attachments and future hopes are destroyed by the brute present immediacy of pain. Sheila Cassidy, an English doctor who was tortured in Chile, writes of her stay at Villa Grimaldi, "It was as though I was suspended over a pit: the past had no relevance and I could see no future. I lived only for the minute that was and in the fear of further pain."[47] The project of the regime steals time as well as space from its subjects.

The future becomes the possession of the regime above all through the indefinite nature of the imprisonment. The prisoner's life stops at arrest; if and when it will begin again is entirely within the power and the knowledge of the security apparatus. Many are confined for months and years with no trial, and no sentence, and so no end in sight. For them, time itself becomes a weapon used against them. Time cannot move forward, because there is no end point for time to approach – the prisoner is never nearer to release. With no eschaton, time runs in circles, always dumping the prisoner back in the anguish of the present. The security forces have an eternity in which to torment the prisoner; they possess, quite literally, *all the time in the world.*

The torturer eliminates not only the future but the prisoner's past as well. The well-regulated mechanism of pain forces the victim to denounce friends, comrades, loved ones, and highest ideals as filth. This is more than a simple conversion and renarration of one's past; it is instead the obliteration of that past. Under intense and virtually unlimited torment, past attachments to people and causes become pale, distant shades, and the victim's larger world is exploded into fragments, bits of flotsam in a sea of pain. Elaine Scarry rightly points out that, given the destruction of the prisoner's world and the elimination of past and future, the word "betrayal" is wrongly assigned to the

---

[46] Ibid., 29–35.
[47] Sheila Cassidy, *Audacity to Believe* (London: William Collins Sons & Co., 1977), 198.

victim's confession, even given the denunciation of all people and causes held dear. One cannot betray what no longer exists. The victim can be made to say anything, and to call this "betrayal" is part of the regime's inversion of the moral world of torture, labeling the victim a betrayer and somehow therefore deserving of mistreatment.[48]

One way to think about this destruction of the victim's world is to say that the effect of torture is the creation of individuals. Pain, as we have seen, is the great isolator, that which cuts us off in a radical way from one another. With the demolition of the victim's affective ties and loyalties, past and future, the purpose of torture is to destroy the person as a political actor, and to leave her isolated and compliant with the regime's goals.[49] Torture is consonant with the military regime's strategy to fragment the society, to disarticulate all intermediate social bodies between the individual and the state – parties, unions, professional organizations – which would challenge the regime's desire to have all depend only on it.[50] Wherever two or three are gathered, there is subversion in their midst.

Torture is intended to alter a person's identity, degrade him and strip him of human attributes, but in most cases not to kill him. The torture apparatus is meant instead for the colonization of the subjectivities of political opponents of the regime, their neutralization as opponents, and their reconstitution as coins in the currency of state power. To be an opponent of the regime does not necessarily entail direct opposition; to unite for any purpose with one's neighbors, to participate in a soup kitchen or a sewing circle, is enough to bring one under suspicion. Strictly speaking, the Pinochet regime was not "Fascist," despite the frequency with which the epithet is hurled at it. "Fascism" is derived from the Italian *fascio*, or bundle; the image is meant to evoke a binding together. The goal of the Pinochet and other Latin American military regimes was just the opposite. Alain Rouquié explains the difference between these regimes and those of Hitler and Mussolini:

---

[48] Scarry, *The Body in Pain*, 29–37. It should be clear that resistance to torture and refusal to talk belong almost exclusively to the realm of movies and cheap novels, not to the modern reality of the secret police apparatus. Sophisticated techniques of torture can deliver virtually unlimited pain without causing death. After Sheila Cassidy broke on the *parrilla*, she asked one of her captors "Does everyone talk, or am I weak?" He replied, "Everyone has their breaking point"; Cassidy, *Audacity to Believe*, 189.

[49] Sofia Salimovich, Elizabeth Lira, and Eugenia Weinstein, "Victims of Fear: The Social Psychology of Repression" in *Fear at the Edge*, 78.

[50] Manuel Antonio Garretón, "Fear in Military Regimes: An Overview," in *Fear at the Edge*, 16.

The mobilization of the middle class stopped with the arrival of Pinochet to power and he never established a party. These regimes, without a single party or mobilizing apparatus, did not have a mass base and did not wish to have one. They did not mobilize the citizens, they depoliticized them; they did not indoctrinate the workers; they urged them to return to their private lives. Far from making them march together in step (*zusammenmarschieren*), they isolated them. Every dictatorship, however ferocious, and every counter-revolutionary regime, is not ipso facto fascist.[51]

The economic strategy of the military regime is further illustration of this point. After consolidating his power, Pinochet turned to a group of economists known in Chile as "Los Chicago Boys" to restructure the economy. They had studied under Milton Friedman and Arnold Harberger at the University of Chicago, and were now given free rein to implement their free-market ideas. They privatized state-run enterprises, slashed public employment, reversed land reform, cancelled wage increases, deregulated banking, and dismantled labor unions. A new entrepreneurial class appeared, spurred by the acquisition of most of the more than 500 state enterprises by a small number of powerful business conglomerates. Meanwhile prices were freed from state control for all goods and services except labor power; wages remained under the control of the state. Unions were atomized, restricted to organizing only within a particular plant. Workers could be fired virtually at will, strikes were prohibited, and unemployment among the poor classes soared.[52] Chile was subjected to market competition, and to Friedman's underlying vision: "a 'country' or a 'society' is a collection of individuals; . . . only individuals can have moral obligations."[53] On a highly publicized visit to Santiago in March 1975, Milton Friedman announced that the Chilean economy needed "shock treatment."[54] This was more than a metaphor to those strapped to the "grill" in Chile's secret prisons. The disarticulation of workers' organizations through the strategy of torture was an essential component of the neoliberal economic model imposed in Chile and other Latin American countries. As Uruguayan writer

[51] Rouquié, *The Military and the State in Latin America*, 268.

[52] James Petras and Fernando Ignacio Leiva, *Democracy and Poverty in Chile: The Limits to Electoral Politics* (Boulder, Colo.: Westview Press, 1994), 17–45; and Constable and Valenzuela, *A Nation of Enemies*, 166–98.

[53] Milton Friedman, "Good Ends, Bad Means" in *The Catholic Challenge to the American Economy*, ed. Thomas M. Gannon, SJ (New York: Macmillan Publishing Company, 1987), 105.

[54] Milton Friedman, quoted in Constable and Valenzuela, *A Nation of Enemies*, 170.

Eduardo Galeano puts it, "people were in prison so that prices could be free."[55]

It is important to be aware of the regime's overall strategy of isolation and fragmentation in order to see how that strategy is reproduced in the bodies of the tortured. Psychologists who work with torture victims point to the destruction of the victim as political actor through the fragmentation of the ego. The feeling and reality of powerlessness in torture is so extreme that the subject is no longer subject, but mere object. The ego is dissolved because it cannot sustain the processes necessary for self-preservation. In fact, death, the very negation of ego, becomes desirable. The regime thereby succeeds in altering or destroying not only the political project, if any, in which the person is involved, but also the entire network of psychic processes which bind the person to others.[56]

The prisoner is put in an impossible dilemma: she is forced to choose between her physical and her psychic integrity. She may choose either to be subjected to limitless bodily pain and mistreatment, which could lead to physical death, or to betray and renounce her beliefs, friends, and family, and thus become the executioner of her life's project.[57] It is a double bind, the mere surviving of which often requires the dissociation of mind and body. The prisoner will often renounce her psychological integrity as a coping mechanism, such that her words become those of another, dissociated from her self. Years later, many victims are incapable of expressing significant parts of the horror they underwent; the tortures remain, in a word, unspeakable. The experiences are remembered vaguely, as those of another, repressed into a hidden corner of the fragmented self.[58]

When Arturo sought therapy in 1982, he was a 25-year-old student worried about a chronic loss of concentration and memory. An uncle's political activity had netted Arturo and much of his extended family a ten-day

[55] Eduardo Galeano, quoted in Weschler, *A Miracle, A Universe*, 147.
[56] Elena Lenhardtson, et al., Mental Health Team of the Center for Legal and Social Studies (CELS), "Some Reflections about Torture," in *Health Services for the Treatment of Torture and Trauma Survivors* (Washington: American Association for the Advancement of Science, 1990), 93–4.
[57] Elizabeth Lira and Eugenia Weinstein, "La tortura. Conceptualización psicológica y proceso terapéutico," in *Psicología social de la guerra: trauma y terapia*, ed. Ignacio Martín-Baró (San Salvador: UCA Editores, 1990), 351–2, 359–61.
[58] Elizabeth Lira, "The Development of a Therapeutic Approach for the Treatment of Victims of Human Rights Violations in Chile and its Impact on Therapists," ILAS, manuscript no. 031, 15–16.

nightmare in the cells of the CNI. "He was as if paralyzed," writes his psychologist:

> he had an absent air, distracted, as if he were thinking about something else; eyes lowered, his gaze opaque, one could sense a bit of irritation in his attitude, although his facial expression was difficult to decipher. He appeared rigid, sad, sly. He spoke slowly, as if stammering, a "mop-like tongue." The tone of his voice was low, colorless. The process of organization of thoughts and communication was very slow; each phrase was followed by a long silence.[59]

Arturo told the therapist of the beatings he had suffered in the clandestine prison, but it was not until many sessions later that he was able to verbalize what he had not even discussed with his family. "I don't know how to explain it to you, or I was not capable of telling you; at this moment I don't know how to explain it . . . They put me on an iron bed, they tied my feet and hands, they questioned me and suddenly I felt sharp blows . . . ; it had to be [electrical] current, and they had me like that the entire morning."[60] Now he has lost all interest in affective relations, and has lost the woman to whom he was engaged. He feels safe only inside the house, becoming frightened when the door is opened. Slowly he tells the therapist, "I feel as though I were not myself."[61]

This feeling of being changed into someone else is common among victims of torture. Indeed the entire torture apparatus functions to break down the subjectivities of prisoners, to throw them into a spinning centrifuge which strips away all the coordinates by which persons identify themselves. Prisoners are subjected to the most harrowing pain and the most miniscule indignities. They are left blindfolded, isolated, subjected to constant noise, perhaps the screams of loved ones, or eerie silence. Their sleep patterns are constantly interrupted and altered, and they are denied access to the toilet. Often the rules are bizarre and seemingly senseless: a clandestine prison in Uruguay made all prisoners for one week wear their uniforms backward, with the buttons on the back.[62] Every detail of the prisoners' daily life is rigidly controlled and altered

---

[59] Elizabeth Lira, "Psicoterapia de un detenido político apolítico," in *Psicoterapia y represión política* ed. Elizabeth Lira and Eugenia Weinstein (Mexico City: Siglo Ventiuno Editores, 1984), 52.

[60] Ibid., 58.

[61] Ibid., 56.

[62] Agusto Murillo Perdomo, "Psicoterapia con víctimas de la tortura," in *Psicología social de la guerra*, 322.

at will. "They forced me to change my skin, my gestures, my voice, my way of walking," says Ramón, another victim of torture; "after months in jail, I didn't recognize myself."[63] The jailers' creation of a power which is both arbitrary and total steadily erases landmarks on the victim's personal map. At the same time it redraws lines to produce a new identity. Victims are scripted into a different socio-political drama, recreated as abused, bastard children of the regime. A team of Argentinian psychologists writes:

> If we think about the first experience of human defenselessness, we see that the life and death of the child depend absolutely on the Other – the mother – who, in giving the child care and affection, strengthens the child's Ego. In the other situation of maximum defenselessness and loss of identifiable references to which the person tortured is regressively reduced, the torturer is the only Other, the only image available to which the Ego, threatened with disintegration, has access. All that this generates – mainly humiliation and guilt for the victim's involuntary dependence – will cause most of those tortured to dissociate and to silence all or part of their experience.[64]

Not only is it difficult for the victims to assign words to the torture itself; torture permanently scrambles their general ability to build a world from words. Years after their release, victims remain silenced, their words swallowed up into the maw of horror which has so mercilessly deconstructed their identities. Aníbal Quijada writes of release from a Chilean prison:

> Yes. I was free. Free to see and hear and even to walk within the occupied city. But I could hardly speak. My movements had been restricted. I knew that I should stay far away from the street and people and be seen as little as possible . . . I was now a branded, muted man. I remained inside the house. That's all – nothing else. Looking at my wife who walked in her own house hardly making a sound, alert, looking fearfully out the window, worrying over the slightest knock on the door, talking in whispers. Later I learned to do the same.[65]

The only voice heard is that of the regime. This is why therapy for torture victims is centered on recovering their voices, allowing them to conceptualize and verbalize their anguish.[66]

---

[63] Ibid., 321.

[64] Elena Lenhardtson, et al., "Some Reflections about Torture," 94.

[65] Aníbal Quijada, "Barbed Wire Fence," trans. Jo Carrillo, in *Chilean Writers in Exile*, ed. Fernando Alegría (Trumansburg, NY: The Crossing Press, 1982), 59.

[66] Lira, "The Development of a Therapeutic Approach," 17. Giving voice to the victims also means contextualizing their anguish as part of an overall strategy of

The silencing of torture victims is akin to the cutting of affective links between the victim and others, a common symptom left by the torturer's tools. Torture victims often experience severe difficulty relating to others and lose those whose support they most desperately need. A great many victims experience, along with an inability to communicate, a loss of warmth and an aversion to intimacy.[67] It is a cruel irony of torture that the conversion of the body to an intense field of sentience leaves in its wake an inability to feel.

A person's self and a person's world are constructed largely of interpersonal relationships – links to others, both significant and peripheral – which help define who one is. In torture's shattering of self and world, those relationships are undone, and the victim is left isolated and alone, that is, without the resources to reconstitute a shared life, and therefore an integrated self. The relationship with the torturer, the only one available to the prisoner during the time she is disappeared, becomes the dark lens through which future relationships are necessarily viewed. For this reason it is crucial to distinguish between traumas caused by natural disasters – floods, earthquakes, fires – and those caused by torture. The horror of torture is magnified by the realization that *this is being done to me by another human being.* It is a perversion and destruction of the very idea of human relationship.[68]

The cruel use of kindness often goes the farthest in breaking the affective links which bind the victim to others. The secret police take full advantage of the prisoner's helplessness through the common juxtaposition of the barbaric torturer with the gentle one who appears to comfort the victim. In contrast to blows, insults, and electricity, the "good cop's" weapons include soft words, caresses, offers of hot coffee and a cigarette.[69] After a brutal session of torture, when the prisoner is demoralized and abandoned, the good interrogator appears to concern himself with the prisoner's welfare. "You poor thing, look what they've done to you," he will say. "It would be best for you to

---

political repression, and not merely a private experience. This allows the victims to circumscribe their pain and assign its cause. It also demands from the therapist a non-neutral political stance which carries its own risks. See ibid., 15, and Elizabeth Lira and Eugenia Weinstein, "Prefacio," in *Psicoterapia y represión política*, 11–19.

[67] Murillo, "Psicoterapia con víctimas de la tortura," 320.

[68] Elizabeth Lira, interview by author, July 12, 1993, Santiago, tape recording. Also David Becker, Elizabeth Lira, María Isabel Castillo, Elena Gómez, and Juana Kovalskys, "Therapy with Victims of Political Repression in Chile: The Challenge of Social Reparation," *Journal of Social Issues* 46, no. 3 (1990), 139.

[69] For firsthand accounts of the use of this technique in Chile, see Politzer, *Miedo en Chile*, 121-8, and Cassidy, *Audacity to Believe*, 179–81.

cooperate. Then I'll make sure that things go better for you." Despite its appearance, this is a technique of exceptionally refined control, for in the prisoner's state of complete abandonment, she will find herself, against her own instincts, leaning on and confiding in one of her own tormentors. The feelings of the victim toward her torturers become fraught with *ambivalence* in a situation which in fact is marked by the clearest imaginable boundaries of right and wrong. Later in therapy, "The discovery that during torture [the victim] felt dependent on one of the torturers is a self-revelation that inundates the affected person with anguish, guilt, and aggression."[70] Habitual forms of interpersonal relationship are shattered, and often the victim's basic ability to trust other people is irreparably impaired.[71]

Another common method of dissolving interpersonal links is the use of sexual torture. Entire DINA facilities were set up to specialize in this type of degradation; rape of both women and men and a host of other unmentionable practices brought horror to the very center of the prisoners' affective life.[72] Street-variety perversity is not enough to account for the extensive use of sexual torture in Chile's clandestine prisons. It is a systematic practice intended to transform the seat of procreation and erotic attraction into a space of helplessness and repulsion.[73]

Arrest and torture have devastating effects on the family life and other social relations of the victims. Besides emotional isolation, the disappearance of the family breadwinner, especially among the poor, often causes financial hardship which can split up the family if the remaining spouse is obliged to leave the home to find work. If and when the arrested person is released, he and his family and friends are stigmatized. Employers hesitate to hire someone who has incurred the wrath of the security apparatus, regardless of the merits of the charges. The constant drumbeat against "extremists" in the media helps maintain the impression that anyone who has had a close encounter with the security forces is dangerous and to be avoided, lest one fall under the same suspicion. In short, write Elizabeth Lira and Eugenia Weinstein, "The most

---

[70] Lira and Weinstein, "La tortura. Conceptualización psicológica y proceso terapéutico," 368.

[71] Ibid.

[72] The DINA center located at Calle Irán no. 3037 in Santiago was known among security agents as *La Venda Sexy* [The Sexy Blindfold]. The team of agents assigned there specialized in rape and other forms of sexual humiliation. Because of the constant background music, the place also earned the nickname *La Discoteca* [The Discotheque]; *Rettig Report*, 487–8.

[73] Ibid., 370–2.

important psychosocial damage that torture generates consists in the destruction or deterioration of collective links."[74]

It should be clear at this point that the psychological scars which torture leaves behind are not intended for the individual victim alone. Through the shattering of his relationships and the silencing of his voice, the victim is forced to suffer the assault on his self-identity in isolation. Ironically, his isolation is intended to reverberate throughout the society and spread his suffering to others, who yet must also suffer alone. As Mary Douglas has shown, the individual body is a mirror of the social body. The physical body is constantly made to emit signs for the benefit of society. To discipline social bodies it is therefore necessary to discipline the body of the individual. If torture has the effect of destroying the relational links between victims and others, it will likewise have the effect of disciplining the society into isolated monads easily made to serve the regime's purposes.

When the survivors of torture are released back into the population at large, their isolation does not prevent them from conveying an implicit message to others. They serve as walking signifiers of the regime's power, spreading fear among others who might be tempted to defy the state. Their own voices silenced, they mutely shout the words of the regime. As Aníbal Quijada suggested, they bear the "brand" of the regime, like a cow marked and claimed by its owner.

Disappearance and torture were important facets of the Pinochet regime's overall strategy, which aimed at dissolving all opposition social groups, such as parties, church groups, unions, and community organizations. Actual action by security forces went well beyond harsh laws restricting the functioning of such groups, such that even legal group activity could be met with torture.[75] At the same time, those who chose to challenge the ban on political activity lived in constant fear and suspicion of even their closest comrades, since informants were widely rumored and the interrogation process was designed to spread feelings of betrayal among members of a group. Victims were commonly told that their companions had already collaborated with the secret police and had already betrayed them. The effects on organizations were devastating.[76]

---

[74] Lira and Weinstein, "La tortura. Conceptualización psicológica y proceso terapeútico," 346–8.
[75] Political parties were placed in "recess" immediately following the coup, and were officially dissolved on March 11, 1977. A 1974 law gave the Junta unlimited power over all other intermediate groups to replace their leaders at its whim; *Rettig Report*, 85–6.
[76] Murillo, "Psicoterapia con víctimas de la tortura," 324.

The repercussions of the system of torture extend far beyond active militants of the opposition, seeping like poison into the groundwater of the subject classes. A joke popular in Chile following the coup went like this: "A terrified bunny rabbit runs off to the border. The guard who stops him on the other side asks, 'What are you running away from?' He answers, 'They're killing all the elephants in Chile.' The border guard soothes him, saying 'That's OK, you're a bunny.' The bunny answers, 'And how am I supposed to prove that?' "[77] The joke reflects the popular fear that seemingly random victims were swept up into the web of repression. It may seem that the secret police would have no reason to draw its tentacles around people with no political or church or union activity, but it occurred often, and the apparent randomness bears the imprint of a sinister design. If "mistakes" were made, then no one could feel entirely secure, and anxiety could spread through the society like a virus. The security of some states is made to depend on the insecurity of its citizens. The citizens then become self-disciplining, which is far more effective than the use of brute force.

The self-isolation and self-regulation of the population were served by the deliberately vague limits the repressive apparatus put on group activities. At times during the Pinochet regime, meetings were allowed; at other times they were violently suppressed. Most people stayed away from any group activity. The isolation itself fed the fear, for accurate information gave way to unsubstantiated rumors and dark stories of atrocities.[78] People learned to live in an environment of fear and anxiety, avoiding as much as possible anything but the most superficial contact with neighbors and co-workers. "The myth of the omnipresent security apparatus became so great that no one wanted to take risks," recalled Carlos Gálvez, formerly a labor organizer. "You would confide only in people you were absolutely sure of, and even then there was always a seed of doubt."[79] Chile's flourishing public life was driven indoors and privatized. A community leader during Allende's government summed up his life under Pinochet: "I spent years swearing at the television set."[80]

If disappearance and torture worked to isolate and transform the identity of its direct victims, the same dynamic applied to the rest of society as well. Aníbal Quijada writes:

[77] Garretón, "Fear in Military Regimes: An Overview," 25 n. 5.
[78] Ibid., 18.
[79] Carlos Gálvez, quoted in Constable and Valenzuela, *A Nation of Enemies*, 147–8.
[80] Quoted in Constable and Valenzuela, *A Nation of Enemies*, 148.

There was a fence that came out of the detention centers and around the city. You could see it in the streets around every house, surrounding the people, with its barbs ready. Those barbs had acquired many forms: they patrolled the streets in dark cars, they were in the threatening weapons of the soldiers and police, they were fixed in watchfulness, they had the sound of metal in the sly footsteps that hounded people, they were writers in lists and accusations, they became voices and actions in the events of every hour, by day and by night.[81]

The idea of torture is perhaps the most effective generator of fear, since torture reaches to the very limits of horror, turning the body against the person to such an extent that death appears as something desirable.[82] Fear of torture, fear of death, were concrete fears that only began to articulate the hidden anxieties which lurked not far beneath the surface of Chilean society.[83] The net effect of this strategy was the disappearance of social bodies which would rival the state.

Anxiety is such an effective tool for the regime's strategy of disarticulating social bodies because of its peculiar character as an essentially private phenomenon which nevertheless can be produced simultaneously in millions of persons within a given society.[84] The regime's practices do not merely isolate, but also create new subjectivities which form a "community" of atomized selves scripted into the regime's drama of anxiety and fear. Paradoxically the isolation experienced is accompanied by a feeling of *having lost one's sense of privacy*.[85] People feel themselves to be labeled and watched by the regime, yet feel themselves to be alone in this experience, as if they were the only one. The state thus succeeds in separating people from each other yet creating a direct and powerful link between the state and the individual. The state does not merely wish to make its citizens feel as independent as possible from each other, but also seeks to make them as dependent as possible on the authority of the state.

Michel Foucault's memorable image of the Panopticon captures this arrangement superbly. Modern power, Foucault claims, can be characterized

[81] Quijada, "Barbed Wire Fence," 59.

[82] Elena Lenhardtson, et al., "Some Reflections About Torture," 93–4.

[83] Anxiety is the inability to specify the content of the threat felt, the "dark room." Anxiety becomes fear when the source of the threat is identified, the "dog that bites"; see Garretón, "Fear in Military Regimes," 14 and Salimovich, Lira, and Weinstein, "Victims of Fear," 73.

[84] Elizabeth Lira, and María Isabel Castillo, "Psicología de la amenaza polítia y del miedo y conducta colectiva en Chile," (Santiago, ILAS, 1991), 175.

[85] Salimovich, Lira, and Weinstein, "Victims of Fear," 74.

by its likeness to Jeremy Bentham's design for a prison, with its central surveillance tower surrounded by cells.

> By the effect of backlighting, one can observe from the tower, standing out precisely against the light, the small captive shadows in the cells of the periphery. They are like so many cages, so many small theatres, in which each actor is alone, perfectly individualized and constantly visible . . . Each individual, in his place, is securely confined to a cell from which he is seen from the front by the supervisor; but the side walls prevent him from coming into contact with his companions. He is seen, but he does not see.[86]

The possibility of subversive community is eliminated; the subject, attached by invisible spokes to the hub of the state, learns to respond only to the central disciplining apparatus. But at the same time the authority in the tower remains invisible; Bentham cleverly designed his Panopticon never to betray the presence or absence of a guard in the surveillance tower. Unsure at any moment if she is being watched, but sure at all times of its possibility, the subject becomes self-disciplining. In Pinochet's Chile this process was taken one step further, because generalized anxiety made each person an observer, and the "surveillance tower" itself, the secret police apparatus, was invisible. A decentralized, hyper-panopticism resulted, with each citizen playing the simultaneous roles of watcher and watched. This is the apex of power, for as Foucault shows, power is most powerful when it functions invisibly.[87]

3 The Striptease of Power

It may seem odd for me to subscribe to Foucault's comments on the invisibility of modern power when Foucault himself illustrates this point by showing the movement *away from* torture and other direct attacks on the body. Part One of *Discipline and Punish* is entitled "Torture," and it begins with a horrific account of the public mutilation and dismemberment of the regicide Damiens in mid-eighteenth-century Paris.[88] From there Foucault traces the fascinating evolution of Western penal institutions, showing how between the mid-eighteenth and early nineteenth centuries, social control rapidly turned from

---

[86] Michel Foucault, *Discipline and Punish: The Birth of the Prison*, trans. Alan Sheridan (New York: Vintage Books, 1977), 200.

[87] Ibid., 201–3.

[88] Ibid., 3–6.

corporal punishment to incarceration. Criminals are no longer whipped, burned, or hacked to pieces before the anxious eyes of the townspeople. They are put away in prisons, banished from the public view, where their souls, not their bodies, are the ostensible objects of disciplinary attention. The idea is to suspend some of the prisoner's rights, especially that of liberty, but not to inflict pain. The sequestering of the prisoners allows the state not merely to punish but to reform, recreating the person as a more productive social entity.[89] Nothing, it seems, could be farther from the horrors of the South American dungeon and its torture apparatus.

The torture which rent Damiens's body, however, is as dissimilar from Chilean torture as it is similar. Like pre-modern regimes, the Chilean secret police attacked the body of its victims, but like modern regimes, it worked invisibly on social bodies. According to Foucault, torture must meet two demands. First, "It must mark the victim: it is intended, either by the scar it leaves on the body, or by the spectacle that accompanies it, to brand the victim with infamy." Second, "from the point of view of the law that imposes it, public torture and execution must be spectacular, it must be seen by all almost as its triumph."[90] Modern torture in Latin America meets neither of these demands. Techniques of torment taught by the master torturers place great emphasis on leaving no physical marks behind. And torture never surfaces, but does its work in the shadowy realm of the disappeared, in clandestine dungeons with no address and no escape.

Modern torture does not fit neatly into Foucault's narrative of the birth of modern penal institutions, for although it assaults the body, the spectacle is eliminated. Nevertheless, modern torture can be located within the shift to disciplinary societies of the modern type. For although most writing on the subject sees this shift as a humanitarian move away from cruelty and toward reform, Foucault shows, convincingly I think, that as state power has extended into every aspect of modern life, many states have simply found that obvious

---

[89] Ibid., 6–16.

[90] Ibid., 34. Foucault makes no claim that his analysis of torture is meant to cover all uses of the word across historical and geographical boundaries. In fact, he places great emphasis on "genealogical" histories which trace effects through concrete practices over limited spans of time and place. Foucault alludes to modern torture in contrast with judicial torture of the medieval period; he does, however, misdescribe it as "the unrestrained torture of modern interrogations." Medieval torture, he says, contrasts with modern torture in that the former "was certainly cruel, but it was not savage. It was a regulated practice, obeying a well-defined procedure;" 40. Foucault ignores the extent to which modern torture has been ruthlessly routinized.

displays of power, as in direct public attacks on people's bodies, are less effective than more invisible means of coercion.

The Chilean repressive apparatus also was predicated largely on invisibility. Claudio Molina Donoso was picked up on the street September 4, 1986, blindfolded, and taken to a secret CNI prison.

> The tortures were varied. They took me from the cell and submerged me in a type of tub, from the waist up, with my hands tied behind my back. They grabbed me by the hair and put me in at full force. The tub had excrement and other things in it. They took me out when I was losing consciousness or began to flail my arms desperately.
>
> Other times they threatened me forcefully, beat me and put me against a wall, simulating a firing squad . . . Another form of pressure was not letting me sleep for four or five days . . .
>
> On one occasion they stripped me and left me hanging by the handcuffs, some four or five hours in this condition. Because of this my left arm was partially paralyzed for 40 days . . . The next day, in the room called "The Soviet," they interrogated me intensively, progressively increasing the voltage of the electric current. More or less an hour and a half later they released one of my hands and gave me a revolver. They said we were going to play 'Russian Roulette.' They pointed the revolver at my head. In a moment of desperation, in an attempt to end it all, I fired all the chambers of the gun. They were surprised. "So you want to die! . . ." "We're going to give you a slow death."[91]

The important thing to notice about this typical account is that for all the variations of intense torment, both physical and psychological, none of the methods used left any visible mark on the body of Claudio Molina. He was released profoundly affected by the experience, but with no sign to prove what he had undergone. Of the torture techniques listed by the Chilean Commission for Human Rights as used in Chile, few left marks of any kind: besides a range of psychological tortures, the Commission lists electricity, beatings, "the telephone,"[92] sexual torture, forced postures, water torture, the "parrot's perch,"[93] burning with cigarettes, privation of food and water,

---

[91] Claudio Molina Donoso, quoted in René García Villegas, *Soy testigo: dictadura, Tortura, injusticia* (Santiago: Editorial Amerinda, 1990), 94–6.

[92] "The telephone" consists of simultaneous blows to both ears of the victim, causing intense pain and loss of equilibrium. It is used worldwide in countries that torture.

[93] The victim is "hogtied" and hung by a bar passed behind the victim's knees. Hanging upside down, the victim is then usually subjected to electrical current. Because of its Brazilian origin, this torture is usually known by its Portuguese name, "*pau de arara.*"

and bright lights or loud noises.[94] Beatings and burnings that left marks were almost always allowed to heal before the prisoner was released or delivered over to the regular judicial system; the secret detention site at Cuatro Alamos was designated as the place where prisoners could recuperate from torture before surfacing to public scrutiny.[95] The soul was to bear the scars, not the body.

Not only the torturer's craft but the entire repressive machine was predicated on invisibility. The Pinochet regime never admitted the existence of an extensive network of clandestine torture centers to which people were whisked off in the dead of night. In the early years of the DINA's operation, agents would drag people from their beds and drive off into the darkness, but eventually they refined their strategy, moving toward snatching victims off the street, the better to avoid witnesses.[96] The person would simply not come home, just vanish into thin air. Hours or days would pass before the families began their desperate searches, all with the same dreary result: the judiciary and government organs routinely denied that the victims had ever been arrested.

Of the 5,400 petitions of habeas corpus filed between 1973 and 1983 by the Catholic church's Vicaría de Solidaridad on behalf of those kidnapped by security forces, the Supreme Court rejected all but ten.[97] The courts limited themselves to routine queries to the same authorities that had done the dirty work. Invariably officials denied that the arrest had ever taken place,

---

[94] Comisión Chilena de Derechos Humanos, *La practica de la tortura en Chile durante la vigencia de la constitución política de 1980* (Santiago: 1982), 30–1. This is by no means a complete list of tortures used in Chile over the course of the dictatorship (it covers the Commission's findings for 1981–2), but it gives a good idea of the physical tortures most widely used under Pinochet. A listing of methods used in the years 1973–5 is essentially the same; see Katia Reszczynski, Paz Rojas, and Patricia Barcelo, *Tortura y resistencia en Chile: estudio médico-político* (Santiago: Editorial Emisión, 1991), 131–9.

[95] *Rettig Report*, 484. Actor Sergio Buschmann Silva, kidnapped and tortured in 1986, gives this account of the end of his time in a secret CNI center: "I realized because of a sign I saw beneath my blindfold: 'Don't touch,' that we were in the 'cosmetic phase,' that is, in the fixing up of the prisoner, when he will be delivered over to public knowledge"; testimony in García Villegas, *Soy testigo*, 91.

[96] Research of the database of the Vicaría de Solidaridad's archives at the Center for Civil and Human Rights at the Notre Dame Law School reveals a significant shift in the DINA's strategy near the end of 1975 and the beginning of 1976. By the middle of 1976, the DINA had become quite proficient at making people disappear without a trace.

[97] Constable and Valenzuela, *A Nation of Enemies*, 122.

often suggesting that the missing person had "left his wife" or "fled the country," explanations the judges meekly accepted without further investigation. Some of those who had vanished resurfaced – usually after being tortured – in an equally mysterious way, let off blindfolded in a deserted field or street. Others reappeared in legal custody; if the authorities had already denied the fact of their arrest, a back-dated detention order was hastily prepared and an "unfortunate administrative error" quickly concocted.[98] Others, finally, never reappeared at all. After Manuel Cortez Joo was snatched off the street on February 14, 1975,[99] his mother, like so many other mothers, undertook a frantic search for him, filing writs of habeas corpus and shuttling from one government agency to another begging for clues. In response to an inquiry on her behalf by the Interamerican Commission of Human Rights, the Chilean government issued this typical reply:

> Case 2022 – MANUEL EDGARDO CORTEZ JOO. There is no evidence that this person is or has been arrested in Chile. Presumably this person has gone into hiding with the purpose of joining the clandestine extremist movements. The accusation might be due to persons who, with the purpose of defaming the government of Chile, dedicate themselves to fabricating lists of persons who were supposedly arrested.[100]

Manuel Cortez remains disappeared to this day.

The word "disappearance" captures the mysterious quality of the strategy of invisibility. The shift from open executions to disappearance in the six months or so after the coup should not be understood merely as an attempt by the regime to cover up its crimes. The very occult nature of disappearance – the way it obfuscates knowledge of what is really going on – augments the fear and anxiety which separates people from each other. Disappearance also works to discipline the family and friends of the victim. The relatives of disappeared persons, with no body to prove what has happened, live in a limbo world between fantasy and reality. On the one hand, to believe that the person is still alive is to prolong visions of torment to which the victim has undoubtedly been subjected. Chilean poet Ariel Dorfman:

[98] Ibid., 122–4.

[99] *Rettig Report*, 546.

[100] Quoted in a letter dated July 2, 1976 from the Interamerican Commission of Human Rights to Señora Faustina Joo de Cortez, archives of the Vicaría de Solidaridad.

> What I am asking is
> how can it be
> that a father's
> joy
> a mother's
> joy
> is knowing
> that they
> that they are still
> torturing
> their son?
> Which means
> that he was alive
> five months later
> and our greatest
> hope
> will be to find out
> next year
> that they're still torturing him
> eight months later[101]

On the other hand, to decide to assume the disappeared person is dead is, in effect, to kill him in one's own mind.[102] In the face of official denials, the death becomes the family's own invention. The dilemma is exceedingly cruel. It disturbs the normal processes of grief and mourning, and it often succeeds in buying the silence of the victim's family and friends. Unable to know the whereabouts of the victim and thus unable to give up hope, hope is controlled for the regime's purposes, as the relatives cooperate with the authorities for fear that their actions could bring reprisals on their loved one.[103]

The strategy of invisibility is key to understanding state terror in Chile, yet for this type of strategy to be effective, the state's power cannot simply remain hidden. Disappearance and torture is rather a dance of visibility and invisibility, a macabre striptease of power in which the regime both conceals its security apparatus and at the same time assures that its presence is widely known. The sheer terror of torture must be invisible to public scrutiny, but

---

[101] Ariel Dorfman, "Hope," in *Last Waltz in Santiago*, 8.
[102] Elizabeth Lira, David Becker, and Maria Isabel Castillo, "Psychotherapy with Victims of Political Repression in Chile: A Therapeutic and Political Challenge," in *Health Services for the Treatment of Torture and Trauma Survivors*, 107–8.
[103] See *Nunca Más*, 233–4.

its power must nevertheless be manifested for the state to achieve its goals of social control. Disappearance and torture is a game of the shadows, always lurking just out of sight, behind the curtain of the temple. The omnipotence of the state must be made present, but it is most powerful precisely when it is invisible, internalized in the anxieties of the people. The liturgy of torture realizes the state's terrible might, but it remains out of grasp yet palpable, felt like a nausea in the viscera of society.

It is important for the regime, therefore, both to deny and simultaneously to affirm the existence of state terror. In an interview with journalist Patricia Politzer, Colonel Juan Deichler Guzmán exemplifies this double logic. After disputing the number of the permanently disappeared in Chile, Deichler says:

> Besides, I think that all these disappeared people were like rabid dogs, full of rage! [*rabia* = rabies; also rage or fury] And rabies must be eliminated, although by no means do I justify it. Neither in the Army, nor in any institution of National Defense are the disappearances justified. On the other hand, are they all disappeared? A neighbor of mine was crying about a disappeared person and two weeks later he arrived from Argentina. There are a lot of myths about this disappearance thing![104]

Colonel Deichler justifies the disappearances, then denies justifying them, then casts doubt on their existence altogether. Spokespersons for the Pinochet regime became adept at this type of discourse; accusations of human rights abuses were used as proof that opponents of the regime were steeped in Marxist tactics of strategic lying, the regime thus tacitly justifying violence against such devious miscreants.[105] The very denials were simultaneous affirmations. The point of this was not to minimize the violence, to calm the fears of the people while the security forces went about their secret business of eliminating subversion. On the contrary, the point was to stoke the fires of

---

[104] Interview in Politzer, *Miedo en Chile*, 67.

[105] See e.g. the interview with General Manuel Contreras, ex-chief of the DINA, in the newspaper *Las Ultimas Noticias*, March 26, 1991. Asked about accusations of grave violations of human rights under the Pinochet regime, Contreras responds: "False propaganda and vicious rumors by means of a prostrated press are one of the principal weapons for discrediting people according to the guerrilla manual of Che Guevara. So it doesn't surprise me that the Marxists, taking advantage of the freedom they've had to use the press, can say such things and many others. And they have to say such things because in four years we beat them in the subversive war." The "four years" are 1973–77, when the leftist parties in Chile were wiped out by disappearance and torture.

disorder. The state increased fear and the subsequent demand for order, and then presented itself as the only possible solution to the disorder.[106]

In an essay entitled "Terror as Usual: Walter Benjamin's Theory of History as State of Siege," Michael Taussig uses Colombia as one exemplar of Benjamin's idea that the so-called "state of emergency" invoked by various regimes is not the exception to history but the rule.[107] Chile lived virtually all of its seventeen years of dictatorship under one or another of the "states of exception." The forces of order have much to gain from disorder. Disorder is, after all, what gives them their reason to be. Part of the fine art of social control, of generating states of normality, is creating the appearance of a prior chaos.

Here Foucault's notion of control through normalization is turned inside out, for within this type of routinization the abnormal is built-in, and terror becomes the norm: "Combining violence with law, the state in Latin America rules through the strategic art of abnormalizing."[108] What passes for reality in such a world is deeply imbued with fantasy, the "magical realism" captured in the best of Latin American literature. Not only torture victims, but victims of fear and anxiety in general lose their ability to distinguish clearly between reality and fantasy.[109] This becomes a generalized condition under a terrorist state which both undertakes massive and brutal violence against its people, and at the same time imposes a strict denial that such abuses are real.

Part of what it means to have arbitrary power is that the state becomes the arbiter of what is real and what is not. But rather than set firm boundaries between reality and unreality, it is more profitable for the state to leave those boundaries confused and ambiguous. Ambiguity and unknowing create anxiety, which in turn creates the demand for order which the state provides. Power remains invisible; it is rarely seen but it is constantly *felt*. The aim is not to erase the violence but to drive it deep within the recesses of the individual. As Taussig writes,

> The State's interest is in keeping memory of public political protest, and memory of the sadistic and cruel violence unleashed against it, alive! . . . The memory of protest, and the violence enacted against it by the State, best serves the official forces of repression when the collective nature of the memory is broken, when it is fragmented and located not in the public sphere but in the

---

[106] Norbert Lechner, "Some People Die of Fear," in *Fear at the Edge*, 26–35.
[107] Michael Taussig, *The Nervous System* (New York: Routledge, 1992), 11–13.
[108] Ibid., 48.
[109] Lira, "Psicología del miedo y conducta colectiva en Chile," 184–6.

private fastness of the individual self or of the family. There it feeds fear. There it feeds nightmares crippling the capacity for public protest and spirited intelligent opposition.[110]

What is ironic about this game of visibility and invisibility is that through it the state manages to conceal the fact that the state does not, as such, exist. This easily forgotten curiosity has been pointed out many times.[111] One cannot put a finger on the state; what exists instead are certain buildings and tanks and tax forms and custom inspectors and soldiers. But none of these physical bodies are the state, and they only take on their peculiar power when the idea of the state is *believed in*. As Philip Abrams puts it:

> Armies and prisons, the Special Patrol and the deportation orders as well as the whole process of fiscal exaction . . . are all forceful enough. But it is their association with the idea of the state and the invocation of that idea that silences protest, excuses force and convinces almost all of us that the fate of the victims is just and necessary.[112]

The state manages to assert its claims over the bodies of citizens while simultaneously concealing its own imaginary status.

To use the word "imaginary" is not to trivialize or wish away what we find abominable. Obviously there is a sense in which the state has far more reality than the "real," and not simply in the sense that the whole of the state is more fearsome than the sum of its real parts. The state is imaginary in the precise sense of the phrase "make believe." De Certeau uses this phrase (*faire croire*) in describing torture's effects: "Torture is the technical procedure by which the tyrannical power acquires for itself this impalpable primary matter which it itself destroyed and which it lacks: authority, or, if one prefers, a capacity to make believe."[113]

As we have already seen, torture makes real the power of the state on the body of the individual and on the body politic. Torture is a "liturgical" enactment of the imaginative project of the state. Therefore the terrorist state is not just the

---

[110] Taussig, *The Nervous System*, 48.

[111] E.g. Ralph Miliband, *The State in Capitalist Society: An Analysis of the Western System of Power* (New York: Basic Books, 1969), 49; and A. R. Radcliffe-Brown, preface, in *African Political Systems*, ed. M. Fortes and E. E. Evans-Pritchard (Oxford: Oxford University Press, 1970), xxiii.

[112] Philip Abrams, "Notes on the Difficulty of Studying the State," *Journal of Historical Sociology* 1, no. 1 (March 1988), 77.

[113] de Certeau, "Corps torturés, paroles capturées."

agent of torture, but the effect of torture as well. For this reason I refer to torture not as the state's imagination, but as the imagination of the state. The ambiguous genitive helps indicate that the state is not an independent agent invested of its own will, but is better understood as an enacted imaginative drama in which – in some states – torture is the repeated climactic moment.

Modern torture as practiced in Chile is, therefore, not simply a contest over the visible, physical body; it is better understood as a contest over the social *imagination*, in which bodies are the battleground. As Cornelius Castoriadis uses the term in his *The Imaginary Institution of Society*, the imagination of a society is the sense of what is real and what is not; it includes a memory of how the society got where it is, a sense of who it is, and hopes and projects for the future. The social imagination is not a mere representation of something which is real, as a flag represents a putatively "real" nation-state; the imagination of a society is involved when the flag becomes what one will kill and die for. In other words, the social imagination is not a mere image of something more real; it is not some ideological "superstructure" which reflects the material "base." There is no substantive distinction between material and cultural production. The imagination of a society is the condition of possibility for the organization and signification of bodies in a society.[114] The imagination is the drama in which bodies are invested.

This allows for a more adequate way of approaching the distinction between "body" and "soul" in political discourse. As Foucault has it, the body is still the target of the disciplinary society of the modern type, but the "soul" is the instrument of this "political economy of the body." The object is to create "docile bodies" which are productive for the interests of power; the soul – which is the province of educators, psychologists, theologians, and propagandists – is the effect of the power/knowledge which organizes and habituates these bodies. "The soul is the prison of the body."[115]

To grasp torture as the "imagination of the state" is crucial for helping us to see that the state does not simply want the body; it wants the soul as well. This will become especially important in the next two chapters, when we see that Catholic ecclesiology accepted an arrangement whereby the state would have charge of the body and the church would care for the soul. Such an arrangement is a dangerous illusion. The state under Pinochet was involved in a larger drama. It could not but aspire to be an entire worldview, a way of imagining space and time with which that of the church would conflict.

---

[114] See Cornelius Castoriadis, *The Imaginary Institution of Society*, trans. Kathleen Blamey (Cambridge, Mass.: MIT Press, 1987), 115–64.

[115] Foucault, *Discipline and Punish*, 24–31.

In this chapter so far, we have seen that torture and disappearance effect the casting of bodies into the imaginative drama of a certain state project through a subtle strategy of visibility and invisibility. The effect on rival bodies such as the church is to disappear them by breaking them up into individual units easily subjected to the state's discipline and written into its performance. In this contest over bodies, both individual and social, Christian resistance will depend on having a visible body, that is, a counter-discipline and counter-performance. In the fourth and final section of this chapter, I will illustrate this contest by discussing martyrdom, the Christian locus where the contest is most acute. I will show how torture and disappearance work to refuse a visible body to the church by denying it the possibility of martyrs, those who keep alive the subversive memory of Christ through their *public* witness, and thus make the body of Christ visible.

4 Habeas Corpus

Father Patrick Rice's work with the poor did not escape the attention of the secret police. Rice was an Irish worker-priest who had made his home in Villa Soldati, a fetid slum built around and upon a garbage dump on the outskirts of Buenos Aires. Witnessing to hope in a slum can be a perilous undertaking, as Rice discovered one evening in October 1976. That night a young woman named Fátima Cabrera had come to the chapel to ask Rice for medicine for her sister. In a scene repeated countless times throughout Latin America, Rice and Cabrera were snatched off the street by armed men in civilian garb.[116] They were taken to a police station, where they were brutally mistreated. After being tortured there, as Rice tells it, "they took me to a cell, and soon others came to tell me that 'I was going to the Military', that I was going to see that the Romans did not know a thing when they persecuted the first Christians in comparison with the Argentine Military."[117]

Insofar as the police in this case were referring to the magnitude of cruelty delivered by the Romans in their circuses, they were wrong: the Romans knew how to inflict unspeakable pain with a perversely varied creativity that only torture-as-entertainment could foster.[118] With regard to the overall strategy employed by the repressive apparatuses in Latin America, however,

---

[116] Penny Lernoux, *Cry of the People* (New York: Penguin Books, 1982), 3–7.
[117] *Nunca Más*, 339.
[118] See Daniel P. Mannix, *The History of Torture* (New York: Dell Publishing Co., 1964), 27–42.

the police who spoke this way to Father Rice were absolutely right. Many modern states have learned the lessons of the Coliseum summed up in the oft-quoted dictum attributed to Tertullian, "The blood of the martyrs is the seed of the church."[119] Christian resistance to regimes of terror has often appropriated the ancient language of martyrdom to claim for the church a new crop of witnesses to the faith among those who have suffered persecution in Latin America. If we are to understand properly the workings of terror and the church's response, however, we must see the strategies of disappearance and torture as ways to *deny* martyrs to the church. In this section I will first examine some prominent attempts to assimilate the experience of martyrs to the Latin American experience, and argue that they do not adequately account for the ecclesiological dimension of martyrdom. I will show how martyrdom makes the church visible, and then show how torture works to create victims, not martyrs.

Reading through the acts of the early Christian martyrs, it is not difficult to see why the word "martyr," meaning "witness," was assigned to them. Although the accounts are highly stylized, the basic shape of Christian martyrdom under the Romans comes through. The horrible deaths of the martyrs are usually preceded by a lengthy interrogation in which a Roman official offers the prisoner a last opportunity to recant. The martyrs here make their final public confession of fidelity to Jesus Christ, often seizing the occasion to deliver a defense of the essentials of the Christian faith before the unbelieving judges. They are then led away to their deaths, standing before the mocking crowds, awaiting deliverance from this momentary torment into the peace of their assured reward.[120]

To what extent can the experiences of modern victims of violence in Latin America be compared to those of the early Christian martyrs? At all levels of Latin American society, martyrologies abound, and the language of martyrdom appears frequently in accounts of state abuses of power.[121] More famed

---

[119] The actual quote appears in Tertullian's *Apology*, ch. 50, as "Plures efficimur quoties metimur a vobis, semen est sanguis christianorum." (The oftener we are mown down by you, the more in number we grow; the blood of Christians is seed.) See *The Ante-Nicene Fathers*, vol. III, ed. Alexander Roberts and James Donaldson (New York: Charles Scribner's Sons, 1926), 55.

[120] See Herbert Musurillo, trans. and ed., *The Acts of the Christian Martyrs* (Oxford: Oxford University Press, 1972).

[121] E.g. Paul Debesse, *Mártires latinoamericanos de hoy* (Santiago: Ediciones Paulinas, 1991); *Testigos de Cristo hasta la muerte: martirologio latinoamericano* (Buenos Aires: SERPAJ, 1984); and Jaime Escobar, *Persecución a la iglesia en Chile* (Santiago: Terranova Editores, 1986).

victims such as Oscar Romero and the six Jesuits and two women killed in El Salvador are widely revered as martyrs; pictures of Romero hang in the dwellings of the poor all over Latin America. Leftist movements and even the secret police also celebrate their own martyrs.

Even if we limit ourselves to victims of violence who were active Christians and participants in the church in Latin America, there is still nevertheless a great deal of hesitancy by the church hierarchy to lay the mantle of martyrdom upon them.[122] The theological reason for this hesitation is that the traditional definition of martyrdom, "tolerant acceptance of death for the sake of the faith,"[123] would not seem to apply in twentieth-century Latin America. The faith does not seem to be what is at issue in these persecutions, for the killing of Christians is not done *in odium fidei*, given that most of the killers are Christians too, and profess the same doctrines of faith.

Leonardo Boff and Jon Sobrino have both attempted to expand the theological notion of martyrdom so that those fallen in the struggle for justice in Latin America might share the martyrs' glory. Boff does so by suggesting that not only those who die for the sake of Christ, nor only those who die for the sake of actions derived from their faith in Christ, but also those who die for "truth and justice," which is the content of Christ's message, are to be considered martyrs.[124] Sobrino, housemate and brother of the six slain Jesuits, makes a similar move in recommending that a martyr be defined "not only, or principally, as someone who dies *for* Christ, but someone who dies *like* Christ." It follows, then, that "a martyr is defined as not only or principally someone who dies *for Christ*, but someone who dies *for Jesus' cause*."[125] What is crucial, according to Sobrino, is to rethink martyrdom in terms of Jesus' life and death, instead of in terms of faith in Jesus. Jesus died not for the church, but for the Kingdom of mercy and justice, which can be identified in history by the criterion of love. Love has priority over truth, though they are not mutually exclusive: "Both things can be united if we say that in martyrdom

---

[122] See the final document of the Puebla Conference, paragraphs 92, 265, 668, and 1138, where persecution is referred to but the language of martyrdom is avoided; Conferencia General del Episcopado Latinoamericano, *Puebla: la evangelización en el presente y en el futuro de América Latina* (Bogotá: Ediciones CELAM, 1979).

[123] Karl Rahner, "Dimensions of Martyrdom: A Plea for the Broadening of a Classical Concept," *Concilium* 163 (1983), 9.

[124] Leonardo Boff, "Martyrdom: An Attempt at Systematic Reflection," *Concilium* 163 (1983), 12-17.

[125] Jon Sobrino, *Jesus the Liberator*, trans. Paul Burns and Francis McDonagh (Maryknoll, NY: Orbis Books, 1993), 267, italics in the original.

for the cause of justice the martyr is bearing witness to the truth of the God of justice, the truth of the God of the poor, and the practice that leads to martyrdom is often explicitly, or sometimes implicitly, accompanied by a faith in this God."[126]

Boff and Sobrino seem right to amplify the definition of martyrdom so that it might respond to the Latin American experience. In a region where so many identified with the church have suffered great persecution, it is fitting that the people have turned to the martyrs of old for inspiration and guidance in living through their present affliction. The Pope has used the language of martyrdom to describe the present-day suffering of the faithful. During the Holy Week Angelus on March 30, 1980, just six days after the murder of Archbishop Romero, John Paul II offered the following reflection:

> We cannot forget those who in our day have suffered death for the faith and for the love of Christ, those who in different ways have been jailed, tortured, condemned to death and even mocked, despised, humiliated and marginalized socially. The *martyrologium* of the church and Christians of our day cannot be forgotten. This *martyrologium* is written with different characters from the ancient ones. There are other methods of martyrdom and another way of giving testimony; but all springs from the same cross of Christ and completes the same cross of our redemption.[127]

Sobrino is right to emphasize, as does the Pope, the Christoform nature of martyrdom. Martyrdom is an imitation of Christ, a following in the way of the cross. Jesus warned that those who would follow him would drink from the same cup of suffering as he (Mk 10:38). Martyrdom is the clearest exemplification of that following.

Unfortunately, both Sobrino and Boff threaten to deform the *imitatio Christi* by recognizing abstract principles such as "love" or "justice" as more basic to determining who is a martyr and who is not. Boff and Sobrino seem to assume that the content of Christ's life, death, and resurrection can be isolated apart from their form. Thus Sobrino's "central criterion for martyrdom," that it be "unjustly inflicted death for love's sake,"[128] leaves him no choice but to recognize even those who resort to armed violence as potential "martyrs by analogy." Their status as martyrs depends on their successful overcoming in love of the dangers of dehumanization implicit in the use of

---

[126] Ibid., 269.
[127] Pope John Paul II, quoted in Debesse, *Mártires latinoamericanos de hoy*, 118.
[128] Sobrino, *Jesus the Liberator*, 270.

violence, "and in the end only God can judge where great love has been shown."[129] One difficulty with this account is that it ends up straining analogy to the breaking point. The ancient martyrs are *defined* by their nonviolence; Tertullian asks "For what wars should we not be fit, not eager, even with unequal forces, we who so willingly yield ourselves to the sword, if in our religion it were not counted better to be slain than to slay?"[130] The martyrs choose death rather than apostasy or violent resistance precisely because their deaths mirror that of Jesus on the cross. As *The Martyrdom of Polycarp* makes clear, the martyrs are loved "as disciples and imitators of the Lord."[131] The Acts of the martyrs place moving emphasis on their imitation of the life and death of Jesus as the way to participation in his resurrection and glory.[132] The imitation of Christ is not reducible to some principle such as "love," but is rather a highly skilled performance learned in a disciplined community of virtue by careful attention to the concrete contours of the Christian life and death as borne out by Jesus and the saints.

Sobrino and Boff need not make the move to abstract principles in order to expand the concept of martyrdom to the contemporary Latin American scene. What is needed is rather a more eschatological and more ecclesial notion of what is meant by dying for one's faith, one which does not make sharp distinctions between the "religious" dimensions of confessing Jesus as Lord and the "political" implications of such a confession. The ancient church understood the martyrs' deaths as an inevitable consequence of imitating Jesus, who was put to death for inaugurating a new reign which stood in contrast to the powers and principalities of the world. In Christ's death, God "disarmed the rulers and authorities and made a public example of them, triumphing over them in it" (Col. 2:15). The very presence of the church in the world is an affront to these powers, for the church demonstrates in its life how to be free of the powers. The church of the martyrs saw itself as a "contrast-society,"[133] a holy people called out of darkness to be a light to the nations (1 Pet. 2:9), a people who rejected the sword and

---

[129] Ibid.

[130] Tertullian, *Apology*, ch. 37, in *The Ante-Nicene Fathers*, vol. III, 45.

[131] *The Martyrdom of Polycarp*, in *Early Christian Writings*, trans. Maxwell Staniforth (New York: Penguin Books, 1968), 162 [17].

[132] E.g. "The Martyrs of Lyons," in *Acts of the Christian Martyrs*, 83. See also Michele Pellegrino, "L'Imitation du Christ dans les Acts des martyrs," *Vie Spirituelle* 98 (1958), 38–54.

[133] Gerhard Lohfink, *Jesus and Community*, trans. John P. Galvin (Philadelphia and New York: Fortress Press and Paulist Press, 1984), 122–32, 157–63.

practiced justice and charity not only among their own but among strangers and their pagan neighbors.

At least by the time of Pliny (c. 110), the Christians were viewed by the Roman authorities as subversive to the social order. Pliny applied the emperor Trajan's ban on "political societies" to the Christians in Bithynia, ordering the suspension of their ritual corporate meals. The account of Polycarp's martyrdom some forty years later makes clear that Caesar and Christ were seen as rival monarchs. As N.T. Wright comments on the church of Asia Minor in Pliny's time,

> the litmus test for conviction as a Christian was, as in Polycarp's case, ritual actions and declarations which, small in themselves, carried enormous sociocultural significance. These only make sense on the assumption that Christians of all sorts in the area, who would mostly not have been trained theologians, regarded it as fundamental that their allegiance to Christ cut across any allegiance to Caesar.[134]

Wright considers it uncontroversial to apply this rivalry of Christ and Caesar to a general picture of the early church.

The ancient martyrs often asserted the kingship of Christ in refusing to offer worship or service to the emperors and their gods.[135] The church was, by its nature as Christ's crucified and resurrected body, a challenge to the violence and idolatry of the secular authorities. "In the acts of the military martyrs the refusal of governmental demands takes the form of a choice between the military and the church."[136] If martyrdom is thus put into the context of the conflict between the church and the powers and principalities, it is right and fitting that those who give their lives in this ongoing conflict in Latin America today be recognized as martyrs. From a theological point of view, the conflict is the same; it is the conflict between Christ's body on earth and the powers of the world which refuse to recognize Christ's victory over it. Christians see acts of injustice and state violence as the continuing struggle between the people of God and the forces of death.

Martyrdom makes the body of Christ visible. To the world, the death-acts of the martyrs make visible a disciplined community that will not be

---

[134] N. T. Wright, *The New Testament and the People of God*, vol. I of *Christian Origins and the Question of God* (Minneapolis: Fortress Press, 1992), 350.
[135] Everett Ferguson, "Early Christian Martyrdom and Civil Disobedience," *Journal of Early Christian Studies* 1, no. 1 (1993), 77–82.
[136] Ibid., 81.

conformed to the world (Rom. 12:2). The trial, torture, and execution of each martyr only serve to call the Christians out from among the world and put the conflict into bold relief. Origen writes, "A great multitude is assembled to watch you when you combat and are called to martyrdom. It is as if we said that thousands upon thousands gather to watch a contest in which contestants of outstanding reputation are engaged. When you will be engaged in the conflict you can say with Paul: *We are made a spectacle to the world and to angels and to men.*"[137] The pyres which burn the martyrs' bodies serve as light for the world, not isolating the community of believers but calling all to the city on the hill (Mt. 5:14–16). As the martyr Apollonius proclaimed to the Roman proconsul, "the more they kill those who believe in him, so much the more will their numbers grow by God's aid."[138]

For the church itself, martyrdom disciplines the community and helps it to claim its identity. Sobrino and Boff overemphasize the intention of the individual in determining who is a martyr and who is not. What is most crucial to martyrdom is not whether or not the person killed intended to act out of love or for justice – for then indeed, as Sobrino says, only God would be able to judge – but whether or not those with eyes to see are able to discern the body of Christ, crucified and glorified, in the body broken by the violence of the world. Those seeking to follow Christ in the world look for guidance to the martyrs, those fellow disciples who have most fully imitated the way of Christ on the earth. It is not the heroism of the individual which is most significant, but rather the naming of the martyr by those who recognize Christ in the martyr's life and death. Indeed, what makes martyrdom possible is the eschatological belief that nothing depends on the martyr's continued life; if he dies, nothing is ultimately lost. Christ lives on in the faithful multitude who make Christ present by remembering the martyrs. The recognition of martyrs happens in the base communities of the church as well as in the hierarchy, and is part of the ongoing imaginative process which determines the shape of the church.[139] As such, martyrdom recalls into being a people, the people of God, and makes their life visible to themselves and to the world. They remember Christ and become Christ's members in the Eucharist, reenacting the body of Christ, its passion and its conflict with the

---

[137] Origen, *Exhortation to Martyrdom*, trans. John J. O'Meara (New York: Newman Press, 1954), 158.
[138] "The Martyrdom of the Saintly and Blessed Apostle Apollonius, also called Sakkeas," para. 24, in *Acts of the Christian Martyrs*, 97.
[139] See David Matzko, "Hazarding Theology: Theological Descriptions and Particular Lives" (Ph.D. diss., Duke University, 1993).

forces of (dis)order. The martyrs and all the faithful followers of Christ make up in their own bodies what is lacking in the suffering of Christ for the sake of his body, the church (Col. 1:24).

The body of the martyr is thus the battleground for a larger contest of rival imaginations, that of the state and that of the church. A crucial difference in these imaginations is that the imagination of the church is essentially eschatological; the church is not a rival *polis* but points to an alternative time and space, a mingling of heaven and earth. A strong apocalyptic element is associated with martyrdom from early on in Christian history, at least by the time Acts and Revelation were written. About to be stoned to death, Stephen, the first martyr, raised his eyes and declared "Look, I see the heavens opened!" (Acts 7:56). This was more than a vision of his final resting place; it was instead the outpouring of heaven upon the earth, a foretaste of the final consummation of the Kingdom of God. Martyrdom is a bridge between heaven and earth not because the martyr is soon to travel one way to her eternal reward, but because heaven has been brought to earth in the form of one who, in imitating Jesus the Christ, has cheated earthly death of its sting. A martyr is one who lives imaginatively as if death does not exist. The eschatological imagination sees that, although they presume to kill us, Christ has vanquished the powers of death once and for all. The eschatological imagination of martyrdom is not a vertical ascension to another place and time, a distant heaven; the movement instead brings a foretaste of heavenly space-time to earth.

> Then I saw a new heaven and a new earth; for the first heaven and the first earth had passed away, and the sea was no more. And I saw the holy city, the new Jerusalem, coming down out of heaven from God, prepared as a bride adorned for her husband (Rev. 21:1–2).

As James Alison remarks on this passage, John's vision here is not mere consolation for the individual martyr, but rather a vision for the whole church: "the Church *is* the collective living out of the opening of heaven."[140]

The church is thus a vision of things unseen, but the church is never wholly visible, either in the sense of being entirely subjectively holy or being an institutional rival to the state. In its eschatological imagination, the church waits on Christ's second coming, straining forward toward full consummation of the Kingdom. Its task on earth is a hope-filled witness to the opening of heaven, the revelation of things which the earthly eye now sees only dimly.

---

[140] James Alison, *Raising Abel: The Recovery of the Eschatological Imagination* (New York: Crossroad, 1996), 81.

This is the importance of the Book of Revelation: it is so-called because the hidden truth to which the martyrs have witnessed is revealed as a sign of the coming of the Kingdom.

The function of the terrorist state, then, is to kill the eschatological imagination of the church by preventing this vision from coming to light. The state does so through its own imagination of things unseen, that is, the torture chamber and the entire underground apparatus of anxiety and fear. The state is not fully visible, but not because it lives in a hopeful waiting for the fulfillment of a new time. State use of invisibility is predicated on the foreclosing of hope through anxiety, and the consequent domination of both space and time.

We are now in a position to understand the strategy of repression employed by the Pinochet regime in Chile as not the production of martyrs but rather the denial of martyrs to the church. The effect of the regime's strategy was to produce not martyrs but victims. Martyrs by their public witness build up the body of Christ in opposition to the state. For precisely this reason the regime's strategy was predicated on the elimination of spectacle, and therefore the disappearance of the visible church. The Pinochet regime had learned the lessons of the Coliseum all too well. Rather than allow the public confession of faith, the victims were made to speak the words of the regime in its subterranean chambers. The words of Jesus thus were fulfilled ironically: "When they hand you over, do not worry about how you are to speak or what you are to say; for what you are to say will be given to you" (Mt. 10:19). Moreover, doctors were present at the torture sessions to ensure that the victims would *not die*; in an overwhelming majority of cases, torture in Chile was accompanied by medical intervention designated to determine how much torture the victim could take without dying, and without therefore producing a martyr.[141]

Those that were killed had their bodies disposed of secretly, left in clandestine graves, dumped into rivers or the ocean, or dynamited. On occasion, when bodies surfaced, people were known reverently to pull floating bodies from a river only to have the authorities throw them back in.[142] In the second half of 1976, eighteen bodies were found on the banks of the

---

[141] Paz Rojas Baeza, et al., *Persona, Estado, Poder: Estudios sobre Salud Mental Chile 1973-1989* (Santiago: CODEPU, 1989), 225–9. The problem of doctors' complicity in torture is treated extensively in *The Breaking of Bodies and Minds: Torture, Psychiatric Abuse, and the Health Professions*, ed. Eric Stover and Elena O. Nightingale (New York: W. H. Freeman and Company, 1985).

[142] *Rettig Report*, 142.

river in the Cajón del Maipo, but only one could be identified; the rest had had their faces and fingertips removed or mutilated.[143] It was crucial to the Pinochet regime to have complete control over bodies. The regime understood perfectly well that the body could become a focus of resistance to the state's power.

For the early Christians, the bodies of the martyrs were loci of God's power on earth and had a central place in the memory and formation of the community. *The Martyrdom of Polycarp* reports that the Roman authorities, jealous of the crown that Polycarp had won, confiscated his body and had it burnt to keep it out of Christian hands. Nevertheless,

> after all, we did gather up his bones – more precious to us than jewels, and finer than pure gold – and we laid them to rest in a spot suitable for the purpose. There we shall assemble, as occasion allows, with glad rejoicings; and with the Lord's permission we shall celebrate the birthday of his martyrdom. It will serve both as a commemoration of all who have triumphed before, and as a training and preparation for any whose crown may be still to come.[144]

The grave, fragments of the corpse, even other objects that had touched the body of the martyr thus became privileged channels between heaven and earth. Altars were built on the graves of the martyrs, and these became the centers of Eucharistic celebration. As Peter Brown points out, the graves of the martyrs shattered the barrier between public and private that had surrounded people's graves; the martyr's tomb was public property, accessible to the whole community, and death was brought from the periphery of communal life to its center.[145] The dead bodies of the martyrs took on great importance because of their participation in the strange Christian dramatics of a crucified God whose followers are most alive when they die for him. By imitating the death of Jesus at the hands of earthly powers, the martyrs earned a share in the glory of Christ's resurrection.

The cult of the martyrs overturned the well-established barriers between the living and the dead and appalled the sensibilities of the Romans.[146] The Emperor Julian could not hide his dismay:

---

[143] Ibid., 502.
[144] *The Martyrdom of Polycarp*, 162 [18].
[145] Peter Brown, *The Cult of the Saints: Its Rise and Function in Latin Christianity* (Chicago: University of Chicago Press, 1981), 1–9.
[146] Brown, *The Cult of the Saints*, 1–7.

the carrying of the corpses of the dead through a great assembly of people, in the midst of dense crowds, staining the eyesight of all with ill-omened sights of the dead. What day so touched with death could be lucky? How, after being present at such ceremonies, could anyone approach the gods and their temples?[147]

How indeed. The cult of the martyrs' bodies posed a threat to the Empire's cult of power, for not only was death brought into the realm of the living and honored as glory, but those honored were criminals, executed for refusing to believe in the divinity of imperial authority. As Brown writes, "Their deaths, therefore, involved more than a triumph over physical pain; they were vibrant also with the memory of a dialogue with and a triumph over unjust power."[148] This dangerous memory associated with the body of a martyr – preeminently located in the Eucharist – is what forms and identifies a community as the body of Christ in ongoing conflict with worldly power.

In November of 1978, just days before the Catholic church was to host an international symposium on human rights in Santiago, a disheveled old man wearing a cap and enormous muddy boots made his way into the Vicaría de Solidaridad and asked to speak with a priest. The old man had the unlikely name Inocente de los Angeles, and the tale he had to tell would have a stunning impact on all of Chile. He was a miner who, since his retirement, had dedicated himself to searching the hills of Chile for some clue to the fate of his son, who had disappeared at the hands of security agents. On a vague rumor he picked up in the town of Talagante, he had found a pair of abandoned lime ovens near Lonquén. Inside were human remains.[149]

Fifteen bodies in all were found. They belonged to eleven farm workers and four teenage boys who had been arrested in October 1973. In response to a writ of habeas corpus filed by family members in 1974, the local police admitted having arrested them, but claimed to have sent them to the prisoner camp at the National Stadium in Santiago, and provided documentation to "prove" it.[150] It was just another case of disappearance until a committee from the Vicaría unearthed the bodies. They took a text of their findings, still secret,

---

[147] Julian, *Epistulae et leges*, quoted in Brown, *The Cult of the Saints*, 7.

[148] Brown, *The Cult of the Saints*, 101.

[149] Ascanio Cavallo Castro, Manuel Salazar Salvo, and Oscar Sepúlveda Pacheco, *La historia oculta del régimen militar* (Santiago: Editorial Antártica, 1990), 260-1; Ahumada and Atria, *Chile: La memoria prohibida*, 1. 145–6. The latter work records the man's name as Inocencio de los Angeles.

[150] *Rettig Report*, 238–40.

to the president of the Supreme Court, who registered his irritation: "I am bored with the church's inventions."[151] But the judge could not dismiss dead bodies. It was the first tangible evidence of what had been going on invisibly under the military regime. The name "Lonquén" would become synonymous with the regime's abuses.

Analysis of the bodies at the Legal Medical Institute determined that most of the victims had been buried alive. While the remains were in the possession of the Institute, the government called an emergency cabinet meeting to determine how the bodies should be handled. There was reason to fear that the bones would become the focus of resistance to the regime.[152] A court had ordered the remains turned over to the relatives. The relatives meanwhile had gathered in a Franciscan church in Santiago for a funeral mass. While they waited in the church for delivery of the bodies, the remains were removed from the Legal Medical Institute and dumped in a common grave at the Isla de Maipo municipal cemetery.[153] The legal case was terminated under a 1978 self-amnesty law decreed by the regime, and two books being written on the discovery at Lonquén were banned before they appeared.[154]

The importance of having a body must be underscored when we confront the strategy of disappearance, both the pain felt by its victims and the possibilities for resistance to it. The families, especially the mothers, of the disappeared, even in relative certainty that their loved ones have been killed, search tirelessly, year after year, for their remains.[155] A Chilean woman whose husband was permanently disappeared tells a story of almost unbearable sadness: "When my son turned seventeen, he felt so much that he had to know where his father was that I said to him, 'Son, go down to the cemetery and look for the most abandoned grave. Take care of it and visit it as though it were your father's.'"[156] The termination of the grieving process – and the transformation of that process into resistance and even joy – often depends on having a body. As Jon Sobrino attests, "There is joy when we celebrate the eucharist for one of our martyrs, when we sing for joy in the presence of a corpse."[157]

[151] Ahumada and Atria, *Chile: La memoria prohibida*, 3: 153.

[152] Ibid., 155; Cavallo, et al., *La historia oculta del régimen militar*, 262.

[153] *Rettig Report*, 240.

[154] Ahumada and Atria, *Chile: La memoria prohibida*, 3. 155, 158 n. 7.

[155] "Chile's mothers gain a victory for the disappeared," *Chicago Tribune*, Dec. 5, 1993, sec. 6, pp. 1, 11.

[156] *Rettig Report*, 780.

[157] Jon Sobrino, *Spirituality of Liberation: Toward Political Holiness*, trans. Robert R. Barr (Maryknoll, NY: Orbis Books, 1988), 101.

In order for there to be a martyr, there must be a body; in order for that death to be transformed into resistance and joy, there must be a body of people capable of reading that death as participating in Christ's defeat of the powers.

What is at issue here is the possibility of church resistance to the state's monopoly over the bodies of its citizens. Under the Pinochet regime, legal guarantees of habeas corpus existed and were actually expanded under the Constitutional Acts of 1976.[158] Habeas corpus – literally "you may have the body" – is an important safeguard through which a judge can have a person brought bodily before him or her to ensure that the physical integrity and full legal rights of the person are being respected by the state organisms that are holding that body prisoner. Under Chilean law, judges were also theoretically empowered to visit the places where prisoners were held, but in practice habeas corpus brought no protection to Chile's citizens. In 1975 the Supreme Court president complained in a speech that so many habeas corpus appeals had been filed alleging arrests that the normal channels of justice had become clogged, and the higher courts had "been prevented from attending to urgent matters entrusted to them."[159]

5 Conclusion

The contest between the church and the state over bodies is played out at two interacting levels, that of individual bodies and that of social bodies. As we have seen, the state is imagined as master of its citizens' bodies. Under the Pinochet regime, torture was used as a mode of governance. The state seized bodies and made them emit signs, play roles in a drama, speak the regime's words in order to make ritually present the omnipotence of the state. At the same time, and precisely because of its access to individual bodies, the strategy of torture was an attack on rival social bodies, an attempt to atomize and disappear them. The discipline of fear drove the state's invisible mark deep into the individual, to make each depend only on the state, and not on one another.

Torture is therefore an ecclesiological problem, to do with the church's nature as a communal body. The church cannot confront the torture system simply by treating it as a violation of any individual's human rights. From the church's point of view, torture should be read as aspiring to the disappearance

---

[158] *Rettig Report*, 84–5.
[159] Ibid., 118.

of the visible body of Christ. The techniques of invisibility which the secret police structure perfected were capable of fragmenting the church body while depriving the church of martyrs, visible witnesses to the conflict between the church and the powers of the world. The bodies of the martyrs make the church visible as the body of Christ. The church does not seek martyrdom; to do so would be to invite oppressors to sin, which would be a grave sin in itself. The church also does not recognize all victims as *ipso facto* martyrs. The church does, however, celebrate certain people as martyrs, for they make visible the community of Christ's followers. Martyrdom is never a goal, but the church knows that as the body of Christ it will inevitably come into conflict with the disciplines of the principalities and powers.

What discipline means is essentially the power to script bodies into different performances. For the Christian this discipline consists in becoming a member of the body of Jesus Christ who, as *The Martyrdom of Polycarp* attests, is "the Saviour of our souls, the Master of our bodies, and the Shepherd of the Catholic Church the wide world over."[160] As I will show in the next chapter, the "New Christendom" ecclesiology which dominated the Chilean Catholic church between the separation of church and state in 1925 and the coup in 1973 had theorized the church not as social body but as the "soul of society." The church would be responsible for the souls of Chileans, in effect handing their bodies over to the state for political and military duty. The church would supposedly form their individual consciences, and people would enter public life as individual Christians, but the church as a body would not act politically. I will argue that by imagining that it could become society's soul, the church had already begun to forfeit its own discipline and to disappear itself.

---

[160] *The Martyrdom of Polycarp*, 163 [19].

Chapter Two

THE CHURCH LEARNS
HOW TO BE OPPRESSED

Number 5 in a series of pamphlets which appeared anonymously in Santiago in 1986-7 is entitled "Torture: A State Practice Stronger than Love."[1] The title is a sly twist on "Love is stronger," one of Pope John Paul II's favorite slogans during his April 1987 trip to Chile. In the pamphlet is recounted a dramatic confrontation between General Pinochet and Nolbert Bluem, West German Minister of Labor, captured by a writer from *Der Spiegel*. "I accept the principle of non-intervention in the internal affairs of other states," Bluem is reported to have told Pinochet, "but that principle has one exception: human rights. Here interference is an obligation. Therefore, Mister President, stop torturing."[2]

Pinochet, the story continues, is caught off guard. Often at a loss for eloquence but seldom at a loss for words, Pinochet nevertheless is shocked by Bluem's direct approach and must catch his breath before responding. He throws the Nazi experience back into the face of the German diplomat, but Bluem responds that his own country's grim past gives him not only the right to give his opinion but an obligation to defend human rights wherever they are violated. The soul-searching of the German nation stands in stark contrast to the Pinochet regime's 1978 self-amnesty of human rights abusers. Pinochet is stymied, but quickly retorts, "And what did you do at Stammheim?," a reference to the prison where members of the Baader-Meinhof gang died. Without blinking, Bluem proposes an exchange: Pinochet will get free rein to investigate prisons in Germany if Bluem is allowed the same privilege in Chile. Pinochet retreats once again, this time bothering to deny accusations of torture in Chile. "These [accusations] are lies invented by the communists. I am a

---

[1] "La tortura: práctica estatal más fuerte que el amor," Colección Reflexión y Debate, Serie Derechos Humanos, no. 5 (Nov. 1987).
[2] "La tortura: práctica estatal más fuerte que el amor," 5.

committed Christian and I pray every day. We must combat communism."[3]
The author of the pamphlet draws out the details of the encounter and places delighted emphasis on Pinochet's discomfort at being confronted so boldly from a position of moral superiority. Had it never happened before, in all the years of Pinochet's rule? According to the author, it had not.

> Pinochet is somewhat overwhelmed. Never has he been confronted with such categorical imperatives. He would appear to long for the generic and elusive language, full of conditions, with which the Permanent Committee of the Chilean bishops refer to torture in their declaration of August 13, 1987. How would he not prefer "the authorities whom it may concern are asked to give the country the security that these practices are rejected by them and that there is a disposition to investigate and punish those eventually found guilty" to this grossly direct "Mister President, stop torturing."[4]

A contention such as this may come as a surprise to anyone familiar with the reputation that the Chilean church enjoys abroad for its stand against the Pinochet dictatorship. Chilean bishops have received numerous awards and a chorus of praise from the international community for their stand as the "voice of the voiceless" under brutal repression.[5] In part this aspersion cast at the bishops can be attributed to the license that anonymous pamphleteering confers on the author. But although, as we will see, the good reputation of the bishops' conference is not undeserved, the picture is indeed much more complex. The bishops confronted the first years of military rule with gentle exhortations which only turned to denunciation after the worst years of repression were past.

In this chapter I will trace the trajectory of relations between the state and the Catholic church in Chile over issues of human rights during the military regime. I will argue that the slow evolution of the bishops' position was not due to a lack of courage or information, but rather was a process, never completed, of unlearning a set of ecclesiological presuppositions firmly engrained in the Chilean Catholic church. Just as the first chapter displayed torture as an ecclesiological problem, this second chapter will show how the church's ecclesiology conditioned its response to the military regime and how the possibility of a new ecclesiology began to emerge under the new circumstances

[3] Ibid., 7.
[4] Ibid., 6–7.
[5] See e.g. Hannah Stewart-Gambino, "Redefining the Changes and Politics in Chile," in *Conflict and Competition: The Latin American Church in a Changing Environment*, ed. Edward L. Cleary and Hannah Stewart-Gambino (Boulder, Colo.: Lynne Rienner Publishers, 1992), 22.

of persecution. Specifically I will show how the bishops assumed that the church and state stood in organic relationship as the twin guardians of the Chilean national heritage. The bishops assumed the imagination of the nation-state, such that "Chile" was the natural subject of their discourse. The bishops therefore repeatedly called for unity and reconciliation among all sectors of Chilean society. It was assumed that society constituted an organic whole in which it was the church's duty to act as conscience or soul, exhorting the body, the state, to act for the common good. The church as the province of the soul is what helps define the state as that which has authority over the body. I will show that this amounts to the disappearance of the church as a visible, social body, and therefore leaves the church no resistance to the process of fragmentation and disappearance described in chapter one. It was only through the pedagogy of terror that the official church began to learn how to be oppressed and thus become incarnate in opposition to the state.

This chapter will focus on the ecclesiology of the official Catholic church, available mainly in the documents, statements, and actions of the bishops both individually and together as the Chilean bishops' conference (CECh, *Conferencia Episcopal de Chile*). In the following two chapters I will trace the roots of this ecclesiology and undertake a more theoretical critique of Catholic social thought as exemplified in Chile. Chapters 5 and 6 will focus on three sets of practices of the Chilean church, both hierarchical and grassroots, which point the way to a more Eucharistic understanding of the church as the communal body of Christ.

1 Christians for Socialism

The church hierarchy in Chile was accustomed to having a major voice in national affairs well before the events of 1973. In addition to more traditional ecclesiastical pronouncements the bishops had, since the early 1960s, begun to speak more frequently and more specifically in regard to social questions of general interest to the nation. Just as European industrialization and urbanization had caused Leo XIII to offer *Rerum Novarum* in 1891, so the Chilean bishops responded to similar upheavals in Latin American society in 1962 with a pair of pastoral letters on social problems which would receive widespread attention.[6]

---

[6] Brian Smith, *The Church and Politics in Chile: Challenges to Modern Catholicism* (Princeton, NJ: Princeton University Press, 1982), 109. The two letters were "La iglesia y el campesinado chileno," published in April 1962, and "El deber social y político en la hora presente," published in September.

Besides enormous changes in Chile's traditional agricultural economy in the 1950s and 1960s, ideological pressure for change came from two very different sources in two very different cities: Havana and Rome. The Cuban revolution had lifted the hopes of many for major structural change. There was much talk of an ongoing revolutionary historical process which had found Chile in its path.[7] The Second Vatican Council, in the meantime, was pushing the church toward greater concern with the world's problems, a church in the service of the world and not of itself. It was perhaps inevitable that the two perspectives, somewhat similar in focus on structural change, would both compete and cross-pollinate in Chile.

In the elections of 1964, fear of a Marxist victory had caused many on the right to support the more moderate reform platform of Eduardo Frei's centrist Christian Democratic Party. By the end of Frei's term, however, conservatives had become so alarmed at the pace of change – especially the expropriations of acreage under the land reform program – that they turned back to the Conservative candidate Jorge Alessandri as their choice to throw into reverse the sweeping changes that had engulfed Chilean society. The result was a three-way split among left, center, and right in the 1970 election which the candidate of the Marxist coalition, Salvador Allende, won with a bare plurality of 36 percent of the vote.[8] The revolution was now in office.

"I won't be just another president," Allende announced in his victory speech. "I will be the first president of the first really democratic, popular, national and revolutionary government in the history of Chile."[9] The pace of change accelerated. Companies and banks were nationalized, price and wage controls were set to favor the working class, land expropriations both legal and illegal increased dramatically, and popular movements pressed for immediate realization of Chile's socialist destiny. Chilean society at all levels became intensely politicized, and politics were polarized by mutual suspicion and animosity.[10]

---

[7] See e.g. Christians for Socialism, "Final Document of the Convention," in *Liberation Theology: A Documentary History*, ed. Alfred T. Hennelly (Maryknoll, NY: Orbis Books, 1990), 147–58.

[8] Alan Angell, "Chile since 1958," in *Chile since Independence*, ed. Leslie Bethell (Cambridge: Cambridge University Press, 1993), 146–57; and Smith, *The Church and Politics in Chile*, 144.

[9] Quoted in Angell, "Chile since 1958," 157.

[10] Ibid., 157–77.

During Chile's brief experiment with socialism under Allende's Popular Unity coalition of Communists and Socialists, pressure on the church to commit to specific political options was intense. In April 1971 a group of eighty priests working in poor sectors of the country met in Santiago and issued a statement of commitment to the Popular Unity's "Chilean Way to Socialism." After the meeting the group was organized into Christians for Socialism, which would grow into an extremely well-organized network of several hundred priests, religious, and lay leaders. Their purpose was to critique the ties that bound the church to bourgeois structures and ideologies of exploitation. To them the movement of the Spirit in history was clearly apparent in the Popular Unity government, and demanded an immediate option of Christians to collaborate with the founding of a new social order based on social ownership of the means of production. Priests and religious used their pastoral work to bolster commitment to Popular Unity's mobilization of the poorer classes.[11]

This sort of concrete political option was precisely what Cardinal Raúl Silva Henríquez had tried to head off in a televised talk given in July of 1970, before Allende's election. Entitled "church, Priesthood and Politics," Silva's speech, invoking Vatican II, addressed the pressures on the church to opt for one of the three main electoral choices facing the country. "And immediately a first answer, taken from the spirit and letter of the Council: the church as such does not have, nor is it linked with, any political system or party."[12] Lay Christians, "induced by their Christian conscience," can choose a particular party, as long as they recognize that other Christians, drawn by their conscience as well, can sincerely take another option. Clergy, on the other hand, must not publicly serve any particular political ideology, for to do so would damage the unity of the church. The church, according to Silva, is the

> sign and guarantee that the human person is above and is worth more than any political system or party. . . . [The Church] is the sign and safeguard that men can meet each other and, beyond their political ideologies and options, unite. The most appropriate activity of the Church, the source and summit of its life, is, therefore, the Eucharist: the Sacrament of Unity, in which men commune with God and with each other, feeling themselves and making themselves to be brothers, all equally sinners, and equally redeemed.[13]

[11] Christians for Socialism, "Final Document of the Convention"; and Smith, *The Church and Politics in Chile*, 232–3.

[12] Cardinal Raúl Silva Henríquez, "Iglesia, sacerdocio y política," in *Documentos del episcopado: Chile 1970–73* (Santiago: Ediciones Mundo, 1974), 24.

[13] Ibid.

This vision of church and Eucharist stands in sharp contrast to that of Christians for Socialism. Diego Irarrázaval, a member of the organization's secretariat, outlined that vision in a talk to university students:

> We will celebrate the Eucharist amidst the struggle of the working class and in gratitude for insertion into it. We will give thanks because the people are advancing towards the revolutionary goal of the kingdom of God. . . . This celebration will be possible insofar as each member of the community has a revolutionary commitment and insofar as the community is homogeneous. . . . This new type of community also will have a public political dimension. It will participate as a group in destroying exploitation and creating forms of power exercised by the people.[14]

Far from a celebration of the unity of all Christians above and beyond their political options, the Eucharist here demands homogeneous communities united in their definitive option for the realization of socialism.

Six days after the declaration of the eighty priests on April 16, 1971, the bishops meeting in plenary assembly issued a reply reiterating the Cardinal's position on priests and politics, but also stressing that "fidelity to the Gospel of Jesus Christ demands [of Christians] today that they commit to profound and urgent social renovations."[15] A month later the bishops issued a more substantial "working document" entitled "Gospel, Politics, and Socialisms" in which they repeated their adherence to Medellín's call for social justice, but emphasized that the option for the poor is not made to the exclusion of other sectors of Chilean society. The church does not choose between groups of people, but opts for the whole people of Chile. "In effect, it is that living organic whole that we call the people of Chile that Jesus Christ wants to liberate and revitalize with his divine Life, converting it into an authentic community of brothers and sisters."[16]

Note that the primary subject of much of the Chilean church's discourse is Chile; the bishops tend to think of their constituency in spatial terms of a solid community bounded by the territorial borders which outline the sovereignty of the Chilean state. The bishops' discourse is located within the imagination of the sovereign nation-state. This Chile is imagined to form one

---

[14] Diego Irarrázaval C., "Cristianos, compromiso revolucionario, comunidad de creyentes"; quoted in Smith, *The Church and Politics in Chile*, 239.

[15] "El Evangelio exige comprometerse en profundas y urgentes renovaciones sociales," in *Documentos del episcopado: Chile 1970–73*, 55.

[16] "Evangelio, política y socialismos," in *Documentos del episcopado: Chile 1970–73*, 65.

organic whole. The bishops assume that the role of the nation-state is to produce harmony, the orderly functioning of every part and every class in its assigned place, which will lead to the common good of all.

Under Allende, the bishops met the Marxist avowal of class struggle with the belief that their audience's identity *as Chileans* should unite them into a common cause. The reality of conflict under the Popular Unity's drastic restructuring of society was confronted by the bishops with an insistence on the organic unity of Chile. As civil strife increased in June of 1973, the bishops of Santiago province would write, "Ideologies divide; the history, the blood, the common language, the human love and the similar task that we Chileans have today must help us to form one family."[17]

The hierarchy of the church made it clear during this period that the role of the church in this organic whole was to promote unity by staying above and transcending contingent political matters. This was a difficult balancing act, given the church's resistance to the demands of the Christians for Socialism on the one hand, and the church's desire to contribute to "profound and urgent social renovations" on the other. In their document of May 1971, the bishops describe the suffering of their flock. "It is that inhuman situation of marginalization and misery in which thousands of Chileans live which gives to the question of the socio-economic system and the political option of Christians its character of dramatic urgency."[18] What does the church have to say in the face of this question?

> The answer of the church in this matter is, at root, the same as always: she opts for Jesus Christ resurrected, and, therefore, invites Christians to struggle for those socio-economic structures which make more effective all those *values* of personal and social liberation, of justice and love, contained in her Gospel. This is the only thing the church can say as church, because it is the only thing that she can found on the authority of the Gospel. This [Gospel] does not offer formulas for social, political or economic structuration: it only points out the *values* that should be respected and promoted (because they animate man and the human community) and calls [people] to incarnate them and fight for them, but without specifying the way.[19]

The problem with Christians for Socialism, according to the bishops, is that the proper mandate of the laity to attend to temporal matters is confused with

---

[17] "Solo con amor se es capaz de construir un país," in *Documentos del episcopado: Chile 1970–73*, 166.
[18] "Evangelio, política y socialismos," 67.
[19] Ibid., 67–8, emphasis in original.

the function of the whole church as a body. The bishops operate on a "distinction of planes" ecclesiology, imbibed mainly from the "New Christendom," or "Christian Humanism," approach of Jacques Maritain, which makes careful distinctions between clerical and lay roles. Laypeople are to take the values they learn as members of the church out into the temporal world and "incarnate" those values, each according to his or her judgement.[20] The implication is that the church itself is somehow not incarnate in the temporal realm, not a body but rather the soul of society. In "Christian Faith and Political Action," their final statement on Christians for Socialism composed in August 1973, the bishops write that

> liberation demands the construction of a better world within history, but it is projected also toward a Kingdom, which is the soul of that history and at the same time transcends it. This Kingdom, including in its historical dimension, is not identified with any thisworldly process, economic structure or political regime.[21]

The Kingdom hovers above history, entering it only in the soul. Christians enter the temporal world as individuals; the church does not act as a body in the temporal realm. The church does not have a political body but only a religious body, a *mystical* body, which unites all Christians above the rough and tumble of the temporal. The bishops maintain that "we who act `in the name of Christ, head of his mystical body,'"[22] are situated in a perspective above the particular options of the world. To act otherwise would be a danger for the church: "to convert her into just one more element of the world."[23]

The bishops' response to Christians for Socialism should not be understood as mere fainthearted conservatism in the face of change. The bishops explicitly denounced "that prejudice" that would circumscribe the Christian faith to private devotion while the course of history goes its own way.[24] Christians must act to transform the world, but the bishops feared that, far from a bold step forward, Christians for Socialism constituted a *retreat* into a clericalism

---

[20] "Fe cristiana y actuación política," in *Documentos del episcopado: Chile 1970–73*, 181. The Chilean bishops quote *Gaudium et Spes*, paragraph 76, to back themselves up on this point.
[21] Ibid., 193.
[22] Ibid., 182.
[23] Ibid.
[24] Ibid., 180.

long since overcome in Chile.[25] Their concern was that the clergy would once again try to direct Chilean politics, dragging the church down into sectarian battles which would only further divide the country. The church is a religious body only, and lacks the expertise to signal concrete solutions in the temporal realm. Incarnation of the church's values should be left to "*los técnicos*," the technicians – economists, sociologists, psychologists, politicians.[26] By forbidding priests and religious from participating in Christians for Socialism, the bishops believed they were contributing to the advance of peace and justice in Chile.

This prohibition was published in the lengthy document on Christians for Socialism entitled "Christian Faith and Political Action." Although the document had been intensely argued and anticipated within the Chilean church, its publication caused little notice, even among those priests and religious to whom the prohibition was addressed. They had more urgent matters to which to attend; they were busy either fleeing the country or helping others to do so. Plans for publication of the document, prepared in August 1973, had been interrupted by the sound of gunfire on September 11. "Christian Faith and Political Action" was published posthumously on October 16 in a Chile which was not the same country as the Chile in which it was written.

2 "Torture Isn't Everything"

A Chilean bishop would comment years after the coup, "To resist an atheist dictatorship is easy; what's difficult is to resist a Catholic dictatorship."[27] When the military intervened to defend "Western Christian civilization" in Chile, it did not do so to defend the church in its present form. The military and the conservative elements which backed it had become convinced that the Marxist disease which they had set out to extirpate had not passed by the doors of the church. In the first few weeks after the coup, forty-five priests and religious were jailed, and fifty expelled from the country, a serious blow to a church already chronically short of clergy.[28] After four months the church's figures showed that 106 priests and thirty-two sisters had been

---

[25] Ibid., 190.
[26] "Evangelio, política y socialismos," 69.
[27] Ascanio Cavallo Castro, Manuel Salazar Salvo, and Oscar Sepúlveda Pacheco, *La historia oculta del régimen militar* (Santiago: Editorial Antártica, 1990), 92.
[28] Ibid., 95.

forced to leave Chile, either directly expelled or forced out by threats.[29] Experience proved that such threats were rarely idle. In Valparaíso several days after the coup, Father Miguel Woodward was arrested by a naval patrol and tortured to death on board the ship *Lebu*.[30] Shortly after the coup, Spanish priest Antonio Llidó disappeared. He was last seen in October 1974 at Cuatro Alamos, a facility run by the DINA.[31] On September 19, the Spanish priest Joan Alsina was arrested by Army troops at the hospital where he worked, taken to the Bulnes Bridge in Santiago, and shot. His body was pulled from the Mapocho River and turned up at the Legal Medical Institute on the September 27. The cause of death was dutifully recorded as "multiple bullet wounds" and "lash wounds to the face."[32] At five o'clock in the afternoon on October 21, Father Gerardo Poblete, a philosophy teacher at the Salesian school in Iquique, was arrested at the school. At eight o'clock, his superior was called to the police station to give him last rites, but he was already dead. Four days later the police issued a statement saying that Poblete had slipped and fallen as he was getting out of the police van; the effects were not immediately apparent, but when officers came to his cell a few hours later, they found him unconscious. In fact, witnesses later affirmed, several officers had beaten Father Poblete to death.[33]

The church did not suffer the fate of the political parties and unions, which immediately following the coup saw their properties confiscated and their leaders hunted down. Nevertheless the church – at least that part that identified itself with the poor – in some measure suffered from the beginning the persecution directed against all popular organizations. Many parishes and residences of priests and nuns were violently searched. Two of the four vicariates of the Archbishopric of Santiago were entered by troops. Church publications and radio broadcasts were closed down or censored.[34] Jorge Hourton, bishop of Puerto Montt, was informed by the local military chief

---

[29] Jaime Escobar M., *Persecución a la iglesia en Chile: martirologio 1973–1986* (Santiago: Terranova Editores, 1986), 82.

[30] Ibid., 76; also Cavallo, et al., *La historia oculta del régimen militar*, 94. The *Rettig Report* lists Woodward as a "former" priest; 309.

[31] *Rettig Report*, 538; see also Mario Terrazas Guzmán, *¿Quién se acuerda de Sheila Cassidy?* (Santiago: Ediciones Emete, 1992), 110.

[32] *Rettig Report*, 173; Cavallo, et al., *La historia oculta del régimen militar*, 94. After Pinochet left the presidency, the local people erected a very moving memorial to Alsina at the spot where he was killed.

[33] *Rettig Report*, 263–4; Cavallo, et al., *La historia oculta del régimen militar*, 94.

[34] Cavallo, et al., *La historia oculta del régimen militar*, 94.

that all church declarations would have to be authorized by the military before being promulgated.[35] The Air Force took Saint George's school away from the Holy Cross order, which had opened the elite school to the sons and daughters of the poor. Lay people working with the popular church had the most to fear; arrests and threats against them were common.[36]

Nevertheless, the first statements by the bishops' conference following the coup display a cautious acceptance of the ruling Junta. Two days after the military intervened, the Permanent Committee of the CECh issued a declaration stating in the first place that the bishops had done what they could to prevent a violent denouement to the country's crisis, a "denouement which the members of the Governing Junta have been the first to lament."[37] The bishops proceed to mourn the blood shed in the streets of Chile, to ask moderation of the victors over the vanquished, and to ask the cooperation of all with "those who have assumed the difficult task of restoring the institutional order and economic life of the country, so gravely altered."[38] Finally, the bishops declare their confidence in the tradition of democracy and humanism of the armed forces, and in their promise to return the nation soon to institutional normality.

Although a few bishops were openly jubilant at the defeat of the Marxist government, most kept to the center, neither condemning the overthrow of Allende, nor explicitly endorsing the Junta. The last year of the Popular Unity government had brought chaos to the country. The causes were many and complex – sabotage by the right, arrogance on the left, hostile measures by the United States – but as even one of the most progressive bishops later said, "on September 11, 1973, no Chilean bishop sympathized with the Popular Unity government."[39] Nevertheless, the bishops' conference had maintained a respectful relationship with Allende's government, regarding its representatives as the duly elected officials of the nation.[40] When Allende was overthrown, the church hierarchy was aware that "institutional normality" had been ruptured, and that something less than complete recognition of the Junta would have to suffice. The traditional Te Deum mass celebrated on Chilean independence day had long been the most important symbol of church–state accord. In 1973,

---

[35] Escobar, *Persecución a la iglesia en Chile*, 91.
[36] Ibid., 80.
[37] "Declaración del Comité Permanente del episcopado sobre la situación del país," in *Documentos del episcopado: Chile 1970–73*, 174.
[38] Ibid.
[39] Bishop Carlos Camus, quoted in Eugenio Yáñez Rojas, *La iglesia y el gobierno militar* (Santiago: Editorial Andante, 1989), 55.
[40] See Smith, *The Church and Politics in Chile*, 165–229.

coming just one week after the coup, the Te Deum would carry enormous public weight. The Cardinal refused to cancel it, but he did move the ceremony out of its customary place in the Cathedral and he made a point during the mass of addressing the four members of the Junta as heads of the armed forces and not as heads of state. Still, at the end of the day, it was not clear who had won the battle of symbols. The mass had been moved from the Cathedral but ended up at the church of National Gratitude to the Sacred Heart of Jesus for the Triumph of the Arms and Heroes of the War of the Pacific.[41]

The Junta had been displeased that the bishops' statement of September 13, mild as it was, was issued without their prior approval. This time the Cardinal submitted his Te Deum homily in advance to the military authorities, who found nothing to which they could object.[42] The reconstruction of the fatherland, *la patria*, was Cardinal Silva's theme. He spoke of "the soul of Chile," those values like love of liberty and love of the law which prevent "foreign values, customs or powers" – a reference to Marxism – from sapping the nation's *chilenidad*, its "Chilenicity."[43] The "soul of Chile, gift from God to our people,"[44] appears in the homily as the mystical principle of organic unity for all Chileans: "we must overcome our divisions and struggles, we must forget our differences and our contrasting opinions, we must put an end to hate so that it does not poison and destroy the soul of our fatherland."[45] To this end, Silva offers "all our disinterested collaboration" to those who "in such difficult hours have taken onto their shoulders the extremely weighty responsibility of guiding our destiny,"[46] i.e., the military.

Ten days later, on September 28, the Permanent Committee of the bishops' conference met with the Junta "to express their sentiments of respect and appreciation for the armed forces and national police of Chile" and to thank them for the deference they had shown the bishops.[47] After the visit the

---

[41] Cavallo, et al., *La historia oculta del régimen militar*, 94; and Smith, *The Church and Politics in Chile*, 289. The church of National Gratitude was constructed after Chile's defeat of Peru in the War of the Pacific, 1879–83.

[42] *Los Te Deum del Cardenal Silva Henríquez en el régimen militar*, ed. Ascanio Cavallo Castro (Santiago: Ediciones Copygraph, 1988), 13–14.

[43] Ibid., 17.

[44] Ibid.

[45] Ibid., 16.

[46] Ibid.

[47] "Comunicado de Mons. Carlos Oviedo, Secretario General de la CECH, sobre la visita del Comité Permanente a la H. Junta Militar de Gobierno," in *Documentos del episcopado: Chile 1970–73*, 175.

bishops issued a statement saying they had offered their collaboration in the task of "pacification of spirits" and "developing the social gains of the workers." The statement concludes, "the bishops expressed the desire of the church to collaborate in the spiritual and material development of Chile, within its proper field and with the autonomy that is appropriate to it in the authentic preaching of the evangelical Message, given to all without distinction of groups."[48]

Much had changed since the coup, but the bishops saw their most important task as maintaining continuity. In its official discourse, the hierarchy attempted to maintain the same appearance of political neutrality that it had claimed under Allende. Governments come and go, but the nation-state perdures. Chile remained the focus of the church's efforts. In an October 9 press conference, Cardinal Silva affirmed:

> The Church has always maintained cordial relations with governments of this country. We desire to be of service. The Church is not called upon to install governments or to take power away from them, nor to give or withhold recognition of governments. We accept the governments which the people want and we serve them. There is, moreover, a cordial understanding between Church and state in this task: the task of reconstructing Chile and of removing the great difficulties in which the country now finds itself.[49]

In an interview in late October, Silva said that the church had offered the same cooperation to the military regime that it had given to Popular Unity. But then he continued on to say that the military could even "expect more from us" since they were "Christian" and therefore "we can understand each other in many fields."[50] The Cardinal thus attempted to remain consistent with the church's professed separation of the "political" from the "religious." As under Allende, the church must remain politically neutral. However, insofar as the military is Christian, the church can cooperate with them in the sphere of religion.

Under the military dictatorship, the church would have an even greater stake than it had previously in maintaining publicly that its own actions kept well within the lines of religion, for "meddling in politics" became the Junta's constant refrain against church actions that were less than supportive of the regime. Indeed "politics" itself was a dirty word on the lips of government

---

[48] Ibid.
[49] Cardinal Raúl Silva, quoted in Smith, *The Church and Politics in Chile*, 290.
[50] Ibid., 291.

functionaries, regardless of whether it was applied to the church or the remnants of the legally proscribed political parties.[51] According to General Pinochet, it was *politiquería*, especially as embodied by the parties, that brought Chile to the precipice from which the military had rescued it.

> Our historical experience confirms that political parties, as they were called under the old constitutional framework, tended to transform themselves into monopolistic sources for the generation of power; that they made social conflict more acute; and that in the electoral struggle in which they engaged, ethical limits disappeared, thereby allowing for any maneuver whatsoever to injure their adversaries, including the defamation and dishonoring of individuals and of families.[52]

The Junta's *Declaration of Principles* laid out a plan for the depoliticization of government and all intermediate bodies. Politics had produced sectarianism; the new regime would be based on a disinterested nationalism which would put an end to fraternal conflict and unite Chile into one organic whole.[53] As General Pinochet said "We are trying to unite all Chileans, and if we got the politicians involved, it would produce polarization all over again . . . All the work we are doing would be wiped out."[54]

The similarity between the regime's stated purpose and that of the official church is striking: both claimed that they intended to subsume societal conflict into a single whole free of essential strife. The church sought a mystical communion of Chileans above the party political fray; the military regime wanted to eliminate party politics altogether. It is not difficult to appreciate why a few bishops would maintain that the church had an obligation to support openly the new regime. At a luncheon for General Pinochet in August 1974, Bishop Augusto Salinas Fuenzalida remarked "The church should continue supporting – without niggling distinctions or comparisons – the current government, which is different from the rest, which is not of political parties, which is not about personal services, but is the incarnation of Chile."[55]

---

[51] See Brian Loveman, "Antipolitics in Chile, 1973–1987," in *The Politics of Antipolitics: The Military in Latin America*, 2nd edn., ed. Brian Loveman and Thomas M. Davies, Jr. (Lincoln, Neb.: University of Nebraska Press, 1989), 426–55.

[52] Augusto Pinochet, "Chile Should not Fall into the Vices of the Past," in *The Politics of Antipolitics*, 248.

[53] Junta Militar de Gobierno, *Declaración de principios del gobierno de Chile* (Santiago: n.p., 1974), 25–6, 30.

[54] Augusto Pinochet, quoted in Pamela Constable and Arturo Valenzuela, *A Nation of Enemies: Chile under Pinochet* (New York: W. W. Norton & Co., 1991), 271.

If the church is the soul of Chile, the military is its incarnation, its body. Staying out of politics for the most conservative bishops meant supporting the military regime's "depoliticization" of Chile.

For the majority of Chile's bishops, reformists uneasy with the new authoritarian regime, staying out of politics meant other things. All bishops nevertheless regarded the accusation of meddling in politics as a severe rebuke, one which they had continually to counter with claims that the particular activity or statement in question fell under the category of religion and the church's proper mission of evangelization. Where this supposed line between religion and politics was drawn therefore fluctuated according to the church's present purposes. The definitions of what constitutes politics and what is "pure" Gospel were in constant negotiation both without and within the church. The bishops, for example, were united in their opposition to Christians for Socialism, claiming that its links with the parties of the left overstepped their mandate as ministers of the Gospel. Nevertheless the same bishops, as Brian Smith points out, used their public influence on behalf of the Christian Democratic party in the 1960s, differing only in degree and style from the priests who headed Christians for Socialism.[56] One bishop explains the difference in the following unconvincing terms:

> The identification with the PDC [Christian Democratic Party] was made despite a very prudent stand taken by the Church. There were some who made this identification but this was not the official position of the Church. In any case, it is historically understandable because the leaders of the Christian Democratic Party were activists in Catholic Action. They wanted to implement the principles of the social doctrine of the Church. . .
>
> In contrast, I believe those who wanted to take the Church on the road to socialism made moves which were wrong. They presented politics as absolute and implied that a commitment to the Gospel invariably led one to socialism. This was a betrayal – it was a total identification with a political option. This was not only a practical, but a theoretical mistake.[57]

The malleability of the terms "politics" and "religion" suggests, however, that the real theoretical mistake lies in treating them as two essentially distinct activities occupying distinct "spaces" which can be either mixed or kept

---

[55] Augusto Salinas Fuenzalida, quoted in Cavallo, et al., *La historia oculta del régimen militar*, 96–7.

[56] Smith, *The Church and Politics in Chile*, 269.

[57] Chilean bishop, interview quoted anonymously in Smith, *The Church and Politics in Chile*, 268–9.

separate. The true Eucharistic nature of the church challenges this way of imagining "politics," as I will display in later chapters. For the purposes of the present narrative, it will suffice to note that the church's self-description of its own activities under the military regime was subject to a constant demand, both from within and from without the church, to separate out its true evangelical mission from something called "politics." The church's ecclesiology inherited from Maritain involved the constant denial that the church itself constitutes a type of "politics," that is, a way of inscribing bodies into certain visible communal practices. This would become a problem for the church's self-definition when its own activities put it on a collision course with the regime.

The problem would begin to take shape when people began to knock at the Cardinal's door. In the days and weeks after the coup, tens of thousands of people were killed or taken prisoner. Bodies appeared in the rivers, and the soccer stadiums were filled with supporters of the previous government, rounded up off the streets or hounded out of bed by furious troops intent on cleansing Chile of the Marxist plague. Thousands were fired from their jobs and thousands more went into hiding or sought refuge at one of the many embassies willing to grant asylum. Amid great fear and confusion, the church was the only major civilian organization whose structure survived the military siege. The parishes were inundated with desperate requests for help. Hundreds of people every day climbed the stairs of the Archbishopric of Santiago to the Cardinal's secretary's office on the third floor. Luis Antonio Diaz found a volunteer to help attend to the people, but the lines grew longer each day, and it became impossible to see everyone who came. Within a few weeks of the coup, Cardinal Silva asked auxiliary bishop Fernando Ariztía to head a commission to coordinate assistance efforts; Protestant, Orthodox, and Jewish leaders were also asked to send representatives.[58] On October 9, the Committee of Cooperation for Peace in Chile, or COPACHI, was born.

"We operated without having a clearly delineated office," recalls Argentina Valenzuela, a social worker recruited by Ariztía to work for COPACHI:

> In the hallways we received people who presented the most diverse problems. People came, from the hundreds of people fired from public service jobs to one man who said to me: "I'm on the run; what can you do for me?" After talking

---

[58] Representatives of the World Council of churches, the Baptist, Methodist, Methodist Pentecostal, Evangelical Lutheran, and Orthodox churches, and the Grand Rabbi of the Jewish community were members of the original committee; Cavallo, et al., *La historia oculta del régimen militar*, 96.

with him, he asked me at least to accompany him to the bus. And at that moment I could not begin to consider if what he told me was true or not and what risks it implied. Very much afraid, I accompanied him to the bus.[59]

To get to the offices of COPACHI on the sixth floor of the building on Erasmo Escala street, it was necessary to walk past offices of the Air Force, which shared the building with the Archbishopric.[60] Within a couple of weeks, the Committee moved into less hostile surroundings on Santa Mónica street, and rapidly began to take on more and more responsibilities.[61]

Bishop Fernando Ariztía recalls that in the beginning COPACHI operated without a grand vision of the church's social role. It was rather "a response to an emergency which cried out to us from all sides."[62] COPACHI put out a flier to all the parishes in Santiago, informing them that the church now had a place to attend to those who sought help. Those who came told stories that the Committee members would not hear by turning on their television sets. They found themselves helping to hide people fleeing from the police. The Committee's lawyers provided defense for those charged by War Tribunals. COPACHI began to set up visits of family members to those held in prison camps. For unemployed workers it provided legal recourse and support for efforts at self-employment. COPACHI organized a network of soup kitchens for hungry children. In January of 1974, the first writs of habeas corpus were presented to the courts.[63]

COPACHI soon began to organize its personnel according to different departments: Legal, Emergency Assistance, Labor, Universities, Health, Solidarity and Development, and Campesinos. From Santiago the organization spread to 23 other cities in Chile.[64] With all other popular organizations – even sports clubs – forbidden, the church became an *alero*, a protective roof under which people could gather.[65] According to a newspaper advertisement announcing the Committee, its purpose was to "collaborate in the great

---

[59] *Vicaría de la Solidaridad: historia de su trabajo social* (Santiago: Ediciones Paulinas, 1991), 6.

[60] Isabel Donoso, interview by author, July 2, 1993, Santiago, tape recording. Donoso worked with the Vicaría de la Solidaridad in the early days, and now works with the Archdiocese's Vicaría de Pastoral General.

[61] *Vicaría de la Solidaridad*, 14.

[62] Bishop Fernando Ariztía, interview by author, July 8, 1993, Santiago, tape recording.

[63] Ibid.

[64] Cavallo, et al., *La historia oculta del régimen militar*, 96.

[65] Bishop Fernando Ariztía, interview by author, July 8, 1993.

mission of national pacification, since the WORK OF JUSTICE WILL BE PEACE."[66] According to the regime, the church was meddling in politics. COPACHI would be a constant thorn in Pinochet's side, and he would repeatedly demand its dissolution.[67]

At the same time that Monseñor Ariztía found himself heading a burgeoning network of relief operations and organizations, the episcopal conference was requesting that the church's apostolic movements – the Christian Family Movement, Schönstatt, and especially the various branches of Catholic Action – hew closely to the regime's suspension of social activities. On October 1 the permanent committee of the CECh issued a directive asking the apostolic movements to stick to using the Bible and magisterial documents of the church, and to suspend any meetings for the time being. Such precautions are necessary, the statement reads, because given the country's present circumstances "it is very possible that some wish to use the apostolic movements or church groups as a refuge for political activities."[68]

By no means did the Chilean hierarchy simply turn a blind eye to the suffering unleashed among the supporters of the previous government. They took seriously their role as the soul of Chile and sought above all to aid in the "pacification of spirits." As the body count rose in the early weeks, according to Bishop Carlos Camus, caution in the episcopal conference was not a matter of support for the regime, but rather the conviction that more lives could be saved by cooperation and quiet diplomacy. Church and state in Chile had always operated in tandem, and many in the hierarchy were convinced that the new rulers would be more willing to listen to peacemaking words if they came from a church not openly unfriendly to the new regime.[69]

As the Junta's hunt for "subversives" continued unabated in the weeks following the coup, stories of atrocities began to escape Chile's borders with those people who had been forced to flee. The reports reached the Pope, who on October 7 expressed his dismay to the Roman press over the "bloody repression" taking place in Chile.[70] So moved was Paul VI that he wrote a

[66] *El Mercurio*, Nov. 10, 1973.

[67] The press of this period, all closely allied with the regime, attacked COPACHI's initial efforts to help fired workers as damaging Chile's image before the rest of the world. In *El Mercurio*, Santiago's most influential paper, María Correa Morandé asks why the church offered no help to workers who had suffered under "Marxist slavery" in the previous government; "La imagen de Chile," *El Mercurio*, Nov. 4, 1973.

[68] "Acuerdos pastorales sobre movimientos apostólicos," in *Documentos del episcopado: Chile 1970–1973*, 175–76.

[69] Bishop Carlos Camus, interview by author, July 9, 1993, Linares, tape recording.

[70] Cavallo, et al., *La historia oculta del régimen militar*, 95.

letter to the Chilean episcopate articulating his concern for the violence and bloodshed, the circumstances of the many prisoners, and the failure of safeguards for basic human rights. He emphasized the necessity of a return to democratic institutions. The letter was to be made public, and the consequences could be great. A letter from the Pope so critical of the restorers of "Western Christian civilization" in Chile was surely one of the Junta's worst nightmares.[71]

The letter made its way from Rome to a desk in the Papal Nuncio's residence in Santiago, where it stayed while the Nuncio – Sótero Sanz – and Cardinal Silva conferred. Two days after Paul VI's declaration to the press the four members of the Junta had paid a visit to the Cardinal to complain about the Pope's words and elicit a promise of cooperation from the Cardinal. Now the Nuncio and the Cardinal feared that the letter would explode an already tense situation, give aid and comfort to those tempted to armed resistance, and hinder the church's freedom to aid those being persecuted by the regime. Cardinal Silva was dispatched to Rome. On November 3, 1973, he met alone with Pope Paul VI and convinced him to withdraw the letter. It was a mission that Cardinal Silva would come to regret deeply in the years that followed.[72] Two years later he would ask the Pope's permission to make the letter known. The Pope refused, saying that the opportunity was long past.[73]

The first public criticism of the regime by a bishop came in December 1973. Its source, not coincidentally, was Fernando Ariztía, who through his work with COPACHI knew firsthand what most other bishops knew only by rumor. Ariztía issued an open letter acknowledging certain gains in order since the military takeover, but criticizing the many losses in freedom.[74] His requests for more freedom of press, assembly, and organization were met by a chorus of condemnation in the media.[75] A few weeks later, Bishop Jorge Hourton of Puerto Montt joined his voice to that of Ariztía and, in his Christmas letter to pastoral workers in his diocese, denounced in specific terms the worst abuses of the military regime: torture, massive arrests, arbitrary decisions in the courts, economic discrimination, and lack of freedom of expression and assembly.[76]

---

[71] Ibid.

[72] Ibid.

[73] Ibid., 102.

[74] Smith, *The Church and Politics in Chile*, 293.

[75] E.g. "Carta de FEUC a Obispo Ariztía," *El Mercurio*, December 6, 1973; and "Reflexionando sobre la carta de un obispo," *El Mercurio*, December 17, 1973.

[76] Smith, *The Church and Politics in Chile*, 293.

The first public criticism of the regime's abuses by the episcopal conference as a whole had to wait until April 1974. By that date the smoldering embers of the coup had died out, but a new and more sinister mode of power was making itself felt throughout Chile. The DINA was in full operation and had already established its pattern of nightly disappearances. The lawyers at COPACHI filed their first writ of habeas corpus in January of 1974; they would soon accumulate more experience filing such motions than they cared to have. The bishops heard stories from their priests about the terror gripping the marginalized neighborhoods. The Cardinal himself would feel the cold hand of fear upon him. In early April Manuel Contreras, head of the DINA, paid Cardinal Silva a personal visit. Unhappy with the interference of COPACHI with his work, Contreras had a not-very-subtle message from the intelligence community for Silva. "Cardinal," he is reported to have said, "we know that a lot of crazy people are running around out there. We are afraid that something could happen to you. It would be good if you took care of yourself."[77] Cardinal Silva denounced the threat in his homily on April 13. "Would you believe, my beloved children, that in this moment, according to what they tell me, your Shepherd, your Bishop who is speaking to you, is threatened with death and has to have a bodyguard to defend him? Would you believe that this is possible in this land of ours?"[78]

The people of Chile's poor neighborhoods were rapidly becoming believers; most of the bishops, too, realized that they would have to address the mounting evidence of serious abuses under a regime intent on tightening, not relinquishing, its grip on power. The offices of COPACHI nationwide were providing the bishops with ample proof that the situation in the country was not being "normalized." On April 24, 1974, the Episcopal Conference issued a document entitled "Reconciliation in Chile," partly in response to the Declaration of Principles which the Junta had published in March. In their statement the bishops mention favorably the "explicitly Christian inspiration" of the regime's Declaration and the human rights enshrined therein.[79] But although the bishops state "We do not doubt the just intentions or the good will of those who govern us,"[80] they also list a series of concerns for the state of the nation. They first express concern over the "climate of insecurity and

---

[77] Manuel Contreras, quoted in Cavallo, ed., *La historia oculta del régimen militar*, 46.

[78] Cardinal Raúl Silva, quoted in Yáñez, *La iglesia y el gobierno militar*, 60.

[79] "La reconciliación en Chile," in *Documentos del episcopado: Chile 1974–1980* (Santiago: Ediciones Mundo, 1982), 15–16.

[80] Ibid., 16.

fear" in the country, blaming denunciations, false rumors, and the lack of participation and information. Their second concern is the increase in poverty and unemployment due to the regime's restructuring of the economy to the disadvantage of the workers. The bishops' third concern is the massive overhaul of the educational system being done without the participation of parents and the whole community. Their fourth and last concern refers in indirect terms to the work of the regime's security apparatus:

> We are concerned, finally, in some cases, about the lack of effective judicial safeguards for personal security, which translates into arbitrary or excessively prolonged detentions in which neither those affected nor their families know the concrete charges against them; into interrogations with physical or moral compulsion; into limitation of the possibilities of legal defense; into unequal sentences for the same charges in different places; into restrictions on the normal use of the right of appeal.[81]

The bishops acknowledge that the state may need to suspend temporarily some civil rights under particular circumstances, but that there are some rights which pertain to the "very dignity of the human person" and are therefore absolute.[82]

Although torture appears only under the euphemistic guise of *apremios* (pressure or compulsion), in "Reconciliation in Chile" the bishops knew that they had begun to navigate dangerous waters of confrontation with the regime. Cardinal Silva did his best to give the appearance of cooperation with the military government, sending a delegation of fellow bishops to meet with the Junta before the document was released. In his presentation of the document, Cardinal Silva lauded the Junta which, "informed of the content of the present Declaration, have had the noble attitude of completely respecting our freedom, which constitutes the best proof of the right to dissent that exists in Chile, and of the prevalence of the state of law in our country."[83] Silva stressed that the bishops did not want their reflections to be considered "politics," but only an exhortation to Chileans to work for reconciliation.[84]

---

[81] Ibid.

[82] Ibid.

[83] Ibid., 12. Cardinal Silva wanted to delay the publication of the declaration, insisting to the bishops' assembly that the junta had promised him an edict soon to end the arbitrary detentions. Most bishops saw less evidence of the junta's good intentions, and the declaration was published as planned; see Juan Mihovilovich Hernández, *Camus Obispo* (Santiago: Ediciones Rehue, 1988), 74–5.

[84] Ibid.

Concerning the declaration, Silva also added that, "since we have had to touch on delicate subjects," he felt obliged to make clear, especially to foreigners, the peculiarity of the Chilean situation: any consideration of the present government must take into account the chaos under the previous one, as well as the continued armed resistance against the current regime.[85]

According to the *Rettig Report*, in the last three months of 1973 only three soldiers or policemen were killed by civilian militants.[86] In 1974 the first such incident occurred in September; in the entire period from January 1974 to August 1977 only six soldiers or policemen were killed.[87] The existence of continued armed resistance against the military regime was mainly a creation of the regime itself and its allies in the media. Why would the bishops feel obliged to repeat the government line on the continued dangers of Marxist aggression? It is explicable in part by their lack of access to other information, but it is also the case that the official church's emphasis on reconciliation has certain affinities with the regime's constant demand for order. In other words the church's stress on subsuming conflict into the organic unity of Chile had the effect of causing the church to identify its own interests with those of the nation-state. The church hierarchy in Chile had long seen itself in cooperation with the state as the twin guardians of the Chilean national heritage. In the early days of the dictatorship the church therefore had built-in sympathies with Pinochet's program to impose unity and order on Chile and eliminate the chaos of class conflict caused by "foreign ideologies." Specific abuses such as torture and unfair trials were seen in the church hierarchy not as intrinsic to this order but as aberrations, excesses which could be corrected by appeals to the Christian consciences of Chile's rulers.

During this period Cardinal Silva and Carlos Camus, respectively President and Secretary of the CECh, met often in private with General Pinochet and other members of the Junta to discuss the situation in the country. According to Camus, these meetings were formal but cordial, occasionally tense. "Cardinal Silva Henríquez," says Camus, "always had hopes that he could change Pinochet, that we could change his attitude."[88] Pinochet for his part never admitted the existence of serious abuses, but implied instead that the bishops had been duped by the communists. In fact, says Camus, it was the regime that tried to fool them, and they began

---

[85] Ibid.
[86] *Rettig Report*, 460–1.
[87] Ibid., 620–4.
[88] Bishop Carlos Camus, interview by author, July 9, 1993.

to realize, little by little, that private conversations would have no effect.[89]

The bishops' preference for private conversations in the early days of the regime died hard. Many bishops believed that public denunciations would be crossing the imaginary line into politics. One bishop interviewed in 1975 explains, "There were cases of torture here in my diocese during the first days of this government. I went to the authorities and was successful in my complaints. The form of protest is important. We must avoid politics. At the level of prinicple we have to speak the truth."[90] Others believed that public denunciations would only make matters worse for the members of the church, especially those least able to defend themselves.

> Dinners, private letters, or conversations are more effective than public denunciations. This clearly is not prophetic, but it is also certain that we have to live in this country. We can't leave, and we bishops won't pay the consequences, but the clergy and laity will . . . Torture isn't everything . . . The person tortured affects 50 to 100 persons. But there are many other social and economic problems that affect more Chileans. For many the situation is now better – no strikes, no chaos, order has returned.[91]

"Torture isn't everything"; in this bishop's view it is an excess of the regime which should not wholly detract from the regime's accomplishments in achieving order. For the church to denounce such excesses publicly would be to break with that order, to tear it asunder and thus bring suffering, not healing, to the body politic.

Of the Chilean bishops whom Brian Smith surveyed in mid-1975, 90 percent preferred private conversations with authorities over public denunciations in the face of abuse of power. At the same time, those whom the bishops would protect by avoiding public denunciations – priests, religious, and laity – approved by substantial margins more prophetic public positions from the hierarchy, even though they themselves might be made to suffer for it.[92]

In the weeks following the coup, Father Roberto Bolton, one of the leading voices for a closer priestly presence among the poor, took it upon himself to

---

[89] Ibid.

[90] Chilean bishop, quoted in Smith, *The Church and Politics in Chile*, 298.

[91] Ibid., 299.

[92] Smith, *The Church and Politics in Chile*, 302–4. Priests approved the more prophetic stance over private conversations by a margin of 47.3 to 40.3 percent. For nuns the margin was 57.6 to 12.1, for laity 56.9 to 29.4.

visit many of Chile's bishops to discuss the situation in the country. According to Bolton, his pleas for a more prophetic voice from the hierarchy were met with the same response cited above: through quiet diplomacy, the church was more free to go about saving lives. But Bolton argues:

> At that moment the dictatorship was very weak. It was recently installed, and had not yet entrenched itself or taken all positions of power. But the church was, and always has been, a moral force. If the church speaks very clearly, I believe . . . that the church stops the slaughter. They would not have been able to continue killing. If the church excommunicates, if the church speaks very clearly and breaks with the government . . . I think that it would have prevented the thousands of deaths that came later.[93]

Looking back twenty years after the coup, some bishops have expressed regret that the hierarchy did not speak more forcefully from the beginning. Tomás González, bishop of Punta Arenas, says that little was achieved by means of private conversations; the regime would have responded more to public denunciations of torture and disappearance.[94] Carlos González, bishop of Talca, is more blunt: "Everything done in private was useless."[95] Bishop Alejandro Jiménez puts it this way: "Private conversations were important and had to be done, but they were insufficient. I believe that what the military world most feared and what had the greatest effect on it was the courageous, objective and public denunciation of the situations that existed . . . In cases of extreme violations of human rights, a word from the church was very important."[96]

Jiménez speaks of private conversations he had with an army lieutenant in Talca in the early days of military rule. The lieutenant and the bishop had been boyhood friends, classmates, and were able to speak very frankly and forcefully without jeopardizing their friendship. A cordial reception awaited the bishop when he approached the lieutenant about tortures and other abuses, but little progress resulted. Jiménez explains:

> The problem is that it is not only a matter of personal relationships, because the soldier above all forms part of an institution and has to obey absolutely his

---

[93] Roberto Bolton, interview by author, August 4, 1993, Santiago, tape recording.
[94] Bishop Tomás González, interview by author, July 26, 1993, Punta Arenas, tape recording.
[95] Bishop Carlos González, interview by author, July 28, 1993, Talca, tape recording.
[96] Bishop Alejandro Jiménez, interview by author, July 29, 1993, Valdivia, tape recording.

institution . . . [Private conversations] are valuable insofar as the soldiers have a bit of influence to change some things, but they are insufficient because [soldiers] form part of a body in which not they but their superiors have the final word.[97]

I ask Jiménez "But if the person is a Catholic, aren't you his superior as bishop and he therefore has to obey you?" His response is very revealing of the complex position of the more progressive bishops – of which Jiménez is one – under the military regime.

That was St Thomas More's dilemma, and St Thomas More showed exactly the way that had to be followed. God is God and the king is the king. The king is for temporal things but the conscience belongs only to God. But you can't demand St Thomas' attitude of [the soldier] in this case.[98]

Why not?

Because it depends definitively on his conscience, what he wants to do and how he wants to react. The authority of a bishop is a very strong authority, the most powerful of all because it goes directly to the conscience. But it is the most fragile of all authorities, because for the conscience to accept it or not to accept it depends, in the end, on the person.[99]

The soldier is expected to comply with an order without delay because, as Jiménez says, he is a member of a "body," the Chilean army, an organization of people bound by a common mission and a common discipline. What that common discipline indicates here is control over the soldier's body. When an order comes from a military superior it matters little if the soldier of lower rank agrees in conscience or not; the order must and will be obeyed. As a Catholic, however, the soldier belongs simultaneously to the church, which in this view is not a body in the same sense. The church is not bound by the same sort of discipline, but can only speak to the interior consciences of its members, and hope that those members might freely accept the church's word. When it is considered a body at all, the church is only a "mystical body," uniting all Catholics, torturers and tortured alike, in spiritual, not bodily, union.

As a progressive bishop formed in Catholic Action and later in the spirit of Vatican II, Alejandro Jiménez is careful to respect the freedom of the laity from

[97] Ibid.
[98] Ibid.
[99] Ibid.

what he sees as undue clerical control. He is, nevertheless, clearly frustrated by the "fragility" of his authority over Catholics directly responsible for the most unspeakable acts, often committed against fellow members of the church. Ideally the church pictured itself as the conscience or soul of the Chilean military. In practice the necessities of the body overruled the misgivings of the soul; the lieutenant's conscience may have stirred at the bishop's words, but the lives of the people of Talca were none the better for it.

This trap which New Christendom ecclesiology set for the church often made the church reluctant to challenge the state even on the field of "conscience." The episcopal conference never called for the recognition of conscientious objection to Chile's obligatory military service for males, a suggestion which the military government would vigorously oppose. Bishop Jiménez expresses his support for the right of conscientious objection, but says he could only do so on "a private and personal level. I cannot do it by coercing the conscience of other Christians."[100] It seems odd that advocating a law which respects the possibility for Chileans to opt in conscience out of military service would be considered coercion of conscience. Jiménez explains that the episcopal conference has spoken to the issue, but in terms of general values: reconciliation, respecting the adversary, abandoning the state of war, and so on.[101] It would be up to the laity to translate those values into specific laws according to their own conscience. The problem is that the military state is no respecter of conscience; it operates according to its own particular logic and mission and is disciplined to achieve its ends. The military state well understood that conscientious objection would be a direct threat to itself as a body. The hierarchy of the church was unable to grasp, at least in the early years of the dictatorship, that having its members in military service was a direct threat to the *church* as a body.

3 The Stubborn Monkey

A year and a half separated "Reconciliation in Chile" and "Gospel and Peace," the bishops' next major statement on the situation in Chile. Issued in September 1975, the new declaration wavers little from the hierarchy's determination to speak as the loyal conscience of the regime. Freedom from torture is listed among basic human rights that are preconditions for peace, but

[100] Ibid.
[101] Ibid.

the document does not directly state that torture is a reality in Chile.[102] A critique of predatory capitalism and the burdens it imposes on the poor is balanced with a critique of Marxism,[103] which by this time was alive in Chile only in the propaganda mills of the regime. The bishops nevertheless again thank the armed forces for saving Chile from "a Marxist dictatorship that appeared inevitable and would have been irreversible,"[104] a questionable historical judgment at best. Finally, the declaration concludes with a treatise on "healthy" patriotism – "Jesus was a patriot"[105] – and the dangers of excessive nationalism. Had he been born in Chile, Jesus would have been "one hundred percent Chilean, in love with our countryside and our history, with our way of being and living, an authentic son of our people and our land."[106] The bishops praise the Junta's efforts to rekindle Chilean patriotism and parrot the regime's complaints about "an international campaign against Chile which deforms the truth,"[107] but also criticize a nationalism identified with a particular government or particular class interests. The armed forces of Chile "are not and never have been classist," and the bishops express confidence that the armed forces will be able to resist the efforts of "a few Chileans" to use them for certain class interests.[108] Despite the fact that Junta policies amounted to a virtual war on the poor, the episcopacy continued to cling to the fantasy of Chile as an organic whole.

Although many bishops had by this point privately abandoned hope of taming the military regime, it would take one bishop's off-the-record comments to a foreign journalist on September 30, 1975 to break episcopal discontent into the open. Carlos Camus's frank observations to a few foreign correspondents caused a furor when they were secretly taped by a Bolivian newspaperman and then sold to a Santiago tabloid.[109] In his remarks Camus puts the blame for the "climate of hate" on the shoulders of the regime, and says that church–state conflict is the result of the church's defense of the poor and the persecuted against the "brute force" of the regime. He tells of meeting with people who have been destroyed by torture and the fear that they spread throughout the population. He claims that unemployment far surpasses the

---

[102] "Evangelio y paz," in *Documentos del episcopado: Chile 1974–1980*, 107.
[103] Ibid., 112–23.
[104] Ibid., 110.
[105] Ibid., 123.
[106] Ibid., 124.
[107] Ibid.
[108] Ibid., 126.
[109] Mihovilovich, *Camus Obispo*, 75–9.

already grim figure of 20 percent given out by the government. Camus also acknowledges that some people with Marxist ideas are working in COPACHI.[110]

What is remarkable about the incident is not the content of Camus's comments, but rather that, after two years of brutality, his comments would come as such a shock to the country. Camus was demonized in the media, and the government demanded his removal as secretary of the CECh. The bishops refused, and many rallied to Camus's defense,[111] but the furor that met his remarks is only understandable against the backdrop of the episcopacy's mild public criticisms of the regime up to that point.

In the meantime the condition of the poor majority in Chile was marked by increasing economic hardship and fear of the omnipresent security apparatus. The DINA had expanded rapidly into a quasi-independent power, eliminating any hint of dissent and making its chief, Colonel Manuel Contreras, the second most powerful person in Chile, feared even by the armed forces' top brass. The rate of disappearances escalated throughout the end of 1974 and into 1975, and COPACHI was inundated with reports of midnight arrests and tortures. This period saw the virtual elimination of the MIR (Revolutionary Left Movement) through executions and disappearances.[112]

On the night of October 16, 1975, dozens of DINA agents closed in on a small country house near Malloco, between Santiago and Valparaiso. Inside were those who remained of the MIR's highest leadership, six of the most wanted people in Chile. The DINA agents were unable to surround the house before the shootout began. While Dagoberto Pérez kept the agents at bay, the others escaped. Nelson Gutiérrez, wounded in the leg, and María Elena Bachman handed their baby to a neighbor and fled toward the highway. There they intercepted a red Volkswagen, left its driver standing by the side of the road, and sped towards Santiago. Their destination was a Catholic parish, where Father Fernando Salas, executive secretary of COPACHI, met them.[113]

After two days in hiding at the parish, Gutiérrez and Bachman were moved

---

[110] *El Mercurio*, Oct. 8, 1975. Camus later released a transcript of his own tape of the interview showing that the media had misquoted or taken some portions of his remarks out of context; see Smith, *The Church and Politics in Chile*, 301.

[111] Mihovilovich, *Camus Obispo*, 78.

[112] *Rettig Report*, 525–59.

[113] Sheila Cassidy, *Audacity to Believe* (London: William Collins Sons & Co., 1977), 156–64; and Terrazas, *¿Quién se acuerda de Sheila Cassidy?*, 240. Cavallo, et al., report that Gutiérrez fled with Andrés Pascal Allende; *La historia oculta del régimen militar*, 136.

to the convent of the Notre Dame sisters, meeting up there with Mary Ann Beausire, another of the MIR refugees. It was here that the English doctor Sheila Cassidy would be asked by a priest friend to tend to Gutiérrez's wounds; "I hope to God," the priest told her, "that Christ goes disguised as a wounded Mirista."[114] After being moved to the home of Holy Cross Father John Devlin, Gutiérrez and Bachman were driven to the papal nuncio's residence by another priest in the trunk of his car, and there found diplomatic asylum. Mary Ann Beausire and Andrés Pascal Allende found refuge at the Costa Rican ambassador's house. Sheila Cassidy was not so fortunate. On October 31 she was taken by DINA agents from the residence of the Columban Fathers, where she was tending to a sick friend. At Villa Grimaldi that night she was brutally tortured on the "grill" until she confessed her role in the matter and revealed the whereabouts of another MIR refugee, hiding with two other Holy Cross priests.[115]

When the story became public, the regime and the official press could not contain their incredulous indignation. That so many priests and nuns, even a bishop (Enrique Alvear, auxiliary of Santiago) had been involved at all different levels gave excuse to a spasm of defamation and persecution of the church.[116] Many of the priests and nuns involved were arrested; the foreigners among them, as well as Sheila Cassidy, were expelled from the country. Others, both foreigners and Chileans, sought asylum in various embassies. Public attacks on the church became virulent. The religious and priests involved were accused of active participation in terrorist organizations and acts. The Cardinal and even the Papal Nuncio were accused of Communist sympathies.[117]

Twice on national television Jaime Guzmán, an integralist Catholic and the regime's chief legal adviser, accused the priests and religious involved of active participation in the MIR and attacked the church's hierarchy for defending them. The Archbishopric of Santiago had published a declaration underlining the evangelical requirement to offer mercy to those whose life is endangered regardless of their political beliefs. Guzmán countered with the Chilean penal code, making clear that all who aid those fleeing from justice put themselves outside the law. The Archbishopric's statement, said Guzmán, "contains a grave error" in its interpretation of mercy. He urged, therefore, that all good

---

[114] Cassidy, *Audacity to Believe*, 159.

[115] Ibid., 165–94.

[116] The press accounts surrounding the incident are collected in Terrazas, *¿Quien se acuerda de Sheila Cassidy?*; see esp. pp. 197–202, 231–49.

[117] Ibid., 305–6.

Catholics be good Chileans and turn in anyone fleeing from justice, even if they seek the protection of the church.[118]

The hierarchy reacted swiftly and decisively in a lengthy reply on November 10. The statement makes clear the anti-evangelical nature of Guzmán's definition of mercy and threatens him with excommunication for undermining the authority of the bishops, according to canons 2331 and 2344 of the 1917 Code of Canon Law. The statement concludes "The Catholic church will not allow the authority of its Pastors to be usurped or undermined, nor the honor of the name 'Catholic' to be injured, with grave detriment to its unity and its mission of service to the people of Chile."[119] The forcefulness of the bishops' reply was an indicator that relations between church and state had entered a new phase.

With the expansion of the DINA and the catastrophic effects of economic restructuring on the poor throughout 1975, COPACHI also stepped up its activities and grew into a rival organization worthy of the regime's most focused ire. Between September and November ten functionaries of COPACHI were arrested on various charges. On October 3 the co-president of the Committee, Lutheran Bishop Helmut Frenz, was refused reentry to Chile after a visit to Europe.[120] Finally, when the events of Malloco unfolded and it became clear that members of COPACHI were involved in hiding the Miristas, the regime had in its grasp the perfect opportunity to close in on the Committee. In early November General Pinochet summoned Cardinal Silva to his office and demanded the dissolution of COPACHI, which had become, in Pinochet's words, a "hotbed of subversion." "If you don't want to dissolve it," the General told the Cardinal, "I'll dissolve it myself."[121] Silva asked Pinochet to request it in writing. On November 11 General Pinochet addressed a letter to Cardinal Silva, stating that COPACHI had become "a means of which Marxist-Leninists take advantage in order to create problems which upset the tranquility and the essential peace of the citizenry, which it is my principal governmental duty to maintain."[122] The Cardinal was in a very difficult position; he believed that further confrontation with the regime had to be avoided for the sake of peace in Chile. The Orthodox and Baptist

---

[118] "Comentario de Jaime Guzmán Errázuriz transmitido por Televisión Nacional el 6 de Noviembre y repetido el 8," *Mensaje* 24: 596–7.

[119] "Evangelio y misericordia: réplica a un comentarista de TV Nacional," *Mensaje* 24: 597–9.

[120] Terrazas, *¿Quién se acuerda de Sheila Cassidy?*, 332.

[121] Augusto Pinochet, quoted in *Vicaría de la Solidaridad*, 52.

[122] Pinochet, ibid., 53.

churches had already withdrawn from COPACHI, believing it had become too "political." Cardinal Silva flew to Rome to consult with the Pope. In his absence Auxiliary Bishop Enrique Alvear read a declaration written by Silva announcing that on December 31, 1975, COPACHI would cease operations. According to Alvear, the closing of the Committee was a gesture of peace meant to maintain good relations between church and state, "relations which are esteemed to be of maximum importance for the tasks of development and peace that urgently confront the nation."[123] Once again the bishops had understood their contribution to peace in terms of the maintenance of cordial relations with a regime which had long since become the church's fiercest enemy.

The regime's reaction proved the fruitlessness of the Cardinal's attempts at making peace. Rather than reciprocating with a lessening of hostilities, the DINA understood the Committee's dissolution as a sign of weakness and attacked like wolves on a wounded deer. Dozens of people associated with COPACHI were arrested, tortured, or threatened in December.[124] The DINA had regarded COPACHI as something like the church's own intelligence operation with which it was in direct competition.[125] The DINA could now assume it was entirely without rival.

Those who had worked so hard to defend the regime's victims were disconsolate. Many felt that the Cardinal had abandoned them in one of the darkest hours of an already bleak and furtive life under the dictatorship. In Rome the Cardinal appealed to Pope Paul VI to allow him to publish the letter he had asked the Pope to withdraw two years before in the wake of the coup. The Pope refused, but he did give Silva permission to tell Pinochet that the Pope considered the persecuted priests in Chile as "martyrs of Christian charity."[126] The Pope knew the importance of martyrs in a situation filled with victims. His comments were not published, however, and the DINA's victim mill ground on.

Cardinal Silva was not finished, however. Following his return from Rome, the Archbishopric planned a mass in support of the Cardinal at the Temple of Maipú on December 8. The regime understood its import, and issued an order prohibiting massgoers from arriving in groups or with banners or signs. The CECh responded by cancelling the annual ceremonies in honor

---

[123] Bishop Enrique Alvear, quoted in Terrazas, ¿Quién se acuerda de Sheila Cassidy?, 336.
[124] Cavallo, et al., La historia oculta del régimen militar, 102.
[125] Ibid., 127; see also 259.
[126] Ibid., 102.

of the Virgin of Carmen, patroness of Chile's armed forces.[127] At the same time, conversations about how to continue the church's work for the oppressed in the absence of COPACHI had given birth to an ingenious idea: the Cardinal Archbishop of Santiago would create a new Vicariate. The ecumenical structure of COPACHI's governance had given it an ambiguous legal standing; the regime's lawyers had drafted a decree declaring it an "illicit association" which they would have used had Silva refused to dissolve it. A Vicariate, on the other hand, would depend directly on the ordinary of the Archdiocese of Santiago, which enjoys the legal standing of *persona de derecho público*, "person of public law."[128] It would be much more difficult legally to interfere with the work of a *vicario*, who stands as a direct representative of the ordinary of the Archdiocese. COPACHI officially ceased operations on December 31, 1975. On January 1, 1976, Cardinal Silva signed a decree creating a new vicariate, with Father Cristián Precht as vicar. The Vicariate of Solidarity, soon to be known throughout Chile simply as the *Vicaría*, was born.[129]

The news of the birth did not bring felicitations from General Pinochet. "Stubborn monkey! He's like a stubborn monkey!" Pinochet exploded.[130] He summoned Silva to his office and their conversation is reported as follows.

———— What's all this about a Vicariate, Cardinal? You're not going to tell me that you're going back to filling the church with communists!
———— General, I told you that the church cannot and will not abandon the defense of human rights . . .
———— So we're going to start with the same thing again! It seems that the church doesn't want to understand!
———— You can't interfere with the Vicariate! And if you try to, I'll put the refugees under my bed if necessary![131]

The Vicaría was installed in spacious offices right next to the Cathedral on the Plaza de Armas, giving it both high visibility and symbolic proximity to the goals of the Catholic church. The Vicaría expanded rapidly to become, in the words of political scientist Brian Loveman, "the foundation of moral and legal resistance to the military dictatorship."[132] Pinochet turned his frustration with

---

[127] Ibid.
[128] *Vicaría de la Solidaridad*, 55.
[129] Ibid., 54.
[130] Cavallo, et al., *La historia oculta del régimen militar*, 125.
[131] Ibid., 125–6.
[132] Loveman, "Antipolitics in Chile, 1973–87," 432. See also *Vicaría de la Solidaridad*, 59.

the Cardinal into efforts to harass the new organization. The Vicaría was financed to a great extent by foreign sources, such as the German Catholic church, the World Council of churches, and the Inter-American Foundation. The regime therefore tried to create the impression that foreign powers were financing subversion in Chile through the Vicaría. General Pinochet made public accusations of this nature, and the Chilean Central Bank tried to freeze funds destined for the Vicaría from the Inter-American Foundation.[133] The regime also targeted Vicaría personnel. Between April and August of 1976 three of the most prominent lawyers working with the Vicaría were expelled from the country, and a fourth was jailed.[134]

Relations between church and state continued on a downward trajectory throughout 1976. Cardinal Silva's frank May Day speech lamenting the atomization of the workers and the disappearance of their organizations is evidence that the hierarchy was beginning to believe in the importance of open denunciation.[135] The true breaking point came in August. During the same week that the bishops were vigorously protesting the expulsions of the Vicaría lawyers, three Chilean bishops were arrested and expelled from Ecuador along with forty-five other bishops, nuns, laypeople, and priests participating in a pastoral conference in Riobamba. Seventeen bishops were among those rounded up at gunpoint and jailed for subversion in a ham-handed attempt by the Ecuadoran government to embarrass the church. Those arrested were released the following day after a storm of protest from the US, Venezuelan, and Argentinian embassies, but no objection from Chilean diplomats was heard. In fact, the regime was busy preparing an unpleasant homecoming for the Chilean participants in the Riobamba conference. When Bishops Ariztía, Alvear, and Carlos González landed at Santiago's Pudahuel airport, they were met by a hostile crowd carrying placards denouncing them as leftist revolutionaries and subversives. The bishops were shoved, shouted at, and insulted as they tried to make their way to their car, which was met by a hail of rocks. Except for arresting several relatives of Bishop Alvear, the police made no attempt to intervene, for they were under orders to let the scene unfold. The entire demonstration was orchestrated and carried out by agents of the DINA.[136]

Against a media chorus of accusations against the church, the Permanent

[133] Smith, *The Church and Politics in Chile*, 328–9.
[134] *Vicaría de la Solidaridad*, 56.
[135] Yañez, *La iglesia y el gobierno militar*, 68.
[136] Penny Lernoux, *Cry of the People* (New York: Penguin Books, 1982), 137–42; and Cavallo, et al., *La Historia oculta del régimen militar*, 128–32.

Committee of bishops issued a declaration which finally recognized that the church was confronted with a hostile power which meant to do it harm. The declaration makes clear the responsibility of the DINA whose agents had been clearly identified directing the airport mob. It condemns the actions of those involved and names two newspapers and a television channel whose coverage of the incident was especially intended to paint the bishops as traitors to Chile and the faith. The declaration recognizes as well that these attacks "are not isolated."

> They are linked in a process or system of perfectly defined characteristics which threatens to rule without rival in our Latin America. Always invoking the justification of national security, from which there is no appeal, a model of society is increasingly confirmed which stifles basic liberties, tramples on the most elementary rights, and represses citizens within the framework of a feared and omnipotent Police State.[137]

For those carrying out the attacks on the bishops, the declaration reminds them that they automatically incur the penalty of excommunication reserved, according to canon 2343, for those who commit violence against a bishop or archbishop. Furthermore, excommunication is the penalty, according to canon 2334, for anyone who promulgates laws and decrees against the liberty of the church, or those who impede the exercise of ecclesiastical jurisdiction. After laying out these penalties, the bishops say that, although the church believes in dialogue and persuasion, the nature of its mission can lead the church occasionally to resort to these "extreme measures. . . to safeguard its identity and efficaciously move the conscience of its children."[138]

The bishops hasten to add that in defending its liberty the church does not wish to present itself as an "alternative power";[139] they continue to speak of the church in this declaration as the "conscience and soul of the world."[140] As is clear from their remarks on excommunication, however, the bishops recognize that sometimes the conscience needs to be moved "efficaciously," that is, given a bit of a bodily shove through external sanctions such as excommunication. Given that those to whom the sanctions applied were never directly named, however, the sanctions remained ambiguous, and it was left to the conscience of the offenders to identify themselves.

---

[137] "Declaración sobre la detención y ataque en Pudahuel a 3 obispos chilenos detenidos en Ecuador," *Documentos del episcopado: Chile 1974–1980*, 161.

[138] Ibid., 160–1.

[139] Ibid., 161.

[140] Ibid.

The forcefulness of the bishops' response is thus somewhat mitigated. On the one hand, the bishops express their gratefulness for the opportunity to suffer bodily in solidarity with others persecuted by the regime:

> Many other brothers and sisters, who are not Bishops, have suffered and suffer equally condemnable outrages, also arbitrarily deprived of their freedom and their honor or prevented from exercising the fundamental rights of the human person. Here the reflection of the Lord is fitting: "If they have done this with green wood, what won't they do with the dry wood?" (Lk. 23:31). We give thanks to the Lord for this privileged opportunity to experience in our own flesh the sufferings of so many who cannot defend themselves like a Bishop can.[141]

On the other hand, the bishops seem willing to take "extreme measures" like excommunication only when they personally are attacked. The declaration reserves excommunication for situations in which the identity and integrity of the church is at risk. Unfortunately, the integrity of the church is narrowly defined as a matter of respecting the position of the institutional church, especially its hierarchy. As in the case of Jaime Guzmán, the explicit reasoning given for threatening the "extreme measure" of excommunication had to do with a challenge to the authority of the bishops, and not with the systematic abuses daily inflicted by the regime's apparatus of order. The bishops have not properly understood that the disappearances and tortures suffered by their "brothers and sisters who are not Bishops" *are* in fact attacks upon the identity and integrity of the church. They have not, in other words, understood torture as an ecclesiological problem, the subject of the first chapter of this work. The bishops are rightfully grateful for the chance to experience in their own flesh the sufferings of the regime's victims. They need, however, to discern the bodily nature of the church, to feel that the sufferings of others are in fact their own sufferings, torturing the Body of Christ, which is also the church.

From this point on, nevertheless, there was an unmistakable change in the stance of the bishops toward the regime. As Eugenio Yáñez puts it in his study of church–state relations in Chile, the tone of their statements changed from exhortation to criticism or denunciation.[142] The idea that the state and the church were united in earnest pursuit of peace was simply not being borne out by events. The DINA was at the height of its terrible power, and 1976 saw the destruction through disappearances of the Communist Party, the last

---

[141] Ibid., 161.
[142] Yáñez, *La iglesia y el gobierno militar*, 71.

viable party of the left in Chile. The parties of the center came under attack as well. In response to criticisms of the government by the Christian Democrats, the party's radio station was closed in January 1977, then all parties were officially declared dissolved in March.[143]

On March 25, 1977, the bishops' conference issued a major declaration entitled "Nuestra Convivencia Nacional" (Our Life Together as a Nation). The bishops continue to use the language of Christian Humanism, or New Christendom thought, but use it here to criticize the human rights record of the military regime. The bishops say they have found agreeable Pinochet's professions of adherence to the priniciples of Christian Humanism, which puts above the state and all else the dignity of the human person. This is followed by a call on the Pinochet government to clear up the fate of the disappeared once and for all, without which there will never be peace nor will Chile's image in the world be improved.[144] Once again the bishops echo the government's claim that "an international campaign against our Government, promoted mainly by Marxist governments and parties" has unfairly prejudiced world opinion against Chile.[145]

Nonetheless, for the first time the bishops made bold to question the legitimacy of Chile's military rulers and to acknowledge that violations and abuses were not occasional lapses, but were woven into the fabric of the current system.[146] They also took on delicate matters of political parties, freedom of expression, and the economic situation, chastising the regime for the lack of opportunities for participation and the undue burden the poor bore under the economic policies of the regime's "technocratic elite."[147]

The reaction of the regime and the media exceeded even the usual hostility. Chile's most influential newspaper, *El Mercurio*, attacked the bishops for meddling in politics and running astray of their pastoral duties.[148] Minister of Justice Renato Damilano got personal. He called the bishops "stooges, ambitious, bad-intentioned and resentful" who "abandon their sacred ministry to take the place of those parties which in one way or another contributed to the destruction of the country." The bishops, said Damilano, "forget that the kingdom of Christ is not of this world," and so they "abandon the cure

---

[143] Smith, *The Church and Politics in Chile*, 308.
[144] "Nuestra convivencia nacional," *Documentos del Episcopado: Chile 1974–1980*, 165–6.
[145] Ibid., 169.
[146] See Smith, *The Church and Politics in Chile*, 309.
[147] Ibid., 166–71.
[148] "Posición política de los obispos," *El Mercurio*, March 27, 1977.

of souls" to "launch a political and hypocritical attack on the government."[149] In a letter to Damilano, the bishops exclaimed that never in the history of Chile had a government official referred in such pejorative terms to the bishops of the Catholic church, "whom the government itself includes among the 'authorities' of the country."[150] Clearly, church–state relations had entered uncharted waters. Damilano was forced to step down from his cabinet post, but the government took no action on the bishops' call for reform, and it was clear that Damilano's opinion of the bishops was not in the minority among the regime's functionaries. Damilano, for his part, was openly unrepentant, and denied that the Catholic bishops had anything but "religious" authority over their adherents, among whom he counted himself.[151]

In the wake of the publication of "Our Life Together as a Nation," the regime and the media furiously admonished the church to hew carefully to the spurious distinction of the religious and the political planes, a distinction of which, as we have seen, the hierarchy itself had made much in its dispute with Christians for Socialism.[152] The bishops did not explicitly repudiate this distinction – nor the correlate distinction between moral values and technical solutions – but from this point on, what counted as "politics" underwent something of a redefinition, and the hierarchy became increasingly unwilling to leave concrete solutions to the "Chicago Boys" and others of the "technocratic elite" they had denounced in their latest statement.

Two examples of church discourse from this period should make this clearer. The first is Father Pedro Azócar's keynote address at an April 1977 conference on "Our Life Together as a Nation." Azócar gave a brief historical overview of church denunciations of abuses in Chile, including the 1626 excommunication of those trafficking in slaves brought from the Cuyo Province, a move which led the governing authorities to question the church's competence in temporal affairs. According to Azócar, the church can never be restricted to a sphere of the personal and the spiritual because human life is social, and the religious lives of people are interwoven with the political,

---

[149] Renato Damilano, quoted in "Carta al Sr. Ministro de Justicia, Don Renato Damilano, respecto a calificaciones públicas hechas sobre los obispos," *Documentos del episcopado: Chile 1974–1980*, 173. "Stooges" is my translation of *tontos útiles*, a phrase which literally means "useful fools."

[150] Ibid.

[151] " 'No estoy arrepentido y mantengo lo que dije, en toda la línea,' " *La Tercera*, 18 April 1977.

[152] See Jose Aldunate Fernando Castillo, and Joaquim Silva, *Los Derechos Humanos y la Iglesia Chilena*, 116–18, 123.

economic, and cultural processes of society. "Entrusted by Christ not with 'souls' but with 'men,' nothing human can be alien to [the church]."[153] There is no limit, therefore, to the types of subjects on which the church can pronounce. Just as the church should not be surprised that historians would take an interest in Jesus of Nazareth, those in the political arena should not object if the church does not guard silence with regard to contingent matters of politics.[154]

A second, and more important, example of the shift in church discourse is the working document "The church: Its Mission Yesterday and Today," published by the bishops' Permanent Committee in May 1977. The statement reflects a growing awareness among the bishops that the church is subject to a deliberate strategy of "divide and conquer." For this reason the document puts a heavy emphasis on the visible and the communal aspects of the church.

The first half of the main body of the document, dedicated to the mystery of the church, begins with an exposition of the church as the "prolongation of Christ" on the earth. The church "is the mystery of the *invisible* God who, after being manifested *visibly* in the Lord Jesus, continues to manifest himself *visibly* to men in his church."[155] Just as incarnation produced the irresolvable paradox of Christ's divine and human natures, so too the church lives in the mystery of its own divinity and humanity, the tension between the "spiritual church" and the "visible church." The world, the bishops warn, works to separate the two aspects. Some want a discarnate church, a church (the bishops quote Peguy) " 'with clean hands . . . but without hands.' " But can we really imagine that God does not care about malnourished children, terrorism and torture, or the rights of his people to work with dignity? If so why would God have founded a church which is "human, historical, visible"? Others, the bishops continue, want the church to be merely a social force, a "simulacrum of a political party." But were this the case, where would its relationship with God be? How would the church have produced "those thousands of saints that are the visible expression of the divine force that lives in her? How would she have managed, over 2,000 years, all the persecutions from outside and all the poverty inside, intact in her eternal youth, full of life in spite of a thousand scars?"[156]

[153] Pedro Azócar, "No hay límites en los temas que debe tocar la iglesia," *El Sur*, Concepción, April 22, 1977.
[154] Ibid.
[155] Ibid., 176, emphasis in original.
[156] Ibid., 177–8.

There follows in the document a reflection on the church as community. According to the bishops, the liberalism of the nineteenth century had yielded in the church an emphasis on the relation of the individual with God which was only overcome by the Second Vatican Council. There the church recovered a greater sense of itself as the new Israel, a truly social body of active members, bound to one another in fraternal solidarity, closely united especially with those who suffer.[157] The bishops therefore underscore the importance of the church for salvation, which is social. The second half of the document, on the mission of the church, begins by pointing out that Christ did not simply announce salvation; he *is* salvation incarnate. But since Christ is not with us in visible form, the church prolongs Christ and makes salvation visible in itself to all people.[158] It does so by imitating Christ's sacrifice to the Father. The Eucharist unites all members of the church, who join the sacrifice of their own lives to Christ's self-offering.[159]

The examples of this salvific self-giving to which the bishops point add up to a virtual listing of the activities of the Vicaría de Solidaridad: when the church participates "in commitees of fraternal aid, in soup kitchens for children, in cooperatives for the unemployed, in handicraft workshops, when it concerns itself for the poor, the unemployed, the oppressed, the defenseless man without a voice, it is evangelizing without saying so explicitly."[160] The bishops stress once again that the church is concerned with the concrete person in concrete circumstances. Therefore the church

> [d]oes not let itself be circumscribed only to the "religious" field, often arbitrarily defined by persons interested in removing the church from other fields. Neither does it permit its message to be identified with a determinate *political*, much less *party*, option. It serves neither to legitimate power nor to legitimate the revolution. It knows that there are those who want to use it: this is a risk inherent in every incarnation. But it knows that absence and silence imply a danger similar to that of word and presence.[161]

This passage is extremely important, because it goes beyond a mere defense of the church's relevance to the political sphere to question the very categories in which the debate is framed. By putting quotation marks around the word

[157] Ibid., 178–9.
[158] Ibid., 181.
[159] Ibid., 182.
[160] Ibid., 183–4.
[161] Ibid., 183, emphasis in original.

"religious" and acknowledging the arbitrary way in which it is often defined, the bishops allude to the fluidity of any division between "religion" and "politics." By refusing to identify the church with any of the available secular political or party options, the bishops leave open the possibility for the church to define its own type of alternative "political" space and time, the "politics of Jesus." The church is, in other words, a communal body *sui generis*, willing to give neither the souls nor the bodies of its members over to another type of discipline.

Set against the growing confrontation between church and state in Chile in 1977, this remarkable document is a vindication of the nature of the church as the sign of Christ's salvation, which is nothing if not incarnate in this suffering world Christ came to redeem. "The Church: Its Mission Yesterday and Today" is thus an important indicator of the reappearance of the visible church in Pinochet's Chile. It reflects an awareness among the bishops that the regime's concerted attempts to silence, fragment, and remove the church to a religious sphere must be met with an insistence on the church as a visible social body. This insistence would invite the wrath of the regime. But as the bishops say, there is "a risk inherent in every incarnation."

4 "I Am Jesus, Whom You Are Persecuting"

Just ten days after the Pinochet regime celebrated its third anniversary in power, a car carrying Orlando Letelier, the ex-foreign minister of Allende's government, was ripped apart by a bomb as it drove through the embassy district of Washington, DC. Letelier – one of the Pinochet regime's most vocal critics in exile – and his aide Ronni Moffit were killed in the blast. It did not take long for suspicion about the case to come to rest on the DINA and its head, Manuel Contreras. Throughout 1977 the pressure mounted as the FBI pieced together the details of the DINA's work with Cuban exiles in planting the bomb.[162] Many within the military regime had come to believe that the DINA's pretensions to power had become a peril to the regime itself. The DINA had become an object of scrutiny; "Its power had begun to be too visible."[163] It had overplayed the subtle striptease of visibility and invisibility, and had revealed too much. Still vehemently denying his regime's role in the Letelier assassination, Pinochet dissolved the DINA on August 13, 1977. The same day Pinochet created by decree the *Central*

---

[162] Constable and Valenzuela, *A Nation of Enemies*, 103–7.
[163] Cavallo, et al., *La historia oculta del régimen militar*, 140.

Nacional de Informaciones, the CNI, which took over the DINA's property and staff.[164]

With the advent of the CNI under new chief Odlanier Mena, the volume of disappearances and tortures decreased, but the church's calls for greater freedoms continued to go unheeded throughout the rest of 1977. President Pinochet did call for a national referendum on his government on January 4, 1978, but the terms of the vote were so ludicrously stacked in Pinochet's favor that the bishops felt obliged to protest. The voters were asked to respond yes or no to the following statement: "Faced with the international aggression unleashed against our Fatherland, I support President Pinochet in his defense of the dignity of Chile and I reaffirm the sovereign legitimacy of the government of the Republic to lead the process of institutionalization of the country."[165] The regime ignored the church's call to cancel the referendum, and it was passed by a three-to-one margin.[166]

The official church's lack of enthusiasm for joining in the celebration did nothing to endear it to its enemies in the regime. Attacks on the church escalated in 1978, with the Vicaría taking precedence as the target of choice. Regime functionaries accused the Vicaría in the press of spying for the Soviet Union, committing treason against Chile, being an illicit association, and violating the political recess imposed by the military government. First Lady Lucia Hiriart was quoted referring to the Vicaría as "esa canallesca institución" (that institution of scoundrels)."[167]

The church for its part was more visible than ever. The programs of the Vicaría expanded to new levels.[168] The episcopacy began to raise its voice in criticism more often and in more concrete detail. In May the bishops' Permanent Committee issued a document sharply critical of the government's proposal to address the problem of unemployment in Chile. The document takes on a minute analysis of the government's plan, discussing in detail such matters as the forms of financing social spending, the retirement age and minimum wage, the amount of severance pay, and the formation of anony-

---

[164] *Rettig Report*, 88; 635–41.

[165] Cavallo, et al., *La historia oculta del régimen militar*, 185.

[166] "Carta del Comité Permanente a la Junta de Gobierno sobre la Consulta Nacional," *Documentos del episcopado: Chile 1974–1980*, 207–8.

[167] Yáñez, *La iglesia y el gobierno militar*, 82–3.

[168] Cavallo, et al., *La historia oculta del régimen militar*, 259. See also Brian H. Smith, "Chile: Deepening the Allegiance of Working-Class Sectors to the Church in the 1970's," in *Religion and Political Conflict in Latin America*, ed. Daniel H. Levine (Chapel Hill, NC: University of North Carolina Press, 1986), 163–6.

mous societies which would gut the agrarian reform law. The bishops claim that they are not competent to provide full-blown alternatives, but it is clear from the specificity of their criticisms that they are no longer content to defer to the authority of the "Chicago Boys" or other of the regime's technocrats.[169]

The bishops continued finding their voice. In October 1978 the Permanent Committee of the CECh issued yet another major document on the relationship between the church and politics, this time dedicated, at least in part, to justifying the greater role in political affairs that the church had taken on. "Christian Humanism and the New Institutionality" was set against the background of what the bishops called a "profound political crisis" infecting not only Chile's political institutions but the moral basis of the entire society.[170] The bishops' definition of the crisis as moral allowed them, as churchmen, to claim a greater competence to address it. The document is introduced with a brief history of Catholic church interventions in Chilean national life, obviously intended to provide a pedigree for church interventions in the present.[171]

As we might expect from the title "Christian Humanism and the New Institutionality," the bishops continue to speak the language they learned growing up in New Christendom, a language learned at the knee of Maritain and others, as I will show in chapter four. The accent, however, has changed. First, the bishops are careful to reject the "reduction" of faith "to the interior of mere individual consciences."[172] Second, the bishops distinguish two "levels" of church participation in politics, first that of general principles, the responsibility of the clergy, and second that of political action, under the primary care of the laity. The two levels, however, are notoriously difficult to keep apart, a point which the bishops acknowledge: "It is certain that these two levels do not constitute two separate and independent worlds between which there is no relation . . . Therefore, it is not outside the competence of the church to pronounce judgment, in the name of Christian morality, on concrete policies when they put into play fundamental factors of Christian humanism."[173] This formula is left sufficiently vague to allow the bishops room to maneuver when accused of interfering in contingent political matters beyond their proper ken.

---

[169] "Declaracíon sobre el plan propuesto por ODEPLAN para atender al desempleo," *Documentos del episcopado: Chile 1974–1980*, 327–9.
[170] "Humanismo cristiano y nueva institucionalidad," *Documentos del episcopado: Chile 1974–1980*, 355–7.
[171] Ibid., 345–8.
[172] Ibid., 348.
[173] Ibid., 349.

When the progressive Latin American church appropriated Maritain in the 1930s and 1940s, it did so to argue against clerical involvement in politics. Here in 1978, the bishops' implicit purpose is quite the opposite. Times have changed. As the bishops write, quoting the French Episcopal Conference,

> New problems have arisen in these last few years . . . They come in particular from the double movement that compels the church and its leaders, on the one hand, to take a certain distance with respect to public powers and all political entities and, on the other hand, to intervene more often in political matters in the very name of its religious mission.[174]

The bishops claim that putting this distance between the church and the powers that be respects the "autonomy of political society," but is especially important in order to allow the church to register the demands of the Gospel in political matters and to criticize freely those policies which are unacceptable.[175]

The bishops spend the latter part of the document doing just that. They lay out a lengthy list of human rights derived, they emphasize, not merely from the "old individualistic liberalism"[176] but from the biblical revelation that all are images of God and members of Christ's body.[177] The bishops then describe at length the way in which the Doctrine of National Security and the anti-subversive war have been used to trample the human rights of Chileans under the military government. Under the guise of a war against Marxist enemies internal to the nation, the regime has tarred anyone working for the betterment of the poor as adversaries and has systematically eliminated the basic rights of all but a small elite associated with "liberal capitalist economic power."[178] Reasons of order and reasons of state have been used to "prolong and almost institutionalize the state of emergency."[179] Here we recall Benjamin's and Taussig's comments on the state of emergency as not the exception but the rule. The forces of order perpetuate their rule by stoking the fires of disorder and emergency.[180]

The subject of the disappeared had, by this point, moved from private

[174] Ibid., 350.
[175] Ibid., 351.
[176] Ibid., 366.
[177] Ibid., 362.
[178] Ibid., 372.
[179] Ibid., 369.
[180] Michael Taussig, *The Nervous System* (New York: Routledge, 1992), 11–13.

conversations between bishops and military men to public denunciation. In June 1978 the bishops publicly called on Interior Minister Sergio Fernández to clear up the fates of all those who remained disappeared.[181] The Episcopal Conference's declaration on November 9 registered their exasperation with the regime's response. "On various occasions, we have dealt with government functionaries regarding the problem of the disappeared. The answers obtained up to now *have not been satisfactory.*" The bishops proceed to announce, again with emphasis, their certainty that the disappeared were in fact arrested "*by the government's security services.*" The bishops, through the work of the Vicaría, have provided the government with detailed information on hundreds of cases, but "unfortunately, we have come to the conclusion that the government will not carry out a thorough investigation of these occurrences." The declaration condemns the disappearances in the strongest terms, mentioning torture as well, and demands that the abuses stop.[182] Three weeks after the bishops' declaration, the grisly discoveries at Lonquén would, for the first time, allow them to back their words on the disappeared with bodily evidence.

The government was not listening, but at least the bishops had become fully aware that it was not. The regime's expulsion of a large group of seminarians from the Catholic University's theology faculty and its amnesty for those responsible for the Lonquén disappearances were fresh wounds when Cardinal Silva penned the text of his Te Deum homily in 1979. In it Silva recalls the bishops' statement two days after the coup in 1973, calling for moderation in dealing with the vanquished, and expressing confidence that Chile's new military leaders would respect the gains made by the working classes under previous governments and return the nation soon to institutional normality. Many times since, Silva writes, the church has sounded the same basic themes, clearly lighting the way toward a just and peaceful society. Then comes the punchline: "We must humbly confess that we have not always been successful in our petitions and our voice has not been listened to on many occasions. What's more, it has been the occasion for very harsh criticisms and very deep misunderstandings."[183] The Cardinal continues with a lengthy discourse on human rights. Unfortunately, the massgoers in the Cathedral never heard this

---

[181] "Declaración sobre la huelga de hambre de los familiares de los detenidos-desaparecidos," *Documentos del episcopado: Chile 1974–1980*, 330–1.
[182] "Declaración acerca de los detenidos-desaparecidos," *Documentos del episcopado: Chile 1974–1980*, 391–2, emphasis in original.
[183] Cardinal Raúl Silva, "Texto completo de la homilía del Señor Cardenal en el Te Deum del 18 de septiembre de 1979," in *Los Te Deum del Cardenal Silva Henríquez en el régimen militar*, 110.

from the Cardinal's own lips. Military censors had obtained the text ahead of time and cut it down to a few inoffensive paragraphs; the full text was distributed as people left the Cathedral. The wives of the members of the junta never received either version of the homily; they had decided to boycott the Te Deum. According to Ascanio Cavallo, this incident was the "point of no return" in Cardinal Silva's relationship with the military regime.[184]

By May 1980, relations between the church and the regime had become so bad that the bishops' Permanent Committee issued a document addressed to the Catholics of Chile entitled "I Am Jesus, Whom You Are Persecuting." The bishops decry the persistent attacks against themselves in the media and the more serious assaults on Christian communities, such that "in some places they don't dare even to have catechism meetings for fear of being denounced for engaging in politics."[185] The bishops ask Catholics to have courage and not to be led astray by attacks on the church. It would be easier to ignore the anguish of the poor and the cries of the abused and tortured, write the bishops, but that would be to neglect our duty.[186]

Taking this duty a step further, in December 1980 a group of seven bishops issued a decree of excommunication for those responsible for torture, not only those participating in the actual torture but also those who order it or are in a position to stop it but do not. Torture was on the rise in Chile; in July the head of the CNI, Odlanier Mena, had been sacked for being too soft, and CNI abuses under new boss Humberto Gordon had markedly increased.[187] The bishops who excommunicated torturers were moved to do so in some cases by seeing with their own eyes the effects of torture on a member of their flock.[188]

The decree written by Bishops Camus, Jiménez, and Carlos González, begins with a moving recognition that their hands were consecrated to bless and to pardon, and not to condemn. Nevertheless, they were also given the power to bind and to loose. In cases where especially grave sins affect "the common good, the dignity of persons and the sense of unity that signifies communion," a bishop is charged with using excommunication to "avoid disturbing the order that God desires."[189] The argument is a remarkable

---

[184] Cavallo, *Los Te Deum del Cardenal Silva Henríquez en el régimen militar*, 108.

[185] "Yo soy Jesús, a quien tú persigues," *Documentos del episcopado: Chile 1974–1980*, 429.

[186] Ibid.

[187] *Rettig Report*, 635–41; and Cavallo, et al., *La historia oculta del régimen militar*, 300–8.

[188] Bishop Tomás González, interview by author, July 26, 1993; and Bishop Carlos González, interview by author, July 28, 1993.

[189] Mons. Carlos González, Mons. Alejandro Jiménez, and Mons. Carlos Camus, "Excomunión a torturadores," *Mensaje* 296 (January–February 1981), 68.

variation on the same language used to promote cooperation with the regime just a few years before. Here the language of unity and order is used not to promote an organicist vision of harmony between church and state, but instead buttresses an act of ecclesial discipline against the state. "Unity" and "order" here refer to the boundaries which excommunication draws around the church to make clear that those responsible in any way for torture put themselves outside of, and in opposition to, the church. These bishops have understood torture not simply as a matter of corrupt secular polity but as a subject for ecclesial discipline. Excommunication is an exercise of church order which makes, however temporarily and faintly, the true church visible as an alternative society of peace and justice where torture has no place.

5 The Church as Russia

Relations with the regime never did improve. Eugenio Yáñez sums up the church's position under Pinochet in the 1980s in these terms: "Relations with the Government are conflictive, and the tensions become more acute. . . The negative attitude is maintained and reaffirmed; the bishops now do not limit themselves to making a call to the conscience; they also seek structural and institutional changes."[190] For its part, representatives of the regime recognized that the church is "the only really serious problem that we have."[191]

The bishops continued to produce sharp denunciations of regime policies regarding human rights, unemployment and workers' rights, military spending, neo-liberal economics, educational policy, and a host of other issues.[192] In December of 1983 the entire Plenary Assembly of the Episcopal Conference subscribed to the excommunication for torturers and their accomplices that the seven bishops had previously issued in their own dioceses. In the same declaration the bishops demanded a thorough reform of the CNI and other security organisms in order to put an end to torture and other abuses.[193] At the same time the grassroots church increased its activism, producing among other groups the Sebastián Acevedo Movement against Torture, in which priests,

---

[190] Yáñez, *La iglesia y el gobierno militar*, 88.

[191] Quoted in ibid., 94.

[192] See e.g. "La reforma educacional," *Documentos del episcopado: Chile 1981–1983* (Santiago: Ediciones Mundo, 1984), 16–30; "El renacer de Chile," ibid., 107–9; and "Censura que impide la participación," *Documentos del episcopado: Chile 1984–1987* (Santiago: 1988), 42.

[193] "Un camino cristiano," *Documentos del episcopado: Chile 1981–1983*, 147.

nuns and laypeople of the church took leading roles in street protests.

Progressive elements in the church feared the worst when in May 1983 the Vatican filled the Archbishop of Santiago's chair vacated by the retiring Cardinal Silva with Francisco Fresno, known in poor areas as Archbishop "Frenos" ("brakes"). As Archbishop of La Serena, Fresno had made gestures supportive of the regime, especially in its early years. Upon hearing of his promotion, First Lady Lucia Hiriart was said to have exclaimed, "At last God has listened to us."[194] Cardinal Fresno, however, did not find the regime any more willing to listen to him than Cardinal Silva had. Fresno did not try to rein in the activism of the church, and the intensity of attacks on the church gradually increased his resolve in the face of the regime.[195]

The church was made a particular target of the fierce wave of repression unleashed in the years 1983–6 in response to a popular movement of street protests meant to topple the Pinochet regime. Numerous priests were expelled from the country and held in prison.[196] The head of the Vicaría, Monseñor Ignacio Gutiérrez, was denied reentry to the country after a trip abroad.[197] Another priest, Andrés Jarlan, was killed during a protest in his neighborhood. Members of church communities, especially youth groups in poor parishes, were repeatedly arrested and tortured.[198] Churches and other church buildings were searched, shot at, bombed and burned: a partial listing of such occurrences by Jaime Escobar cites over fifty in the years 1980–5 alone.[199] The hierarchy was not immune from the attacks. When a bullet was fired into the residence of Miguel Caviedes, Bishop of Osorno, the President and Secretary of the Episcopal Conference wrote him: "The bullet directed at you was aimed at our entire College of Bishops."[200]

The military regime left no stone unturned in their attempts to silence the church. In April 1984 Pinochet even sent his representatives to Rome to try in secret to arrange a concordat between the Chilean state and the Vatican.

---

[194] Lucia Hiriart, quoted in Yáñez, *La iglesia y el gobierno militar*, 93.

[195] Ibid.

[196] Escobar, *Persecución a la iglesia en Chile*, 82; and "Declaración ante expulsión de sacerdotes franceses," *Documentos del episcopado: Chile 1984–1987*, 169.

[197] Escobar, *Persecución a la iglesia en Chile*, 82.

[198] "Declaración del Departamento de Educación del Episcopado (DECH) sobre acontecimientos que atañen a la educación," *Documentos del episcopado: Chile 1984–1987*, 107.

[199] Escobar, *Persecución a la iglesia en Chile*, 83–90.

[200] "Obispos respaldan a Monseñor Caviedes," *Documentos del episcopado: Chile 1984–1987*, 163.

The General prized above all the right of *patronato*, the ability of the state to nominate bishops within its borders. The Vatican rebuffed Pinochet's clumsy attempt at influence over the church and immediately notified the nuncio in Santiago and the Chilean Episcopal Conference.[201] That the regime could have imagined that such a scheme would work was a sign of its desperation to solve the problem of its most intractable enemy, the church. After losing the 1988 plebiscite which would have extended his reign until 1997, a stunned General Pinochet compared himself to Christ, rejected by the people in favor of Barabbas. In the same speech he listed the church along with Russia, the US, and the European countries as the great powers against which he had had to fight. Later in the speech he was more precise, saying it was not the whole church as such that he had fought, only "certain priests." Bernardino Piñera, the President of the bishops' conference, fired off a declaration contending that the church had never fought against the government, but only in favor of human rights, social justice, participation, dialogue, reconciliation, under-standing, and peace. Besides, Piñera asked, if Pinochet only had to fight against " 'certain priests,' how could he compare them with great world powers like Russia or the United States?"[202] Piñera intended to deny the comparison of the church with great world powers; his rhetorical question could just as easily be read, however, as denying that Pinochet had only had to fight a certain few priests.

In this chapter I have traced the movement of official Catholic ecclesiology under the Pinochet regime from legitimating a position above the "political" fray to qualified support for the church's immersion in it. This movement is of course not uniform across the ranks of the bishops. Bishops began in different positions and some moved farther than others. Bishops named in the late 1980s under Pope John Paul II tended to be of a more conservative stripe. Furthermore, most of the documents of the episcopal conference on which I have primarily relied are the work of committees, and individual bishops might not always be in conformity with the end result. The movement of church ecclesiology is not uniform chronologically either. There is no neat march from less prophetic to more prophetic; the equivocal episcopal statement on torture which begins this chapter is from 1987. Nevertheless, there is a clear shift apparent from a church which thought of itself as the soul

---

[201] Cavallo, et al., *La historia oculta del régimen militar*, 448.
[202] "Declaración referente al discurso del Presidente de la República en aniversario de CEMA-Chile," *Documentos del episcopado: Chile 1988–1991* (Santiago: CENCOSEP, 1992), 99–100.

of society to one which could be compared in worldly influence to Russia.

Official Catholic ecclesiology had helped create an autonomous political sphere of arbitrary power by withdrawing to a "religious" terrain in civil society. It was the task of the layperson, acting on general "values" learned in the church, to enter the political realm as an individual and incarnate those values in concrete policies. Unfortunately, this individualization and disappearance of the visible church is also the effect of the military regime's strategy of torture and disappearance described in chapter 1. Chapter 2 describes how ill-prepared the official church was to meet this strategy, since its own ecclesiology had already, in effect, disappeared the church as a social body.

The division between "religion" and "politics" had served to ensure that the church would stand above the sectarian strife of politics as a source of interior unity for all Chileans. The official church saw itself, especially through the Eucharist, as the guarantor of reconciliation, so that Chile could function as an organic whole, free of essential conflict, especially between classes. As the bishops found themselves immersed in conflict under the military regime, they did not so much abandon their aversion to politics as reimagine the categories of "religion" and "politics." In the face of constant accusations of interfering in politics, the church gradually made clear its refusal to leave bodily matters such as employment and torture to the state – in other words, to hand over the bodies of its members to the state. At the same time the bishops were quite clear that they would not simply revert to a Christendom model of ecclesiology in which the church threw its weight behind a political party and obliged the faithful to do the same. What we have, therefore, is the possibility of a different kind of ecclesial counter-politics, one which neither makes irrelevance to the political a point of pride nor is beholden to the autonomous power politics of party and state. In chapters 5 and 6 I will display some exemplary forms this ecclesial "body politics" took in Pinochet's Chile, and explore more positively and normatively the church's resources for realizing such a body. But first I will trace, in chapters 3 and 4, the roots of Catholic social thought in Chile and provide a more theoretical analysis of Catholic thinking on politics and human rights, and the nature of the church.

Part Two

ECCLESIOLOGY

Chapter Three

THE ECCLESIOLOGY OF
A DISAPPEARING
CHURCH

Father Roberto Bolton is one of the most prominent of a small but significant group of Chilean clergy, native to the more elegant districts of Santiago, who have taken up residence on the other side of town. Bolton has lived and worked for many years in Villa Francia, an extremely poor and politically active *población* on the west side of Santiago. His "rectory" is a small wooden shanty, warped and weathered by the winter rains. The inside is insulated by a haphazard collection of posters and photos. Archbishop Oscar Romero figures prominently, as does Joan Alsina, a Spanish priest killed on the banks of the river in the early days of Pinochet's coup. There is a poster of the Vergara brothers, young revolutionaries from Bolton's neighborhood shot by security forces. There is a photo of Father Andrés Jarlan slumped over his Bible, a bullet in his neck. Sitting at his table, Bolton speaks of the hierarchy's cautious acceptance of the military regime following the coup. "I suppose it was out of good will, and not because of cowardice; I don't believe that Cardinal Silva is a coward. Rather it was because of theory, of theology, mistaken ecclesiology, because the church did not see itself as called to break with the government."[1]

My task in this chapter and the next will be to outline this ecclesiology, identify its sources, and critique it. In this chapter I will follow the development of what is known as "social Catholicism" in Chile from the separation of church and state in 1925 up to the advent of the military regime. I will first

---

[1] Father Roberto Bolton, interview by author, August 4, 1993, Santiago, tape recording: "Yo supongo por buena voluntad y no por cobardía; yo no creo que el Cardenal Silva sea cobarde. Sino que es por teoría, por teología, eclesiología equivocada, porque la Iglesia no se veía llamada a romper con el gobierno."

show how the Chilean church fit into Pope Pius XI's strategy of abandoning the "political" sphere in favor of a "social" presence in civil society, exemplified by Catholic Action. I will then narrate the rise of Catholic Action in Chile. My objective in this chapter and the next will be to show that social Catholicism in Chile in fact resulted in the abandonment of social space to the state. When the state turned its strategy of torture and atomization on the Chilean people, the church lacked the resources to resist, having already been "disappeared" by its own ecclesiology.

In focusing on the ecclesiology of the church in Chile, by no means will I imply any direct causality from "theory" to "praxis," or vice versa. Indeed, I have no stake in any clear distinctions between theology and praxis. There are no such things as disembodied causative ideas; neither is there any spontaneous pre-theoretical praxis which is only subsequently theologized in a secondary act of reflection. Theory originates within a social context, and praxis arises already embedded in narrative structures, in a "text" which gives it shape.[2] Neither Pius XI's nor Maritain's thought, therefore, were the *cause* of the praxis of a significant sector of the Chilean church, but rather provided the imaginative context necessary not merely to understand that praxis but to move it forward.

1 An Amiable Divorce

Church and state in Chile had been bonded to each other, for better or for worse, since colonial days. Under the terms of the *Patronato Real de las Indias*, the Spanish Crown had been granted tremendous power over the church in Latin America in exchange for certain privileges. The Catholic church was guaranteed a religious monopoly in Spanish America; priests were not subject to civil courts, but enjoyed the *fuero eclesiástico*, the right to be tried by special church tribunals. All family law was governed by canon law, and Catholic religious education was mandatory for students of all schools, public and private.[3]

The toll exacted by the Crown for the propagation of the Catholic faith, however, gave the colonial authorities a stranglehold over the church. Spain controlled all appointments to bishoprics and the creation of new dioceses.

---

[2] See John Milbank, *Theology and Social Theory* (Oxford: Basil Blackwell, 1990), 249–52.
[3] Timothy R. Scully, *Rethinking the Center: Party Politics in Nineteenth & Twentieth Century Chile* (Stanford, Cal.: Stanford University Press, 1992), 31.

The *fuero eclesiástico* only produced a relative autonomy; decisions by church courts could be appealed to the Crown. All procedural changes within the church and even the promulgation of church teachings required approval by the civil authority. Independence from Spain did not alter this arrangement. The constitution of 1833 transferred the terms of the *patronato* into the law of the new republic.[4]

As long as the elites in Chile remained committed to the Catholic faith, the church hierarchy was content with the close bond of church and state. When European liberalism began to make inroads among the powerful in Chile, however, the church hierarchy became increasingly uneasy with secular control over sacred things. Secularizing moves by liberal elites were met by Archbishop Valentin Valdivieso's attempts to annul the *patronato* and increase the church's influence over public education and the press. In 1857 church leaders and aristocratic lay people formed the Conservative Party to defend and extend the Catholic church's position in Chilean society. The remainder of nineteenth-century politics in Chile would be marked by a sharp cleavage between clerical and anticlerical factions.[5] The conflict would reach its zenith in 1873 when Archbishop Valdivieso excommunicated President Federico Errázuriz and other liberal lawmakers for abolishing the *fuero eclesiástico* and tithes. Throughout these struggles the Conservative Party was recognized as the Catholic party, and mutual loyalty between the official church and the Party was taken for granted.[6]

Toward the end of the nineteenth century, industrialization, urbanization, and the creation of a significant export economy had begun to alter the political landscape. As a politically active proletariat emerged, class conflict replaced the clerical–anticlerical axis as the most important motivator in Chilean electoral politics. The traditional parties – Conservative, Liberal, and Radical – continued to define themselves according to church–state issues and tried to absorb urban labor into the old conflicts. As social unrest became more widespread, working-class parties were formed to reflect the interests of labor, and class conflict surfaced as the crucial political cleavage of the early twentieth century.[7]

The tenure of Crescente Errázuriz Valdivieso as archbishop of Santiago

---

[4] Ibid., 31–2.
[5] Ibid., 20–61.
[6] J. Lloyd Mecham, *Church and State in Latin America: A History of Politico-Ecclesiastical Relations*, revised edn (Chapel Hill, NC: The University of North Carolina Press, 1966), 210–11.
[7] Scully, *Rethinking the Center*, 62–105.

from 1919 to 1931 was a time of great change for the Catholic church in Chile. After the victory of Chile's first middle-class president – Arturo Alessandri Palma of the Radical Party – in 1920, the old liberal desire to separate church and state finally appeared an inevitability, but under the guise of truce instead of conflict. Alessandri presented a bill for the separation of church and state to Congress in 1923.[8] Alessandri was not an enemy of the church. He was convinced that a peaceful separation on good terms for the church would deflate Conservative attempts to use defense of the church to garner Catholic support for their own efforts to block real social reform.[9] In an interview in Rome, Alessandri convinced Pius XI's Secretary of State, Pietro Gasparri, that his intention was to ensure that the strife of previous times between the church and the government would become a distant memory. The traditional Catholic opposition to the separation of church and state had been restated as recently as 1885 in Leo XIII's *Immortale Dei*.[10] Nevertheless, anxious to avoid the kind of bitter and fruitless battles to resist separation which had cost the church so dearly in Portugal (1911), Mexico (1917), and Uruguay (1919), Gasparri agreed not to resist. Before leaving, Alessandri sought and received assurances from the Cardinal that he would not be excommunicated, as President Federico Errázuriz had been, for his actions.[11]

Archbishop Crescente Errázuriz and the Chilean hierarchy opposed church separation from the state in theory, but agreed to put up no opposition. They saw a certain advantage to extricating the church from its constant involvement in state politics. Employing the distinction between "thesis" and "hypothesis" formulated by Félix Dupanloup,[12] Errázuriz accepted the

---

[8] Mecham, *Church and State in Latin America*, 217–20. Under the terms of the new Constitution, the Roman Catholic church was the only legally recognized church, but other religious bodies would be allowed freely to erect their own houses of worship and purchase property, all of which would be exempt from taxation. The Catholic church lost all control over public education but would be free to maintain its own private schools. The church also would henceforth be free to appoint its own bishops and communicate with the Vatican without civil authorization.

[9] Brian Smith, *The Church and Politics in Chile: Challenges to Modern Catholicism* (Princeton, NJ: Princeton University Press, 1982), 72.

[10] Pope Leo XIII, *Immortale Dei* in *The Papal Encyclicals 1878–1903*, ed. Claudia Carlen (Raleigh: The Pierian Press, 1990), 107–31.

[11] Fidel Araneda Bravo, *Historia de la Iglesia en Chile* (Santiago: Ediciones Paulinas, 1986), 709–10.

[12] After Pius IX's promulgation of the Syllabus of Errors in 1864, Félix Dupanloup, bishop of Orleans, distinguished between accepting the separation of church and state in "thesis," or theory, which would be contrary to Catholic teaching, and accepting

separation of church and state as a lesser of two evils, the alternative being the renewal of conflict between the church and the governing powers of Chile. In the Archbishop's mind, it was crucial that church and state remain unified in cooperation for the good of Chile as a whole. After the promulgation of the new Constitution, Errázuriz declared:

> It is just to note that the authorities of Chile, in establishing this separation, have not been actuated by the spirit of persecution which characterizes other countries where Catholicism has been attacked. By the sacrifice of separation, the Church acquires, at least, the liberty which divine law accords it; and, finally, the State is separated from the Church; but the Church is not separated from the State, and will always be ready to serve it.[13]

The arrangement was more or less a friendly one, a rarity in the history of church–state separations in Latin America. As one observer put it, it was accomplished in Chile not "by repudiation, but by divorce through mutual consent."[14]

Desire for unity and harmony was also behind the other significant controversy of Errázuriz's tenure. Although he and virtually all of the Chilean clergy were partisans of the Conservative Party, Errázuriz forbade clerics' participation in party politics.[15] For this the clergy and other bishops accused him of selling out the church's power to affect society for the good. Errázuriz realized, nonetheless, that the hatreds and divisions produced by the clergy's frequent politicking on behalf of candidates for election could only harm the church in the long run. The divisions cut one way only; the lower classes knew that the loyalties of the church lay with the Conservative aristocracy, and Errázuriz knew that this had cost the church the love of the people.[16]

In 1922 Errázuriz issued a pastoral letter proscribing party political activity by the clergy. As private citizens, they are entitled to their opinions. In the

---

it in "hypothesis," or practice, which can be tolerated as a lesser evil if separation appears inevitable. In the face of the general trend toward separation in Europe, this distinction gave Catholics a way to deal with the new political realities in the nineteenth century. Pius IX accepted the distinction; ibid., 709.

[13] Archbishop Crescente Errázuriz, quoted in Mecham, *Church and State in Latin America*, 220.

[14] Quoted in Mecham, *Church and State in Latin America*, 219.

[15] Archbishop Crescente Errázuriz, quoted in Araneda, *Historia de la Iglesia en Chile*, 699.

[16] Araneda, *Historia de la iglesia en Chile*, 705.

pulpit, however, and in any official capacity, priests should refrain from even the appearance of support for any particular party. Priests must not attend political meetings or manifestations, nor should they frequent the company of party leaders. The day of the elections should find them far from the polling places, except in the personal act of casting their votes. In all of these measures, the clergy would act so as not to "excite the passions" of the people for political strife, but to the contrary, "bring their spirits serenity and peace."[17]

In issuing these directives the Archbishop had no intention of simply abandoning Chilean politics to secular forces. The injunction to stay out of party politics "does not mean, however, that the priest should keep silent about the duties that the citizen has in conscience, but he must speak of these matters with great prudence, and only with regard to the religious aspect of such duties."[18] According to Errázuriz, priests should, for example, urge their parishoners to vote for "worthy, upright men, lovers of order" who will guarantee "the exalted interests of religion and of the fatherland."[19]

This way of placing the locus of the church's political activity in the conscience of the Catholic citizen was new to the church in Chile, and was not well received by a clergy closely linked to the Conservative Party. Gilberto Fuenzalida Guzmán, bishop of Concepción – and therefore second most powerful churchman in Chile – strongly opposed Errázuriz, contending that the latter's prudence was producing political disorientation among Catholics.[20] In 1919 Fuenzalida had already issued a pastoral letter urging unity among lay Catholics in a political crusade against secularizing tendencies and economic liberalism. Inspired by the social teachings of the Catholic church and under the direction of the bishops, the church in Chile should form a disciplined body for political action, since

among us every political struggle is at the same time a religious struggle. . . . As in an organized body, all the members discharging their proper functions cooperate in its activity for the common good of the body . . . Discipline is vital, and every [Catholic] association is eager to execute orders from above.[21]

Following on Crescente Errázuriz's pastoral letter forbidding clerical participation in party politics, Fuenzalida responded in 1923 with a letter of his own,

---

[17] Archbishop Crescente Errázuriz, quoted in ibid., 703–5.
[18] Ibid., 704.
[19] Ibid.
[20] Araneda, *Historia de la iglesia en Chile*, 705.
[21] Ibid.

making use of a letter from Pope Pius XI's Secretary of State, Cardinal Gasparri. Fuenzalida's pastoral letter specifically attacked the attempts to create separate spheres for religion and politics. According to Gasparri, religion and politics cannot be separated, since laws cannot be effective if they are not informed by principles of the Christian faith. Fuenzalida takes this to mean that religion ought to "direct" the political life of the nation.[22] According to Gasparri, when religious questions ignite conflict between parties, the church should take sides against those parties hostile to the church. Fuenzalida takes this to mean that, given that the church "recognizes in the Conservative Party her best sons," the Catholic's duty is to "occupy his rightful place in the ranks of the Christian Party, remain closely united with his coreligionists, submit in everything to the discipline of the party, and give his vote to its candidates."[23]

As a fierce critic of secularization, Fuenzalida was only able to demand Catholic submission to the orders of a political party by assuming that the Conservatives were merely the political arm of the Catholic church. It is not that the bishop made no distinction between "religion" and "politics"; he instructed his priests to use the pulpit to deal with political matters only as they affected religion.[24] Nevertheless, in Fuenzalida's organicist view, the conflicts at issue between the parties of the time were essentially religious, and only improperly construed as class conflicts. At the same time, party conflicts were political conflicts, and he assumed the church was not, strictly speaking, a political entity. A Catholic party was therefore necessary to provide the disciplined body necessary to defend the church's interests in the political realm.

Fuenzalida was convinced that the church was engaged in mortal conflict with the powers of secularization, atheism, and revolution; lingering above his prose is the faint smell of gunpowder. He often refers to Catholics as "soldiers for Christ" in the battle to transform a world in rebellion against the church.

---

[22] María Antonieta Huerta, *Catolicismo social en Chile* (Santiago: Ediciones Paulinas, 1991), 299.

[23] Bishop Gilberto Fuenzalida, quoted in Huerta, *Catolicismo social en Chile*, 300–1.

[24] Ibid., 302. In a letter to Crescente Errázuriz, Fuenzalida writes, "It has also been a constant tactic of theirs (of the anti-Catholics) to call 'politics' everything which figures in the programs of the parties, even if they be direct attacks against the dogmas or sacraments of the church. They never distinguish between politics as such and antireligious politics. And they avoid this distinction precisely in order to apply to the intervention of the clergy in the antireligious struggles the arguments and reasons that are valid for purely political struggles"; quoted in Araneda, *Historia de la iglesia en Chile*, 746.

This struggle, he is sure, must not be waged along class lines. Inspired by *Rerum Novarum*, the church's task is rather to unite all sectors of society once again under the tutelage of the church.[25] In this struggle all fronts must be manned. Catholic workers' associations and Catholic social aid societies are important but not sufficient. The example of Spain, according to Fuenzalida, makes this clear. With the Catholic social apostolate in full flower in Spain, the country still faces perdition at the hands of anarchistic socialism. The church must keep up the fight in both the "social" and the "political" spheres.[26]

Although Archbishop Crescente Errázuriz was an opponent of secularization, he had no intention of fighting such a battle, and thought the interests of the church and the nation were served better by ceding the political sphere to the direction of the laity and concentrating the church's efforts in the area of the social apostolate. In the social sphere Errázuriz had no intention of cutting the laity loose to do the bidding of their individual consciences. His pastoral letter on "Social Action" quotes Pius X to this effect: "It is better not to do a work than to do it against the will or without the consent of the bishop."[27] Errázuriz's point in stressing the role of the bishops was precisely to take Catholic associations out of the hands of Conservative Party politicians.[28]

Although written into the histories as a progressive figure in the Chilean church, Crescente Errázuriz retained a quite clerical vision of Catholic social action and even – by removing the Catholic social apostolate from the direction of lay Conservatives – headed off any trend toward greater lay leadership in Catholic associations. At a more fundamental level, however, Errázuriz was a pioneer in the movement to carve out a semi-autonomous sphere for the laity called "politics," understood as party political activity, and another sphere called the "social" in which the clergy would predominate. It was this movement which Gilberto Fuenzalida so vigorously resisted. The two became engaged in an acrimonious and quite public dispute over the issue, much of this dirty laundry being aired in the liberal press of the times.[29] When Errázuriz died in 1931 at the age of 92, Conservatives hoped to regain the church's official support. Two years later, following alarming electoral advances by Marxist parties and a short-lived socialist republic in 1932, the

[25] Huerta, *Catholicismo social en Chile*, 293.
[26] Ibid., 301.
[27] Archbishop Crescente Errázuriz, quoting Pope Pius X's encyclical *Graves de Communi* in Araneda, *Historia de la iglesia en Chile*, 700.
[28] Araneda, *Historia de la iglesia en Chile*, 700.
[29] Ibid., 743–8.

church hierarchy gave its official endorsement once again to the Conservative Party.[30]

The second honeymoon of the church and the Conservatives would not last long. In 1934, Pius XI's Secretary of State Eugenio Pacelli, the future Pope Pius XII, issued a letter to the Papal Nuncio in Chile strongly reaffirming Archbishop Errázuriz' position on political parties. In the judgment of the Vatican, "It is evident that the church could not bind itself to the activity of a political party without compromising its supernatural character and universality of its mission."[31] Pacelli cites the Plenary Council of Latin America, which had written that "Holy Religion . . . must be above all human things and unite the spirits of all citizens with a bond of mutual charity and benevolence."[32] No party, Pacelli maintains, even if it profess Catholic inspiration, can claim to represent all Catholics, since the laity are free to support any party which respects the "rights of the church and of souls." Only when those rights are threatened should the hierarchy call for political union of all Catholics. This is not to say that Catholics should be uninterested in political matters. To the contrary, Pacelli recommends that the Chilean hierarchy encourage the formation of cells of Catholic Action so that the individual Catholic's political activity might be inspired by Catholic social teaching, as long as Catholic Action itself stay completely free of party involvement.[33] Crescente Errázuriz had won a posthumous victory, and Chilean church histories would remember him as a "prophet" for the development of the progressive church in Chile.[34]

Political scientists have pointed out that the way in which the church extricates itself from alliances with the state and with traditional party alliances can determine whether or not the church will become an agent for progressive change.[35] In the case of Chile it is clear that the absence of hostility in the separation process left open a greater possibility for mutual influence between

---

[30] Smith, *The Church and Politics in Chile*, 78-9.
[31] Eugenio Pacelli, "Carta del Emmo. Cardenal Pacelli al Sr. Nuncio en Chile," in *La iglesia y la política* (Santiago: Ediciones Paulinas, n.d.), 83.
[32] Ibid., 84.
[33] Ibid., 85–92.
[34] Fernando Aliaga Rojas, *La iglesia en Chile: contexto histórico* (Santiago: Pontificia Universidad Católica de Chile, 1985), 150; and Araneda, *Historia de la iglesia en Chile*, 713.
[35] See Ivan Vallier, "Extraction, Insulation and Re-entry: Toward a Theory of Religious Change," in *The Church and Social Change in Latin America*, ed. Henry A. Landsberger (Notre Dame, Ind.: University of Notre Dame Press, 1970), 9–35.

the church on the one hand and left-leaning parties and the masses who supported them on the other.[36] I hope to show, however, that the process of extrication from the state and party alliances, and the consequent removal of the church to a "social" sphere, is not as unambiguously positive as most authors assume.

In Chile the Vatican employed the same strategy for church–state relations that it was simultaneously pursuing in Europe. Following World War I, the political situation in Europe was highly volatile, with the emergence of new states and dictatorships of the right and the left. In the late nineteenth century parties representing Catholic interests had arisen in Germany, France, and Italy to defend the church against virulent anti-clericalism. The Popes had lent their support for these parties, but Pius XI opted for a different course after his election in 1922. In this transitional phase of Europe's history, he decided, the church's interests must not be compromised by close association with any particular party. Beyond the fickle winds of political conflict lay the church's permanent interests, and those could be best defended precisely by staying out of partisan political struggles.[37] As the British ambassador to the Vatican put it, "Pius XI wishes to withdraw the Church as far as possible from politics, so that Catholics may unite on a religious and moral basis."[38]

In Pius XI's vision, the locus for such "religious and moral" unity was the sphere of social action. He threw his concerted efforts behind Catholic Action, an organization of lay Catholics under clerical direction dedicated to penetrating the various organs of civil society with Catholic teaching and remedying the ills of the modern world. At the same time, Pius XI moved to end official Catholic support for political parties. In 1924 he ordered all priests out of political parties in Italy and ordered the complete dissociation of Catholic Action and its charitable, social, and youth organizations from the Popular Party. In 1926, Pius XI condemned outright Action Française, not an officially Catholic party but the party which championed monarchist and ultramontane Catholic interests versus the liberal Third Republic.[39] In 1933, Pius withdrew official support for the German Catholic Center Party in a concordat with Adolf Hitler.

Sicilian priest Luigi Sturzo had founded the Popular Party in 1919 based on the combination of principles from *Rerum Novarum* and a moderate program of agricultural and social reform. Within two years, the party had

[36] Smith, *The Church and Politics in Chile*, 69–70.
[37] Anthony Rhodes, *The Vatican in the Age of Dictators 1922–1945* (London: Hodder and Stoughton, 1973), 11–21.
[38] Sir O. Russell, quoted in Rhodes, *The Vatican in the Age of Dictators*, 15.
[39] Ibid., 103–11.

110 deputies in the Italian parliament and presented the only significant opposition to Mussolini, after the Communists were suppressed. Mussolini, knowing that the Pope wanted to be extricated from party politics, offered friendly terms to the church in exchange for his abandoning the Popular Party. Pius was wary of the Fascists, but felt at the same time that Italy owed them a debt of gratitude for eliminating the Communist threat to the church. The years 1919 and 1920 had seen massive strikes and worker takeovers of factories and whole villages. But for the intervention of Mussolini, many on both sides were sure that what had happened in Russia would be repeated in Italy. The Fascists, however, brooked no opposition, and soon turned their attention to the Popular Party. As Fascist violence escalated, Pius felt the church would be better able to carry out its social apostolate in peace in a united Fascist country free of political strife. When the Pope withdrew his support, the Popular Party collapsed, Sturzo fled into exile, and Mussolini consolidated his hold over Italy.[40] Pius XI said in 1929 he would negotiate with the Devil himself for the sake of souls. That same year he agreed to a concordat with Mussolini's regime, negotiated by Cardinal Gasparri, in which the Pope gave up claims to the Papal States in exchange for autonomy for Catholic Action, authority over moral matters in Italy, and sovereignty over the 108.7 acres of the Vatican City.[41]

The lesson was not lost on Adolf Hitler; within two months of assuming power in 1933, Hitler opened negotiations with the Vatican aimed at the elimination of the Center Party, the last obstacle in the *Reichstag* to approval of dictatorial powers for the Führer. The Center (also called the Catholic) Party was formed in Leo XIII's reign to resist Bismarck's *Kulturkampf*. Based on the teachings of *Rerum Novarum*, the Center Party spawned the most advanced trade unions in early twentieth-century Europe.

> The word "party", as indicating a body of men elected to achieve certain well-defined political ends, had little if any meaning when applied to the Centre. It represented no particular class or interest, but existed solely to further the affairs of Catholics, be they employers or employees, landlords or peasants. It was a parliament in miniature, comprising every shade of political thought. It contained feudal landlords as well as farmers; there were bishops and priests, a

---

[40] Ibid., 23–35. Mussolini's friendliness toward the church was of fairly recent vintage. As late as December 1919, he wrote in the party newspaper "Detesting as we do all forms of Christianity, that of Jesus as of Marx, we feel an immense sympathy with the modern revival of the pagan worship of strength and courage"; ibid., 27.

[41] Ibid., 37–52.

cross-section of the bourgeoisie, as well as Catholic trades union leaders, whose ideas about social progress were indistinguishable from those of the Socialists. All these men sat together in the Reichstag and voted in unison, not because they necessarily thought alike, but because they had a common goal, to promote the interests of Catholics.[42]

Pope Pius XI destroyed the Center Party in one stroke. On July 20, 1933 he signed a concordat with Hitler, withdrawing church support for the Center Party in exchange for guarantees of freedom for Catholic Action and all Catholic educational and charitable efforts. The Pope was no fan of Nazism; he hoped that by buying the church some sort of juridical protection for its efforts to penetrate society with the Gospel, he was avoiding a greater evil.[43]

As is well known, the Gospel did not penetrate far in Nazi Germany. Within months of signing the concordat, the Nazis began a determined effort to eliminate Catholic influence over the country's youth. Parents sending their children to Catholic schools would receive from the local Nazi party headquarters a note like the following to a railway employee: "I must remind you that it is not in keeping with the dignity of a State official to allow his children to be educated by organisations which are hostile to the State."[44] In 1933 65 percent of parents in Munich sent their children to Catholic schools; by 1937 the figure was 3 percent. Catholic Action organizations were attacked by decree and by direct violence. Priests and nuns from the Pope to the sisters teaching catechism were subjected in the official press to insults and accusations of increasing fury. They were painted as mongrels of Jewish ancestry, perverts and thieves, playing politics and undermining the German nation and state. Catholic masses and meetings were broken up and participants beaten.[45]

After meeting with German bishops in 1937, Pius XI was moved to issue the encyclical *Mit brennender Sorge*, perhaps the most blunt denunciation of a political regime ever issued by the Holy See. Obviously feeling jilted, the Pope begins the encyclical with an explanation of his concordat with Hitler. "[D]espite many and grave misgivings" the Pope signed the agreement in the hopes of sparing the German people what they were now undergoing. The church has remained faithful to the concordat; all blame for the current crisis must fall on the German state which has so egregiously violated its terms.[46] The

---

[42] Ibid., 162.

[43] Ibid., 173–83.

[44] Quoted in ibid., 186.

[45] Ibid., 185–210.

[46] Pope Pius XI, *Mit brennender Sorge* in *The Papal Encyclicals 1903–1939*, pp. 525–6, paras. 3–5.

problem, in other words, is not the concordat itself, but rather the fact that it has been violated. The "aggressive paganism" of the German state has tried to raise the merely mortal state and its leader above the church and its head. In circumstances where the Catholic is forced into a choice between the church and the nation-state, the Pope leaves no doubt as to where the loyalty of the faithful should lie. According to Pius XI, however, the problem is not loyalty to Germany as such, but the fact that it has been put into opposition with the Christian faith.

> No one would think of preventing young Germans establishing a true ethnical community in a noble love of freedom and loyalty to their country. What We object to is the voluntary and systematic antagonism raised between national education and religious duty . . . He who sings hymns of loyalty to this terrestrial country should not, for that reason, become unfaithful to God and His Church, or a deserter and traitor to His heavenly country.[47]

Pius XI had already issued a similar, if milder, encyclical critical of Mussolini's encroachments on Catholic Action in Italy. A mere two years after securing freedom for the educational and social work of the church with the Lateran Treaty and concordat, the Pope found himself forced to protest the "many acts of brutality and violence . . . even to the striking of blows and the drawing of blood" unleashed on Italian Catholic Action.[48] The Catholic youth organizations had been disbanded as a political threat to the security of the state. Pius' response stresses the strictly religious and social nature of Catholic Action, whose "fundamental law" is "abstention from every political activity."

> The regime and the party which seem to attribute such a fearful and feared strength to those who belong to the Popular Party for political reasons, should show themselves grateful to Catholic Action, which removed them precisely from that sphere and required them to make a formal pledge not to carry out any political activities, but to limit themselves to religious action.[49]

The church has kept to its part of the bargain; the Fascist ingrates have not, and are usurping the church's proper territory, the moral education of Italy's youth.

In his encyclical, Pius XI protests the Fascist oath of absolute loyalty to the

---

[47] Ibid., p. 532, para. 34.
[48] Pope Pius XI, *Non Abbiamo Bisogno*, in *The Papal Encyclicals 1903–1939*, p. 447, para. 11.
[49] Ibid., p. 450, para. 25.

state "which even little boys and girls are obliged to take . . . Takers of this oath must swear to serve with all their strength, even to the shedding of blood, the cause of a revolution which snatches the young from the church." He declares the oath unlawful, but allows Catholics to take it provided that they would "make for themselves before God, in their own consciences, a reservation such as 'Saving the laws of God and of the church' or 'In accordance with the duties of a good Christian,' with the firm proposal to declare also externally such a reservation if the need of it arose."[50] Ironically one of the terms agreed to in the concordat with Mussolini was the introduction of an oath of loyalty to the Italian state to be taken by the bishops.[51]

Pius XI sought organic harmony between church and state, or at least to avoid conflict enough to win for the church a sphere of autonomy where it might evangelize without interference. The problem, as Luigi Sturzo wrote in exile, is that the state wants more.

> [T]he totalitarian State demands not resignation but consent, not a sullen opposition but joyous surrender. Thus all the more interesting expressions of collective and personal life have passed into the hands of the State – youth associations, sport, wireless, the cinema, newspapers and publications of every kind, private and public schools of every grade and type. Nor is this enough. There must be a discipline of mind, will and body.[52]

The state would not and could not abandon a fictional "social" or "moral" sphere to the church. The Fascists knew that the spheres are not so easily separable. Indeed their theoretical separation is often a ruse of the state to enervate the church. The Italian state realized, as the church did not, that the two were unavoidably rivals. Sturzo identifies this rivalry as a dynamic not only of Fascist states, but of modern states as such.

> The modern State aspires to be a *Weltanschauung*, a conception of the world and of life, in substance, a religion. Christianity too is a *Weltanschauung*, besides being a supernatural religion. Between Christianity and the modern State conceived as a *Weltanschauung* conflict is inherent and inevitable.[53]

---

[50] Pope Pius XI, *Non Abbiamo Bisogno*, p. 455, paras. 56–9.
[51] Luigi Sturzo, *Church and State*, trans. Barbara Barclay Carter (Notre Dame, Ind.: University of Notre Dame Press, 1962 [1939]), 490.
[52] Ibid., 481.
[53] Ibid., 535.

Clearly the situation Pius XI confronted in Europe was not immediately paralleled in Chile. The parties that Pius XI helped eliminate in Italy and Germany were socially progressive parties; the Conservative Party of Chile – which at any rate would remain a viable force in Chilean politics until the coup – represented oligarchic interests. In Italy and Germany, right-wing totalitarian parties benefitted from the Vatican's actions; in Chile, more progressive elements took advantage. Because of this, the suppression of the official Catholic party in Chile is hailed by progressive Catholics in Chile as a crucial step in building the tradition of "social Catholicism" in Chile, a tradition which has championed social justice and human rights for Chile's disadvantaged. There is, however, a more melancholy side to this arrangement. The church erred first in identifying all "politics" with party activity, and second in deliberately removing itself as a body from the sphere of "politics." The church created a confined sphere for itself called the "social" in which alone it could act as a church, thereby creating a vacancy in the "political" to be occupied by increasingly powerful state interests. It would take several decades more before a totalitarian regime would assume control in Chile, but the church's inability to resist would have the same roots as the church's weakness when jackboots pounded the streets of Europe.

2 The Rise of "Social Catholicism"

When Pius XI withdrew church support for confessional parties, he did not thereby signal a simple retreat of the church into the hearts and minds of individual Catholics. On the contrary, Pius XI wrote his celebrated 1931 encyclical *Quadragesimo Anno* in part to combat the "evil individualistic spirit" of the age.[54] Confronted with the gray specter of Stalinism on the one hand and the wreckage of capitalism in the depth of the Great Depression on the other, Pius laid out an alternative vision based on an array of vocational groups, or *ordines*, reminiscent of the medieval guild system. Such organizations would remedy the individualism of the capitalist system and also protect the individual from the depredations of the totalitarian state. The result was not a complete abandonment of free enterprise, but rather a modified corporatism meant to blunt the pernicious effects of competition and class conflict.[55]

In Pius XI's scheme, the key to reconstructing a Christian social order was

---

[54] Pope Pius XI, *Quadragesimo Anno* in *The Papal Encyclicals 1903–1939*, para. 88.
[55] Ibid., para. 101. Also Donal Dorr, *Option for the Poor* (Maryknoll, NY: Orbis Books, 1992), 75–94.

Catholic Action, "the apple of our eye" as the Pope put it.[56] Catholic Action "neither engages in politics nor brings an undesired rivalry, but solely seeks to make good Christians living their Christianity, and by that very fact elements of the first order for the public good."[57] The seeds of Catholic Action were sown in the collaboration of laity and clergy in various clubs, sodalities, and charitable enterprises which had operated since the reign of Pius IX. Pius XI's predecessors in the chair of Peter had even used the phrase "Catholic action," but it was Pius XI who capitalized the "A" and articulated a vision and a structure for this association of associations. His official definition of Catholic Action, often repeated, was "the participation of the laity in the hierarchical apostolate."[58] Concerned about the shortage of clergy, the church's loss of the proletariat to Marxist parties and unions, and the epidemic secularization of modern society, Pius envisioned a brigade of committed laypeople, under the direction of the hierarchy, who would take the Gospel into the everyday world and rewin society for Christ.

Catholic Action was meant simultaneously to resist the privatization of religion in bourgeois societies and to disentangle the church from its dysfunctional relationships with party politics. The kind of groups included in Catholic Action, therefore, were of a peculiar kind, neither purely devotional nor purely worldly. Groups which met to say the rosary and nothing more were not Catholic Action; neither were Catholic labor unions or professional associations, their aims being purely temporal.[59] Catholic Action was meant to be an indirect link between the spiritual and the temporal, the religious and the political. The formation that participants received was spiritual, directed at their souls. Such formation, at the same time, was meant to prepare them for the "real world." They were to take their strengthened faith to work with them on Monday and apply it, each in her or his own way, to the problems they encountered. As Pius XII put it, the church "does her work in each one's heart, but it affects the whole of life and every individual activity. In men thus formed, the Church prepares a secure foundation for human society."[60]

[56] Pope Pius XI, "Allocution to the College of Cardinals, December 24, 1938," quoted in Sturzo, *Church and State*, 535 n. 1.

[57] Ibid.

[58] Pope Pius XI, letter to Cardinal Bertram, Nov. 13, 1928, in *The Lay Apostolate: Papal Teachings*, ed. Benedictine Monks of Solesmes (Boston: St Paul Editions, 1961), 289. See also Yves Congar, *Lay People in the Church: A Study for a Theology of Laity*, revised edn, trans. Donald Attwater (London: Geoffrey Chapman, 1985 [1964]), 360–2.

[59] Congar, *Lay People in the Church*, 363.

[60] Pope Pius XII, quoted in Congar, *Lay People in the Church*, 382.

Underlying the ideology of Catholic Action is a crucial distinction between the spiritual and temporal spheres. Pius XI lays this and corollary distinctions out in the following way:

> like the mandate entrusted to the Church by God, and like the apostolate of the hierarchy itself, this Catholic Action is spiritual, not temporal, supernatural, not of this world, religious, not political. However, it deserves no less because of this to be called social action; for its purpose is precisely to extend the kingdom of Christ and by this extension to procure for society the greatest of all benefits, from which all others spring, that is to say all those which concern the organization of a nation and which are termed political.[61]

Catholic Action is to be the linchpin of "social" Catholicism which, because the Kingdom is not of this world, is yet not "political" Catholicism.

This is not to say, as Pius XI points out, that the political order will not be a beneficiary of the church's social action. As Pius X had asserted, Christ is not simply absent from the political; the desired reconquest of all civilization for Christ is based on the fact that no part of creation was beyond Christ's redemptive power. Christ's power nevertheless obeys a direct/indirect duality which corresponds precisely with the neoscholastic dualities of supernature and nature, spiritual and temporal, and clergy and laity. "In the absolutely universal scope ('all things') of Christ's redemption and kingship, they imply an area of direct and full efficaciousness, which is spiritual, and an area of indirect, suggested or partial efficaciousness, which touches nature or creation itself."[62] The church, which is properly spiritual or supernatural, relates to the temporal or political world indirectly, which means not through its official representatives – the clergy whose task is above nature – but through its laity, who find their proper place in the temporal world. The priest must not become mired in secular affairs. Instead he forms the laity in Catholic Action with a formation which is strictly religious. In so doing laypeople develop a Christian conscience which will serve them well in the workaday world and in their political commitments. The Gospel finds its way to that world indirectly, through the labors of the individual layperson.[63]

The logic of Catholic Action makes use of a neoscholastic distinction between the natural end of the work itself and the supernatural end of the

---

[61] Pope Pius XI, letter to Cardinal Bertram, in *The Lay Apostolate*, 290–1.
[62] Congar, *Lay People in the Church*, 351.
[63] Michael Williams, *The Catholic Church in Action* (New York: P.J. Kenedy & Sons, 1958), 320–2.

person who does the work. When a Catholic formed in Catholic Action goes forth as a doctor to care for the sick or a politician to enact legislation, he or she can do so with the inward final intention of God's glory. The action itself, however, retains an intrinsically natural end. The techniques of operating on a sick person or writing legislation to regulate the economy are beyond the competence of the church, which is religious. The intrinsic aims of temporal structures and activities remain temporal and natural, even when influenced by Christian people. Nevertheless, those people remain Christians whose end is in Christ, and whose work is sanctified and given final meaning by Christ. The supernatural is confined to the subjective final intention of the person, and does not in any direct way impinge on the purely natural end of the action itself.[64]

Pius XI believed he had found a solution to the dilemma of a church which had lost the last vestiges of its temporal power and yet was unable by its very nature to accept the modern privatization of religion. The church would be involved in worldly affairs, yet not directly. Across Europe and Latin America, the state was separating from the church. The church, however, sought still to influence the state and to tie their fates together. Catholics well-formed must avail themselves of the rights and duties of the citizen "for the good of religion, which is inseparable from that of the State."[65] Of Catholic Action, Pius XI would write, "Is it not destined to provide society with its best citizens, and the State with its most upright and skillful magistrates?"[66] It must be, because training in Catholic Action, though essentially religious, produces laypeople with properly formed conciences for action in the world. "For every true Catholic, trained in accordance with Catholic doctrine, is by that very fact found to be an excellent citizen, a sincere lover of his country, and a loyal and obedient subject under any legitimate form of government."[67]

The relationship of church and state for Pius XI was not so much a dichotomy as a division of labor. The state has a broad range of rights and duties within its proper competency and role, "a role which, though certainly not only bodily and material, is by its very nature limited to the natural, the terrestrial and the temporal."[68] The proper competence of the church concerns the "sacred and inviolable rights of souls." For this reason, the Pope says, he has waged the good

---

[64] Congar, *Lay People in the Church*, 385–7.

[65] Pope Pius XI, letter to the Mexican bishops Feb. 2, 1926, in *The Lay Apostolate*, 278.

[66] Pope Pius XI, letter to Cardinal Bertram, Nov. 13, 1928, ibid. 293.

[67] Pope Pius XI, *Divini Illius Magistri*, Dec. 31, 1929, ibid. 308.

[68] Pope Pius XI, *Non Abbiamo Bisogno*, in *The Papal Encyclicals 1903–1939*, p. 453, para. 45.

fight for liberty of consciences from state interference.[69] Pius XI's constant concern for Catholic Action was the salvation of souls. It is not that he was unconcerned with the body or ready to abandon it to the state. Rather, as Congar comments, salvation in this life is properly spiritual and inward, since the full outward establishment of Christ's power will come only in the Kingdom at the end of time. "What elements of transformation or anticipation of the final renewal that there really are in this world seem to us to be too closely connected with the spiritual life of individual persons to be very socialized."[70] In the meantime, the church works inwardly, not through worldly power but through spiritual influence. The church is a body "mystical"; it is not of the bodily and the material as such, but rather penetrates it, inspires it, vivifies it.[71]

When Pius XI claims that his vision of Catholicism can properly be called "social," therefore, it must be understood against the backdrop of this emphasis on interiority. Catholic Action cells are indeed to take up and, at the level of general principles, deal with the great "social" problems of the day – unemployment, unjust economic relationships, the dissolution of the family – that is, all problems which have to do with people in society with other people. The emphasis, nonetheless, is on personal formation of the individual for action in the world. "Social Catholicism," therefore, is Catholicism which generated a set of "values" applicable to the realm of social problems which exist "out there," outside of the church. There is no sense that the church itself is meant to be a body in any way analogous to other social bodies.

3 Catholic Action in Chile

Catholic Action had an enormous impact on the church in Latin America. An entire generation of Catholic leaders, both lay and clerical, was trained in a style of addressing social issues from a Catholic perspective. Social change was not simply tolerated but embraced as an imperative for Catholics, and Catholics saw themselves in the vanguard of constructing a more just society. Although the movement did not reach as far into the marginalized classes as some have supposed,[72] it is credited with providing the church with

---

[69] Ibid., para. 39–41.
[70] Congar, *Lay People in the Church*, 92.
[71] Ibid., 384–5.
[72] Brian Smith points out that membership in Catholic Action in Chile was between 1 and 2 percent of the total Catholic population – for example, 58,071 adults and youths in 1945 out of a Catholic population of 4.8 million. Membership was

the structures of lay participation in small groups which would prefigure the base community movement.[73] The Catholic Action methodology of See-Judge-Act placed great importance on a close analysis first of the reality of the situation, much as liberation theologians emphasize a first moment of social scientific reading of the situation before a theological analysis is applied. In fact, many important liberation theologians, such as Gustavo Gutiérrez and Juan Luis Segundo, began their social activism in Catholic Action.[74]

The most important aspect of Catholic Action in Latin America was its ability to provide a space for the church's social action while the church was in the process of officially disaffiliating itself from political party alliances. In Chile this process got a boost, interestingly enough, from the corporatist dictatorship of General Carlos Ibáñez which lasted from 1927 to 1931. Ibáñez was convinced, as General Pinochet would be several decades later, that hopes for the harmonious functioning of civic responsibility were brightest in a Chile without the strife of party *politiquería*. Ibáñez's Republican Confederation for Civic Action, or CRAC, became in effect the official state party, while Chile's other parties cooled their heels under an obligatory political "recess."[75] Unintended beneficiaries of this arrangement were the Catholic apostolic movements which would become Catholic Action when Ibáñez fell. The most active of the elite Catholic youth, looking for alternatives to the banned political parties, flocked to groups such as ANEC, the National Association of Catholic Students, the most important building block of Catholic Action

---

primarily drawn from the upper and middle classes; Smith, *The Church and Politics in Chile*, 95–96. Nevertheless, Enrique Dussel calls the Chilean Agrarian Youth Movement "the most outstanding Catholic youth movement in the world"; Enrique Dussel, *A History of the Church in Latin America: Colonialism to Liberation*, trans. Alan Neely (Grand Rapids, Mich.: William B. Eerdmans Publishing Company, 1981), 109.

[73] Edward L. Cleary, OP, *Crisis and Change: The Church in Latin America Today* (Maryknoll, NY: Orbis Books, 1985), 1–6; Christian Smith, *The Emergence of Liberation Theology: Radical Religion and Social Movement Theory* (Chicago: University of Chicago Press, 1991), 79–81; and Ana María Bidegaín, "From Catholic Action to Liberation Theology: The Historical Process of the Laity in Latin America in the Twentieth Century," Notre Dame, Ind.: Kellogg Institute Working Paper #48, Nov. 1985.

[74] Smith, *The Emergence of Liberation Theology*, 81.

[75] Brian Loveman, *Chile: The Legacy of Hispanic Capitalism* (New York: Oxford University Press, 1979), 247–53.

in Chile. Ironically the university students would play a key role in the ouster of Ibáñez in 1931, at the head of the general strike that would force his resignation.[76]

In 1928 Father Oscar Larson took over as advisor to ANEC upon his return from studies in Belgium. There he had been exposed to the most advanced Catholic Action cells in Europe, and with that experience he transformed ANEC. With the See-Judge-Act methodology, Larson exposed a significant group of future lay Catholic leaders to the most notable trends in Catholic social thinking, especially Pius XI's *Quadragesimo Anno* and the "New Christendom" ideas of Jacques Maritain. In the first years of Larson's tenure as advisor, ANEC formed many of those who would found the Chilean Christian Democratic Party, including Eduardo Frei and Bernardo Leighton, future president and vice-president of Chile. Also included in that early group was Jaime Eyzaguirre who, as influential professor at the Catholic University, would form some of the Pinochet regime's main ideologues.[77]

ANEC and other apostolic movements came under the aegis of Catholic Action when it was formed officially in October 1931 on the feast day of Christ the King. In its early years, Catholic Action was a motor for the most progressive elements of the church in Chile, often despite the intentions of the bishops. While most in the hierarchy, such as bishops Fuenzalida and Campillo, wanted Catholic Action to channel its youngest participants into the Conservative Party, advisors such as Larson and Father Fernando Vives Solar, SJ formed Catholic students quite critical of the Conservatives, especially for their support of liberal economic arrangements which the students saw condemned in *Rerum Novarum* and *Quadragesimo Anno*.[78] The young cadres of Catholic Action were the first to take *Quadragesimo Anno* seriously and propagate its ideas; the Conservative-controlled newspaper refused to print the encyclical, one of its directors lamenting that it was sometimes "necessary to protect Catholics from the imprudence of the Pope."[79] The conflicts between the mainstream of the Conservative Party and the young progressive Catholics formed in Catholic Action came to a head in 1938, when the latter group broke away from the Conservative Party and

---

[76] Huerta, *Catolicismo social en Chile*, 412–14; and Loveman, *Chile*, 253. Students from ANEC occupied the main building of the University of Chile in downtown Santiago, one of the key stands of the general strike; Araneda, *Historia de la iglesia en Chile*, 726.

[77] Araneda, *Historia de la iglesia en Chile*, 724–9.

[78] Huerta, *Catolicismo social en Chile*, 414.

[79] Quoted in Araneda, *Historia de la iglesia en Chile*, 727–8.

formed the National Falange, which would become the Christian Democratic Party two decades later.[80]

There is an urgency and a dynamism in the rhetoric of Catholic Action which suggests the awakening of a long-slumbering church. It would have been difficult to sleep through the 1930s. The Chilean Communist Party was formed officially in 1922, the Socialist Party in 1933; the former would grow into the largest Communist party in Latin America and both would become major forces in Chilean national life. At the same time, Fascist sympathizers were many in the 1930s, especially in Catholic circles. A sizable Nazi party appeared and tried its hand at a coup in 1938.[81] Conservatives grew alarmed and defensive. The more instability rocked the country, the more the bishops wished to bring the battling elements under the tutelage of the church, to bring Chile back to its Catholic heritage and incorporate all into the spiritual unity of the mystical body of Christ. Catholic Action was to be the instrument. It was meant especially to steal the Marxists' clothes by offering an alternative vision of improved conditions for the worker.

The organicist vision and anti-communism combined to produce a strong sense of patriotism among the Catholic Action cadres, among both conservatives and progressives. The need was to produce good citizens for the *Patria*; the subject of Catholic Action discourse in Chile was very often Chile itself. For example, the official prayer of the Chilean Young Catholic Students (JEC) branch of Catholic Action asks Jesus "Give us a sense of our student responsibilities, thus preparing us to serve the Fatherland, in case tomorrow we are called on to act."[82] In his 1941 book *Catholic Action in the Schools*, Father Florencio Infante, Vice-Director of Catholic Youth and later Military Bishop and supporter of the Pinochet regime, explains the patriotic formation given in Catholic Action to combat Marxist indoctrination. "The aspirant must have a thorough knowledge of the history of his fatherland in order to be able to love it passionately; it would be appropriate often in the meetings to cite examples of our history, to make them see how it has unfolded in its entirety united with the Cross."[83] This patriotism was by no means limited to conservatives in Catholic Action. The following is from Manuel Larraín, one of the leading promoters of Catholic Action in Chile, national director of

---

[80] Loveman, *Chile*, 307–8.

[81] Loveman, *Chile*, 213–76.

[82] Mario González G., *Nuestra J.E.C.* (Santiago: Editorial del Pacífico, 1952), 57.

[83] Florencio Infante, SS.CC., *La Acción Católica en los colegios* (Santiago: Editorial Splendor, 1941), 19.

Catholic Action after 1952, founder of CELAM, hailed as one of the most progressive bishops in all of Latin America from the 1940s until his death in 1966.

> The very sign of the cross, which knits the poem of the life of the citizen, gives heroic feeling to our history. It is an ideal of God and Fatherland and a cry to Mary on the lips which animates the soldiers of the Independence.[84]

Larraín continues on to name some of the great campaigns of the armed forces in Chile's history. He comes to the battle of Yungay, in which General Manuel Bulnes defeated the forces of Peru and Bolivia in 1839.

> When the afternoon of Yungay brought victory to Bulnes, the great soldier – opening his chest and displaying the image of Mary – said that he owed the triumph to his "*Lady of Carmen*," the good fortune of Chilean arms.[85]

According to Roberto Bolton, it was said that the triumph of Our Lady of Carmen over Our Lady of Merced, Peru's patroness, was due to the fact that Our Lady of Carmen had the baby Jesus in her arms, while Our Lady of Merced, sadly, did not. At any rate, patriotic military rhetoric in Catholic Action was common, and served to make the unity of the nation-state its natural field of discourse.

The unity among Catholics that the bishops had sought to combat the ideological strife rending Chilean society now had a unified structure to promote it. In actual fact, however, Catholic Action did not unite the competing classes of society into one. It was a movement of elites, overwhelmingly middle and upper class. The leaders of Catholic Action came out of prestigious schools such as the Jesuit Colegio San Ignacio, where Fernando Vives, Jorge Fernández Pradel, and later Alberto Hurtado formed two generations of progressive Catholics.[86] The natural cultural environment of social Catholicism in Chile was the university, not the factory. The Papal Nuncio in 1950 declared that the salvation of Chile lay in Catholic "profes-

---

[84] Bishop Manuel Larraín Errázuriz, "Congreso Eucarístico Nacional, Homilia (1941)," in *Mons. Manuel Larraín E.: escritos completos,* vol. I, ed. Pedro De La Noi (Santiago: Ediciones Paulinas, 1976), 170.

[85] Ibid., 170–1.

[86] The biography of Father Hurtado provides an excellent picture of the social activism at San Ignacio in the 1910s and 1920s; see Alejandro Magnet, *El Padre Hurtado* (Santiago: Editorial Los Andes, 1990), 27–67.

sionals" and "intellectuals."[87] The talks and conferences on the social question given in Catholic Action had a profound effect on a group of future leaders of the church and center parties, but, as Eduardo Frei later recognized, Catholic Action never made significant advances into working-class culture. While Catholic Action went to the poor, it was not successful in coming from the poor.[88]

This elitism was written into the idea of Catholic Action. Papal documents on the subject were paternalistic, often stressing the importance of seeking first the most talented laypeople for Catholic Action, those most capacitated to be apostles, to take the message to others.[89] This strategy was often echoed in writings on Catholic Action in Chile. Fernández Pradel, for example, wrote that first one must have talented leaders, then good *militantes* capable of the apostolate, and finally "with the leaders and the militants one must act among the *masses*."[90] The position of the masses themselves tended to be a passive one. There was no deliberate intention to exclude talented members of the working or peasant classes. As it was, however, the lower classes had been neglected by the Chilean clergy, and Catholicism in the lower classes revolved around feast days and traditional pieties, not around weekly Mass, much less the church's latest social teachings. At the same time, the ideology of Catholic Action was based on *influence*, on the penetrating of society with its ideals. The working classes were beginning to organize, but had no access to the board rooms and editorial offices usually associated with attempts to exert influence on society at large. Although Catholic Action was intended to unite all the different environments where people lived and worked, in practice its own ideology doomed its efforts to penetrate the lower classes to limited success.

Starting in the 1940s, Catholic Action itself also tried new strategies to penetrate working class and peasant culture, increasingly adopting the specialized model of Catholic Action favored in France and Belgium. This model traced its roots to the work of Father Joseph Cardijn, himself a product of a working-class family, beginning in 1912. Cardijn founded the Jeunesse Ouvrier Catholique, or JOC, in the factories around Brussels. There he

[87] Maximiliano Salinas Campos, *Historia del pueblo de Dios en Chile: La evolución del cristianismo desde la perspectiva de los pobres* (Santiago: Ediciones Rehue, 1987), 210.
[88] Smith, *The Church and Politics in Chile*, 96 n. 17. See also Smith, "Chile: Deepening the Allegiance of Working-Class Sectors to the Church in the 1970's," in *Religion and Political Conflict in Latin America*, ed. Daniel H. Levine (Chapel Hill, NC: University of North Carolina Press, 1986), 159–60.
[89] Congar, *Lay People in the Church*, 376–7.
[90] Jorge Fernández Pradel, quoted in Huerta, *Catolicismo social en Chile*, 424.

employed his famous See-Judge-Act method to apply the Catholic faith of the young workers to the concrete situation of the working class.[91] Cardijn's model differed from the Italian model of Catholic Action in that it was based on what could be called "affinity groups" or cultural environments – workers, students, peasants – instead of being centered on the parish. JOC was founded in Chile in 1942, along with AUC, the Association of Catholic University Students, thus inaugurating a new era of specialization in Chilean Catholic Action.[92] Cardijn himself gave a strong push to this trend with his visit to Chile in 1948.[93]

The major reason for resistance to specialization up to this point in Chile was fear of disunity, specifically class conflict. Those who pressed for a move to specialization were careful to stress the oneness of the church's mission. In a 1946 article in the *Bulletin of Catholic Action* entitled "Unity and Specialization," Father Rafael Larraín writes "Undoubtedly Catholic Action is 'one': the laity participate in the hierarchical apostolate which is 'one.' One Christianizing action on society. The unity of Catholic Action dictates its spirit, objective and general plan, identical for all its components."[94] The point of all this protesting the unity of Catholic Action is to set up his argument for bringing different manifestations of Catholic Action to the different classes of society. We must recognize differences in classes, wrote Larraín, but not different classes based on "divisions, selfishness, or accidental circumstances." The church does not accept the division of society into upper, middle, and lower classes, since this division obeys no proper function worthy of the church's respect. Rather, the church recognizes three *ambientes*, environments or settings. These are (*a*) the class of leaders (*la clase dirigente*), those with influence over the economic, social, and administrative life of the country. This class is characterized by being "*at the service of the society* in its *orientation and direction*"; (*b*) the working class; (*c*) the peasant class.[95] In the 1940s and 1950s Catholic Action movements were organized to correspond to these three settings.[96]

[91] Ana María Bidegaín, "From Catholic Action to Liberation Theology," 6–8.
[92] Huerta, *Catolicismo social en Chile*, 439–41.
[93] Ibid., 476.
[94] Father Rafael Larraín, quoted in Huerta, *Catolicismo social en Chile*, 453.
[95] Ibid., 454.
[96] The new statutes of 1953 organized Catholic Action into three branches: general, workers, and peasants. The general branch took in all the student movements, it being understood that the students would form the class of leaders for society, plus the adult women's branch; Huerta, *Catolicismo social en Chile*, 494.

While the advocates of specialization found it necessary to downplay potential conflict between the *ambientes* and foster an organic view of the nation, the impetus behind specialization was the realization that the Marxists, advocates of class struggle, had succeeded in organizing Chilean youth, workers, and campesinos to a much greater extent than the church had. Church leaders viewed the growth of Marxist organization with alarm, and realized that the church must go on the offensive if society was to be rescued from Marxism, atheism, secularism, and a host of other menaces. The idea behind specialization was to go to people in their reality, just as it was, and Christianize it. Just as the different settings in which people lived were different, so also Catholic Action must be differentiated and specialized. The mission of Catholic Action, according to Bishop Emilio Tagle, is to "communicate the spirit of Christ to the Social Body"; to pretend that the body was homogeneous would be to ignore the reality of the different *ambientes*.[97]

The term *ambiente* is defined in the *Official Bulletin of Catholic Action* in 1949 in the following terms: "men gathered by the same way of living, of thinking, of acting, of cultivating themselves, of conceiving of science, art, politics, of amusement; that have the same reactions, the same sympathies or antipathies. Together with the psychological bonds which unite them in the same conduct of life."[98] One might think that this would not be a bad start on a definition of the church as a community where virtue is produced and reproduced, but the ecclesiology of Catholic Action would regard this as a confusion of the temporal and the spiritual planes. For the ecclesiology represented by Catholic Action, the church itself is not an *ambiente*, that is, it is not properly understood as a social entity. Joseph Cardijn had told the gathering of JOC advisors in Chile, "*we must not create a separate Catholic ambiente*."[99] An *ambiente*, as Bishop Tagle says, is part of the social body, meaning the nation; the church is a mystical body, repository of the spirit of Christ which is sent forth to penetrate the various *ambientes*. Implied is that the church itself is not properly a social performance, a discipline, a *Weltanschauung*, a way of living and acting, a way of imagining and organizing the world. This is not to say that the church does not have its own *values* regarding the political. Catholic Action was meant to form Catholic leaders in these values, to habituate them into Catholic ways of thinking, to sink this ethos so deep into their bones that they could not help but radiate it in their sojourns into contingent matters of politics. Cardijn was

---

[97] Archbishop Emilio Tagle, quoted in Huerta, *Catolicismo social en Chile*, 448.
[98] Sara García de la Huerta de Eyzaguirre, quoted in Huerta, *Catolicismo social en Chile*, 458.
[99] Joseph Cardijn, quoted in Huerta, *Catolicismo social en Chile*, 475, italics in original.

correct in not wanting to create a separate Catholic ghetto. Nevertheless, the process is one of sending out; to engage the contingent, one must leave the church. The church, however, does not leave the individual, but is carried with the individual in an interior way.

Catholic Action correctly intuited that the church must not be reduced to just one *ambiente* among many in civil society, for the church is broader than any particular class or cultural group. In Paul's vision, the many different people are all to be gathered into the body of Christ, in which there is neither "Jew nor Greek, slave nor free, woman nor man" (Gal. 3:28). At the same time, differences among people are not effaced, but harmonized into a true sharing of charisms (I Cor. 12:12–26). In the body of Christ each person retains the particularities of her cultural setting, but those particularities are embraced as contributions to the catholicity of the community. Particularities are embraced but divisions between oppressor and oppressed are overcome. The result is not a procedural egalitarianism but a true equality based on honor and care for the weakest members of the body (I Cor. 12:22–6).

Catholic Action is a parody of Paul's view, however, in that the nation-state and not the body of Christ is the field of unity for the various *ambientes*. Genuine reconciliation is supplanted by an attempt to subsume class conflict into a common patriotism and devotion to the imaginary project called "Chile." Catholic Action failed among the poor because it occluded rather than resolved the endemic class war between the Chilean elites and the peasants and workers. The interiorization of the church made impossible any attempt to enact a specifically Christian imagining of a socio-political order capable of true social unity. Any attempt to enact the body of Christ was defined as a confusion of the spiritual and the temporal. Individual Christians were left with a vague interior "spirituality" of politics which left the imagination of the nation-state untouched.

In a few short decades the church in Chile had moved from a "Christendom" ecclesiology to what was being called a "New Christendom" model. The change is virtually always narrated as an entirely positive movement. Chilean church historian Fernando Aliaga Rojas, for example, sums up the process this way:

> The old ecclesiological conception . . . confused the church as subject of the faith with [the church] as contingent political actor. This theological notion put a strong emphasis on all the juridical dimensions that permitted the clear sociological demarcation of those who were outside or inside of the church, which underlined its character as perfect society, possessed of it own ends and with the adequate and unrelenting means to achieve them. The renovation of

the 1950s is grounded in traditional theology, enriched by the new conception of the "mystical body of Christ," which puts forth a demand for greater lay participation in the hierarchical church. This orientation coincides with a new concept of what the action of the church should be with regard to the political, which is manifested principally in the recognition of the autonomous character of [the political] and in the need for the church not to intervene as an institution in questions of contingent politics. . . . These ideas correspond with the intention to construct a "new Christendom" in the midst of a world which progresses towards secularization, democracy, and political pluralism.[100]

In the next chapter we will see that the story did not in fact have such a happy ending.

---

[100] Aliaga, *La iglesia en Chile*, 183.

Chapter Four

A DISTINCTION OF PLANES

Although the New Christendom ecclesiology commonly associated with French Catholic philosopher Jacques Maritain did not spring vigorous and fully-grown from his pen, Maritain's influence on Catholic ideas of church and politics from the 1930s into the 1960s was immense. In chapter 3 I began the theoretical elaboration of the church's removal from an autonomous political sphere by situating this ecclesiology within the encyclicals of Pius XI and the spread of Catholic Action. In this chapter I will complete that elaboration by addressing the work of Maritain, who gave theoretical expression to the reconfiguration of the church's politics for many in both Europe and Latin America. I will show Maritain's influence in Chile, present the major themes of his ecclesio-political work, and criticize its effect on the church.

1 Maritain among Us

Maritain's name is often linked to the rise in Latin America of both Catholic Action[1] and Christian Democracy.[2] As one of his Latin American admirers wrote

[1] E.g. Enrique Dussel, *A History of the Church in Latin America: Colonialism to Liberation*, trans. Alan Neely (Grand Rapids, Mich.: William B. Eerdmans, 1981), 107; and María Antonieta Huerta and Luis Pacheco Pastene, *La iglesia chilena y los cambios sociopolíticos* (Santiago: Pehuén Editores, 1988), 156.

[2] "No other European would equal the influence of Maritain among Latin American Christian Democratic intellectuals"; Edward A. Lynch, *Religion and Politics in Latin America: Liberation Theology and Christian Democracy* (New York: Praeger Publishers, 1991), 69. See also Paul Sigmund, "Maritain on Politics," in *Understanding Maritain: Philosopher and Friend*, ed. Deal W. Hudson and Matthew J. Mancini (Macon, Ga.: Mercer University Press, 1987), 165–9; and Brian Loveman, *Chile: The Legacy of Hispanic Capitalism* (New York: Oxford University Press, 1979), 303–8.

in 1948, "The Thomist renovation in America as well as the Christian solution of the social problems of the New World owe to Maritain more than to any other modern thinker the vigor of their current expansion."[3] His influence in Chile was especially profound. Maritain himself wrote in 1966 that the only place his ideas of a Christian politics had really taken root was Chile under Eduardo Frei.[4] A book entitled *Maritain Among Us,* published by Frei and Ismael Bustos on the eve of Frei's election, refers to Maritain as "the greatest thinker of our time."[5]

Eduardo Rojas, executive secretary of the Vicariate of the Social Pastorate, comments "I believe that the ideas of Maritain are the foundation for the majority of Catholics who participate in politics in Chile."[6] Rojas traces Maritain's influence not only to the Christian Democrats in the center, but also to Catholics in parties of both the left and the right. This pluralism of political options for Catholics, endorsed by Vatican II, is in fact Maritain's most enduring legacy, according to Rojas: "Every position of the autonomy of the temporal ultimately comes from Maritain."[7] Although this assessment might overstate the direct causative influence of Maritain, it is clear that Maritain's ideas can be fairly taken to represent the kind of Latin American thought on politics and religion I have been tracing.

Maritain's thought began to enter the seminaries and the Catholic University of Chile on the back of a neo-Thomist revival in the late 1920s. The Catholic University had been founded in 1888 to counter the increasingly secular nature of the University of Chile. As such, *La Católica*'s founding charter decreed that its teaching would be rooted in that of Thomas Aquinas, true to the plan of Leo XIII's *Aeterni Patris* to restore the unity of human and divine sciences under the healing auspices of the Angelic Doctor. In this environment interest in Maritain's neo-Thomism grew.[8]

---

[3] Tristán de Athaide, "Maritain et l'Amerique latine," *Revue Thomiste* 48 (1948), 17. Tristán de Athaide was the pen name of Alceu Amoroso Lima of Brazil, one of the founders of Christian Democracy in Latin America. See also Alceu Amoroso Lima, "Testimony: On the Influence of Maritain in Latin America," *The New Scholasticism* 66, no. 1 (Winter 1972), 70–85.

[4] Jacques Maritain, *The Peasant of the Garonne: An Old Layman Questions Himself about the Present Time,* trans. Michael Cuddihy and Elizabeth Hughes (New York: Holt, Rinehardt and Winston, 1968), 23.

[5] Eduardo Frei and Ismael Bustos, *Maritain entre nosotros* (Santiago: Instituto de Educación Política, 1964), 10.

[6] Eduardo Rojas, interview by author, August 2, 1993, Santiago, tape recording.

[7] Ibid.

[8] Jaime Caiceo Escudero, "Principales expresiones de la filosofía tomista en Chile," *Anuario de Historia de la Iglesia en Chile* 8 (1990), 108, 116–18.

At first Maritain's impact was felt through his more speculative writings. Soon, however, the founders of social Catholicism in Chile – Julio Restat, Fernando Vives, Jorge Fernández Pradel, Oscar Larson, Alberto Hurtado – began to imbibe Maritain's ideas of building a new Christendom and make them their own. Maritain's political ideas were seized upon by a significant section of Christian thinkers and activists looking for a way to escape the Conservative Party's monopoly on Catholic political expression. Cardinal Pacelli's 1934 letter on the right of Catholics to choose any political party not contrary to the church's vital concerns was followed by the publication in Chile of excerpts from Maritain's *Letter on Independence* of 1935, which reinforced the idea of the political freedom of Catholic laypeople.[9] At the same time, periodicals of different stripes, from the Conservative *Diario Ilustrado* to the progressive *Política y Espíritu* began to publish articles and reviews on and by Maritain.[10]

It was the Catholic youth of Chile who took on Maritain with revolutionary fervor in the 1930s. Under Oscar Larson's direction, the National Association of Catholic Students (ANEC) formed study circles to analyze his writings.[11] Articles in ANEC's journal, as well as the *Journal of Catholic Youth* and the *Bulletin of Catholic Action*, began to reflect Maritain's influence.[12] Through participation in international conferences of Catholic youth, the young cadres of Catholic Action were exposed to the Catholic intellectuals of Europe, most notably Jacques Maritain.[13] In 1933 ANEC sent Manuel Garretón and Eduardo Frei to Rome for the Iberoamerican Congress of Catholic University Students, of which Frei was elected Secretary General. Frei and Garretón stayed on in Europe, visiting Cardinal Pacelli in Rome, attending Maritain's lectures in Paris, and visiting Catholic social movements in Belgium. Frei would write of Maritain, "When we formed the National Falange and later the Christian Democratic Party, his ideas exercised a determinative influence."[14]

---

[9] An abbreviated version, translated into Spanish by Julio Gómez de la Serna, was published in Argentina's periodical *Sur* in July 1936. The excerpts in *El Diario Ilustrado* were taken from the Argentine version; see Jacques Maritain, "Carta sobre la independencia," *Sur* (July 1936), 54–86.

[10] Jaime Caiceo E., "Influencia de Maritain en los orígenes del social-cristianismo chileno, en su expresión política (1930–1950)," *Estudios Sociales*, no. 67, trimestre 1 (1991), 192.

[11] Araneda, *Historia de la iglesia en Chile*, 729–30.

[12] Huerta, *Catolicismo social en Chile*, 344–5.

[13] Aliaga, *La iglesia en Chile*, 172.

[14] Eduardo Frei Montalva, *Memorias (1911–1934) y correspondencias con Gabriela Mistral y Jacques Maritain* (Santiago: Editorial Planeta, 1989), 54. See also George W. Grayson, Jr., *El Partido Demócrata Cristiano Chileno* (Buenos Aires and Santiago: Editorial Francisco de Aguirre, 1968), 117–19.

In prominent circles of Catholic youth involved in the ferment of the 1930s, Maritain became known as *El Maestro*.[15] Maritain's followers, all active in Catholic Action, were arrayed in two groups. The first consisted of those who had followed the prodding of the Archbishop of Santiago, Horacio Campillo, and joined the Conservative Party. In this group were Frei, Garretón, Bernardo Leighton and others who would figure prominently in the Falange. The second group of Maritainites were those like Jaime Eyzaguirre, Julio Phillipi, and Alfredo Bowen, "integrists" who thought that Christian social concern should remain outside of politics of any stripe.[16]

Frei later commented, "At that time to be Catholic and to be Conservative were practically synonymous."[17] The young Catholic Actionists were extremely wary of the Conservative Party for its resistance to change, its corruption, its compromises with Ibáñez's dictatorship, and above all for its embrace of liberal economics. Frei sums up the situation in a letter to Maritain.

> In Chile there has occurred a universal phenomenon: a deep divorce between our generation and the old one. Our generation, being formed in Catholic Action, differs fundamentally from the other in its formation, in its sensibility, in its sense of things and in its conception of what the Christian ought to be in this world. Catholicism in Chile has taken refuge in the bourgeoisie and the aristocracy.[18]

Oscar Larson resisted Archbishop Horacio Campillo's instructions to guide his bright young charges in ANEC into the Conservative Party, but the pressure was insistent and unsubtle, and Larson asked to be transferred to Peru in 1934. Bernardo Leighton then convinced his fellows in the first group of Maritainites that the only way to realize Maritain's "concrete historical ideal" would be through party political action.[19] They joined the Conservative Youth, but from the start many Conservatives were not happy that their Party had been crashed. The Maritainites combined papal social teaching with Maritain's thought to envision a communitarian society free of capitalist conflict, characterized by social pluralism, civil liberties, and a state-directed redistri-

---

[15] Frei, *Memorias*, 157-8.

[16] Caiceo, "Influencia de Maritain en los origenes del social-cristianismo chileno, en su expresión política (1930-1950)," 192.

[17] Frei, *Memorias*, 25.

[18] Ibid., 166.

[19] Grayson, *El Partido Demócrata Cristiana Chileno*, 104-9; Caiceo, "Influencia de Maritain en los origenes del social-cristianismo chileno, en su expresión política (1930-1950)," 192.

bution of wealth, all of which was greeted with groans of distaste by the Conservative leadership. By 1938 the differences had become irreconcilable, and the National Falange was formed as a separate party.[20]

Maritain's influence in Latin America increased with his visits to the continent in 1936 and 1938.[21] In Chile and Argentina the spread of Maritain's thought ignited furious controversy between his defenders and those who were threatened by the decoupling of the church from conservative oligarchic interests. In Argentina the attack was led by traditionalist Julio Meinvielle, who accused Maritain of selling out the church to liberalism. In his book *From Lammenais to Maritain*, Meinvielle excoriated Maritain for his supposed belief in necessary progress, religious indifferentism, and liberal rights, all contributions to the perdition of modern society.[22] Meinvielle's attacks were taken up and expanded in Chile by Luis Pérez, who, in the words of one of Maritain's defenders, made "anti-Maritain criticism a central preoccupation of his existence."[23] Pérez adopted the concern of many conservative Catholics over the division of the Catholic vote by the Falange, which by refusing to support the coalition candidate of the Conservative and Liberal Parties in the 1938 elections contributed to the victory of the Marxist-backed Popular Front candidate Pedro Aguirre Cerda.[24] Pérez spearheaded the attack on Maritain's influence in Chile for over ten years, prompting an acrimonious controversy involving many of Chile's leading political and church figures.[25]

In his book *In Defense of Maritain*, Falange theorist Jaime Castillo Velasco takes on the charge that Maritain simply capitulates to modernity in his defense of democracy and pluralism. To the contrary, Castillo contends, Maritain is extremely critical of the modern world's atomistic individualism, its unfettered competition, its anthropocentric atheism, its idolatrous statism.[26] At the same time, Maritain is able to appreciate what is good in modernity, for

---

[20] Grayson, *El Partido Demócrata Cristiano Chileno*, 109-63. Conservative leader Rafael Luis Gumucio once remarked "Las encíclicas me cargan," which, loosely translated, means "The encyclicals are a pain in the neck"; ibid., 84.

[21] Sigmund, "Maritain on Politics," 165.

[22] Julio Meinvielle, *De Lammenais à Maritain* (Buenos Aires: Ediciones Theoria, 1967 [1945]), 9-22.

[23] Jaime Castillo Velasco, *En defensa de Maritain* (Santiago: Política y Espíritu, 1948), 9.

[24] Eduardo Frei, letter to Jacques Maritain, in *Memorias*, 165-70.

[25] See *Una polémica sensacional. Jacques Maritain,* ed. Rafael Luis Gumucio (Santiago: Gutenberg Impresores, 1944).

[26] Castillo, *En defensa de Maritain*, 17.

example its emphasis on liberty. Maritain neither accepts liberalism nor wishes a return to medievalism; unlike the medievals, he recognizes the proper autonomy of the temporal, but unlike the liberals he subordinates it clearly to the spiritual. Maritain's critics, says Castillo, are mired hopelessly in the nineteenth century, wishing to impose the Catholic faith with a temporal force the church no longer possesses.[27]

Jesuit Father Julio Jiménez Berguecio also responded to Maritain's critics with a book in 1948, entitled *The Orthodoxy of J. Maritain*. According to Jiménez, Maritain's acceptance of religious liberty and pluralism is based on a practical, not a dogmatic tolerance. In other words, Maritain is not a liberal indifferentist; religious pluralism is not a good in itself, but can be accepted as an "hypothesis" given the disastrous prospects should the church try to impose the Catholic faith through temporal power.[28] Jiménez uses a similar argument to rebut Pérez' claims that Maritain privileges democracy as the only normatively Christian political system. The church cannot be enfeoffed to any form of temporal power, even democracy, since, as Maritain points out, there is a fundamental distinction between the things of Caesar and the things of Christ. For this reason a Christian was still a Christian in the Roman Empire, even though he accepted the institution of slavery.[29]

Maritain's defenders would win the battle for the ideological center of the Catholic church in Chile. Although the majority of practicing Catholics would not transfer their allegiance from the Conservative Party to the Christian Democrats until the early 1960s, Jaime Castillo rightly pointed out in 1948 that even Maritain's opponents operated on the same presuppositions of democracy, rights, and religious pluralism. As Castillo wrote, "the ideas of the French philosopher are nothing but the expression of the general Catholic environment."[30] The next generation of Catholic bishops, those who would lead the church in the 1960s and 1970s, were steeped in Maritain's thought, much of it imbibed through participation in Catholic Action.[31]

---

[27] Ibid., 19–25.

[28] Julio Jiménez Berguecio, SJ, *La ortodoxia de J. Maritain* (Talca: Ediciones de la Libreria Cervantes, 1948), 12–17.

[29] Ibid., 74–5.

[30] Castillo, *En defensa de Maritain*, 44.

[31] Most of the bishops I interviewed had been involved in Catholic Action. The influence of Maritain on their thought is attested to by many sources, for example Jose Aldunate, Fernando Castillo, and Joaquim Silva, *Los derechos humanos y la iglesia chilena* (Santiago: Educación y Comunicaciones, n.d.), 19: "Many of our Bishops who participated in Medellín and Puebla, through their own pre-Vatican formation, bear deep-rooted mental structures of a Maritainian personalism."

2 The Minimum of Body

Maritain's first major political book was *Primauté du spirituel*, rendered in English as *The Things That Are Not Caesar's*. The book was published in France in 1927 as Maritain's response to the papal condemnation of Action Française a year before. The Vatican edict had produced consternation and crisis among the Catholic supporters of Action Française, who were many, and who were in the habit of describing themselves as "the best Catholics in France."[32] Though the leader of the movement, Charles Maurras, was a self-professed pagan, his monarchist, anti-liberal vision drew a great deal of its support from Catholics angered by the disintegration of traditional society and the travails of the church under the Republic. Maritain, himself a severe critic of modernity in his early writings, had been quite sympathetic with Maurras.[33] When Pius XI condemned Action Française, however, Maritain put his full support behind the Pope's position and counseled filial obedience to the Pontiff's orders despite the anguished sense of betrayal among the movement's many staunch Catholics.[34]

Action Française was born in the Dreyfus affair of 1899 to champion the broad interests of France's nationalist right against liberalism, socialism, and Jewry. Its interests were diffuse, but tended to congregate around a unifying anti-modernism and a hatred of the Third Republic. Although not a Christian, Maurras was a mystic possessed of a vision of France and her traditions preserved under a restored Crown and a church returned to her privileged position. Traditionalist Catholic sentiment was drawn to Action Française by its opposition to the liberal Republic's anti-clerical legislation in 1905, increased with the papal condemnation of modernism in 1910, and continued to grow with post-war reaction to the Bolshevik triumph.[35]

Maurras and his movement had come under Vatican scrutiny in 1914, but it was not until December 1926 that Pius XI moved to condemn Action Française. The condemnation fit into Pius XI's strategy to remove the church from political entanglements and move its efforts into Catholic Action. Pius

---

[32] Jacques Maritain, *The Things That Are Not Caesar's*, trans. J.F. Scanlan (New York: Charles Scribner's Sons, 1931), 48.

[33] Bernard E. Doering, *Jacques Maritain and the French Catholic Intellectuals* (Notre Dame, Ind: University of Notre Dame Press, 1983), 6–36.

[34] Ibid., 49.

[35] Joseph Amato, *Mounier and Maritain: A French Catholic Understanding of the Modern World* (University, Ala.: University of Alabama Press, 1975), 72–4.

XI felt that Maurras, an infidel, had made the church a mere pawn in a political game, and had only embittered the church's relationship with the Republic. Catholic youth in France and Belgium were being drawn away from Catholic organizations, and Action Française – by claiming to represent Catholic interests – was eroding the church's teaching authority. When the condemnation came, Maritain submitted at once to the Pope's authority. It was an important turning point in Maritain's development. It forced him to engage political matters more directly, and it put his strongest attacks on modernity behind him.[36]

Many French Catholics did not submit to the Pope's directive. They openly accused Pius XI of overstepping the proper bounds of papal power and intervening directly in politics. The purpose of *Primauté du spirituel* was to establish in this case that the Pope acted for a purely spiritual end which had an only secondary effect on the political. In order to accomplish this, Maritain situated this particular controversy within a full exploration of the proper distinction of the temporal and the spiritual for Catholic thought.

Superficially, the Action Française complaint that the Pope had transgressed the boundary between the spiritual and the temporal would seem to obey the same sort of distinction on which Maritain bases his argument. Maritain not only defends Pius XI from the charge – which Maritain assumes would be a serious one if true – but in fact turns the charge against Maurras and his Catholic defenders. They had protested that the Pope's order was in effect asking them to sin against their country, "to murder their mother," since the salvation of France lay in Catholic political activity. Maurras was convinced that the church was useful to France as the cultural custodian of Latin civilization and true social order. This is, according to Maritain, a mere naturalization of the church, a temporalization of the spiritual, a transformation of the "mystic body of Christ" into "a power of this world whose supposed conflict with the mother country then became insoluble."[37] It is the disobedient Catholics, then, and not the Pope, who have confused the temporal and the spiritual and damaged national interests. Maritain contends that nothing "could have done France *greater harm* than to have exposed it, through disobedience to the supreme authority, to a schism between Catholics and to have excited national passions against the spiritual power."[38]

The first chapter of *Primauté du spirituel* is dedicated to a careful delineation

---

[36] Anthony Rhodes, *The Vatican in the Age of the Dictators 1922–1945* (London: Hodder and Stoughton, 1973), 103–11; Amato, *Mounier and Maritain*, 71–6.
[37] Maritain, *The Things That Are Not Caesar's*, 58.
[38] Ibid., 59, italics in original.

of the church's powers with regard to the spiritual and the temporal realms. St Thomas Aquinas remarks that as head of his body, the church, Christ exerts both an interior and an exterior influence over the limbs. According to Maritain, the former corresponds to the interior influence of grace through the sacraments. The latter refers to the juridical power of the church, its laws and teachings, under the earthly direction of Christ's vicar, the successor of Peter. This exterior power applies in a direct way over spiritual things, that is, "the province of faith and morals, of salvation." Over temporal things the church has an indirect power, but only as those things affect the spiritual order of salvation of souls.[39]

In order to limit the church's direct power to a purely spiritual realm, Maritain must resort to an array of discriminations which sometimes fail to convince. Maritain first dispenses with the idea that the church ever did exercise direct power in temporal things, as some medieval theologians claimed. After the French edition of *Primauté du spirituel* was published, Austrian theologian Karl Winter accused Maritain of putting forth an ahistorical notion of the church's indirect power by ignoring the use of direct power over the temporal in both theory and practice in the Middle Ages. Maritain responded in the preface to the English edition of his book that, *"without ever adopting the doctrine of the 'direct power,'* [the church] made use of her 'indirect power' in such a way as might sometimes *seem* to suggest such a doctrine."[40] When Bellarmine in the sixteenth century put forth his theory of indirect ecclesiastical power over temporal rulers, therefore, he was only giving new formulation to the church's traditional doctrine, which had been expressed in different modalities according to historical circumstances.[41]

What Maritain means by "direct power" seems to be power over temporal things themselves for purely temporal interests. This can be surmised from his definition of indirect power as "the right of intervention which the spiritual power possesses *over temporal things themselves* from the strict point of view of moral and spiritual interests, when superior interests of that kind happen to be involved in the temporal event."[42] Such intervention is not done for the sake of some temporal good but rather for the avoidance of sin for the sake of souls. In other words, if the church intervenes in the temporal sphere, it can only be to remove some obstacle to the spiritual salvation of the individual soul or the freedom of the church which mystically binds those souls together.

---

[39] Ibid., 7–9.
[40] Ibid., x, italics in original.
[41] Ibid., viii–x.
[42] Ibid., xii, italics in original.

Two characteristics of Maritain's thought come through clearly in his theory of indirect power: the autonomy of the temporal and the superiority of the spiritual. According to Maritain the foundation of Christian political thought is Jesus' famous admonition to render to Caesar what is Caesar's and to God what is God's. "He thereby distinguished the two powers and so doing emancipated the souls of men."[43] The pagans had confused the two powers, absolutizing the state and making an idol of it. It would take until modern times for the state to achieve "full 'laic' stature,"[44] but the desacralization the state has undergone in Western history and the proper distinction of spiritual and temporal is nothing less than the working out of the Gospel idea. Says Maritain, "It is common knowledge that the distinction is the achievement of the Christian centuries and their glory."[45]

In Maritain's telling of Western history, Christianity was needed not only to distinguish the spiritual from the temporal but to subordinate the latter to the former. The ancients, Aristotle included, did not realize the freedom of the human act to escape all earthly ties and belong solely to God. The temporal must be subject to the spiritual because the ultimate end of the soul is God, not the state. The state is "the most perfect natural community . . . which mankind can form in this world,"[46] but it remains a natural community with a natural end.

> Although *formally considered as part of the State*, every act of his can be referred to the common good of the State, man, *considered in the absolutely peculiar and incommunicable quality of his liberty and as ordered directly to God as to his eternal end*, himself enjoying therefore the dignity of a whole (to a more eminent degree than the entire physical universe, because God is much more intimately the end of a soul than of the whole universe of bodies), under this formal aspect escapes inclusion in the political ordination.[47]

What we should note about this sentence (other than the obvious fact that it should have been three sentences) is the way in which the spiritual is identified with an interior, incommunicable realm, while the body is left to the state. Maritain has no intention of leaving the state to its own devices, and for that reason he stresses the subordination of the common good of the state to supernatural ends. St Thomas, he writes, compared the subordination of the

---

[43] Ibid., 2.
[44] Ibid., x.
[45] Ibid., 1.
[46] Ibid., 2.
[47] Ibid., 4, italics in original.

temporal to the spiritual to the subordination of the body to the soul.[48] Maritain considers it unproblematic to identify Thomas's medieval "temporal" with the modern "state," because the modern state in Maritain's view is simply the product of the proper differentiation of the temporal from the spiritual.

In this work Maritain is remarkably sanguine about the desacralization of the modern state, which he sees as the honored heir of the Christian era instead of its undertaker. While rightly applauding the extrication of the church from entanglement with coercive state power, Maritain seems unable to contemplate the possibility that the modern distinction of temporal and spiritual, body and soul, has also served to subjugate the church by creating a sphere of purely temporal power which is by definition property of the state alone. Thus Maritain tells the reader that the church in the Middle Ages had need to exercise indirect power because of the "menace which the imperial despotism held over the liberty of the spiritual." In the modern era, in contrast, Maritain believes the church will exercise her indirect power over the temporal only in the form of "*counsels* or *directions*, which the nations will always expect from her supreme moral authority."[49] Such counsel does not require strict obedience, Maritain contends, but rather operates on the same principle as Pius XI's Catholic Action, which is "supra-political," and "not unconcerned with things in the temporal and political order, but . . . affects them, not by a process of authority and jurisdiction, but by a vital and spiritual influence, animating from within and impregnating with Christian spirit the activities which concern them."[50] The church's temporal activity in the modern era is characterized by a spiritual penetration and animation of the temporal, not by a harsh discipline.

Where, then, does the condemnation of Action Française fit into this narrative? Maritain reports that, despite initial appearances, the condemnation was not an instance of the use of indirect power, since its object was not Action Française as a political party, but rather the party's teachings on the relations of politics, morals, and religion, which is a purely spiritual matter. The condemnation was therefore not an instance of indirect church intervention in temporal things, but a direct exercise of spiritual power obliging obedience. Any repercussions in the temporal realm were only secondary.[51]

Pius XI therefore acted for a spiritual good by making clear that linking the fortunes of the church to a political party is a confusion of temporal and

---

[48] Ibid., 14.
[49] Ibid., xii, italics in original.
[50] Ibid., xv; see also 26–9.
[51] Ibid., 46–54; xii.

spiritual which ultimately jeopardizes the church's role as saver of souls. According to Maritain, individual Catholics *as citizens* are entitled to support any party not condemned by the church. *As Catholics*, however, they are required to stand above every political party. The church, in other words, is a source of "metapolitical unity." As such "it is just and required by the law of God that there be union and collaboration between the church and the public authority which is the incarnation, so to speak, of the common good of the nation," but once a party has fallen from power, it is just one party among others, no longer represents the temporal unity of the nation, and thus no longer may claim the church as an ally.[52]

The church's collaboration with government naturally includes, in dangerous times, support for military preparedness. Indeed, Maritain claims,

> As Catholics in the different countries are as a rule and very normally the element most devoted to the principles of natural law, it is also understandable that from this point of view they should be conscious, as citizens, of specially grave duties and be the first to require from their governments all the strength of action and preparation necessary for the protection of their native land.[53]

While Catholics of the different countries are preparing to kill each other, Maritain would also have them simultaneously called to the task of uniting in spirit across national boundaries. Despite the apparent contradiction in the two duties, Maritain says, the best hope for peace is the strength of the nation and genuine spiritual communion among people of all nations.[54] The Catholic church, therefore, while ready to serve legitimate governments, cannot be bound to any temporal space. The Pope is the

> visible head of the mystical body, essentially supra-temporal, supra-political, supra-national, supra-cultural . . . His kingdom is not of this world, and, if he does possess a temporal sovereignty, it is as the minimum of body required precisely to assure the full liberty of the spiritual sovereignty peculiar to him; if he is sovereign of the Vatican City, it is precisely so that he shall be neither Italian nor American, neither French nor Chinese.[55]

Many of the ideas Jacques Maritain began working on in *The Things That Are Not Caesar's* (*Primauté du spirituel*) would appear again in his future works. In

[52] Ibid., 63–6.
[53] Ibid., 88.
[54] Ibid., 90.
[55] Ibid., xx.

a short work entitled *Religion and Culture*, published in France in 1930, Maritain again addressed the relationship of the spiritual and the temporal, this time exploring more of the philosophical background of the distinction. His main concern is to trace the relationship between "culture," which he defines as natural and particular, and "religion," which, if true, is supernatural and universal. He thus continues the theme of the extrication of the spiritual from the contingencies of the temporal which was so present in his work of three years before.

Culture, says Maritain, is the material and moral development which is proper to humans and leads to a dignified life on this earth. Insofar as its specifying object is terrestrial life, it belongs by nature to the temporal sphere. This is not to say that culture is essentially a stranger to the supernatural. On the contrary, Maritain quotes Charles Journet to the effect that there is no such thing as a state of "pure nature;" God has spread grace "like a tablecloth" over the whole world.[56] It cannot, however, be said that Maritain here allies himself with the Transcendental Thomists and the *Nouvelle Théologie* thinkers whose theology of a "graced" nature would eventually triumph at the Second Vatican Council. While he is concerned not to quarantine the temporal and the spiritual from each other, a more abiding interest of Maritain will be to guard jealously the freedom of the spiritual, in his view so much in danger of enslavement in the modern world. This accounts for much of the spleen he directed toward Vatican II and its champions in his 1966 book, *The Peasant of the Garonne*.

Culture is a joint venture of nature and reason, which belong to the temporal sphere. Culture is natural in that it obeys the deepest inclinations of human nature, oriented by the natural law to God.[57] Culture must therefore be subordinated to its true spiritual end. A culture or civilization so ordered will perform its earthly work in an elevated fashion. True religion should penetrate the culture, but this is not to say that religion and culture must be one. Only what Maritain calls "the imbecile dogma of positivist sociology" would reduce all religion to a mere byproduct of a particular social clan.[58] In fact, says Maritain, it is pagan civilization which absorbs religion into the culture, deifying the state as well as shackling religion to the contingent particulars of a local tribe or nation. What sets Israel, and thus Christianity, apart is its universalism; the Decalogue appeals to the consciences of all

---

[56] Jacques Maritain, *Religion and Culture*, trans. J.F. Scanlan, in *Essays in Order*, ed. Christopher Dawson (New York: Sheed & Ward, 1940, 9–10).

[57] Ibid., 3–8.

[58] Ibid., 33.

humankind, the new Jerusalem is to be a purely spiritual "country of souls," and the Kingdom of God is found in the hearts of people of all nations.[59]

If Christianity cannot be bound to a particular culture or civilization, then neither can the church itself be considered a culture. "Culture or civilisation . . . is rooted in the soil of natural life, whereas the Church has her roots in the sky of the supernatural life."[60] The church is not a party, not a state, not a culture, and nothing is gained for the Kingdom of God by any temporal conquest in the name of Catholicism. The death of Christendom, says Maritain, should be seen as a repudiation once and for all of "sociologism," a liberation for the church from all the dead weight of temporal culture which held down the Spirit for so long.[61]

So what are we now to make of this liberation? Should the Catholic reject "culture" and attend only to the life of the spirit, far from the unclean world? Surely not; to eschew culture is to eschew reason and the natural law implanted in God's creation.[62] The temporal is to be used as a means for the spiritual, keeping in mind a certain hierarchy of means. "Rich temporal means" are those heavily implicated in matter, such as state administration and the fighting of wars. They involve a certain expectation of tangible, worldly success, and as such are remote from pure poverty of spirit, yet to reject them would be absurd; "they are necessary, part of the natural stuff of life. Religion must consent to receive their assistance."[63] Nevertheless, "poor temporal means" are higher, closer to pure spirit, and therefore less encumbered by matter and less visible. Such are the works of Mozart and St Thomas, Dante and St Paul. At the summit of the hierarchy is Christ himself, the "spiritual man *par excellence*," who gave no speeches, wrote no books – "that again was a means of action too heavily weighted with matter" – and relied only on the poverty of preaching.[64] The world is saved by the purely spiritual, but the spiritual is served by temporal means.

Culture, then, though sinful, is not to be despised. Maritain reminds us that the book of history is written under God's will, even though at times Satan holds the pen. More specifically, Western culture is still subject, willy-nilly, to the ferment of the Gospel leaven planted in it so many centuries ago. The modern emphasis on subjectivity and freedom, while falsely turned inward on

[59] Ibid., 10–12.
[60] Ibid., 35.
[61] Ibid., 38–51.
[62] Ibid., 5.
[63] Ibid., 46.
[64] Ibid., 47–8.

itself and away from God, is nevertheless to be reckoned a gain.[65] Maritain recognizes the fragility of such advances; "be that as it may, the idea of slavery or torture or the use of military methods to impose constraint upon consciences and a certain number of similar ideas are, it would appear, spontaneously repugnant at the present day to more people than formerly."[66]

We can forgive Maritain his *faux pas* regarding torture and modernity insofar as he merely errs in historical judgment or fails to predict the ferocity with which torture would reappear a few decades hence. What is important about his analysis is not what kind of appraisal he puts on the modern world; he is actually quite harsh in his critiques. What is truly interesting is the way this historical judgment fits into his conclusion that culture as a whole cannot be rejected. In other words, he sets up the problem such that there is a monolithic "culture" structured by the state and coterminous with the temporal sphere, confronted by a purely spiritual "religion" which is the responsibility of the church. Meant to be free by essence from entrapment in "culture," yet unable by natural law simply to reject "culture," the church is bound to work on "culture" spiritually, to penetrate it, transform it, and redirect it toward God.

The result is to be a "New Christendom." Modernity has swept away the old Christendom, turning its back on the church but at the same time freeing the mystical body from its cultural encumbrances and entanglements with the state. Where others see ruin, Maritain sees opportunity. He sees a new and more true Christian culture, no longer confused with the church. The proper autonomy and independence of culture from the church is to be recognized, yet at the same time the Christian spirit will impregnate the culture and the organs of the state.

> [I]n the new world, an authentical Christian culture will arise, "a culture no longer gathered and assembled, as in the Middle Ages, in a homogeneous body of civilisation occupying a tiny privileged portion of the inhabited earth, but scattered over the whole surface of the globe – a living network of hearths of the Christian life disseminated among the nations within the great supra-cultural unity of the Church."[67]

The church is scattered, the better to make "culture" Christian.

---

[65] Ibid., 14–23; 50–2.

[66] Ibid., 16.

[67] Ibid., 28. Maritain quotes the passage in quotations from his earlier work entitled *St Thomas Aquinas*.

3 New Christendom

Jacques Maritain's most complete blueprint for the New Christendom is laid out in *Integral Humanism*, the most influential of his books for his Latin American followers. First published in book form in 1936, *Integral Humanism* originated as a series of lectures in Spanish at the University of Santander in August 1934. With the rise of Fascism and Bolshevism, Maritain sensed that the post-World War I peace was only the eye of the storm. His writings from this period betray a sense of urgency to envision a "new historical ideal" capable of nothing less than saving Europe.

Laid out before him was the specter of a failed bourgeois individualism melting into collectivisms of both left and right. His theoretical solution to the problem was ingenious. Based on the distinction of temporal and spiritual, Maritain made a corollary distinction between the individual and the person. As an individual, one participates in the social, political, and economic activity proper to the temporal sphere, and subordinates oneself to the temporal common good as structured by the state. The common good is not a mere collection of private goods, but neither does it amount to a dissolution of the human subject into the collective will, because the human being in the Christian tradition is simultaneously a *person*, a spiritual whole oriented toward God whose dignity transcends any ultimate claims the state makes on her. The common good is a good of human *persons* in communion with each other, and it is common both to the whole and to the parts. At the same time, then, the human is both a natural and a supernatural being, and can enter into the common projects of building the earthly city without thereby surrendering her inviolable freedom.[68] Maritain calls his vision of human being a "theocentric humanism," in which human being finds its center not in itself but in God.

Such an overcoming of both individualism and collectivism depends on a proper understanding of the ends of the temporal and spiritual spheres. The spiritual sphere is directed to an eternal end, and for this reason transcends the temporal. At the same time as it is subordinated to the spiritual, however, the temporal has its own natural "infravalent" end which is possessed of its own proper autonomy. This, says Maritain, is a "real historical gain" over medieval Christendom, which tended to view the temporal as a mere means, or instrumental cause, for the spiritual. In a new Christendom, the temporal would be a

---

[68] Jacques Maritain, *Integral Humanism*, trans. Joseph W. Evans (New York: Charles Scribner's Sons, 1968, 9–10. See also Jacques Maritain, *Scholasticism and Politics* (London: Geoffrey Bles, 1940), 55–6.

"secondary principal cause," that is, one with its own immediate ends to accomplish.[69] What this means in effect is that there is trash to be picked up, businesses to be run, wars to be fought. These things are not our ultimate end, but neither are they simply cut loose from any spiritual significance. The spiritual life of persons is to animate and superelevate all their temporal activities. Reciprocally, the earthly ends of the temporal order are meant to serve the eternal end of the person, to facilitate the attainment of supernatural life with God.[70]

The New Christendom is a lay and secular civilization. For Maritain "secular" does not indicate the absence of Christianity or the strict privatization of religious life, but rather that the church itself will refuse to be bound to particular cultural forms and will not wish to direct the administration of temporal affairs. The concrete technical aspects of trash collecting and war fighting are best left to the laypeople who know how to do it right. Those laypeople, insofar as they are Christians and members of the church, will bring the values and social teachings of the church to bear on the concrete tasks in front of them. The Christian, however, "finds himself engaged more and more not as Christian or as member of the church, but as member of the temporal city, I mean as Christian member of this city."[71] The distinction to be made is between the action of Christians and of Christians *as such*:

> on the plane of the spiritual, I appear before [others] *as a Christian as such*, and to this extent I engage Christ's Church; . . . on the plane of the temporal, I do not act *as a Christian as such*, but I should act *as Christian*, engaging only myself, not the Church, but engaging my whole self. . . who by my faith, my baptism, and my confirmation, and insignificant as I may be, have the vocation of infusing into the world, wherever I am, a Christian sap.[72]

The distinction Maritain wants to make becomes clearer in his discussion of Catholic Action. Here Christians gather as Christians for a dose of Christian sap, but they do not engage in concrete political analysis. Catholic Action is an organization directed by the hierarchy of the church, which has no definite political solutions for social problems such as inflation and unemployment but rather seeks to create in laypeople "an essentially Christian state of mind."[73] Catholic Action strictly speaking is not of the temporal sphere. Once Christians do enter the temporal to engage in political action, it is important

[69] Maritain, *Integral Humanism*, 176–7.
[70] Ibid., 97–8.
[71] Ibid., 119.
[72] Ibid., 294.
[73] Ibid., 269. Also Maritain, *Scholasticism and Politics*, 166.

that they form parties which are not Christian parties as such, but rather parties of Christian inspiration in which all, Christian and non-Christian alike, are welcome. Thus no single party can claim the church's backing, Christians militate in a pluralism of parties across the political spectrum, and the supra-political position of the church is secured.[74] For Christians, unity should be the rule on the spiritual plane, and diversity the rule on the temporal. "When the objective is the earthly life of men . . . it is normal that a unanimity whose center is of the supratemporal order should break up, and that Christians who receive Communion at the same table should find themselves divided in the body politic."[75]

If politics is an affair of non-Christians as such and Christians who do not act as Christians as such, then in what sense can this be called a Christian social order? Maritain stresses that his embrace of pluralism is not to be a simple reproduction of liberal tolerance. The New Christendom is not indifferent to truth, nor does it consider the right to propagate falsehoods to be a good in itself. Tolerance in the new order is not dogmatic, but a prudential respect for extraterritoriality of the conscience of the person.[76] The juridic structure of the body politic would not be indifferent to truth, but would be "oriented" toward "the form of common life that is best in accord with the supratemporal interests of the person."[77] Note that unity in the body politic is not posited at the supernatural or dogmatic level, but only at the level of the temporal common good which serves the person's supratemporal development. Christianity will enter the body politic not through a confessional state but through the leadership of virtuous individual Christians. If this political and social order is to be integrally and vitally Christian, it will be "because the bearers of this Christian conception will have had enough spiritual energy, enough force and political prudence to practically exhibit to men capable of comprehension that such a conception is in conformity with sound reason and with the common good."[78]

The key words here are "prudence" and "practically." The Christian politician will have to convince his fellows on a practical level, without resorting to explicitly Christian language. Maritain rejects any attempts to secure the unity of the social body in a common profession of faith or

---

[74] Maritain, *Integral Humanism*, 258–64. See also Maritain, "Carta sobre la independencia," 70–86.
[75] Maritain, *Integral Humanism*, 301.
[76] Ibid., 165–72, 180–1.
[77] Ibid., 167–8.
[78] Ibid., 174.

philosophy. He rightly points out that such an attempt to secure minimal theoretical agreement among different creeds and convictions only produces "intellectual mediocrity and cowardice, weakening minds and betraying the rights of truth."[79] The Christian politician proceeds not on the basis of some watered-down platitudes, but on the basis of the full Christian truth. However, for Maritain that truth must remain interior to him or her, for the Christian truth is not directly applicable to concrete problems in the political sphere. Indeed here we find the main reason that Maritain so emphasizes the prudential nature of practical moral science of which politics is a part. Practical morality for Maritain is not simply a matter of applying moral principles, given by the church, to particular cases. In practical morality, politics especially, the individual, *inspired* by the teachings of the church, makes prudential decisions within the freedom from direct church intervention that the autonomy of the temporal affords.

Maritain is attempting to walk a tightrope between Constantinianism and liberalism. He claims that his pluralist body politic, "though much less concentrated than the mediaeval body politic, is much more concentrated than the 'liberal' one."[80] What he means by "concentration" is the state's legal duty and ability to instill virtue and pursue the common good. On the one hand, in an attempt to decentralize state power and direct the church's effort to civil society, Maritain cites Pius XI's "principle of subsidiarity": " 'It is an injustice, a grave evil and a disturbance of right order for a larger and higher organization to arrogate to itself functions which can be performed efficiently by smaller and lower bodies.' "[81] Maritain envisions a pluralism of intermediate associations – professional societies, cooperatives, unions, corporations – between the individual and the state. Maritain's political ideas in the 1930s drew inspiration from Pius XI's suggestions on the establishment of guilds which would operate – contrary to the Fascist model – with as much independence as possible from the state. Such associations would limit the power of the state by adjudicating potential conflicts within natural communities without need of recourse to the state.[82] On the other hand, Maritain still relies on the state to be much more "concentrated" than the liberal state, in order to avoid the dissolute fate of bourgeois liberalism. Law in his new order will regain "its moral function, its function as *pedagogue of freedom*."[83] The state

---

[79] Ibid.
[80] Ibid., 183.
[81] Ibid., 164. The quote is from Pius XI's encyclical *Quadragesimo Anno*.
[82] Ibid., 162–202.
[83] Ibid.

will be secular, and all faiths will be tolerated, yet it will pursue a "general line of legislation leading towards the virtuous life," *oriented* by natural law and Christian law.[84] Individual Christians work within the pluralist body politic not to realize the Kingdom of God on earth, but to establish the temporal common good. The Kingdom is eternal, and Christians look for it "outside time."[85] Though inspired by the Gospel, the law is a temporal thing, entirely within time; its task is to realize an earthly community, imperfect yet oriented toward respect for the dignity of the human person and her spiritual vocation.[86]

For the pagans, Maritain tells us, " 'holy' was synonymous with 'sacred,' i.e. with that which is physically, visibly, socially in the service of God. . . . The Gospel profoundly changed this by interiorizing in the heart of man – in the secret of the invisible relations between the divine personality and the human personality – the moral life and the life of sanctity."[87] The purity of the Kingdom of God is thereby removed from historical time; those engaged in the building of culture "are engaged in time and in the vicissitudes of time. Moreover, it can be said that none of them has clean hands."[88] The Christian cannot flinch from incarnation in history, but in the darkest hours must make use even of cruel and terrible means, provided they not be intrinsically evil.

> It is clear that force and, generally speaking, what I have called the carnal means of war are not intrinsically bad, because they can be just. Theologians and moralists explain to us on what conditions these are just, and thereby they perform a work of mercy, enabling us to live on this earth. They do not take the lead, it is not their business to open new doors to violence; but once these doors are open, they justify what can be done, and give us light in order to advance into the dark defiles of history . . . The worst anguish for the Christian is precisely to know that there can be justice in employing horrible means.[89]

Presumably Maritain would consider torture intrinsically evil means. Nevertheless, one shudders at the following: "We cannot touch the flesh of the human being without staining our fingers. To stain our fingers is not to stain our hearts."[90]

---

[84] Ibid., 167.
[85] Ibid., 101.
[86] Ibid., 203–4.
[87] Ibid., 124.
[88] Ibid., 98.
[89] Ibid., 246–8.
[90] Ibid., 249.

Despite Maritain's avowed aversion to the individualism of modernity, in trying to protect the person from the intrusions of collectivities he does not seem able to resist the pull of interiority and the essential individuality of the spiritual life. He is undoubtedly a foe of the modern disease of privatization which permits the same person to obey Christ on Sunday and Machiavelli the rest of the week. His desire with regard to the temporal and spiritual planes is to "distinguish in order to unite," not to separate them.[91] Nevertheless, the spiritual is in need of transmission and translation *through the individual* before it can touch on the social.

In *Integral Humanism* Maritain tries to clarify the relationship between the individual and the social by introducing a third plane of activity intermediate to the temporal and spiritual planes. There are, says Maritain, spiritual truths which provide general principles for Christian political life but do not engage in the particular contingencies of the political. At the same time, there are spiritual matters such as marriage and education which are "mixed" with the concerns of the earthly city. Both of these kinds of spiritual concerns belong to this third plane, which is that of the spiritual as touching on the temporal. This third plane belongs essentially to the spiritual order, and differs from the purely spiritual plane only by an "accidental" distinction; the "intermediary plane is the plane of the spiritual itself as inflected on the side of the temporal and joining the latter."[92] Maritain is desperately trying to maintain a spatial distinction between the spiritual and temporal, but his introduction of a third plane should make the reader question the terms under which the distinction is offered.

Maritain identifies this intermediary plane, which is the plane of Catholic Action, as a plane of social action, but, as he says, only "a *certain* social action."[93] In his *Scholasticism and Politics*, published four years after *Integral Humanism*, Maritain emphasizes that the third plane covers Christian social action but not social activity as such. "[T]he social is by its nature concerned with the second level, the level of the temporal, on which we act as members of the earthly city, and on which we ought to act *in a Christian manner*, on our own responsibility and on our personal initiative, at our risk and peril, but not *professedly* as Christians and sent by the church."[94] When Maritain speaks of "social" Catholicism, therefore, he does it in the same way as Pius XI. Christian social action provides the individual Christian with principles and orientations

---

[91] See, e.g. Maritain, *Scholasticism and Politics*, 159.
[92] Maritain, *Integral Humanism*, 296–7.
[93] Maritain, *Scholasticism and Politics*, 165.
[94] Ibid., italics in original.

which can be applied in different ways to the social plane. The spiritual life itself, however, is interior and can never properly be socialized, even though the spiritual life is supported by and enriches social life. The church as well is a "mystical" body, not properly a social body, since the social as such belongs essentially to the temporal.

It is odd that this should be the case in Maritain's scheme, given that the temporal is also the realm of the individual. When Maritain writes of the social, however, he means the society of individuals who are subject to the purely natural laws of association. As an individual, the human being is corporeal and "subject to the determination of the physical world."[95] Individuality, as Aquinas taught, is rooted in matter and the material world. As a person, however, the human being is free, spiritual, directly oriented to God, and transcends the natural world; "the Western metaphysical tradition defines the person by independence."[96] Here we find a strong resemblance not to Aquinas but to Kant; as phenomenon the human being is determined, as noumenon he is free. Maritain intends to preserve the freedom and transcendence of the human person, but in so doing he seriously qualifies and limits the possibility of the supernatural acting directly in the world. For example, he claims that Christians working out their salvation in their private lives do, by their resistance to hate and testimony to love, have an imperceptible but real effect on the temporal world. However, this effect belongs to a "higher causality" which, however important, "does not *suffice* for the development of social life required by nature and by Providence."[97] In private we are to exercise the natural and supernatural virtues of Christian life. In public, however, we need the natural virtues ("guided and elevated by the supernatural ones") proper to social and political life by which a direct causality is exerted on the temporal plane.[98] The theological virtues – faith, hope, love – are denied any direct access to temporal action, and in the political sphere one must also discipline oneself not to expect miracles.

Maritain's distinction between the individual and the person is the basis for his theory on human rights, which he lays out in his 1943 book *The Rights of Man and Natural Law*, the most important source for Catholic thinking on human rights in Latin America in the three decades following its publication. This is Maritain's first extended treatment of rights, which he had heretofore regarded as of liberal, and therefore questionable, ancestry. World War II,

[95] Ibid., 49–50.
[96] Ibid., 51.
[97] Ibid., 184.
[98] Ibid., 184–5.

however, marked a shift in Maritain's thinking toward a more favorable view of American-style liberalism.[99] A theory of universal human rights purged of its liberal basis in human self-rule became an important part of Maritain's agenda for the reconstruction of the post-war world.

It was not difficult to fit a scheme of rights onto the framework of his previous work. Absolute and inviolable human rights are based on the human person's status as a totality, a whole which is not merely part of a larger collectivity. The individual as a temporal being will always take part in the common project of the body politic, but the person remains a whole with a dignity that transcends the state. As Maritain puts it, "Man finds himself by subordinating himself to the group, and the group attains its goal only by serving man and by realizing that man has secrets which escape the group and a vocation which the group does not encompass."[100] Maritain hoped thereby to create a reciprocity between the individual and the state, rather than use rights as a mere trump card of the isolated individual against the state. The problem with liberal rights, according to Maritain, is their roots in the Rousseauian idea that "man" must "obey only himself." When such rights proved illusory, many turned against the idea of rights altogether.[101] Maritain would refound the language of absolute rights on the person's supernatural relationship with God, the Absolute.[102]

Maritain defines natural law as "the ensemble of things to do and not to do which follow therefrom in *necessary* fashion, and *from the simple fact that man is man*."[103] If human rights are those things due a person just by virtue of being a human person, then it follows that human rights should be based on the natural law. The natural law is not a detailed code to be read off nature by human reason, but rather an unwritten law in human nature according to which we attune ourselves to the true ends of the human being. Consciousness of this law, implicit in pagan antiquity, was awakened by the Gospel and made explicit throughout the world by Christianity. Therefore, human rights in Maritain's conception are universal, and yet find their true source in the Christian religion.[104]

---

[99] See his *Reflections on America* (New York: Charles Scribner's Sons, 1958); also Amato, *Mounier and Maritain*, 146–63, and Sigmund, "Maritain on Politics," 156.

[100] Jacques Maritain, *The Rights of Man and Natural Law*, trans. Doris C. Anson (New York: Gordian Press, 1971, 18.

[101] Ibid., 41–3; 66–7. See also Jacques Maritain, *Christianity and Democracy* (London: Geoffrey Bles, 1945), 47–8.

[102] Maritain, *The Rights of Man and Natural Law*, 1–5.

[103] Ibid., 63, italics in original.

[104] Ibid., 60–8.

As part of the natural law, human rights come under the purview of the state, the source of authority on the temporal, natural plane. Of course, Maritain as always hastens to subordinate the state's power to the supernatural inviolability of the person. The result in theory is an elegant balance: the state pursues the good of the commonality and enforces rights and obligations, but at the same time the state itself is limited by, and in service to, those very rights of the person. Thus the state cannot intrude in the realm of the soul and the conscience, the universe of science and wisdom and art and religion, the personal freedom to live where and with whom one wishes, all of which belong to the eternal and absolute order which stands above the political.[105] But to this Maritain adds some important qualifiers. In the face of a threat to the state, it has the right to requisition our bodies and force us to risk our lives in a just war. Furthermore, if one's chosen "religious path goes so very far afield that it leads to acts repugnant to natural law and the security of the State, the latter has the right to interdict and apply sanctions against these acts. This does not mean that it has authority in the realm of conscience."[106] Although Maritain again acknowledges the pedagogical function of the state, the fact that it "tends to develop moral virtues,"[107] he still claims that the state is not and cannot be the standard of conscience. What is apparent, though, is that given the importance of the state in the construction of the common good, the security of the state tends to become the condition of possibility for the development of conscience. The state, as in liberalism, becomes the primary guarantor of human rights.

We find Maritain acknowledging this in his *Man and the State*, published in 1951 and often seen as the benchmark of his turn toward American liberalism in the post-war world.[108]

> I should finally like to point out that the people have a special need of the State, precisely because the State is a particular agency specializing in the care of the whole, and thus has normally to defend and protect the people, their rights and the improvement of their lives against the selfishness and particularism of privileged groups and classes.[109]

---

[105] Ibid., 76–80.
[106] Ibid., 82 n. 1.
[107] Ibid., 77.
[108] E.g. Amato, *Mounier and Maritain*, 157–8.
[109] Jacques Maritain, *Man and the State* (Chicago: University of Chicago Press, 1951), 26.

At the same time Maritain was far from lapsing into a simple statism; indeed, the purpose of *Man and the State* was precisely to limit the state's power by attacking the entire idea of sovereignty. According to Maritain the state is neither to be confused with nor separated from the body politic. The state is simply the topmost part of the body politic, that part which has as its special function to promote the good of the whole, that is, the common good, and to maintain public order through a monopoly on the means of coercion.[110]

Maritain tells an interesting story about the rise of the sovereign state in Western society. In the medieval period, the prince was possessed of supreme power within his realm, but medieval theorists understood this as a vicarious exercise of the people's natural right to self-government. In the modern period, however, the concept of sovereignty was invented by Bodin to represent a *transfer* of the right of government to the prince, who transcends the body politic. Hobbes and Rousseau as well understood sovereignty as the people's abandonment of their power to a fictional Man or a General Will, which stood above and over against the people.[111]

Although medieval jurists in a remote way helped prepare the ground for the modern notion of sovereignty, it was essentially a creation of Bodin and the age of absolute monarchies in the sixteenth and seventeenth centuries.[112] Maritain acknowledges that the very word and concept "state" only appeared in the early modern era. Nevertheless, he wishes to separate the development of the state from the development of sovereignty as two movements, one positive and one negative, that unluckily got mixed up together. "According to a historical pattern unfortunately most recurrent, both the normal development of the State – which was in itself a sound and genuine progress – and the development of the spurious – absolutist – juridical and philosophical conception of the State took place at the same time."[113] The concept of the state as a sovereign whole was adopted by democratic theorists as well, preying "like a parasite" on true democratic principles. Liberal democracy tended to absorb all the individual wills of its subjects into the state and substitute the state for the people, alienating the latter from the political process. The wars of the nineteenth century were the result of the absolutization of the democratic state. The wars of the twentieth century, worse still, were the result of the full flower of the absolute state in totalitarian regimes of left and right.[114]

---

[110] Ibid., 9–24, 40–2.
[111] Ibid., 14–19, 28–53.
[112] Ibid., 36–7.
[113] Ibid., 14–15.
[114] Ibid., 14–19.

What is needed for the state to become a true respecter and protector of rights and liberties, according to Maritain, is a limitation of the state to its true and proper function as the topmost part of the body politic. But this does not mean, he continues, a deprecation of the phenomenal growth of the state in the modern era, which is part of "normal progress." The state is the necessary instrument for the realization of social justice and the common good. Since the nineteenth century especially, large-scale state intervention has been needed to compensate for the rampant disregard for the basic rights of the human person. The ideal, however, is not a plodding bureaucracy managing in detail the enterprises of the various organs of civil society, but rather a state which merely supervises and regulates these autonomous activities for the sake of the common good.[115] As long as the state is limited to the temporal and is not sovereign, then all people should be able to participate in its activities without jeopardizing or compromising their spiritual beliefs.[116]

As Maritain realizes, however, it takes some kind of faith, some sort of ideological glue, to get people to work together for something as complex as the common good. Democracy implies fundamental agreement on at least some things, such as the importance of freedom. The problem with bourgeois liberal democracy, he contends, is that it claimed to be neutral with regard to *all* beliefs, even the belief in democracy itself. Small wonder that bourgeois democracies had succumbed to identity crises in the early twentieth century. In the personalist democracy with which Maritain wanted to replace them, there would have to be some kind of common belief, a "creed of freedom." And yet such a creed would not be a religious one, given the pluralism of religious beliefs in contemporary society. It would have to be, then, a "democratic secular faith," a churchless creed which belongs strictly to the temporal plane. People would agree on a basic charter of rights and obligations for citizens and the state, including basic positions regarding justice, equality, respect for religious freedom, love of country, human dignity, and so on. They would agree regardless of the diverse justifications they would give for holding such things dear.[117]

Maritain recalls a meeting of the French delegation to UNESCO in which people of conflicting ideologies came up with a common list of human rights. They could agree provided they were not asked *why*.[118] Because human rights

---

[115] Ibid., 19–23.
[116] Ibid., 108–9.
[117] Ibid., 109–13.
[118] Ibid., 76–80; and Jacques Maritain, *The Range of Reason* (New York: Charles Scribner's Sons, 1952), 165–72.

are based on the natural law, we should not be surprised to find that people should come to an initial understanding of them not on the basis of theoretical rationality but by what he calls the "*inclinations* of human nature."[119] This does not mean that the Gospel is unimportant to the foundation of democratic faith and human rights. On the contrary, Maritain contends that Christianity is the true justification for the "creed of freedom," and the more the body politic is penetrated by Christian conviction on the spiritual plane, the more it will adhere to the democratic secular faith on the temporal. This is because the democratic faith "has taken shape in human history as a result of the Gospel inspiration awakening the 'naturally Christian' potentialities of common secular consciousness, even among the diversity of spiritual lineages . . . "[120] Maritain's post-war writings focus less on the rechristianization of Western society and more on the conviction that Western society is *already* Christian in its marrow, whether it recognizes it or not.

4 The Disappearance of the Church

This short journey through some relevant aspects of Maritain's political thought should, I hope, give the reader a sense of the audacity of Maritain's attempt to save European civilization. Although audacious it may be, it is a project born not of ego but of sanctity. Jacques Maritain was a great man and a holy man, not possessing but possessed by a vision of individual freedom and common good under a limited state and a benevolent God. Hemmed in by atheisms, individualisms, and collectivisms, Maritain took the valid insights proper to each and imagined a new civilization which would correct the errors of both present and past. My task in the remainder of this chapter will be to diagnose the failure of this project in one context, that of Chile, a context which may be instructive for Christian political practice in other contexts.

At least part of the difficulty with translating Maritain's ideas into the Chilean context is that they were largely imagined for Europe between the wars. By the time Maritain started to address specifically political problems, Europe was becoming painfully aware that the Treaty of Versailles had brought the curtain down on the first act of European hostilities only to allow the stage to be set for a second, bloodier, act. Maritain's emphasis on the transnational character of the church is at least understandable given the antagonisms among nations in Europe between the wars. The same dynamic

[119] Maritain, *Man and the State*, 80–97.
[120] Ibid., 113.

was absent from the Latin American context. Also absent was the virulent atheism and secularism Maritain encountered in Europe. Maritain's removal of the church from political activity was in many ways a *fait accompli* in Europe in which Maritain found great positive potential. In Latin America the situation was decidedly different.

In his landmark 1971 book *A Theology of Liberation*, Gustavo Gutiérrez voiced what has become the standard view among church progressives of Maritain's impact in Latin America. The New Christendom mentality represents an important stage in the growth of Latin American Catholicism toward becoming a true liberating force. It freed the laity to become agents for change by recognizing the autonomy of the "world" from church domination. Maritain imbibed from St Thomas an appreciation for the ends of nature, which is not overcome by grace, but perfected. Maritain's work, according to Gutiérrez, made possible an autonomous political action based on justice and human rights rather than on the agenda of the church.[121]

Nevertheless, Gutiérrez's gratitude to Maritain has its limits. The New Christendom approach "amounted to a timid and basically ambiguous attempt."[122] On the one hand it bred moderates, children of the elites with an increasing tendency toward modernization and bourgeois developmentalism. The distinction of planes model allowed them to maintain the fiction of a "lyrical spiritual unity of all Christians" in a church perched above the political fray. On the other hand, many of those involved in Catholic Action, especially the youth, got their first taste of social awareness there and then found themselves wanting to make commitments more radical than the hierarchy controlling the lay movements could allow. They wanted to commit themselves on the temporal plane, the realm of the political, but the distinction of planes model would not allow them to do so "as Christians as such" and remain in Catholic Action. As Gutiérrez rightly points out, Catholic Action went into crisis when the youth movements discovered that they "could not separate religious formation from political formation."[123] They discovered through experience that these distinctions were fictional.

Although Maritain's model had been taken on by progressives in the 1930s and 1940s to distance the church from alliances with the Conservative Party, by the 1960s it was being used to stifle the more radical elements of the church

---

[121] Gustavo Gutiérrez, *A Theology of Liberation*, revised edn, trans. Sister Caridad Inda and John Eagleson (Maryknoll, NY: Orbis Books, 1988), 35–6.
[122] Ibid., 36.
[123] Ibid., 36–41. Gutiérrez was involved in Catholic Action as national advisor to the Catholic Student Movement in Peru.

by keeping the church out of political activity which – because belonging to the "temporal sphere" – was out of the church's competence. As Gutiérrez comments, the church's supposedly "supra-political" position as "soul of human society" was in fact a political option in favor of the status quo and against direct action on behalf of the poor. "The distinction of planes banner has changed hands. Until a few years ago it was defended by the vanguard; now it is held aloft by power groups, many of whom are in no way involved with any commitment to the Christian faith."[124]

Gutiérrez's criticisms of the distinction of planes hit their mark. Unfortunately, in trying to get beyond Maritain and articulate a true Christian theology of the political, Gutiérrez often only compounds the problems in Maritain's thought. Gutiérrez believes the New Christendom model fails because in it the church "continues to be, in a certain way, at the center of the work of salvation. A certain ecclesiastical narcissism is still evident."[125] A theology that would move beyond this approach must jettison the idea of "a society inspired by Christian principles"; Maritain's "profane Christendom" is a Christendom nonetheless. In the modern world, secularization has opened our eyes to a human-centered approach to history. Humans now see themselves as agents of their own destiny; God has created the world as the proper sphere for human activity and has established humankind as "lord of this creation." Rather than see the world in terms of the church, today the church is seen in the world's terms. "In the past, the church used the world for its own ends; today many Christians – and non-Christians – ask themselves if they should, for example, use the influence of church to accelerate the process of transformation of social structures."[126]

But Gutiérrez claims that the full autonomy of the world is not the only positive result of contemporary theology. He says that Vatican II endorses this more positive attitude toward the world by pointing to the omnipresence of God's grace in the world. Therefore we are no longer dealing with two histories, one sacred and one profane. The history of salvation is a unity; we cannot properly distinguish two separate realms, spiritual and temporal, with different ends, one transcendent and the other natural. The lines between church and world are blurred. There can be no state of pure nature; all nature is already "graced." The human being can be construed with Rahner as "transnatural," not possessed as such of supernatural life yet oriented toward it.[127]

---

[124] Ibid., 41.
[125] Ibid., 36. A version of this critique of Maritain by Chilean commentators is found in Huerta and Pacheco, *La iglesia chilena y los cambios sociopolíticos*, 154–7.
[126] Gutiérrez, *A Theology of Liberation*, 42.
[127] Ibid., 43–6.

These appear to be two contradictory movements: the world is autonomous, yet permeated by God's grace. How can the boundaries between church and world disappear and yet the world claim autonomy? It can only be because, as Gutiérrez says, the church has now become part of the world's story. The world has absorbed the church into itself. This signals both the final destruction of a church practice of the political, and the abandonment of specifically Christian discourse in favor of a social scientific reading of reality. The disappearance of the church as a social body, already begun by Maritain, is completed in Gutiérrez's reconstrual of the church–world axis. As John Milbank puts it, for this line of thought

> to take account of the social is to take account of a factor essentially 'outside' the church and the basic concerns of theology. . . . The social is an autonomous sphere which does not need to turn to theology for its self-understanding, and yet it is already a grace-imbued sphere, and therefore it is *upon* pre-theological sociology or Marxist social theory, that theology must be founded. In consequence, a theological critique of society becomes impossible. And, therefore what we are offered is *anything but* a true theology of the political.[128]

If the true legacy of Vatican II is the breaking down of false spiritual/political, clerical/lay dichotomies – and not simply the emptying out of the church into the world – then we must go beyond Gutiérrez and liberationist thought in order to mount a critique of Maritain and the New Christendom. I will attempt to locate a Christian contribution to liberation from oppressive state disciplines not in the subsumption of the church under supposedly autonomous social processes but instead in the church's own character as a *contrast society*, a counter-performance of the body to that of the state. To do so I will need first to rebut the idea that the church is not properly considered a social body in its own right.

A general definition of "social body" has its limits in that, from a Christian point of view, the church is not simply one of a generic group of such bodies whose dynamics can be studied by an independent "science" such as sociology. My only point in calling the church "social" is to emphasize that it is not to be reduced to an interiorized "spirituality" in the hearts of its members. The church is a body *sui generis*. As a body it cannot be analyzed apart from the body of Christ, which I will do in chapter 5. Maritain, therefore, is right for the wrong reasons when he claims that the church in its essence can never be subjected to sociological critique.[129] Maritain would protect the

---

[128] John Milbank, *Theology and Social Theory* (Oxford: Basil Blackwell, 1990), 208.
[129] Maritain, *Religion and Culture*, 36.

mystical body from reduction to a merely natural community subject to the same laws of power as the state and other temporal bodies. Instead of challenging the autonomy of the temporal, however, his thought has the effect of promoting it, aiming at the same time to carve out an untouchable "spiritual" space for the church which is both interior to the person and transcendent to the state. Maritain does not allow the possibility that the Gospel may have its own bodily performances, its own "politics," its own set of social practices which are neither purely otherworldly nor reducible to some "purely temporal" discourse.

The New Christendom model found in Catholic Action and Maritain is unable to envision the church as anything like a "culture," that is, a set of specific social practices. For Maritain, his laudable desire to protect the church from the encroachments of the state leads him to posit a dualism of "religion" and "culture" which obeys a Kantian logic of noumenal and phenomenal. A culture is part and parcel of the contingent, the phenomenal, the relative, the realm of conflict and compromise. Religion, on the other hand, belongs to the supernatural, the realm of a kind of noumenal freedom which, as *supernatural* is not subject to phenomenal cause and effect, but also cannot directly intervene as cause. As a result the supernatural virtues are in effect excluded from the "realm of the dirty hands." For this reason Maritain's thought has been charged by several Chilean commentators with a tendency towards political "Machiavellianism."[130]

At this point Maritain would undoubtedly object that he has simply been misunderstood, for he takes great care to subordinate the natural *telos* of virtuous political action to the supernatural *telos* of the person. Maritain deliberately distances himself from Machiavelli, as the following illuminating excerpt from *Man and the State*, worth quoting at length, illustrates:

> For human life has two ultimate ends, the one subordinate to the other: an ultimate end *in a given order*, which is the terrestrial common good, or the *bonum vitae civilis;* and an *absolute* ultimate end, which is the transcendent, eternal common good. And individual ethics takes into account the subordinate ultimate end, but *directly aims* at the absolute ultimate one; whereas political ethics takes into account the absolute ultimate end, but its *direct aim* is the subordinate ultimate end, the good of the rational nature in its temporal achievement. Hence a specific difference of perspective between those two branches of Ethics.
>
> Thus it is that many patterns of conduct of the body politic, which the

---

[130] Aldunate, Castillo, and Silva, *Los derechos humanos y la iglesia chilena*, 18.

pessimists of Machiavellianism turn to the advantage of political amorality – such as the use by the State of coercive force (even of means of war in case of absolute necessity against an unjust aggressor), the use of intelligence services and methods which should never corrupt people but cannot help utilizing corrupt people, the use of police methods which should never violate the human rights of people but cannot help being rough with them, a lot of selfishness and self-assertion which would be blamed in individuals, a permanent distrust and suspicion, a cleverness not necessarily mischievous but yet not candid with regard to the other States, or the toleration of certain evil deeds by the law, the recognition of the principle of the lesser evil and the recognition of the *fait accompli* (the so-called "statute of limitations") which permits the retention of gains ill-gotten long ago, because new human ties and vital relationships have infused them with new-born rights – all of these things are in reality ethically grounded.

The fear of soiling ourselves by entering the context of history is not virtue, but a way of escaping virtue.[131]

As we have seen, for Maritain the natural virtues needed for social and political life are "elevated" by the supernatural virtues. He insists, as did St Thomas, that the politician who is caretaker of the common good must be *bonus vir*, a virtuous man in every respect, that is, natural and supernatural. Temporal civilizations cannot be left to leaders possessed of merely natural virtue; they achieve their full dignity by being "elevated in their own order" by the "influence" of those virtues belonging to God and not Caesar.[132] The charge of Machiavellianism at face value against Maritain is therefore unfair. Nevertheless, there is plenty in the passage above which should give us pause. If only "individual ethics" can aim at the highest end, because entering "history" means "soiling ourselves," then we are left in a world where the police "cannot help being rough with" people.

At the heart of the problem are at least two serious distortions of St Thomas's teaching on virtue. The first distortion is that for Maritain politics is ethical if it "takes into account" the absolute end, while aiming somewhat lower. In Aquinas, however, the supernatural virtues *transform* the natural virtues to direct them to their proper end. When Aquinas says that charity is the form of the virtues, he does not mean that charity must simply somehow be "taken into account" while acting in history. Charity transforms both the status and the *content* of the natural virtues, which is precisely the importance in Aquinas's account of *infused natural virtues*, which are essentially different from acquired

---

[131] Maritain, *Man and the State*, 62–3.
[132] Maritain, *Scholasticism and Politics*, 181.

natural virtues because of the end to which they are directed. So Thomas makes clear that the moral virtues cannot exist without charity, saying "only the infused virtues are perfect, and deserve to be called virtues simply: since they direct man well to the ultimate end."[133] Maritain acknowledges that the acquired moral virtues need to be "elevated" by the infused moral virtues in order to be fully effective,[134] but he is unable to give an account of how the very definition of "justice," for example, could be transformed by Gospel norms. The second distortion of Thomas comes from Maritain's inattention to the fact that Aquinas placed his entire discussion of the virtues in the *Summa* within his analysis of habituation. Virtues are a type of *habitus*. They are complex sets of skills learned by habit within the context of a community of virtue.[135] Charity, for example, is a skill learned within the community of those who know what charity is only by performing (differently) the concrete life and practices of Jesus. Charity is not reducible to some ghostly "influence" added on to natural virtues which are learned outside of Christian practices in some autonomous social and political world.

These distortions of Thomas are driven by Maritain's spatial dualism of temporal and spiritual, nature and supernature – despite his efforts to "distinguish in order to unite" – such that the supernatural virtues are precluded from any direct transformative effect in history. "The pure essence of the spiritual," Maritain claims, "disturbs no single atom on earth in order to touch the heart of God."[136] On this score Maritain may have been served poorly by his reliance on the sixteenth- and seventeenth-century Dominican commentators on St Thomas, rather than on Thomas himself. As Gerald McCool writes, "Maritain can be fairly called the great twentieth-century representative of the Thomism of the classical commentators," that is, "Cajetan and John of St. Thomas."[137] It is precisely the formulations of Cajetan, Suarez, and John of St Thomas on the relation of nature and supernature against which Henri de Lubac's classic 1946 study *Surnaturel* was directed, a study which earned its author a decade of disfavor with Pius XII before his vindication in the Second Vatican Council. De Lubac showed that the Dominicans' understanding of a hypothetical state of "pure nature" and

---

[133] St Thomas Aquinas, *Summa Theologiae*, I–II.65.2.
[134] Jacques Maritain, *Science and Wisdom*, trans. Bernard Wall (New York: Charles Scribner's Sons, 1940), 145–54.
[135] St Thomas Aquinas, *Summa Theologiae*, I–II.49–55.
[136] Maritain, *Religion and Culture*, 47.
[137] Gerald McCool, SJ, *From Unity to Pluralism: The Internal Evolution of Thomism* (New York: Fordham University Press, 1989), 116.

the resultant dual finality of human nature was nowhere to be found in Thomas. Maritain, of course, did not subscribe to a closed realm of nature in which a purely natural end is naturally fulfilled; the human's natural end is always subordinated to, and elevated by, the supernatural end. Nevertheless, Maritain does retain the importance of a twofold human finality corresponding to distinct spiritual and temporal tasks, and does not, as we have already seen, succeed in conveying the *permeation* of the natural by the supernatural that is found in Thomas. In his groundbreaking studies on "Christian Philosophy," Etienne Gilson found Maritain's philosophy of nature inadequate in its perpetuation of the "separated" philosophy of the Dominican commentators, for example, in its removal of metaphysics from its context in theology. Gilson objected that Maritain's philosophy, which followed an ascending order from contingent finite being to necessary cause, was indebted to Thomas's commentators and not Thomas himself, who built his Christian philosophy within the descending order of theology from revelation.[138] As McCool documents, the research of Gilson and de Lubac led to the eclipse of Maritainian Thomism in the post-Vatican II era.[139]

An important corollary of Maritain's separation of nature and supernature is a dualism of time and eternity, or history and Kingdom. There are two sides to this dualism: the elimination of the Kingdom of God from history, and the simultaneous insistence that Christians cannot reject history as such. Maritain works hard to qualify this dualism, but he makes quite clear that culture is enmeshed in the vicissitudes of time, and the Kingdom, as a result, is essentially timeless, belonging to the eternal and not to the temporal. He takes Jesus' saying "My kingdom is not of this world" (John 18:36) to mean "My kingdom is not *in* this world." Maritain's attempts to support his dualism with this passage are defeated by the consensus of scholarship on John's Gospel. The Greek *ek* is properly translated *from*, not *of*; the question is one of origin. Jesus is telling Pilate that Jesus' kingly authority comes from God, or, in Dean Brackley's paraphrase, "Pilate, my politics are radically different from yours."[140] Brackley criticizes Maritain from a liberationist point of view for divorcing salvation from any earthly struggle for justice. The temporal good can prepare individuals and history for the coming of the meta-historical Kingdom of God, but ultimately only individual dispositions and not the fruits of our works

---

[138] Ibid., 193–4, 165–70.
[139] Ibid., 200–30.
[140] Dean Brackley. SJ, *Divine Revolution: Salvation and Liberation in Catholic Thought* (Maryknoll, NY: Orbis Books, 1996), 33.

will perdure in the Kingdom. The beatific vision is, for Maritain, an act of utter solitude, the individual person alone with God.[141]

Maritain's eschatology is unable to recognize the "already but not yet" character of the Kingdom; it is always partially present in history. I will expand on the true eschatological aspect of the church in chapter 5. For now it is worth noting with regard to Maritain's division of temporal and spiritual that in Augustinian eschatology the temporal is not a space which is cordoned off from the spiritual; the temporal is rather a time, a time between the times, between the first and second comings of Jesus Christ. The task of the church in the temporal is to embody what Christ has already accomplished in history by re-membering his broken and victorious body. Christ's victory is already won, and the Kingdom is to have transformative effects on Christian practice in history. The task of the church is to live as if this is the case, until Christ comes again and fully consummates his reign.

Maritain often seems to await the second coming as if the first were just a rumor. Indeed, for all Maritain's undoubted personal devotion, Jesus makes only cameo appearances in his political works. Most often Maritain's argument features "the spiritual" or "the supernatural." Occasionally the subject is "God," more rarely is it "the Gospel." Virtually never is the reader exposed to the actual content of the Gospel, the concrete contours of the life of Jesus Christ. The "vitally Christian society" of which Maritain speaks is based on the very thinnest account of Jesus Christ himself. Absent are the Sermon on the Mount, Jesus' identification with the hungry and the imprisoned, Jesus' death at the hands of the powers. Maritain's dichotomy between spiritual and temporal serves as a philosophical *a priori* into which the Incarnation fits very awkwardly. As we have seen, Maritain's Jesus is made of the most ethereal flesh; he floats daintily through Galilee disdaining things "too heavily weighted by matter."[142] In Maritain's view God became human in Jesus to universalize and interiorize the moral life in human hearts; the logic of the Incarnation thus works against itself. In similar fashion, Maritain echoes Wellhausen in claiming that Yahweh's choice of Israel is manifested not in the particular bodily practices of the Jewish people but by a universal "country of souls" that overcomes limitation by a particular culture.

At the same time that the New Christendom's dualisms serve to banish Christ from incarnation in culture, there is a contrary insistence that the church take a positive attitude toward culture as such and work within it to transform it. If Christianity has no culture of its own, and cannot simply retreat

---

[141] Ibid., 32–44.
[142] Maritain, *Religion and Culture*, 48.

from culture, it must embrace culture as it is. What this means is an acceptance of the autonomy of the temporal, those structures of power which have asserted their "proper" autonomy from the church in the modern age. Specifically what is demanded is acceptance of modern political and economic arrangements, especially as embodied in the state. Such structures, as part of the natural world, are sinful of course, but it is assumed that they are natural just as the human being, by virtue of her bodily character, is natural. Just as the soul animates the body, the Christian animates the temporal order, working within, never outside of, the given structures.

This "animation" is a mysterious process which in the writings of Maritain, Pius XI, and Catholic Action also appears as "penetration," "influence," "inspiration," "vivification," "elevation," and a host of other terms which succeed, first, in setting up the Gospel as something essentially alien to "culture" which must come at it from afar, and second, in leaving the impact of the Gospel on culture indirect and maddeningly vague. We are offered no concrete narratives with which to identify where and when the Gospel has in fact made a real impact on the world. To look for the specific practices of Jesus or the New Testament communities in historical time would be a mistake, since the Gospel as such does not appear in its own cultural forms. Instead Maritain offers us assurances that the Gospel has penetrated Western culture, and what good things we find there today – democracy, freedom, human rights – are thanks to the Gospel still working its magic in the secret of the individual soul, even those souls which have explicitly rejected it.

This faith in the perdurance of "Western Christian civilization," a faith ironically often echoed by the Pinochet regime, allows Maritain to give a faint Christian gloss to the "democratic secular faith" he would require of all citizens. Here we find ambiguity and hesitation in Maritain's thought. Recognizing that the common good requires a common faith, he puts forth his idea of a secular faith in freedom and rights. This, he says, is not a supernatural faith, merely a temporal one, yet he still wishes to claim for Christianity some privileged position in its perpetuation. It may be that he intuits the difficulty in maintaining a distinction between secular and spiritual faiths. His own comments on communism in *Integral Humanism* indicate as much. Communism, while atheist, has "religious" significance; it "is a complete system of doctrine and life" with its own ethical and social expressions which replace all other religions.[143] Maritain believes that careful distinguishing of the spiritual and temporal planes prevents this from happening in true democracies. He does not fully appreciate to what extent many

[143] Maritain, *Integral Humanism*, 36.

modern states have *already* replaced, or at least displaced, other religions, including Christianity, either through the privatization of religion or the hostility of an ever-expanding state. The task of limiting the state's power once it has been charged with maintaining a secular faith is at least more difficult than Maritain makes it out to be.

Maritain is correct to suggest that people of various religious faiths can come to pragmatic agreement on certain issues without necessarily giving up those traditions. He is mistaken, however, to think that those traditions can be sequestered from the construction of a common ethos without fundamentally distorting them. In his own thought, Maritain believes that the social order can be built on ideas such as human rights and democracy while Christianity remains only an inchoate inspiration behind these ideas. Especially in his writings after World War II, the language of rights expresses for Maritain the social order implicit in the Christian faith. Although Maritain wishes to purge rights language of its basis in liberalism and locate its inspiration in the Gospel, it is the Gospel which ends up being supplanted, precisely because it is banished in effect from explicit insertion into public discourse. Just as an immigrant language will die if it is not spoken outside the home, so Christian language will eventually cease to provide "inspiration" for rights language as long as such inspiration is closed away in the interior of the human soul.

In laying out his "democratic secular faith" Maritain attempts to baptize the language of rights and provide it with a Christian underpinning which will go beyond the individualism of liberal rights theories. Nevertheless, Maritain's work on rights – and indeed the entire Catholic post-World War II turn to rights language exemplified by Pius XII and John XXIII[144] – was motivated by the desire to attain a universal language for dialogue with a "pluralistic world." In other words the importance of rights language was precisely to try to find a way of talking about human dignity and human destiny without requiring habituation in Christian practices and beliefs. This seems like an admirable goal for Christians to pursue in a world of many different practices and beliefs. Unfortunately, this strategy has failed, and we must finally begin to recognize this and ask why. Why has appeal to human rights not protected more people from the most atrocious abuses, in Chile and in many other parts of the world? Why did appeals to human rights have so little apparent effect on the Pinochet regime?

Critics of the idea of human rights often point to the incoherence of the idea

---

[144] For a history of the development of papal human rights theory, see David Hollenbach, SJ, *Claims in Conflict: Retrieving and Renewing the Catholic Human Rights Tradition* (New York: Paulist Press, 1979), 41–106.

of their universality, that is, that human rights are not given by custom or positive law but belong to human beings as such. As Alasdair MacIntyre has said, "there are no such rights, and belief in them is one with belief in witches and unicorns." Even if there are universally necessary goods, the claim that one has a *right* to such goods presupposes socially established rules and institutions which are not universal, but come about in very particular times and places. Rights may be locally conferred by custom or positive law, but universal human rights do not exist precisely because there is no such thing as a human being as such, that is, a human being prescinded from all historical and cultural context.[145] Admiral Merino, you will recall from chapter 1, was able to justify the regime's oppression of Marxists by calling them "humanoids." One reason that the language of human rights had no effect on the Pinochet regime was precisely that it did not think that it was torturing human beings; it thought it was torturing Marxists.[146] Human beings are formed within widely varying communities of practices which reduce the thin notion of "human being as such" to practical meaninglessness. As MacIntyre points out, notions of entitlement or rights are highly specific to particular cultural milieux, and such notions always presuppose particular practices and social institutions.[147]

In his account of nineteenth- and twentieth-century Thomisms in *Three Rival Versions of Moral Enquiry*, MacIntyre locates Maritain among the "systematic" Thomists (contrasted with "historical" scholars of Thomism such as Gilson) who erred in presenting Thomas's thought as an answer to false problems set by post-Cartesian philosophy. Their error lay in duplicating the modern turn to epistemology as the primary philosophical task, assuming that Thomas would aid in the vindication of some account of rationality-in-general.[148]

> And so Maritain . . . would formulate what he mistakenly took to be a
> Thomistic defense of the doctrine of human rights enshrined in the United

---

[145] Alasdair MacIntyre, *After Virtue*, 2nd edn (Notre Dame, Ind.: University of Notre Dame Press, 1984), 66–70.

[146] Richard Rorty makes a similar argument, for rather different purposes, in his "Human Rights, Rationality, and Sentimentality" in *On Human Rights: The Oxford Amnesty Lectures 1993*, ed. Stephen Shute and Susan Hurley (New York: Basic Books, 1993), 111–34.

[147] MacIntyre, *After Virtue*, 67.

[148] Alasdair MacIntyre, *Three Rival Versions of Moral Enquiry: Encyclopedia, Genealogy, and Tradition* (Notre Dame, Ind.: University of Notre Dame Press, 1990), 68–77.

Nations Declaration of Human Rights, a quixotic attempt to present Thomism as offering a rival and superior account of the same moral subject matter as do other modern nontheological doctrines of universal rights alleged to attach to individual persons.[149]

Aquinas acknowledged a natural knowledge of divine law within every human being. But for Aquinas all rights are only warranted by divine law and are thus secondary to law. MacIntyre agrees with Maritain that for Aquinas the "plain prephilosophical person" has certain moral capacities. "But what Maritain failed to reckon with adequately was the fact that in many cultures and notably in that of modernity plain persons are misled into giving moral expression to those capacities through assent to false philosophical theories" such as that of universal rights prior to all law.[150] At the root of this problem is Maritain's inability – following that of Thomas's sixteenth-century commentators – to appreciate that Aquinas's account of rationality presupposes that enquiry takes place in a craft-tradition in the Aristotelian sense of *techne*, situated within a particular type of community of virtue. There is no timeless reason which inheres in the individual mind. Because of the tendency of the will to be misled, the will must be guided by the authority of a virtue-guided community. Rational progress is achieved historically through the open-ended enquiry of a craft-tradition toward excellence in both theoretical understanding and practical embodiment, which are specified by a theological narrative of the *telos* of human life.[151] For Aquinas true rights emerge only from particular tradition-formed communities.

The key to Maritain's difficulty, then, is his inattention to the kinds of communities and institutions from which true rights emerge. With his interiorization of the church, Maritain ultimately is unable to avoid leaving the nation-state as the key institution presupposed by his account of human rights. In Maritain's thought the state, as responsible for the common good, is also the guarantor of the rights of its citizens. Maritain dissents from the liberal state in acknowledging the pedagogical function of the state, the fact that it "tends to develop moral virtues."[152] What we have is a state which becomes the community of moral habituation and discernment for the person with regard to her social existence. Church and state will not become rivals provided the

---

[149] Ibid., 76.
[150] Ibid.
[151] Ibid., 58–81.
[152] Maritain, *The Rights of Man and Natural Law*, 77.

division of temporal and spiritual is strictly respected and the natural virtues inculcated by the state are subordinated to, and elevated by, the supernatural virtues which are the province of the church.

For Maritain everything hinges on the propriety of the modern differentiation of spiritual and temporal into two distinct planes which intersect only in the individual. According to Maritain the desacralization of the state following the Reformation was the proper fulfillment of the true Christian ideal of a pure spiritual life unburdened by cultural and tribal particularities. Jesus articulated this ideal in his pithy reply to the agents of the scribes and the chief priests: "Render to Caesar what is Caesar's and to God what is God's." The true meaning of this passage remained implicit for many centuries as the spiritual and temporal powers struggled towards proper differentiation. Finally in the sixteenth and seventeenth centuries the church was freed from the state but, by an unfortunate coincidence, the absolutist notion of the state arose at the same moment in history, worsening in the nineteenth and twentieth centuries. The world still awaits, says Maritain, the full realization of the Gospel ideal of the properly profane state well-tamed by the spiritual order.

New Christendom ecclesiology rests on this very influential, and entirely spurious, fairy tale. This fable is based on a series of anachronisms and misreadings of history that are more often asserted than argued for. To begin, it is illegitimate to read the modern division of religion and politics back into the story of Jesus and the coin. Not only would the very ideas of "religion" and "politics" as separate things have been unthinkable for a first-century Jew, but the story itself makes no sense unless the reader assumes some overlap or competition between the things that are Caesar's and the things that are God's. If Jesus had taught that they belonged to two distinct planes on different levels of reality, then those who posed the question could hardly have expected to trap Jesus with it and use his words to denounce him to the authorities.[153] As it is, the question is posed in the context of mounting conflict between God and Caesar, as a prelude to the Passion in all three synoptics (Mt. 22:15-22; Mk 12:13-17; Lk. 20:20-6). Mark and Luke place the story immediately following the parable of the wicked tenants' murder of the son, and shortly before Jesus' apocalyptic predictions that his followers will be imprisoned and "brought before kings and governors for my name's sake" (Lk. 21:12). If Jesus preached the distinction of planes, his conflict with the authorities remains

---

[153] On this passage see John Howard Yoder, *The Politics of Jesus* (Grand Rapids, Mich.: Wm. B. Eerdmans Publishing Co., 1972), 52–3.

incomprehensible. The Cross itself needs some explanation. Although precise interpretation of the story of Caesar's coin is difficult, I concur with Oliver O'Donovan's judgment that this passage "allows us to rule out the view that Jesus assigned Roman government a certain uncontested sphere of secular right."[154]

Also in need of some accounting for is the absence of the "distinction of planes" interpretation of this passage until at least the late medieval period. According to Maritain, it is simply "common knowledge" that the distinction of spiritual and temporal and the creation of the desacralized state is "the achievement of the Christian centuries and their glory,"[155] an assertion he seems to offer in order to bluff his way out of presenting any evidence that such is the case. Undoubtedly the distinction gradually took form during the Christian centuries, but it would be odd to call "their glory" what in fact coincided with their demise. Maritain's contention that the best of liberal freedoms and universal human rights is the fruit of the Gospel's subterranean work in Western culture similarly is based on mere assertion. In the face of evidence that those ideas originated in the Enlightenment context of an *explicit rejection* of Christianity and the church, Maritain sprinkles a bit of holy water on them and declares that what is good in them is due to the Gospel's invisible influence.[156] Although he is certainly right to endorse the disentanglement of the church from coercive state power, we should expect Maritain at least to acknowledge that the desacralization of the state is not historically separable from the very privatization of Christianity and rising nation-state ambitions to power that Maritain himself abhors.

Maritain's claim is that the creation of the state as separate from an individualized "spiritual" order was proper and only coincidentally mixed up with state pretensions to absolute power. Absolutist theorists such as Bodin and Hobbes, however, saw and explained quite clearly that the state's power is *predicated on* the domestication of the church and an unfettered resort to the means of violence. The more apparently tolerant Locke went even further in reducing religion to purely interior belief. Locke held that the state cannot coerce religious belief because it is a matter of the internal conscience. But for the very same reason he flatly denied the social nature of the church, defining it as merely a free association of like-minded individuals, a semi-private club. When Locke's ideas were enshrined in England's Toleration Act of 1689,

---

[154] Oliver O'Donovan, *The Desire of the Nations: Rediscovering the Roots of Political Theology* (Cambridge: Cambridge University Press, 1996), 92.
[155] Maritain, *The Things That Are Not Caesar's*, 1.
[156] Maritain, *Christianity and Democracy*, 25.

Catholics were explicitly excluded from the Act, precisely because they had as yet refused to interiorize the church and transfer their ultimate loyalty to the sovereign.[157] Maritain was painfully aware of the violence and restrictions on freedom which nation-states had visited on the modern world. He tried to distinguish this, however, from the "astonishing growth" of the state in modern times, which is "normal growth," needed to protect the rights of citizens and enforce social justice.[158] What Maritain did not fully appreciate is that the "normal growth" of the state's supervisory capacities is easily turned to the kind of surveillance I described in chapter 1. The discourse of rights usually presupposes a large state bureaucratic apparatus to police the many ways that people can interfere with one another's freedoms. At the same time in Maritain's scheme, rights are meant as protection for the individual as person from state interference. The effect of rights is to build a protective wall around the individual. To do so, however, the state often assumes greater control and surveillance capabilities. The result, as Rousseau saw, is that the object of the state is to make citizens as independent as possible from each other and as dependent as possible on the state.[159] Marx makes similar observations on rights and the state: if the state is the guarantor of rights, then those rights must be abrogated as soon as they interfere with the security of the state.[160] The panopticon constructed in Chilean society by the secret police is not an aberration, a throwback to darker ages, but is, as Foucault points out, a part of the "normal growth" of the many modern states which are constructed as the guarantor of the rights of its citizens.[161] Ironically, then, appeals to the state

[157] William T. Cavanaugh, " 'A Fire Strong Enough to Consume the House' : The Wars of Religion and the Rise of the State," *Modern Theology* 11: 4 (Oct. 1995), 397–420.

[158] "The growth of the State, in modern centuries, as a rational or juridical machine and with regard to its inner constitutive system of law and power, its unity, its discipline; the growth of the State, in the present century, as a technical machine and with regard to its law-making, supervising, and organizing functions in social and economic life, are in themselves part of normal progress"; Maritain, *Man and the State*, 19–20.

[159] Jean-Jacques Rousseau, *The Social Contract*, trans. Willmoore Kendall (South Bend, Ind.: Gateway Editions, 1954), 58 [book 2, ch. XII].

[160] Karl Marx, "On the Jewish Question," in David McLellan, ed., *Karl Marx: Selected Writings* (Oxford: Oxford University Press, 1977), 54–5.

[161] "The general juridical form that guaranteed a system of rights that were egalitarian in principle was supported by these tiny, everyday, physical mechanisms, by all those systems of micro-power that are essentially non-egalitarian and asymmetrical that we

to protect human rights often fail because state protection of such rights follows the same atomizing and individualizing pathology as does the very apparatus of torture.

Maritain, of course, is keen in theory to circumscribe the state's power by limiting the state to purely temporal pretensions and subordinating the temporal to the spiritual. What he does not see is that this very distinction of planes can function to augment the power of the state by eliminating the interference of the church. Maritain may declare that only God, and not the state, is truly sovereign, but once the church has been individualized and eliminated as Christ's body in the world, only the state is left to impersonate God. As the state itself becomes guarantor of rights, human rights become tied, in bitter irony, to the security of the state.

In Chile this irony is exemplified by a 1979 book entitled *The Security of the State and Human Rights* by Christian Democratic jurist Hernán Montealegre Klenner, who himself suffered imprisonment by the regime. Montealegre remarks that human rights violations are normally justified by appeals to the security of the state. But, he argues, a state is made up of three elements: territory, government, and inhabitants. The state, he contends in Maritainian fashion, is not above the people but in part is made up of them. When the government violates the human rights of the people, therefore, it should be interpreted as a *threat to the security of the state,* since one part of the state is attacking another. Human rights violations can lead to instability in the state by, for example, inciting opposition to the government.[162] As we saw in chapter 1, however, human rights violations can be used to foment opposition in order to justify increased power for the state. Montealegre's argument turns on a naive view of the state as a neutral arbiter of conflict in civil society, and assumes therefore that the security of the state should be our prized goal. Stopping torture and disappearances is apparently a matter of convincing the soldiers somehow that what they thought was state security really was not.

Surely Maritain cannot be accused of simply aggrandizing the state. As we have already seen, he invokes Pius XI's "principle of subsidiarity" to espouse an organic pluralist civil society comprised of multiple autonomous associa-

---

call the disciplines . . . The real, corporal disciplines constituted the foundation of the formal, juridical liberties. The contract may have been regarded as the ideal foundation of law and political power; panopticism constituted the technique, universally widespread, of coercion"; Foucault, *Discipline and Punish,* 222.

[162] Hernán Montealegre Klenner, *La seguridad del estado y los derechos humanos* (Santiago: Academia de Humanismo Cristiano, 1979).

tions which limit state pretensions to power. "In this conception, which avoids *étatisme* as much as possible, the organic City would be ruled not by the wheels of a bureaucratic machine but by decisions taken by men chosen as leaders of their several organisations."[163] Nevertheless, in eliminating any direct temporal relevance for the church, Maritain cannot resist the necessity to make the state the pedagogue of virtue. Thus Maritain says that the state is to these intermediate associations as the church hierarchy is to the religious orders, though they should be as free of the state as possible.[164] In *Integral Humanism*, Maritain envisions in charge of the common good a kind of Gaullist executive indirectly elected and standing above the fray of party politics, advised by a multitude of intermediate associations.[165] The ideal is the "progressive self-regulation" of these autonomous societies. As an example, Maritain offers the writers' guild:

> Let me suggest that in virtue of an institutional status various groups of publicists and writers, assembled in an autonomous body, would have a progressive control over the duties of their profession. Then we would see whether, through the natural severity with which the potter judges the work of the potter, they would not be able to exercise an efficacious control; it would rather be to protect the individual from his associates that the supreme judicial organs of the State would have to interfere.[166]

The goal of the state's pedagogy is that people would cease to need it, since they would become self-disciplining.[167] Similarly, the state would launch cooperative business enterprises based on the social function of private property, but then leave these enterprises to others. "Thus the State itself would launch a movement of progressive decentralization and 'destatization' of social life."[168]

Unfortunately, asking the state to "destatize" usually works as well as putting a wolf in the henhouse to protect the chickens from predators. As Alfred Stepan has shown, the organic-statist model, derived from Aristotelian–Thomist and papal sources and attempted in various Latin American countries, rests on a

---

[163] Jacques Maritain, *Freedom in the Modern World*, trans. Richard O'Sullivan (New York: Charles Scribner's Sons, 1936), 57.
[164] Maritain, *Integral Humanism*, 171.
[165] Ibid., 175. Also Sigmund, "Maritain on Politics," 160.
[166] Ibid., 182.
[167] Ibid., 183.
[168] Maritain, *Man and the State*, 22.

contradiction. On the one hand, the "principle of subsidiarity" aims to protect the "natural" associations of the body politic from infringement by the state. On the other hand, this model envisions a state strong enough to order the community toward its *telos*, the common good, and overcome antagonisms among various groups in civil society. The predictable outcome of such a scheme, as Stepan shows, is that, in order adequately to coordinate the common good, the state will find it necessary to build such strong controls of the intermediate associations into the system that meaningful participation and autonomy for these groups will be squelched. If the associations are initially allowed a real measure of autonomy, some will acquire control over others, eventually necessitating state intervention for the common good.[169]

For those interested in a Christian theology and practice of the political, the key difficulty with Maritain's project is that he makes the Christian community the repository of purely supernatural virtue which stands outside of time, and thus interiorizes and individualizes the Gospel. The soul is the province of the church, and the state has charge of the body. Because he has sequestered political virtue from any direct habituation in Christian community, the state becomes that community of habituation, the pedagogue of virtue. This is not at all to imply that the Aristotelian–Thomist tradition of Catholic political thought is incoherent. Rather, we would do well to heed Alasdair MacIntyre's reminder that modern nation-states simply are not the kind of community through which true virtues can be fostered and the common good achieved. Where Aristotelian–Thomist communities of practice appear in the modern world, they constitute *resistance* to the nation-state. MacIntyre allows that some evils can be resisted by ad hoc cooperation with certain enterprises of some nation-states. Nevertheless, the "state as a bearer of values always imperils those values."

> The modern nation-state, in whatever guise, is a dangerous and unmanageable institution, presenting itself on the one hand as a bureaucratic supplier of goods and services, which is always about to, but never actually does, give its clients value for money, and on the other as a repository of sacred values, which from time to time invites one to lay down one's life on its behalf. As I have remarked elsewhere . . . it is like being asked to die for the telephone company.[170]

Nation-states are fetishes. They have power because people believe in the

---

[169] Alfred Stepan, *The State and Society: Peru in Comparative Perspective* (Princeton, NJ: Princeton University Press, 1978), 29–45.

[170] Alasdair MacIntyre, "A Partial Response to my Critics," in *After MacIntyre: Critical Perspectives on the Work of Alasdair MacIntyre*, ed. John Horton and Susan Mendus (Notre Dame, Ind.: University of Notre Dame Press, 1994), 303.

need for their security. They have power because people will kill and die – and sometimes torture – for them. Christians in modernity have often bought into a devil's bargain in which the state is given control of our bodies while the church supposedly retains our souls. This arrangement would be bad enough if it stopped there. But the state cannot be expected to limit itself to the body; it will colonize the soul as well. A secular faith will not stay long confined to some temporal sphere; the secular god is a jealous god. As Luigi Sturzo pointed out, the nation-state tends to develop its own *Weltanschauung*, a worldview and a discipline which aspires to train us in certain virtues, to mold our thoughts and our actions. It does so by taking hold of our bodies.

In Christian conceptions of virtue, there is a unity of body and soul which cannot be sundered. For most medieval writers on virtue, "it is discipline imposed on the body which forms virtue. Body and spirit are but one: disordered movements of the former betray outwardly (*foris*) the disarranged interior (*intus*) of the soul. But inversely, 'discipline' can act on the soul through the body . . . "[171] As Talal Asad explains, it is this concept of discipline that allows medieval writers to make an equivalence between the human body and the political community.[172] In the body politic Maritain would subordinate, as did St Thomas Aquinas, the temporal to the spiritual as the body to the soul. For St Thomas, however, the relation of soul and body is unmediated. Aquinas teaches that the church has the power to excommunicate rulers and absolve their subjects from obedience to them.[173] For Maritain the power of the spiritual in the temporal must take the form of inspiration and mere counsels which do not require obedience. The result is a dysfunction between body and soul, a false soul haunting a body which receives its orders from elsewhere. What this looks like in practice is the case of the bishop, cited in chapter 2, who can speak a word to the conscience of the Catholic soldier, but cannot override the soldier's orders from his army superior to torture his fellow Christians. The army functions as a true body, a *corpus verum*, but the church, according to this conception, does not.

What I have been tracing in this chapter is the recreation of the church as the "soul of society" and its consequent inability to resist the bodily disciplines of the state. The point to reclaiming the power of the church over bodies, however, is decidedly *not* to reclaim the power of physical coercion for the church, to

[171] J.C. Schmitt, quoted in Talal Asad, *Genealogies of Religion: Discipline and Reasons of Power in Christianity and Islam* (Baltimore: The Johns Hopkins University Press, 1993), 138.
[172] Asad, *Genealogies of Religion*, 138.
[173] St Thomas Aquinas, *Summa Theologiae*, II–II.12.2.

rebuild the Old Christendom on the ruins of the New. If we understand the unity of body and soul, we must understand that what is really at stake is not body-power versus soul-power, but competing types of soul/body disciplines, some violent and some peaceful. Christians must understand that the state's control of the body is a control of the soul as well. The church must see that its own disciplinary resources – Eucharist, penance, virtue, works of mercy, martyrdom – are not matters of the soul which may somehow "animate" the "real world" of bodies, but are rather body/soul disciplines meant to produce actions, practices, habits that are visible in the world. For the church to be a true social body it must reclaim not only its body but its soul from the state, and institute a discipline which is truly Christlike – a power based in compassion and martyrdom, suffering and reconciliation, and not in a revived Christendom.

5 The End of the Story

What happened to "social Catholicism" in Chile? Catholic Action collapsed virtually overnight in the wake of Eduardo Frei's election as President in 1964. The bishops I interviewed said that the major reason for the demise of Catholic Action was the defection of young Catholics into the Christian Democratic party and administration. The social programs that the church had sponsored – campesino unions, neighborhood associations, educational projects, housing cooperatives – also disappeared as the new government set up similar programs and Catholic activists opted for the latter.[174] As the sixties wore on, elements of active Catholic laity became increasingly radicalized and joined leftist parties or formed leftist parties of Christian inspiration, such as the Christian Left and the Movement for Unitary Popular Action (MAPU). In the election of 1970, Socialist Salvador Allende defeated both Conservative Jorge Alessandri and Christian Democrat Radomiro Tómic to become the first democratically elected Marxist head of state in the West. Three years later General Pinochet and his Junta assumed control.

On March 11, 1974, the six-month anniversary of the coup, the Junta issued a Declaration of Principles which would set the course for the military government. Its primary author was Jaime Guzmán Errázuriz, the young legal counsel who would become chief ideologue for the Pinochet regime. During

---

[174] In my interviews, Bishops Bernardino Piñera, Camilo Vial, Tomás González, Alejandro Jiménez, and Carlos González all repeated this analysis of the fall of social Catholicism in the 1960s. Brian Smith gives the same appraisal in *The Church and Politics in Chile*, 137–8.

his student days, Guzmán had become a nationally-known figure as one of the founders in 1965 of the *Movimiento Gremial*, an attempt by right-wing Catholics to counter the influence of progressives in the Catholic University. The movement quickly spread beyond university walls, opposing agrarian reform and railing against leftist influence in the church and in society. The movement got its name from its broad vision of replacing political parties with *gremios*, or guilds, of students, professionals, and workers, all coordinated for the common good by the state. Guzmán drafted Chile's new Constitution for the regime in 1980, and remained an ardent public apologist for the regime until his death at the hands of assassins in 1990.[175]

Jacques Maritain would no doubt have strongly disapproved of the Junta which seized power in 1973. He would perhaps have been puzzled by the Declaration of Principles which Jaime Guzmán wrote for them, however, for the document reads for the most part as if it had been penned by *El Maestro* himself. At the Catholic University, Guzmán had been a disciple of Jaime Eyzaguirre, the influential historian at the Catholic University who was one of Maritain's early followers in Chile.[176] Eyzaguirre was active in Catholic Action and trained many integralist Catholics important in right-wing politics. Among Eyzaguirre's most important students was Guzmán, for whom also Maritain became the single most significant philosophical influence.[177]

Maritain's ideas and vocabulary leap off every page of the Junta's Declaration of Principles. According to the document, the military intervened to save Chile from the twin threats of Marxist totalitarianism and a flaccid liberalism which espoused ideological "neutrality." The new government is not neutral, but based upon the Christian view of "man" passed down in Western society. As such, the Junta recognizes the "dignity of the human person," which gives him "natural rights anterior and superior to the state."[178] The state must regulate the exercise of those rights, but can never deny them because they are given by the Creator. The state therefore guarantees all fundamental human rights, "protecting the weak from all abuses by the strong."[179] Liberty of conscience is respected, but the state must put limits on freedom to dissent in order to protect others.

---

[175] *Jaime Guzmán: su legado humano y político* (Santiago: Ercilla, 1991), 3-22. See also Smith, *The Church and Politics in Chile*, 139–40 n. 26.

[176] Caiceo, "Influencia de Maritain en los orígenes del social-cristianismo chileno, en su expresión política (1930–1950)," 192.

[177] Smith, *The Church and Politics in Chile*, 83; 139–40 n. 26.

[178] Junta Militar de Gobierno, *Declaración de Principios del Gobierno de Chile*, 9-10, 13, 26–7.

[179] Ibid., 23.

The state is not neutral towards those doctrines which would destroy the state. Marxism, therefore, is prohibited in its public expression.[180]

The person has priority over the state by virtue of his ultimate end, for "while societies and States run their course in time and history, man transcends them, since he lives in history but is not consumed by it."[181] The state, nevertheless, has its own proper end. "The end of the state is the general common good," defined as "the total of social conditions which permit all Chileans and each Chilean to reach their full personal fulfillment." The common good, therefore, is neither a collection of individual goods, as in liberalism, nor a totalitarian whole which eliminates the good of each person.[182]

The reconstruction of Chile laid out in the Declaration is to obey a strict distinction of the political and the social. The political lies in the exclusive ambit of the state. The military took over political power in the realization that, beyond a simple change in administration, it was essential "to change the mentality of Chileans," to open the way "to new generations of Chileans formed in a school of healthy civic habits."[183] The social, meanwhile, consists in all intermediate organizations between the individual and the state. It is imperative that these organizations be completely "depoliticized." At the same time they are to take on added importance as the state directs the "decentralization of power" and the functions arrogated to the state under the Marxist government are returned to their proper place in the "social" sector. Chile is to be ruled by the "principle of subsidiarity," the idea that the state as a higher power should only do what the lower organizations cannot do for themselves. Although the state "coordinates" these intermediate associations, all "statism" is to be avoided. The military government is to serve as an apolitical overseer, arbitrating conflicts in civil society under a National System of Planning. The result will be a "democracy" that is "organic, social, and participatory."[184]

The central contradiction of this scheme is that what goes under the guise of devolving power from the state to a variety of lesser social bodies occurs under the aegis of a ruthless authoritarian dictatorship. Just as we saw in Maritain's writings, the ostensible desire to limit the state's power over the person masks an individualization of the social and an increase in state power.

---

[180] Ibid., 26–7.
[181] Ibid., 13–14.
[182] Ibid., 14–15.
[183] Ibid., 28–9.
[184] Ibid., 16–32.

According to the Junta's Declaration, "the principle of subsidiarity supposes the acceptance of the right of private property and of free enterprise in the area of economics."[185] The idea is "to make of Chile a nation of property owners and not proletarians."[186] The authoritarian regime used privatization, that is, a drastic decrease in the state's share of the economy, to take power from workers and other marginalized groups and return it to powerful business interests.

As Alfred Stepan has shown, the state in Chile was "marketized" in order to dissipate and fragment opposition to the state. Social security was given over to a variety of private firms offering different plans in order to "depoliticize" the issue of social security and remove the incentive for groups to organize against the state on this issue. Union activity and collective bargaining was limited by law to the plant level, supposedly so that workers and managers could work out disputes locally without mass mobilization or the involvement of the state or political parties.[187] This is decentralization of power only in Foucault's sense of making power more powerful by making it less visible. The real point of the depoliticization of the social is not to take power from the state but rather to further the process of atomization of social bodies which would rival the state, and thus to advance the economic and political power of elites linked to the state.

Two Christian Democratic governments, those of Patricio Aylwin and Eduardo Frei (son of the former President), have held power following the transition from military rule in 1990. As significant as this transition was, at least symbolically, James Petras and Fernando Leiva have illustrated the overwhelming continuity in the Chilean state between the Pinochet years and the Christian Democratic governments. An examination of five key structures of the state – armed forces and police, the courts, the civil bureaucracy, the central bank, and the universities – show continuity of both personnel and policy. Governments change, but states remain.[188] Most significantly, the Christian Democrats have continued the Pinochet regime's economic and social policy, so much so that Jaime Guzmán himself would register his

---

[185] Ibid., 18.

[186] Ibid., 19.

[187] Alfred Stepan, "State Power and the Strength of Civil Society in the Southern Cone of Latin America," in Bringing the State Back In, 317–43.

[188] James Petras and Fernando Ignacio Leiva, with Henry Veltmeyer, Democracy and Poverty in Chile: The Limits to Electoral Politics (Boulder: Westview Press, 1994), 2–3, 85–9. Amnesty International has continued to condemn Chile for human rights abuses in their annual reports in the 1990s.

satisfaction that the Aylwin government had preserved "the central lines of the development strategy supported by the previous government . . . and persevered in following serious and orthodox macroeconomic management."[189] Christian Democratic strategists have embraced the neoliberal model of the Pinochet regime while incorporating elements of "neostructuralist" theory which has become prominent in Latin America as a less aggressive alternative to neoliberalism. Neostructuralism differs from left and center-left "structuralist" strategies of state-centered economic planning, agreeing with neoliberalism that the state should not interfere with market mechanisms. On the other hand, neostructuralism departs from neoliberalism in seeing a key role for the state in generating social and political consensus toward the common good. Rather than resolve social conflict by atomizing intermediate associations through repression, the new Christian Democratic governments have pursued a strategy of channeling social conflict into the common goal of insertion into the world economy. A key to this strategy is the co-opting of social organizations by the state. Alejandro Foxley, Finance Minister and chief architect of the Christian Democratic economic strategy explains the danger of independent social organizations in these terms:

> Once the autonomy of social organizations expands – a prerequisite for strengthening civil society vis-a-vis the state – these organizations do nothing more than reproduce the main conflicts in society. If these conflicts involve class contradictions or antagonistic ideological currents, each autonomous organization will but passively mirror such conflict. As a result, these conflicts will be strengthened and amplified, increasing society's polarization instead of reducing it. The system becomes more unstable.[190]

The neostructuralist strategy thus aims at the subsumption of social conflict into the state. Petras and Leiva document the dissolution of grass-roots organizations in the post-Pinochet era. International funds previously channeled directly to such organizations, or indirectly through NGOs, are now detoured through the state, such that NGOs have increasingly become appendages of the state. Neighborhood councils have very little autonomy, and grassroots organizations have been severely divided by the choice of either accepting state tutelage or retaining autonomy and forgoing funding. In short, the new

---

[189] Jaime Guzmán, in *El Mercurio*, March 10, 1990, C3, quoted in ibid., 46.
[190] Alejandro Foxley, "Algunas condiciones para una democratización estable: el caso de Chile," *Colección Estudios CIEPLAN* no. 9 (Dec.) (Santiago: CIEPLAN, 1982), pp. 159–60, quoted in Petras and Leiva, *Democracy and Poverty in Chile*, 56.

governments have succeeded in continuing, if not advancing, the disarticulation of social bodies.[191]

It would be more than a bit unfair simply to claim the Junta, its ideologues, and its successors as the true heirs of Jacques Maritain and the New Christendom. That his thought should play such a prominent role in their principles should perhaps give us pause, but certainly they are a corruption of Maritain's intentions. I do not wish to argue that New Christendom thought is responsible for the rise of the Pinochet regime. What I want to argue is rather that this type of ecclesiology has sapped the church's ability to resist regimes such as that of General Pinochet. The story of this chapter is a melancholy one for the church. What began as a liberation of the church from alliances with the state and party entanglements ends with the privatization of the church and its domination by the state. The promise of a "social Catholicism" did not materialize because it was misconstrued from the start. The problem with "social Catholicism" is that it was never truly social. The church was interiorized more radically than before, relegated to a ghostly "mystical" body unable to resist the fragmenting disciplines of the state. To look for a true alternative Christian social practice – a true body – we must look elsewhere than "social Catholicism" and the New Christendom. In the next chapter I will take up that search.

---

[191] Petras and Leiva, *Democracy and Poverty in Chile*, 140–63.

Part Three

EUCHARIST

Chapter 5

THE TRUE BODY OF CHRIST

In the early days of the military regime, Chile was driven indoors. Behind some doors, champagne corks popped; behind others, there was only an anxious silence. In the streets the military patrols sped by on their hungry search for enemies. Those labeled as enemies faced a terrible dilemma. They could stay at home and await capture, or they could attempt to flee, a choice which would take them out into the streets ruled by the regime. Among those who chose to run was a young pair of leftists who, three days after the coup, arrived panicked at the doorstep of a priests' residence in the center of Santiago. They were received, but they were not allowed to stay. Back out into the street, they would have to try their luck elsewhere. That evening as the community prepared for Mass, a seminarian spoke up and objected to the celebration of the Eucharist under the circumstances. He said Christ had been turned away at the door of the residence. Communion in the body of Christ had already been denied in the denial of the two seeking asylum.[1]

What could be the connection between the fates of two unknowns, perhaps criminals, possibly non-Christians, and the sublime, if routine, ritual of the Eucharist? In this chapter and the next I will develop the strange claim that the Eucharist is the church's "counter-politics" to the politics of torture. I want to do more than suggest symbolic connections between the ritual and what happened in the "real world." I want to explore nothing less than the actual and potential impact of the Eucharist on the dictatorship. For Catholic Christianity there is nothing more real than the real presence of Jesus Christ in the Eucharist. Eucharist makes real the presence of Christ both in the elements and in the body of believers. The church becomes the very body of Christ. If the church is to resist the disappearance described in chapters 3 and

---

[1] Ascanio Cavallo Castro, Manuel Salazar Salvo, and Oscar Sepúlveda Pacheco, *La historia oculta del régimen militar* (Santiago: Editorial Antártica, 1990), 93.

4, it must realize its true nature as a locus of social practices, the true body of Christ capable of resisting the discipline of the state. This chapter and the next will serve as the mirror image of chapter 1, in which I describe the logic of torture. This chapter displays the logic of Eucharist as an alternative economy of pain and the body. Torture and Eucharist are opposing *disciplinae arcanorum* using different means and serving different ends. Where torture is an anti-liturgy for the realization of the state's power on the bodies of others, Eucharist is the liturgical realization of Christ's suffering and redemptive body in the bodies of His followers. Torture creates fearful and isolated bodies, bodies docile to the purposes of the regime; the Eucharist effects the body of Christ, a body marked by resistance to worldly power. Torture creates victims; Eucharist creates witnesses, *martyrs*. Isolation is overcome in the Eucharist by the building of a communal body which resists the state's attempts to disappear it.

Perhaps most importantly, the eschatological imagination of the Eucharist overcomes the secular imagination of separate spiritual and temporal planes which, as we saw in chapters 2–4, abetted the regime's disciplining of the body politic. Whereas New Christendom ecclesiology would cordon off the Kingdom of God into a space outside of time, in the Eucharist the Kingdom irrupts into time and "confuses" the spiritual and the temporal. The Eucharist thus realizes a body which is neither purely "mystical" nor simply analogous to the modern state: the true body of Christ.

To say that the Eucharist does in fact realize the body of Christ is not in any way to idealize the church as institution or those who hold authority in it. As previous chapters should make abundantly clear, the church militant is always flawed and sinful. Although inseparable, the church militant is not simply identical with the church triumphant as realized in the liturgy. In the Eucharist the church is always called to become what it eschatologically is. The Eucharist does make the church *ex opere operato*, but the effects are not always visible due to human sin. Christians are called to conform their practice to the Eucharistic imagination. And, as I hope to have made clear in chapter 1, to use the term "imagination" is not to imply unreality. Rather the Eucharistic imagination is a vision of what is really real, the Kingdom of God, as it disrupts the imagination of violence.

My first task in this chapter will be a genealogy of the bad politics embedded in the designation of the church as "mystical body," so prevalent in New Christendom thought. I will show how this designation accompanied an obscuring of the Eucharistic nature of the church as true body of Christ, and the creation of the temporal as an autonomous space from which the church was removed. I will then explore the Eucharist in its eschatological fullness as that which provides the resources for the construction of a true counter-body or counter-performance. The eschatological imagination of the Eucharist will be the key to reconfiguring the temporal not as a space but as a time, namely, the time connecting Christ's first coming with His second. I will draw mainly on scriptural and patristic sources, not to provide anything like a history of the Eucharist in the early church, but to mine the early tradition for resources for an adequate theological practice of the Eucharist.

This chapter is divided into four sections. In the first section, I venture an historical reading of the term "mystical body of Christ," *corpus mysticum*, and show how its use in reference to the church has accompanied the relegation of the church to an apolitical sphere. I therefore argue for the recovery of the church as "true body of Christ," *corpus verum*, and show, in sections 2–4, how a Eucharistic ecclesiology can and should provide the basis for the church's social practice. I have organized these three sections according to the future, past, and present temporalizations of the Eucharist.

1 The Mystical and the True

A genealogy of the term "mystical body of Christ" as applied to the church will serve us both to expose the faulty politics inherent in New Christendom ecclesiology and, more importantly for this chapter, to point us toward a more adequate ecclesiology based on the Eucharist. The designation of the church as "mystical" rather than "true" body of Christ has often served the imagination of a disincarnate church which hovers above the temporal, uniting Christians in soul while the body does its dirty work.

As we saw in the previous chapter, the theology of the church as "mystical body of Christ" was very important to New Christendom ecclesiology – in Europe, the US, and in Chile. In her history of social Catholicism in Chile, María Antonieta Huerta remarks, "The constitutive elements of the New Christendom can be summed up in the ecclesiological renovation of *the church as Mystical Body of Christ*, which implies a harmonious and hierarchical community."[2] "Mystical body" is Maritain's favored expression for the church.[3] In the literature of Catholic Action, the mystical body is often the

[2] Maria Antonieta Huerta, *Catolicismo social en Chile* (Santiago: Ediciones Paulinas, 1991), 408, italics in original.
[3] In addition to the examples cited above in chapter three, see Jacques Maritain, *The Peasant of the Garonne: An Old Layman Questions Himself about the Present Time*, trans. Michael Cuddihy and Elizabeth Hughes (New York: Rinehardt and Winston, 1968),

only image for the church employed.[4] Pius XI and Pius XII both connected Catholic Action with the mystical body.[5] The first World Congress of the Lay Apostolate held in Rome in 1951 took the mystical body as one of its major themes.[6] Upon his return from the Congress to Chile, Bishop Manuel Larraín wrote that the Congress and his visits to Spain, Italy, and France "made me feel . . . the Catholic laity's adoption in extraordinary depth of the doctrine of the mystical body of Christ."[7]

All this interest in the mystical body constituted a remarkable movement in theology which reached its peak in Europe between the World Wars and would continue to hold sway until the Second Vatican Council. As one commentator has written of the period between the wars, "Few other phrases in theology occasioned so much passion and spilled ink during these years as did the Pauline description of the church as the 'Body of Christ.'"[8] The twentieth-century explosion of interest in the mystical body can be traced to the period immediately following World War I. By the 1930s countless articles and books had been published putting the image of the mystical body at the center not only of ecclesiology, but christology, moral theology, ascetic theology, and theology in general.[9] By 1936, French theologian Emile Mersch's historical study of the doctrine of the mystical body could say of the doctrine, "So many theologians are now teaching it that we shall make no attempt to enumerate them, much less to class them

---

176–83, and *On the Church of Christ: The Person of the Church and Her Personnel*, trans. Joseph Evans (Notre Dame, Ind.: University of Notre Dame Press, 1973), 1–23.

[4] Among many examples, see Sebastian Tromp, SJ, *El Cuerpo Místico de Cristo y la Acción Católica*; Jeremiah Newman, *What is Catholic Action?: An Introduction to the Lay Apostolate* (Westminster, Md.: The Newman Press, 1958), 8–9; and Martin Quigley, Jr. and Monsignor Edward M. Connors, *Catholic Action in Practice* (New York: Random House, 1963), 3–19.

[5] See e.g. Pius XI's writings in *The Lay Apostolate: Papal Teachings*, ed. Benedictine Monks of Solesmes (Boston: St Paul Editions, 1961), 347–8, 383, 401; and Pius XII's encyclical *Mystici Corporis Christi*, paras. 8 and 98, in *The Papal Encyclicals 1939–1958*, ed. Claudia Carlen (Raleigh, NC: The Pierian Press, 1990), 38, 57.

[6] Newman, *What is Catholic Action?*, 8.

[7] Bishop Manuel Larraín, *Escritos Completos*, vol. I, 210.

[8] Ron William Walden, "The Concept of the Church in Recent Roman Catholic Theology" (Ph.D. diss., Yale University, 1975), 63.

[9] Ibid., 64–6. Interest in the designation of the church as the mystical body of Christ also appeared sporadically in nineteenth-century Germany in ways which suggest the influence of Romanticism; see Henri de Lubac, *The Splendour of the Church*, trans. Michael Mason (New York: Sheed and Ward, 1956), 61–3.

into schools. Again, its proponents are so recent that it is as yet too early to devote a historical study to them."[10] The mystical body craze did not bypass Chile; in 1948 Chilean theologian Egidio Viganó would report "The doctrine of the mystical body is in fashion today."[11] The movement reached its climax in 1943 with Pius XII's encyclical *Mystici Corporis Christi*, which gave official sanction to the popularity of this image. Mystical body theology would remain in vogue until the ascendancy of the "People of God" image for the church in the late 1950s and early 1960s. The mystical body image is still sometimes used, especially among conservatives in the church, but the period of its greatest popularity in church discourse coincided with that of the New Christendom ecclesiology.

The embrace of the mystical body in the twentieth century is largely explained as an attempt to counterbalance the juridical and institutional emphasis found in Catholic ecclesiology for three centuries following the Counter-Reformation. This emphasis is typified by Robert Bellarmine's insistence against the Reformers that the church is a *societas perfecta*, a structured society with organizational features and powers of coercion analogous to the Kingdom of France and the Republic of Venice. Bellarmine was still the primary authority of Catholic textbook ecclesiology at the beginning of the twentieth century.[12] This vision of the church was increasingly difficult to square with reality after World War I accelerated the crumbling of what remained of Constantinianism in Europe. The ecclesiology of the mystical body was important for New Christendom ecclesiology precisely because it deemphasized the visible, juridical aspects of the church and regarded it instead as a spiritual communion of people bonded by faith.[13] The church, then, is not to be seen as a cold and forbidding institution, a kind of divine IRS.

---

[10] Emile Mersch, SJ, *The Whole Christ: The Historical Development of the Doctrine of the Mystical Body in Scripture and Tradition*, trans. John R. Kelly, SJ (Milwaukee: The Bruce Publishing Company, 1938), 557. This is an English translation and slightly abridged version of the second edition of Mersch's *Le Corps mystique du Christ: étude de théologie historique*. Mersch's other major works include *Morale et corps mystique* and *La Théologie du corps mystique*.

[11] Egidio Viganó, SDB, *La solidaridad elemento esencial en la constitución del cuerpo místico según la doctrina de la "Summa Theologica" de Sto. Tomás de Aquino* (Santiago: Escuela Tipográfica Salesiana "La Gratitud Nacional," 1948), 9.

[12] Walden, "The Concept of the Church in Recent Roman Catholic Theology," 44–5, 52–3.

[13] Ibid., 67–9; and Avery Dulles, SJ, *Models of the Church*, expanded edn (Garden City, NY: Image Books, 1987), 47–55.

Instead it is both a *body*, that is, a connection with other people, and *mystical*, a connection of the heart.

As Henri de Lubac pointed out, mystical body ecclesiologists of the twentieth century had a regrettable tendency to set up a dichotomy between, on the one hand, the external, institutional church, and on the other hand, the body of Christ which is "interior," "hidden," "invisible" – all aspects which came to be associated with the term "mystical." So wide had this gap become that Louis Bouyer complained that in the term "mystical body," "the adjective has swamped the noun."[14] An example of this overemphasis is Sebastian Tromp's book *The Mystical Body of Christ and Catholic Action*, which devotes five pages to the "juridical concept of the church" and forty-one pages to the "mystical concept of the church."[15] A corrollary danger, according to de Lubac, was that the institution of the church, as "mystical" body, could not be a "real," organic body, a social body in any sense. The link to Christ Himself therefore was attenuated, and theologians in the 1930s and 40s wrote of the mystical body *of the church*. As a result the church as institution could become subject to a merely sociological analysis.[16]

Just as progressive Catholics used New Christendom political theology to distance Catholic political action from the institutional church, liberalizing elements in the church used the mystical body emphasis on the invisible church to distance themselves from institutional, especially Vatican, control. As could be expected, this produced opposition, from other theologians and from the Vatican, which also employed the image of the mystical body. Pius XII's *Mystici Corporis Christi* was written both to advance the use of the image and to reemphasize the juridical aspects of the church. Pius XII tried, as Avery Dulles puts it, "to harmonize the 'Mystical Body' concept with the societal concept of Bellarmine."[17] For Pius XII the church is primarily a spiritual union, but that union is held together by the visible hierarchical institution over which the Pope presides. The visible and invisible aspects of the church cannot be separated, though the institutional structure of the church is inferior to the divine spirit which animates it.[18] The church, therefore, is above merely human institutions like states and civil societies. The church does not constitute a social body. Its visibility and unity rather consists in the external

[14] Louis Bouyer, cited in de Lubac, *The Splendour of the Church*, 91.
[15] Sebastián Tromp, SJ, *El Cuerpo Místico de Cristo y la Acción Católica*, trans. Isabelino Fernández (Buenos Aires: Editorial Difusión, 1943), 5–51.
[16] de Lubac, *The Splendour of the Church*, 87–91.
[17] Dulles, *Models of the Church*, 52.
[18] Pope Pius XII, *Mystici Corporis Christi*, paras 60–6.

bonds of sharing the same profession of faith, the same rites, the same church laws, and above all the same allegiance to the Pope's guidance.[19]

Though Pius XII puts more accent on the institutional aspects of the church than do other mystical body theologians, both positions vis-a-vis the political order correspond with New Christendom arrangements. We recall that it was Pius XII as Cardinal Pacelli, Pius XI's secretary of state, who ordered the Chilean bishops in 1934 to avoid politics. Pius XII shared his immediate predecessor's view that the church should serve as a suprapolitical plane of unity for a troubled and conflictive world. Indeed, Pius XII declares this as his motivation for issuing his encyclical on the mystical body during the darkest days of World War II, June 1943. As he writes, "towns and fertile fields are strewn with massive ruins and defiled with the blood of brothers"; such calamities "naturally lift souls above the passing things of earth to those of heaven that abide forever."[20] To the church the world looks for hope, for while nation bloodies nation, the mystical body of Christ retains a "divinely-given unity"; those outside the church "will be forced to admire this fellowship in charity, and with the guidance and assistance of divine grace will long to share in the same union and charity."[21] It is the war, then, that has made proclamation of the doctrine of the mystical body urgent and significant.

> We have had the great consolation of witnessing something that has made the image of the Mystical Body of Jesus Christ stand out most clearly before the whole world. Though a long and deadly war has pitilessly broken the bond of brotherly union between nations, We have seen Our children in Christ, in whatever part of the world they happened to be, one in will and affection, lift up their hearts to the common Father, who, carrying in his own heart the cares and anxieties of all, is guiding the barque of the Catholic Church in the teeth of a raging tempest. This is a testimony to the wonderful union existing among Christians; but it also proves that, as Our paternal love embraces all peoples, whatever their nationality and race, so Catholics the world over, though their countries may have drawn the sword against each other, look to the Vicar of Jesus Christ as to the loving Father of them all, who, with absolute impartiality and incorruptible judgment, rising above the conflicting gales of human passions, takes upon himself with all his strength the defence of truth, justice and charity.[22]

It is not difficult to sympathize with Pius's efforts to bring some hope of comm-union to a world riven with strife. Nevertheless, one can imagine that the Pope's

---

[19] Ibid., para. 63, 69.
[20] Pope Pius XII, *Mystici Corporis Christi*, para. 4.
[21] Ibid., para. 5.
[22] Ibid., para. 6.

words would be slight comfort to the Christian on the battlefield who finds that a fellow member of the mystical body of Christ is trying to blow his legs off. What has gone wrong here? How is it that the doctrine of the mystical body of Christ could have come to mask, rather than witness against, the violence of the nations? Tracing the genealogy of the term "mystical body" may give us a clue. Though the twentieth-century proponents of mystical body ecclesiology rightly claimed that the expression *corpus mysticum* has a fairly early origin, the identification of the *corpus mysticum* with the church does not. Patristic and early medieval tradition, drawing on the Pauline images of the body of Christ, spoke of a threefold distinction of Christ's body: (1) the historical body, meaning the physical body of Jesus of Nazareth, (2) the sacramental body, or Christ as present in the Eucharistic elements, and (3) the ecclesial body, that is, the church.[23] The *corpus mysticum* was identified with the sacramental body, and the *corpus verum* with the church. However, around the twelfth century, as Henri de Lubac's important study *Corpus Mysticum* shows, there is an inversion of meaning. In subsequent centuries the altar would be the site of Christ's *corpus verum*, his true and knowable body, and the church would be his *corpus mysticum*.[24]

In the older understanding, according to de Lubac, the sacramental body and the church body are closely linked, and there is a "gap" between this pair and the historical body.[25] The Eucharist and the church, both of which are understood by the term *communio*, are together the contemporary perform-ance of the historical body, the unique historical event of Jesus. Christians are the *real* body of Christ, and the Eucharist is where the church *mystically* comes to be. The church and the Eucharist form the liturgical pair of visible community (*corpus verum*) and invisible action or mystery (*corpus mysticum*) which together re-present and re-member Christ's historical body. The gap is a temporal one. The link between past event and the present church is formed by the invisible action of the sacrament. The "mystical," then, is that which "insures the unity between two times" and brings the Christ event into present historical time in the church body, the *corpus verum*.[26]

In the newer, inverted conception of *corpus verum* and *corpus mysticum*, the relationships have changed. Now the historical and sacramental bodies

---

[23] Henri de Lubac, *Corpus Mysticum: L'Eucharistie et L'Église au moyen âge*, 2nd edn (Paris: Aubier, 1949), 34–9.

[24] Ibid., 13–19.

[25] Ibid., 288.

[26] Michel de Certeau, *The Mystic Fable*, vol. I, trans. Michael B. Smith (Chicago: University of Chicago Press, 1992), 82–3.

form a pair, and the gap is between them and the ecclesial body. The Eucharistic host has become *corpus verum*, and has taken on a "thingly realism," a visible and available sign in the here and now which produces reverence and awe. Eucharist is increasingly described in terms not of action but of object, such that the scholastic concentration is on the miracle produced in the elements, and not on the edification of the church by the presence of Christ in the sacrament.[27] At the same time, the church is identified as *corpus mysticum*, whose essence is hidden. The visibility of the church in the communal performance of the sacrament is replaced by the visibility of the Eucharistic object. Signified and signifier have exchanged places, such that the sacramental body is the visible signifier of the hidden signified, which is the social body of Christ. Henceforth the Eucharist, as Michel de Certeau puts it, "acts as the visible indicator of the proliferation of secret effects (of grace, of salvation) that make up the real life of the church."[28] Looking for this "real life" in history becomes problematic. The real life of the church is relegated to the "mystical," the hidden, that which will only be realized outside of time in the eschaton. Rather than linking the present with Jesus' first – and, we should add, second – coming, the mystical is now cordoned off from historical space and time. At this point in Christian history the temporal is beginning to be construed not as the time between the times, but as an increasingly autonomous space which is distinct from a spiritual space.

In documenting this historical inversion, de Lubac by no means sought to cast doubt on the real presence of Christ in the elements or the doctrine of transubstantiation. In fact, he thought that the best way to emphasize "eucharistic realism" was precisely through an "ecclesial realism" which sees Christ's real presence in the elements as *dynamic*, working toward the edification of the church.[29] What concerned de Lubac about the inversion of *verum* and *mysticum* was its tendency to reduce the Eucharist to a mere spectacle for the laity. The growth of the cult of the host itself in the later medieval period (the feast of Corpus Christi began in the thirteenth century) was not necessarily an advance for Eucharistic practice. As Sarah Beckwith puts it, "The emphasis was increasingly on watching Christ's body rather than being incorporated in it."[30]

During the later Middle Ages, the training of clergy became much more

---

[27] de Lubac, *Corpus Mysticum*, 78; 269–75.
[28] Ibid., 84.
[29] See Paul McPartlan, *Sacrament of Salvation: An Introduction to Eucharistic Ecclesiology* (Edinburgh: T. & T. Clark, 1995), 57.
[30] Sarah Beckwith, *Christ's Body: Identity, Culture and Society in Late Medieval Writings* (London: Routledge, 1993), 36.

specialized, and the distance between the clergy and the laity grew. Theology became more technical and farther removed from popular piety. Increasing clerical power was linked to the priest's ability to produce the host.[31] As more of the parts of the Mass were arrogated to the priest alone, laypeople were increasingly left to silent contemplation of the awesome spectacle, and this corresponded with a diminishing of the communal nature of the Eucharist and an individualizing of Eucharistic piety. Dom Gregory Dix describes this period in these terms: "The old corporate worship of the eucharist is declining into a mere focus for the subjective devotion of each separate worshipper in the isolation of his own mind. And it is the latter which is beginning to seem to him more important than the corporate act."[32] The image of the panopticon is useful again here. The individual Christian relates not to other Christians but directly to Christ as to the center of the circle, instead of incorporation with one's fellow Christians into the body of Christ, which has a head, but no center. Furthermore, the increased localization of the sacred in the Eucharistic host in effect secularized all that lay beyond it.[33]

Ernst Kantorowicz' classic study *The King's Two Bodies* displays how the inversion of *corpus mysticum* and *corpus verum* was associated not only with changes in the liturgical life of the church, but also with the reconfiguration of the relationship of the church and the civil authorities in the late medieval period. As the emerging self-sufficient secular polities developed their own sacred pretensions independent of the church, and as the church began to be structured as an increasingly organized institution with a centralized administration, the term *corpus mysticum* grew in importance for the church. Kantorowicz comments,

> the new ecclesiological designation of *corpus mysticum* fell in with the more general aspirations of that age: to hallow the secular polities as well as their administrative institutions. When in the twelfth century the Church, including the clerical bureaucracy, established itself as the 'mystical body of Christ,' the secular world sector proclaimed itself as the 'holy Empire.' This does not imply causation, either in the one way or the other. It merely indicates the activity of indeed interrelated impulses and ambitions by which the spiritual *corpus*

---

[31] de Certeau, *The Mystic Fable*, 85–7.

[32] Dom Gregory Dix, *The Shape of the Liturgy* (New York: Seabury Press, 1982 [1945]), 599.

[33] John Bossy, *Christianity in the West 1400–1700* (Oxford: Oxford University Press, 1985), 57–75; Catherine Pickstock, *After Writing: On the Liturgical Consummation of Philosophy* (Oxford: Blackwell Publishers, 1998), 146–9.

mysticum and the secular *sacrum imperium* happened to emerge simultaneously – around the middle of the twelfth century.[34]

In the early medieval era, St Augustine's theory of the relationship of spiritual and temporal held sway. The two cities, one formed by the love of God and one formed by the love of self, occupy not two different spaces but two different times. The earthly city is not everlasting. Its ends are perishable, while the heavenly city which sojourns with the earthly "shall dwell in the fixed stability of its eternal seat, which it now with patience waits for."[35] Aristotle's definition of a *polis* is that form of common life which is responsible for the highest good. For Augustine and his successors this was not the civil authority but the church triumphant, whose end was God. The City of God is the true *res publica*.[36] In the political theory of the early middle ages, the civil authority tended to exercise a purely functional office. The *regnum* was not a state occupying a fixed territory but rather a function of government fulfilled by certain persons. When Charlemagne and Otto the Great were crowned emperor, they acquired no new territory but rather new rights, duties, and functions. Kings were rulers of peoples, not of territories. Medieval society was a network of spatially overlapping personal loyalties.[37]

Theories of kingship in the early Middle Ages were dependent on the Chalcedonian formulation of the two natures of Christ. Christendom was one body, the body of Christ. The dual roles of king and bishop corresponded to the dual natures, human and divine, of Christ, which were inseparable yet unmixed. The king exercised a "liturgical" function as the "vicar of Christ" or "image of Christ" insofar as Christ is King as well as Priest.[38] Kingship and temporal authority were by no means found spatially "outside" the church. Indeed, the anointing of a king was considered by some a sacrament comparable in importance to baptism and ordination.[39] The continuity of the office of kingship was conferred by the church.[40]

[34] Ernst Kantorowicz, *The King's Two Bodies:* A Study in Medieval Political Theology (Princeton, NJ: University Press, 1957), 197.
[35] St Augustine of Hippo, *The City of God*, I, preface; also XV. 4.
[36] Ibid., II. 21; XIX. 21.
[37] Gerhart B. Ladner, "Aspects of Medieval Thought on Church and State," *Review of Politics* 9 (1947): 403–7; and Colin Morris, *The Papal Monarchy: The Western Church from 1050 to 1250* (Oxford: Clarendon Press, 1989), 14–21.
[38] Kantorowicz, *The King's Two Bodies*, 87–97, 56 n. 30.
[39] Ibid., 318–19.
[40] Otto Gierke, *Political Theories of the Middle Age*, trans. F.W. Maitland (Cambridge: Cambridge University Press, 1922), 12–13.

We see a shift beginning in the eleventh century. In the Investiture Controversy, the offices of king and bishop became increasingly independent of each other, and kingship was stripped of its connections to the altar. The title "vicar of Christ" came to refer to the Pope alone, and theories of kingship named the king as vicar or image of *God*; "as opposed to the earlier 'liturgical' kingship, the late-mediaeval kingship by 'divine right' was modelled after the Father in Heaven rather than after the Son on the Altar, and focused in a philosophy of Law rather than in the – still antique – physiology of the two-natured Mediator."[41] The church contributed to this movement in its attempts to assert the uniqueness of its function over against the rising sovereignty of the civil authorities. At the beginning of the thirteenth century, Pope Innocent III issued a decree "On Holy Unction" which separated anointments for bishops and kings and stressed that the royal unction did not confer the Holy Spirit.[42]

Perhaps the most significant change in this period came in the way that church and civil authority were related in *time*. Early medieval political theory operated on the Augustinian assumptions exemplified by the famous letter of Pope Gelasius I to the Emperor Anastasius in 494. According to Gelasius, church authority ranges more broadly than civil authority because the former is eternal and the latter only short-term.[43] Coincident with the separation of crown and altar, however, the nascent territorial states began to theorize a sempiternity for the state centered on an abstract concept of Law instead of on Christ.[44] It was thus that the "temporal," which had previously indicated that the coercive force of kingship was "temporarily" necessary while awaiting the second coming of Christ, would come to mean an autonomous sphere which pursues its own perpetuity.

Thus the fading of the liturgical kingship was accompanied by the *imperium*'s adoption of sacral aspirations independent from, yet parallel to, the church. As the civil authority began to aspire to sempiternity, it borrowed sacral symbols and images from the church for its own purposes. Kantorowicz remarks that

[41] Kantorowicz, *The King's Two Bodies*, 93, 87–9.
[42] Ibid., 319–21. Kantorowicz remarks, "As so often, the Roman Pontiff appears here as the chief promoter of precisely that 'secularism' which in other respects the Holy See tended to fight."
[43] Pope Gelasius, "Letter Twelve to Emperor Anastasius" in Hugo Rahner, SJ, *Church and State in Early Christianity*, trans. Leo Donald Davis, SJ (San Francisco: Ignatius Press, 1992), 173–6. See also Steven Ozment, *The Age of Reform 1250–1550: An Intellectual and Religious History of Late Medieval and Reformation Europe* (New Haven: Yale University Press, 1980), 138–9.
[44] Kantorowicz, *The King's Two Bodies*, 192.

the new territorial and quasi-national state, self-sufficient according to its claims and independent of the Church and the Papacy, quarried the wealth of ecclesiastical notions, which were so convenient to handle, and finally proceeded to assert itself by placing its own temporariness on a level with the sempiternity of the militant Church. In that process the idea of the *corpus mysticum*, as well as other corporational doctrines developed by the Church were to be of major importance.[45]

Kings adopted the trappings of episcopal authority, and the theological concept of martyrdom was now applied to death for the earthly *patria*.[46] Parallel to the rise of the state-as-church came the development of the church-as-state. At the same time that kingship was abandoning the altar, the *corpus verum* of Christ was increasingly confined there to serve as the visible, knowable signifier of a mystery which was becoming increasingly hidden behind the institutional structure of the church. Following on the Investiture Controversy, the church began to parallel the empire, developing a far more centralized and organized administrative apparatus and with it a proliferation of legal decrees to ensure its regular functioning. By the thirteenth century canon lawyers were making a routine distinction between the power of ecclesiastical jurisdiction (*potestas jurisdictionis*) and the sacramental power (*potestas ordinis*).[47] Priestly ordination conferred the ability to transubstantiate the host and produce the *corpus verum* of Christ. Consecration of a priest as bishop added nothing to these sacramental powers; what the bishop received, therefore, were jurisdictional powers, the power to govern the *corpus mysticum*.[48] The separation of episcopacy and Eucharist is a decisive indication that not only the temporal power but the church itself was beginning to locate its source not in the sacrament of the Lord's body but in formal legal concepts.

The term *corpus mysticum* became the vehicle used by the jurists to accentuate the character of the church as a legal corporation. What mattered about the term was its organic connotations and not any connection with the sacramental body of Christ. Theologians and jurists would come to use the term on analogy with natural bodies. They could thus refer frequently to

[45] Ibid., 207.
[46] Ibid., 193, 232–72. Colin Morris notes that in eleventh-century writings the term *patria* still "referred more commonly to the heavenly country than the earthly"; *The Papal Monarchy*, 18.
[47] Francis Oakley, *The Western Church in the Later Middle Ages* (Ithaca, NY: Cornell University Press, 1979), 27–8.
[48] Paul McPartlan, *The Eucharist Makes the church: Henri de Lubac and John Zizioulas in Dialogue* (Edinburgh: T. & T. Clark, 1993), 102.

the "Mystical Body of the church" and the "Mystical Body of God," such that what mattered was the corporate aspect of the body image, and the connection with the Eucharist was severed.[49] "Undeniably the former liturgical concept of *corpus mysticum* faded away only to be transformed into relatively colorless sociological, organological, or juristic notion."[50] By the fifteenth century, the connection with the liturgical body of Christ had been lost to such an extent that Jean Gerson could speak of the "Mystical Body of France."[51]

The application of the term *corpus mysticum* to the church was a legal fiction used to stress the juridical bonds linking the church to its head, the Pope. Innocent IV, for example, used the doctrine of the mystical body to deny the customary assumption that *dominium* over church property was invested in the local community. It was instead, said the Pope, invested in the entire mystical body of Christ, with the implication that the head of the body on earth, the Pope, could dispose of all ecclesiastical property on earth as he saw fit.[52] It became possible to assert that the mystical body is present not where the consecrated host is, but where the Pope is.[53]

The Popes used the doctrine of the mystical body in an attempt to reassert unity under the Pope in a world where secular control was rapidly on the rise and the political unity of Christendom was being fragmented into sovereign nation-states. Boniface VIII's famous 1302 bull *Unam Sanctam*, one of the most strident declarations of papal supremacy, was directed against Philip the Fair of France, one of the principal architects of the modern French state. Boniface invoked the image of the church as mystical body in order to insist that, despite the political divisions in Christendom, the primary allegiance of all Christians must be to the spiritual power represented by the Pope.[54] It was undeniable, however, that the temporal realm was becoming established as an autonomous power. In 1303 Pope Boniface VIII was taken prisoner at Anagni and humiliated by Philip's troops. As Joseph Strayer writes, "during the thirteenth

---

[49] Kantorowicz, *The King's Two Bodies*, 200–6. Kantorowicz notes that it was easier to conceive of the Pope as the head of the mystical body of the church than it was to conceive of the Pope as the head of the mystical body of Christ.

[50] Ibid., 202.

[51] Francis Oakley, *The Political Thought of Pierre d'Ailly: The Voluntarist Tradition* (New Haven, Conn.: Yale University Press, 1964), 59.

[52] Brian Tierney, *Foundations of the Conciliar Theory: The Contribution of the Medieval Canonists from Gratian to the Great Schism* (Cambridge: Cambridge University Press, 1955), 140–1.

[53] Kantorowicz, *The King's Two Bodies*, 203–5.

[54] Ibid., 194.

century leadership passed from the church to lay governments, and when the test came under Boniface VIII it was apparent that lay rulers, rather than the pope, could count on the primary allegiance of the people."[55]

In Boniface VIII's use of the term *corpus mysticum*, we can see clearly that, rather than occupying two different *times*, the church and the temporal authorities were being separated into two distinct *spaces* or jurisdictions. By the end of the thirteenth century, it had become common to distinguish the international church from the secular polities within which it operated. church and state had become more or less autonomous jurisdictions, parallel institutions legally separated. The church had attempted to meet the power of the rising state by stressing its own jurisdictional power. The first treatises on the church as an organization were written only in the early fourteenth century, with the purpose of establishing the church as an "ecclesiastical kingdom" parallel to the secular polity. The full interiorization of the church would have to wait several centuries more, but it was clear at this point that the construction of a separate and sempiternal political space outside the church was well underway.[56]

That the designation of the church as *corpus mysticum* was used to accentuate the growing institutionalization of the church does not mean that the church was becoming more "visible" in the sense of embodying in history the true social body of Christ. It is exactly the opposite. The church was becoming, as de Certeau says, more "opaque."[57] Hans Urs von Balthasar puts it this way: "The medieval, nonreflective aesthetic system of the correspondence between the inner nature of the Kingdom of God and its outward appearance had to give way to a stronger sense of tension . . . between the organized hierarchical Church as form and the inscrutable central mystery as content."[58] Increasingly with the rise of the sovereign state and the fragmentation of Christendom, the real life of the church was being internalized. As the church lost social and communal relevance to the emerging temporal power, a split developed between the visible church institution and a proliferation of "mystical" discourses which were defined as separate from the institution.[59] Simultaneously, the Eucharist was losing its significance as a communal re-membering of the body of Christ.

[55] J.R. Strayer, "The Laicization of French and English Society in the Thirteenth Century," *Speculum* 15 (1940), 76.
[56] Oakley, *The Western church in the Later Middle Ages*, 27–8, 157–60.
[57] de Certeau, *The Mystic Fable*, 86.
[58] Hans Urs von Balthasar, "The Contemporary Experience of the Church," in *Explorations in Theology*, vol. II (San Francisco: Ignatius Press, 1991), 18.
[59] de Certeau, *The Mystic Fable*, 85–9.

This genealogy of the designation of the church as mystical body of Christ, though obviously incomplete, may serve us not only to highlight some of the problems of New Christendom ecclesiology but also to point to a more adequate ecclesiology based on the Eucharist. Although certainly it would be a mistake simply to transpose the problematics of the later Middle Ages onto the twentieth century, in many ways, *mutatis mutandis*, the discourse of the mystical body serves similar functions in both eras. The obvious difference lies in the difference between Christendom and New Christendom; the church of the thirteenth century, though losing power to secular governments, had no intention of abandoning temporal space to them. Nevertheless, Boniface VIII no less than Pius XII recognized the new reality of a semi-autonomous, permanent temporal space essentially *outside* the spiritual power into which it was the church's right, under certain circumstances, to *intervene*. The doctrine of the mystical body is, in both cases, a plea for trans-political unity under the Pope's guidance in a world where a certain political and social unity fostered by the church was being torn asunder by nationalism and statism. The church, as a body *mystical*, must lose its transparency to the body of Christ, which is individualized and commodified in the host, and whose effects become a reality hidden in the interior of the individual heart. The chasm between visible and invisible churches widens. The adjective "mystical," when applied to the church, in the cases we have studied, signals a retreat in varying degrees from any interruption of historical time by the Kingdom of God. We look for the Kingdom outside of time. The eschatological significance of the body of Christ, and the sacramental action which produces it, is effectively denied. Christ comes to the individual upon her death, but the parousia as the end of history and its anticipation within history are rendered incomprehensible by a state and an earthly *patria* which declare their own indispensability and insist on their own perpetuity.

My purposes in constructing this genealogy of the term "mystical body" are limited. First, the reader should by no means infer an endorsement of, or nostalgia for, all pre-twelfth-century socio-political configurations of the church. The shadow cast by Constantine over early medieval Christianity, for example, warns us against any romanticization of that period. This is not a narrative of the "fall" of the church from some pristine perfection, only a tracing of broad changes in the church's relationship to civil authorities concomitant with the rise of the secular nation-state. These comments apply with equal force to church–state alliances in Chile. There should be no question of a return to pre-1925 "Christendom." Second, I do not mean to disparage all uses of the term "mystical body" in reference to the church. I have tried to call attention to some dangerous tendencies associated with the use of the term in two separate but related instances – late medieval official theology and twentieth-century New Christendom ecclesiology. The image of mystical body of Christ for the church does not carry with it some magical poison which will work its harm regardless of how it is employed. As an image for the church, its uses are many, varied, and quite malleable. I have tried to expose some of the bad politics that mystical body theology is capable of concealing.

It may be useful for our purposes to contrast two twentieth-century uses of mystical body theology. In the writings of Dorothy Day and the Catholic Worker movement, the mystical body of Christ image is used to name the church's responsibility to tend to the needs of all people, whether or not they are explicit members of the church. As Dorothy Day wrote after the start of World War II, "St. Augustine says that we are all members or potential members of the Mystical Body of Christ. Therefore all men are our neighbors and Christ told us we should love our neighbors, whether they be friend or enemy."[60] The contrast with *Mystici Corporis Christi*, written during the same war, is extremely telling. For Pius XII the doctrine of the mystical body unites in soul those Christians opposed in mortal combat on behalf of their respective countries; for Day the doctrine of the mystical body of Christ would render Christian participation in the carnage simply inconceivable. In the theology of the Catholic Worker, the mystical body of Christ does not hover above national boundaries but dissolves them, making possible Christian resistance to the nation-state's violent designs.

This brief look at mystical body ecclesiologies should serve to illuminate what is at issue in the church's attempt in Chile to recover itself as a disciplined body in opposition to the state. First, I hope to have prepared the way to develop a politics embedded in the liturgy – that is, accomplished *by Christ in the Eucharist*, and not by the church's imitation of the empire, or its reassertion of authority over the state. Discipline in the church can only make sense as a Eucharistic discipline. The body of Christ is liturgically enacted, not institutionally guaranteed. It should be apparent, second, that Eucharistic resistance to the state must abolish the idea of the temporal and the spiritual as two distinct spaces and recover the eschatological dimension of time. For this reason the following three sections will develop a Eucharistic theology based on the always-overlapping temporalizations of future, past, and present. We will begin with the future to emphasize the eschatological overthrowing of the world's time in the Eucharist.

[60] Dorothy Day, "The Mystical Body of Christ," *The Catholic Worker*, October 1939.

2 Until He Comes

It has been all too easy to regard the Eucharist as a mere representation of a past historical event in order to secure the graces won in that past event. Secular history – the uniform, and literally end-less, progress of time which makes the events of the life, death, and resurrection of Jesus Christ ever more remote from us – has come to predominate over eschatology, with grave consequences for the church. As the church made itself at home in the world's time, the urgent sense of pilgrimage through a temporary world toward an eternal end was muted. The Eucharist became a sacrifice performed for the benefit of the church which re-presented before God the historical process of redemption which had already been achieved in the past. The Eucharist as the inbreaking of the future Kingdom of God into time was suppressed.[61]

Benedict Anderson has traced the different conception of time which arose with the nation-state. The medieval Christian conception is marked by what Walter Benjamin called "Messianic time," that is, the simultaneity of past and future in the present. Representations of biblical figures in medieval dress strike the modern observer as odd, but medieval Christians did not imagine they were separated from the past by a wide gulf of ever-advancing time. The biblical figures were "contemporaries," connected to the present through divine providence. At the same time, the future was also always near; convinced that Christ could come again at any time, medievals tended to think of themselves as living in the end times. It would be difficult for medieval minds to imagine a long earthly future stretching ahead of them and their descendants.[62] Erich Auerbach displays this conception of time in a passage worth quoting at length.

> If an occurrence like the sacrifice of Isaac is interpreted as prefiguring the sacrifice of Christ, so that in the former the latter is as it were announced and promised and the latter "fulfills" . . . the former, then a connection is established between two events which are linked neither temporally nor causally – a connection which it is impossible to establish by reason in the horizontal dimension . . . It can be established only if both occurrences are vertically linked to Divine Providence, which alone is able to devise such a plan of history and

---

[61] Dix, *The Shape of the Liturgy*, 305.
[62] Benedict Anderson, *Imagined Communities: Reflections on the Origin and Spread of Nationalism*, revised edn (London: Verso, 1991), 22–4.

supply the key to its understanding . . . The here and now is no longer a mere link in an earthly chain of events, it is *simultaneously* something which has always been, and will be fulfilled in the future; and strictly, in the eyes of God, it is something eternal, something omnitemporal, something already consummated in the realm of fragmentary earthly event.[63]

By contrast, the secular imagination of history – what Benjamin called "homogeneous, empty time" – is a uniform sequence of cause and effect, measured not by the divine plan, but by clock and calendar. The past is the guarantee of the present and future, hence the importance of locating distant founding fathers and founding wars (even where their antiquity must be invented). The production of the nation-state depends especially on people imagining themselves as contemporaries not with the apostles and the saints, but with all the other presently living French (or Chileans or English). The rise of territorial nation-states implies the creation of a consciousness of time that one is linked with the simultaneous present activity of millions of other fellow-citizens, although one has no idea who they are or what they are up to. Thus is imagined a community which moves linearly out of the past, through the present, and into an endless future.[64]

In contrast with the secular historical imagination, the Christian story is intrinsically eschatological. Unlike the modern nation-state which, under the influence of Roman law, is predicated on its own perpetuity, Christian history has an end. Even stranger, it has an end which has *already come*, and yet time continues. This end of history is Jesus Christ, who announced the Kingdom of God as something which awaits final consummation in the future, but is already present in the form of signs. This is the peculiar "already but not yet" character of the Kingdom of God.[65]

The Eucharist is the true heart of this dimension of the church's life, because it is in the Eucharist that Christ Himself, the eternal consummation of history, becomes present in time. The Eucharist is not a mere reoffering of Christ's sacrifice by the priest before the watchful eyes of the faithful. The earthly Eucharist is the eternal action in time of Jesus Christ himself, "high priest, one who is seated at the right hand of the throne of the Majesty in the heavens" (Heb. 8:1). The Letter to the Hebrews situates Christ's heavenly liturgy

---

[63] Erich Auerbach, *Mimesis: The Representation of Reality in Western Literature*, trans. Willard Trask (Garden City, NY: Doubleday Anchor, 1957), 64, quoted in ibid., 24.
[64] Anderson, *Imagined Communities*, 24–36.
[65] Ibid., 259–63; and Geoffrey Wainwright, *Eucharist and Eschatology* (New York: Oxford University Press, 1981), 7–17.

squarely in the midst of the liturgical gathering of the humble, suffering community of Jewish Christians to whom the letter is addressed.

> You have come to Mount Zion and to the city of the living God, the heavenly Jerusalem, and to innumerable angels in festal gathering, and to the assembly (*ekklesia*) of the firstborn who are enrolled in heaven, and to God the judge of all, and to the spirits of the righteous made perfect, and to Jesus, the mediator of a new covenant, and to the sprinkled blood that speaks a better word than the blood of Abel (Heb. 12:22–4).

At the Eucharist the feast of the last day irrupts into earthly time, and the future breaks into the present. The *ekklesia* or church to which the author refers is not merely the church in its flawed earthly manifestation but the church in its full and proper sense, the eternal gathering of all creation by Christ into the Father's Kingdom.[66]

In his homilies on Hebrews, St John Chrysostom displays the church's belief that Eucharistic celebrations are the link between heavenly and earthly times.

> For although they are done on earth, yet nevertheless they are worthy of the Heavens. For when our Lord Jesus Christ lies slain as a sacrifice, when the Spirit is with us, when He who sits at the right hand of the Father is here, when children are made by the Washing, when they are fellow-citizens of those in Heaven, when we have a country, and a city, and citizenship there, when we are foreigners to things here, how can all these be other than "heavenly things"? But what? Are not our Hymns heavenly? Do not we also who are below utter in concert with them the same things which the divine choirs of angels sing above? Is not the altar also heavenly?[67]

In the Eucharist one is fellow citizen not of other present "Chileans" but of other members of the body of Christ, past, present, and future. The Christian wanders among the earthly nations on the way to her eternal *patria*, the Kingdom of God. The Eucharist makes clear, however, that this Kingdom does not simply stand outside of history, nor is heaven simply a goal for the

---

[66] Paul McPartlan has an excellent reading of Hebrews along these lines in his *Sacrament of Salvation: An Introduction to Eucharistic Ecclesiology* (Edinburgh: T. & T. Clark, 1995), 1–13.

[67] St John Chrysostom, *Homilies on Hebrews* XIV. 3, *Nicene and Post-Nicene Fathers*, ed. Philip Schaff, first series, vol. 14 (Peabody, Mass.: Hendrickson Publishers, 1994), 434, translation slightly altered.

individual to achieve at death. Under the sign of the Eucharist the Kingdom becomes present in history through the action of Christ, the heavenly High Priest. In the Eucharist the heavens are opened, and the church of all times and places is gathered around the altar. Vatican II's *Constitution on the Sacred Liturgy* affirms the scriptural and patristic emphasis on the eschatological dimension of the Eucharist: "In the earthly liturgy we take part in a foretaste of that heavenly liturgy which is celebrated in the Holy City of Jerusalem toward which we journey as pilgrims."[68] The secular historical imagination is thereby radically called into question.

The Eucharist as a meal is a foretaste of the heavenly banquet enjoyed by the blessed. The importance of symbolic meals to Jesus during his ministry is linked to the idea that in the future "people from east and west, from north and south, will come and sit down at the feast in the kingdom of God" (Lk. 13:29; cf. Mt. 8:11). The New Testament evidence suggests that Jesus' meals are understood by his followers as signs which indicate that the Kingdom is *now present* under signs. Patristic writers regarded the Eucharistic action as *mysterion*, in which the elements are in fact the body and blood of Jesus Christ, but what we now behold under the "sensible symbols" of bread and wine, we will behold face to face in the Kingdom.[69] As Geoffrey Wainwright points out in his study *Eucharist and Eschatology*, Christ's gift of his body and blood under the material signs of bread and wine renders impossible any dichotomy between the earthly and the heavenly, the material and the spiritual, or the body and the soul.[70] The form of a meal invites the participants to a physical, not merely spiritual, communion. Heaven and earth are united in the Eucharistic meal, which anticipates the resurrection not merely of the soul but of a glorified version of the same body which now feasts on earth.

The Eucharist has lost much of its eschatological import precisely where the church has come to feel at home in the world, forfeiting its sense of the transitory nature of the Christian sojourn among the earthly kingdoms. Threat of persecution helps keep this in focus; in the early church the Eucharist was explicitly connected with martyrdom. Many early martyrs regarded the Eucharist as the essential preparation and sustenance for their ordeal. During the fierce persecution under Diocletian, the martyrs of Abitinae adopted the motto *sine dominico non possumus*, for they would have seen the Eucharist as an invitation to, and the beginnings of, the heavenly banquet of which they were

---

[68] *Sacrosanctum Concilium* 8, in *Documents of Vatican II*, ed. Austin P. Flannery (Grand Rapids, Mich.: Wm. B. Eerdmans Publishing Co., 1975), 5.

[69] Wainwright, *Eucharist and Eschatology*, 29–42, 47–51.

[70] Ibid., 59.

about to partake in full.[71] The graves of the early martyrs also became special sites for the celebration of the Eucharist, particularly on the anniversary of martyrdom. Peter Brown has commented on how the graves of martyrs became "privileged places, where the contrasted poles of Heaven and Earth met."[72] This disruption of earthly time by the heavenly banquet would serve to maintain the eschatological tension of the Eucharist and thereby keep alive the subversive imagination of both Jesus' and the martyrs' confrontations with the *saeculum*.

In general, the emphasis on the Eucharist as a memorial of Jesus' actions on earth has emphasized his first coming to the neglect of his second. Aside from the problems involved in seeing the memorial as a merely psychological calling to mind of certain historical events and their "meaning," even theologies of real presence have neglected the parousia as a key to understanding the Eucharistic action. There is not a single allusion to the second coming in the old ordinary of the Roman mass.[73] The high and late medieval emphasis on sacrifice made it possible to think that the Eucharist was essentially a this-worldly dispensation of grace to the faithful through the constant propitiatory offering of Jesus' sacrifice to the Father. If the Eucharist is indeed a memorial of the whole Christ, however, then it recalls more than the past events of Jesus' life, death, and resurrection, but also expresses an ardent longing for the future completion of the Kingdom Christ inaugurated. Wainwright puts it this way: "At every eucharist the church is in fact praying that the parousia may take place at that very moment, and if the Father 'merely' sends His Son in the sacramental mode we have at least a taste of that future which God reserves for Himself to give one day."[74] Every Eucharistic celebration therefore recalls the merely temporary status of earthly life and locates the church in the simultaneity of both past and future. The church is ever in its infancy, made new by its Eucharistic participation in Christ's death and resurrection, the very founding moments of the church. And yet in the Eucharist the church also stands at the brink of its own final end, the parousia and the future consummation of the Kingdom.

For this reason it is fitting that the principal celebration of the Eucharist take place on Sunday, the day of the Lord's resurrection. Christ's resurrection stands

---

[71] Ibid., 124. The martyrs saw the Eucharist as a participation in Christ's Passion; see David N. Power, *The Eucharistic Mystery: Revitalizing the Tradition* (New York: Crossroad, 1992), 107–8.

[72] Peter Brown, *The Cult of the Saints: Its Rise and Function in Latin Christianity* (Chicago: University of Chicago Press, 1981), 3.

[73] Wainwright, *Eucharist and Eschatology*, 87–8.

[74] Ibid., 67.

as a promise of the general resurrection of all in the final judgment. But Christ's resurrection also marks his decisive triumph over sin, and thus the beginning of the new age in which we already are living. In the Eucharist Christ's "resurrection appearances" are now no longer spatially limited, but occur wherever the Eucharist is celebrated.[75] The celebration of the Eucharist in a special (obligatory) way on Sundays keeps the resurrection day separate from the world's days of the week and therefore keeps the church in tune with a different time. The endless uniform march of the world's time is denied by the promise and the realization of history's end in the Eucharistic celebration.[76]

If the church is a reimagining of worldly time, then it is necessary to overcome the idea of Eucharistic presence as making Christ available in the here and now in a way which effectively confines Christ to the elements – God in a can. Advocates of the theology of "transignification" have attacked the traditional doctrine of transubstantiation as a freezing of Christ's presence into a readily available, legible "thing" in the present. Philosopher Jean-Luc Marion, in response, has mounted an interesting defense of transubstantiation based on seeing the Eucharistic presence as gift. Christ's presence in the Eucharist, according to Marion, is not the presence of the here and now, the ordinary conception of time, but is rather the present, meaning "gift," of Christ's self in a way that encompasses the whole Christ, past, future, and present.[77]

The secular imagination of time is overcome in the Eucharist by embodying the three temporalizations implicit in I Cor. 11:26: "For as often as you eat this bread and drink the cup, you proclaim the Lord's death until he comes." The present communion is a function of the memorial of the past death of Jesus and his future coming in glory. According to Marion, in the Eucharistic memorial the past is not understood as the dredging up of an accomplished deed, or the recalling of a past fact that is defined by its nonpresence; "It is not at all a question of commemorating a dead person to spare him the second death of oblivion."[78] It is not the present day which determines the reality of the past, but the other way around. In other words, the present sacrifice does

[75] Jonathan Bishop, *Some Bodies: The Eucharist and its Implications* (Macon, Ga.: Mercer University Press, 1992), 42.

[76] Wainwright, *Eucharist and Eschatology*, 74–8. Raymond Moloney refers to liturgical time as "the time that floweth not," in contrast to the relentless forward march of worldly time; see Raymond Moloney, SJ, *The Eucharist* (Collegeville, Minn.: Liturgical Press, 1995), 207–8.

[77] Jean-Luc Marion, *God Without Being*, trans. Thomas A. Carlson (Chicago: University of Chicago Press, 1991), 161–82.

[78] Ibid., 172.

not "produce" the mystery, in the visible form of the elements which make grace available to us. The very present is only possible as an extension of what Christ accomplished in the past.

But if the present is governed by the past, it is only because of the promise made in the past for the consummation of history in the future. The memorial is only valid as a prayer to the Father to hasten Christ's coming again. But this future promised is not a mere utopia, a simple nonpresence which awaits realization outside of history. In the Eucharist the church is "straining forward to what lies ahead" (Phil. 3:13). In the Eucharist the future Kingdom is already incompletely present, so that, as Marion says, "the present itself occurs entirely as this anticipation concretely lived."[79] The Eucharistic community is already a real foretaste of the fullness of the Kingdom.

The present, then, is not a self-sufficient reality defined over against the nonpresence of an extinct past and a not-yet-existent future; in the Eucharist the future fulfillment of the past governs the present. The Eucharistic present is not just one moment in the regular sequence of secular historical time – one damn thing after another. Eucharistic time is marked by charity, the gratuitous and disruptive presence of the Kingdom of God. "Each instant of the present must befall us as a gift."[80] The Eucharist is our *daily* bread precisely in the sense that it is manna, a free gift of God which cannot be stored up for the next day. The Eucharist is not an available thing of which one can take possession. It is never simply here and now, but is always oriented by the past and straining towards the future. The Eucharistic community lives on borrowed time. The temporal is never a stable space autonomous from the spiritual, but is rather the time between the first and second comings of Christ during which the members of the Eucharistic community live as aliens in any earthly country.

As a result of his eschatological analysis of the Eucharistic presence, Marion argues for the restoration of the more traditional designation of the sacramental body of the Eucharist as *corpus mysticum* and the ecclesiastical body as *corpus verum*. The consecrated host is the very flesh of Jesus Christ, truly edible, but it is "mystical" flesh because it defies confinement to a readily available here and now.[81] Marion prefers the term "Eucharistic presence" to "real presence"

---

[79] Ibid., 174.

[80] Ibid., 175.

[81] It should be clear that Marion by no means denies the presence of Christ in the consecrated host. His defense of transubstantiation is based on his contention that the doctrine of transubstantiation alone maintains the Eucharistic presence as an *existence*, that is, as existing outside of the consciousness of the human community; ibid., 169, 182.

– "real" from the Latin *res*, meaning "thing." He offers a recovery of the scholastic couple *res et sacramentum* for the sacramental body. The consecrated bread and wine are *res*, the body and blood of Christ, but are also *sacramentum*, for they serve as signs which point to the building of the ecclesiastical body, which alone can be called purely *res*. If the Eucharist is governed by charity, God's free gift, then one is required not to explain it but to receive it and be assimilated to the body of Christ. It is the communal commitment of charity which is the true *res* of the Eucharist, and therefore the Eucharist aims at the building of the true body of Christ in time, his *corpus verum*, which the church both is and is meant to be.[82]

3 Re-membering Christ

The Eucharist is an *anamnesis* of the past; Jesus commands his followers, "Do this in remembrance of me" (Lk. 22:19). If we understand this command properly, however, the Eucharist is much more than a ritual repetition of the past. It is rather a literal re-membering of Christ's body, a knitting together of the body of Christ by the participation of many in His sacrifice. In earlier chapters I argued that Christian resistance to state oppression depends on the church being the body of Christ capable of resisting the fragmenting discipline of the state. Now we need to look at how the Eucharist conforms the followers of Christ to the true body of Christ, a body able to provide a counter-discipline to state terror. If torture is the imagination of the state, the Eucharist is the imagination of the church.

In *The City of God* Augustine distinguishes true sacrifice from the false sacrifices of pagan Rome's state religion. According to Augustine, the true God does not demand sacrifice as something taken from us in order to fill a need in God. We ourselves become a sacrifice to God, "not because He needs anything, but because it behoves us to be His possession."[83] A true sacrifice does not subtract something from us, but unites us to God in holy fellowship by reference to our eternal end. A human being can become a sacrifice, therefore, by dying to the world and rising with Christ. Augustine quotes Paul: "[P]resent your bodies as a living sacrifice," Paul tells the church in Rome. "Do not be conformed to this world, but be transformed." (Rom. 12:1-2). Christ adopted the form of a servant. His self-gift to humanity, his

---

[82] Marion, *God Without Being*, 176–82.
[83] St Augustine of Hippo, *The City of God*, trans. Marcus Dods (New York: The Modern Library, 1950), 705 [XIX. 23].

complete *kenosis*, is such that he gives over his very identity to the community of his followers, who thereby become in history His true body, which in turn takes the form of a servant. The Christian sacrifice unites us both to each other and to God in the body of Christ, so that we become what is offered on the altar. This, says Augustine, is the import of the Eucharist.[84]

Modern Christians often speak of "hearing" or "attending" the Eucharist; priests "say" the mass. The ancient church, by contrast, tended to speak of "doing" the Eucharist (*eucharistiam facere*) or "performing" the mysteries (*mysteria telein*).[85] The word *anamnesis* had the effect not so much of a memorial, as one would say kind words about the dead, but rather of a performance. The emphasis is thus on the entire rite of the Eucharist as action, and not simply on the consecration of the elements. In the medieval and modern contexts, a shift occurred in the relationship between sacrament and sacrifice. According to Dix, Christians have tended to make the sacrifice dependent on the sacrament: since the consecration turns the bread and wine into the body and blood of Christ, what the church does in the Eucharist must be what Christ did with His body and blood – offer them in sacrifice. In the early church, on the other hand, priority was given to the sacrifice: since we are Christ's body performing His will, what we offer must be what He offered in the events on Calvary, His own body and blood.[86]

Here we see clearly that Christian performance of the Eucharist depends on taking quite seriously the designation of the church as the body of Christ; the church's performance of self-sacrifice is in fact the "proof" of the presence of Christ in the bread and wine. In order for the church at the Eucharistic table to offer what Christ offered, the church must offer its own self in sacrifice, because the community of Christians is nothing less than Christ's *corpus verum*. Dix notes the inversion of the terms *verum* and *mysticum* in Eucharistic theology since the high Middle Ages, and says that the Fathers applied the term *corpus verum* exclusively to the church in order to reinforce the priority of the whole performance to the matter of the sacrament.[87]

It should be obvious that this priority by no means implies anything less than Christ's flesh and blood on the altar under the appearance of bread and wine. In fact the dependence of the sacrament on the sacrifice explains the straightforward literalness with which many ancient writers regarded both the consecrated elements and the church as the body of Christ. If the church truly

---

[84] Ibid., 310 [X. 6].
[85] Dix, *The Shape of the Liturgy*, 12.
[86] Ibid., 245–6.
[87] Ibid., 246–7.

is Christ's Body doing Christ's will, then what it offers at the altar in sacrifice must really be what Christ offered in his sacrifice, his body and blood. Just as Christ was truly incarnated and suffered in human flesh in Jerusalem so many years ago, so the martyrs make a sacrifice of their own flesh. As the sacrifices of the church of the martyrs are not metaphoric, neither is its offering at the altar. The flesh of Christ which Christians consume at the Eucharistic meal is as real as the Christian flesh the lions gnawed in Roman circuses, though the former is consumed under the sign of bread. Ten years before his own death in Rome, Justin Martyr wrote of the Eucharist:

> Not as common bread or as common drink do we receive these, but just as through the word of God, Jesus Christ, our Saviour, became incarnate and took on flesh and blood for our salvation, so, we have been taught, the food over which thanks has been given by the prayer of His word, and which nourishes our flesh and blood by assimilation, is both the flesh and blood of that incarnate Jesus.[88]

It was not uncommon, therefore, for the ancient church to connect failure to recognize Christ in the consecrated bread and wine with failure to treat others as brothers and sisters in Christ. Paul was not alone in chastising certain Christians' reprehensible conduct due to their failure to "discern the body" (I Cor. 11:29). St Ignatius, for example, complains about those who

> have no care for love, no thought for the widow and orphan, none at all for the afflicted, the captive, the hungry or the thirsty. They even absent themselves from the Eucharist and the public prayers, because they will not admit that the Eucharist is the self-same body of our Saviour Jesus Christ which suffered for our sins, and which the Father in His goodness afterwards raised up again.[89]

This is obviously an echo of Matthew 25:31–46, in which Jesus grounds the doctrine of the body of Christ by identifying his own self with the afflicted.[90] Those who truly discern the body and are incorporated into it cannot remain insensate to the sufferings of the weaker members.

One of the peculiarities of the Eucharistic feast is that we become the body of Christ by consuming it. Unlike ordinary food, the body does not become

[88] Justin Martyr, *First Apology*, 66, in *The Eucharist*, Message of the Fathers of the Church, no. 7, ed. Daniel J. Sheerin (Wilmington, Del.: Michael Glazier, 1986), 34.
[89] Ignatius of Antioch, *Epistle to the Smyrnaeans* 6–7, *Early Christian Writings*, trans. Maxwell Staniforth (New York: Penguin Books, 1968), 121.
[90] Dix, *The Shape of the Liturgy*, 250–1.

assimilated into our bodies, but vice versa. Thus Augustine reports in his *Confessions* that he heard a voice from on high say to him, "'I am the food of the fully grown; grow and you will feed on me. And you will not change me into you like the food your flesh eats, but you will be changed into me.'"[91] The fact that the church is literally changed into Christ is not a cause for triumphalism, however, precisely because our assimilation to the body of Christ means that we then become food for the world, to be broken, given away, and consumed. As Raniero Cantalamessa puts it, "the Eucharist makes the Church by making the Church Eucharist!"[92] The Eucharist is under the sign of gift, not of glory. It is true, therefore, that the church is called to embody the very promise of the future Kingdom of God, given long ago, in the present, so that the promise might not be discredited or simply shoved to the margins of history. But it does so not by conquering bodies but by making a sacrifice of its own body. In this sense the church is called to "make up what is lacking in Christ's afflictions" (Col. 1:24). The church is the continuation of the presence of Christ in the world, but the church is most properly the church when it exists as gift and sustenance for others.

Eucharistic sacrifice is the end of the violent sacrifice on which the religions of the world are based, for its aim is not to create new victims but rather martyrs, witnesses to the end of victimization. Assimilation to Christ's sacrifice is not the continuation of the violence and rivalry needed to sustain a certain conception of society, but the gathering of a new social body in which the only sacrifice is the mutual self-offering of Christian charity. Martyrs offer their lives in the knowledge that their refusal to return violence for violence is an identification with Christ's risen body and an anticipation of the heavenly banquet.[93]

While the identification of the church with Christ's true body is much more than metaphor, the earthly church is not, however, to be identified with the whole Christ. Christ is fully identified with the heavenly church; the church in time is the fully realized body only as a foretaste in the Eucharist, when the heavens are momentarily opened.[94] The modern Christian hardly needs

---

[91] St Augustine of Hippo, *Confessions*, trans. Henry Chadwick (Oxford: Oxford University Press, 1991), 124 [VII. x (16)].

[92] Raniero Cantalamessa, *The Eucharist: Our Sanctification* (Collegeville, Minn.: The Liturgical Press, 1993), 21.

[93] Much of the vocabulary here is that of René Girard; see his *Things Hidden Since the Foundation of the World*, trans. Stephen Bann and Michael Metteer (London: Athlone Press, 1987).

[94] See *Lumen Gentium*, 48; also McPartlan, *The Eucharist Makes the Church*, 265-71.

convincing of the manifest sinfulness and unfaithfulness of the church throughout history, not least in our own day. Until Christ comes again, His body on earth is always a body under construction. We live in a construction zone, with all of the dangers that implies. The danger does not lie, however, in the identification of the church with the body of Christ, but rather in the complete identification of the earthly body with the heavenly. Many contemporary Christians have shied away from the image of the church as the body of Christ, for naming the church as Christ's very body rings of the ecclesiastical triumphalism of past eras.[95] If the argument of this book is correct, however, the unfaithfulness of the church in the present age is based to some extent precisely on its failure to take itself seriously as the continuation of Christ's body in the world and to conform itself, body and soul, not to the world but to Christ (Rom. 12:2).

The church *is* the body of Christ, as Paul makes abundantly clear (I Cor. 12), but it is also called to *become* the fulfillment of Christ's body in history. The church is always mandated to become in time what it already is eternally in God's eyes. The Eucharist makes the church, but not in the sense that the church is not the body of Christ until construction is completed. We must avoid a certain Pelagianism which sees the church as a human institution which aspires to be Christlike within the reasonable limits of human failings. The simple fact is that Christ in His cross and resurrection has *already* vanquished sin's hegemony, and continues to be present in history in His body, until He comes in the fullness of glory. We are called to witness to what Christ is already doing in His body. So Augustine admonishes his congregation:

> So if it's you that are the body of Christ and its members, it's the mystery meaning you that has been placed on the Lord's table; what you receive is the mystery that means you. It is to what you are that you reply *Amen*, and by so replying you express your assent. What you hear, you see, is *The body of Christ*, and you answer, *Amen*. So be a member of the body of Christ, in order to make that *Amen* true.[96]

The conduct of the believer makes true the Amen, not what the Amen affirms. It is impossible to understand the church's mandate to become what it

[95] Avery Dulles, *A Church to Believe in: Discipleship and the Dynamics of Freedom* (New York: Crossroad, 1982), 3-6.
[96] St Augustine, "Sermon 272," in *Sermons III/7, The Works of St. Augustine: A Translation for the 21st Century* trans. Edmund Hill, and ed. John Rotelle, (New Rochelle, NY: New City Press, 1993), 300.

already is if we imagine history in the secular sense as a linear sequence of events. *Anamnesis* is not the mere recall of ever-more-distant past events; it is rather, in John Zizioulas's apt phrase, the "memory of the future."[97] The Eucharist enacts the presence not simply of what Christ did in the past, but also and especially the future fulfillment of Christ's work through the Spirit. The past and present receive their significance and continuity from the future, when Christ's salvific will is manifested in full in a new heaven and a new earth. In Eucharistic time the past is not simply an historical object, a given quantity to be parsed by the community; nor is the future Kingdom something simply to be awaited patiently as we muddle through history. In the Eucharist, past and future simultaneously converge, and the whole Christ, the eschatological church of all times and places, is present.

Zizioulas points out how this eschatological disruption of the secular historical imagination also overcomes the individuality of historical existence. For Zizioulas, history is the insistence that being is temporally prior to communion; I exist in my own right before I enter into relationship with others. In the eschatological imagination of the Eucharist, on the other hand, we first have our being in communion as a member of Christ. Individuality is radically overcome by this eternal priority of Christ; Christ in the Spirit contains our destiny, ourselves as we will be. The Eucharist makes present simultaneously our past and our future destiny in communion by incorporating us into the body of Christ.[98]

4 Making the Body Visible

It is the body of Christ's disruption of history that we must keep in focus as we move to an examination of the Eucharist as that performance which makes the body of Christ visible in the present. If the church is to resist disappearance, then it must be publicly visible as the body of Christ in the present time, not secreted away in the souls of believers or relegated to the distant historical past or future. It becomes visible through its disciplined practices, but the church's discipline must not simply mimic that of the state. I will argue that the church's discipline can only be realized as a Eucharistic discipline, and it must therefore assume a conformity to Christ, and therefore an assimilation to Christ's self-sacrifice. Christ in the Eucharist actively

---

[97] John Zizioulas, *Being as Communion* (Crestwood, NY: St Vladimir's Seminary Press, 1985), 180.
[98] Ibid., 101–14, 181–8.

disciplines the church. The church does not simply perform the Eucharist; the Eucharist performs the church.

One of the key texts in this regard is Paul's first letter to the Corinthians. Paul's words in I Cor. 10:16-17 on community in the Eucharist – filched for many a feel-good hymn – are in fact a reprimand issued to the community for its misconduct:

> The cup of blessing that we bless, is it not a sharing in the blood of Christ? The bread that we break, is it not a sharing in the body of Christ? Because there is one bread, we who are many are one body, for we all partake of the one bread.

Paul is appalled at the Corinthians' belief that they can participate in both the Eucharist and pagan worship. To do so is to assault the unity of the church. In verses 20-1 Paul forbids them to participate in both kinds of sacrifice, for by feasting with pagans they feast at the "table of demons," thus entering into a common union with the very forces that Christ came to vanquish. In Paul's view the Eucharist carries with it certain demands. The Eucharist creates unity, it is true, but the Eucharist also *requires* unity. If certain Corinthians wish to partake of the Eucharist, they must first change their conduct.

Is there an "or else?" For Paul it comes in the next chapter of his epistle.

> Whoever, therefore, eats the bread or drinks the cup of the Lord in an unworthy manner will be answerable for the body and blood of the Lord. Examine yourselves, and only then eat of the bread and drink of the cup. For all who eat and drink without discerning the body, eat and drink judgment against themselves. For this reason many of you are weak and ill, and some have died. But if we judged ourselves, we would not be judged. But when we are judged by the Lord, we are disciplined so that we may not be condemned along with the world (I Cor. 11:27–32).

This passage bristles with eschatological expectation. The specific sin Paul addresses here concerns the divisions among the Christians at Corinth, particularly between the wealthy and the poor (11:17-22). As in 10:16-22, unity among Christians is at issue, in the context of the cosmic struggle between the church on the one hand and the demonic forces of the "world," *kosmos*, on the other. Immediately preceding the passage beginning at 11:27, Paul gives instructions for the celebration of the Eucharist "until he comes." The parousia is to be a time not only of redemption but of judgment, when the "world" – meaning that part of creation which refuses the sovereignty of Christ – will be overthrown. As the sacrament which anticipates the parousia now, the Eucharist is also placed in the context of judgment. Those who do

not "discern the body" and become a member of Christ risk condemnation
along with the forces that oppose Christ. The failure to "discern the body"
refers not only to the body on the altar but the ecclesial body as well. The
Corinthians are showing "contempt for the church of God" (11:22) through
their actions. As Paul makes plain, the Lord's "discipline" is meant to save
people from being condemned along with the world. It does so by forming
Christians through the Eucharist into a body which stands in opposition to the
forces of the world.

Although this passage clearly points forward to the future coming of the
Lord in glory, for Paul the effects of the Kingdom are *already* felt in the
community at Corinth in the present. For those who are in Christ, already
"everything old has passed away; see, everything has become new!" (II Cor.
5:17). For those who are not in Christ, judgment likewise does not simply
await the parousia; people are already getting sick and dying as a consequence
of eating and drinking without discerning the body of Christ. Paul is not
speaking metaphorically; *the Eucharist can kill you.* We must stress that it is not
the church which disciplines, but the Lord who disciplines the church.
Furthermore, this is not a matter for the "soul" alone. Those who "eat and
drink judgment against themselves" feel the effects in their very flesh.

What Paul seems to mean by "discipline" is essentially the authority over
the body which produces a visible body of people set apart from the world by
their conduct. In Romans 6, for example, the forces of sin contend with Christ
for control over the body. What one does with the body is a question of slavery
to sin on the one hand versus obedience to Christ, what Paul calls "slavery to
righteousness," on the other (Rom. 6:16-19). Paul commands the Romans,
"do not let sin exercise dominion in your mortal bodies, to make you obey
their passions. No longer present your members to sin as instruments of
wickedness, but present yourselves to God as those who have been brought
from death to life" (Rom. 6:12-13). Christ's followers must be set apart by the
visibility of this life in their bodies now; Christians are "always carrying in the
body the death of Jesus, so that the life of Jesus may also be made visible in our
bodies" (II Cor. 4:10).

In I Cor. 6:18, Paul paraphrases his enemies who contend that "every
sin that a person commits is outside the body." Paul responds, "but the
fornicator sins against the body itself." There is no separating body and soul.
The body is a "temple of the Holy Spirit" which therefore belongs to God
(6:19). "The body is meant not for fornication but for the Lord, and the Lord
for the body. And God raised the Lord and will also raise us by his power. Do
you not know that your bodies are members of Christ?" (6:13-15) At the Last
Judgment we look for the resurrection, not just of the soul, but of the body,

so the body belongs to Christ. The body is enlisted in the cosmic struggle against the demonic forces of the world. It is therefore necessary, as Paul contends in the previous chapter, to except those who seriously misuse the body from the body of Christ (5:1-13). The body is the locus of Christian discipline; the church cannot be relegated to a spiritual realm.

St Cyprian writes similarly of Christian *disciplina* as inscribing the body so as to resist the encroachment of worldly powers against the church. In April of the year 248, Rome began the celebration of its millenium by requiring citizens of the Empire to prove their patriotism in public sacrifice to the Roman gods.[99] For Cyprian, the church is under constant attack from the forces of worldly power, and the battleground is the body of the believer. As Peter Brown remarks, in Cyprian's view "The 'flesh' of the Christian was a bulwark against the *saeculum*."[100] This is most apparent in the martyrs (whose ranks Cyprian would himself join); shaped and strengthened by the Eucharist, they offer their bodies, refusing to capitulate to the Romans under fear of bodily pain. But all Christians are called on to exercise similar discipline over the body in their present lives, a "daily martyrdom." The body's own desires, such as sexuality, must be controlled, but the most serious threats according to Cyprian come from outside the individual body from the powers of the world, which ceaselessly try to use the Christian body for their own purposes. For Cyprian the body of the Christian is a microcosm of the church body which is under constant threat from the *saeculum*. Christian discipline is the antidote to the world's attempts to discipline the body.[101]

For much of the ancient church, the ideal of what would later be called the *disciplina arcani* – the "discipline of the secret" – formed the church into a visible body of people whose outward conduct was, in effect, to be ordered by the Eucharist. Pagans and even catechumens were denied access to the celebration of the Eucharist, which was protected by secrecy and shrouded with trepidation and awe.[102] Participation in the Eucharist was demanding, requiring not simply a proper internal disposition but right conduct. In the *Apostolic Tradition* of Hippolytus, for example, the community is instructed to inquire into the crafts and professions of those who wish to join. Brothel-keepers, idol-makers, gladiators, soldiers, magistrates, prostitutes – all must

[99] Kenneth Hein, *Eucharist and Excommunication: A Study in Early Christian Doctrine and Discipline* (Bern: Herbert Lang, 1973), 365.
[100] Peter Brown, *The Body and Society: Men, Women, and Sexual Renunciation in Early Christianity* (New York: Columbia University Press, 1988), 194.
[101] Ibid., 193–5.
[102] Cantalamessa, *The Eucharist*, 76.

either change occupation or be rejected as candidates for baptism.[103] After completion of a three-year catechumenate, candidates are examined not on points of doctrine but on their lives during this period. "Have they honoured the widows? Have they visited the sick? Have they done every kind of good work?"[104] Only after passing this test are they baptized, and then finally admitted to the Eucharist. The Didache likewise makes conduct the touchstone for participation in the Eucharist. The presider says to the congregation "Whosoever is holy, let him approach. Whoso is not, let him repent." The people reply, "O Lord, come quickly."[105]

This emphasis on the Eucharist as discipline should not be taken as a one-sided emphasis on condemnation, for the Judge who comes at the parousia comes to redeem as well as vanquish. As Wainwright points out, "A judge may acquit as well as condemn!"[106] Indeed, in Matthew's account of the Last Supper, Jesus gives the cup saying "Drink from it, all of you; for this is my blood of the covenant, which is poured out for many for the forgiveness of sins" (Mt. 26:27-8). The Eucharist is a source of forgiveness and reconciliation.

The Eucharist is not a wonder drug which, taken regularly, simply removes the stain of sin from the individual's soul. The Eucharist produces forgiveness by demanding a real unity among people now. The Didache instructs the congregation:

> Assemble on the Lord's Day, and break bread and offer the Eucharist; but first make confession of your faults, so that your sacrifice may be a pure one. Anyone who has a difference with his fellow is not to take part with you until they have been reconciled, so as to avoid any profanation of your sacrifice.[107]

Likewise, from the earliest times, Christians have exchanged the kiss of peace before the Eucharist as a sign that the Eucharist requires reconciliation and forgiveness.[108] Participating in the Eucharist does not earn forgiveness nor compel God to forgive sins which God otherwise would hold bound. The

[103] Hippolytus, *Apostolic Tradition* 16, ed. Geoffrey J. Cuming (Bramcote: Grove Books, 1976), 15–16.
[104] Ibid., 17 [20].
[105] *The Didache* 10, in *Early Christian Writings*, 232.
[106] Wainwright, *Eucharist and Eschatology*, 83.
[107] *The Didache* 14, in *Early Christian Writings*, 234.
[108] The third-century Syrian *Didascalia Apostolorum* reports that during the kiss of peace the deacon would cry out "Is there any man that keepeth ought against his fellow?" as a final precaution lest anyone enter into the Eucharist unreconciled; see Dix, *The Shape of the Liturgy*, 106–7.

Lamb of God has already taken away the sins of the world in His sacrifice. The task of the Christian is to live now as if that is in fact the case, to embody redemption by living a reconciled life, and thereby bring the Kingdom, however incompletely, into the present. St John Chrysostom exhorts Christians to reconcile before partaking of the Eucharist in these terms.

> The Son of God came down for this purpose, to reconcile our human nature to the Lord. But He did not come down for that purpose alone, but also for the purpose of making us, if we do likewise, sharers of His title. For He says: "Blessed are the peacemakers, for they shall be called sons of God" (Mt. 5:9). You, according to human capacity, must do what the Onlybegotten Son of God has done, be an agent of peace, for yourself and for others. For this reason, at the very time of sacrifice He recalls to us no other commandment than that of reconciliation with one's brother, showing that it is the greatest of all.[109]

Discipline, therefore, is not opposed to forgiveness but is its embodiment. What Christ has done in reconciling creation to Himself requires and makes possible a real bodily reconciliation in time. As His body, the church is called to exemplify that reconciliation in its own flesh, and visibly to show forth to a world mired in violence and division what Christ has done. We recall that for Maritain and New Christendom ecclesiology, to be engaged in "the vicissitudes of time" is to get one's hands dirty; "We cannot touch the flesh of the human being without staining our fingers."[110] A true Christian eschatology, on the other hand, makes real reconciliation in time and in the flesh not only possible but urgently necessary. Jesus tells His followers,

> when you are offering your gift at the altar, if you remember that your brother or sister has something against you, leave your gift there before the altar and go; first be reconciled to your brother or sister, and then come and offer your gift. Come to terms quickly with your accuser while you are on the way to court with him, or your accuser may hand you over to the judge, and the judge to the guard, and you will be thrown into prison. Truly I tell you, you will never get out until you have paid the last penny (Mt. 5:23-6).

At the altar in the Eucharist the Christian prays that Christ come again in glory at that very moment. Consequently, the Christian must live as if the Judge is on His way. This is not living under a threat, however – "Wait till your Father

---

[109] St John Chrysostom, *Sermon on the Betrayal by Judas* 6 in *The Eucharist*, ed. Sheerin, 147.

[110] Jacques Maritain, *Integral Humanism*, trans. Joseph W. Evans (New York: Charles Scribner's Sons, 1968), 98, 249.

gets home!" – but under a promise, a promise already being fulfilled. Our sins
have been forgiven and creation has been renewed. Because of Christ's
sacrifice and the Eucharist which bears it through history, it is possible now
to make peace with others. This is why something so terrible can be called
"Eucharist," meaning "giving thanks." The church does not arrogate future
judgment unto itself, claiming to foresee who will be condemned. Eucharistic
discipline does not anticipate future condemnation but rather future reconciliation. Excommunication is the formal offering of reconciliation in the
hope that even the most hardened offender will be saved.

Jesus' admonition to "settle out of court" was carried forward in parts of the
ancient church by means of ecclesiastical councils whose purpose was to
mediate disputes between members and to judge accusations against members.
Paul complains vigorously against the Corinthian Christians' propensity to
drag each other in front of the pagan courts of the state rather than submit to
judgment within the church (I Cor. 6:1-6). The *Didascalia Apostolorum* orders
that mediation of conflict by the bishop and presbyters take place on the
second day of the week, leaving ample time to settle the dispute so that
reconciliation could take place before the Eucharist on Sunday.[111] It is crucial
that the church stand under the judgment of the Eucharist, not merely of the
civil authorities. The church is to be a counter-discipline to worldly discipline
and the standard by which the latter is judged. As Paul says in admonishing the
Corinthians, "Do you not know that the saints will judge the world?" (I Cor.
6:2).

Mt. 18:15-20 outlines one procedure for disciplining members of the
church. Other members of the church get involved only if reconciliation
between the two parties alone fails. Bringing the offender before the whole
ekklesia is a last resort. If the offender refuses to listen even then, he or she is
to be excluded from the assembly, treated as a "Gentile and a tax collector.
Truly I tell you, whatever you bind on earth will be bound in heaven, and
whatever you loose on earth will be loosed in heaven" (Mt. 18:17-18).
Heavenly time is thus brought into earthly time by making future judgment
present.

This harsh attitude of apparent exclusion seems at first thought to contradict
Jesus' attitude of welcoming the sinner. After all, Jesus shares meals with tax
collectors; should the church then exclude sinners from its feast? When the
Pharisees ask why Jesus eats with tax collectors and sinners, he replies, "Those
who are well have no need of a physician, but those who are sick" (Mt. 9:12).
Properly understood, excommunication in the early church was also for

---

[111] Dix, *The Shape of the Liturgy*, 106.

medicinal purposes. Its purpose was not to forsake the sinner but to cure him. In I Cor. 5, for example, Paul is concerned to protect the community in Corinth from contamination by the man who is living with his father's wife: "Drive out the wicked person from among you" (5:13). But this counsel is not only for the benefit of the church: "[Y]ou are to hand this man over to Satan for the destruction of the flesh, so that his spirit may be saved in the day of the Lord" (5:5). What Paul apparently has in mind is that the torments of Satan will eventually bring the man around to repentance; the man is not simply to be abandoned to Satan's final possession. As in II Cor. 12:7 and I Tim. 1:20, Paul believes that Satan can be given as a beneficial and purgative "thorn" to discipline the flesh. The man must die to the flesh (*sarx*) in order that his spirit – and presumably his resurrected body – might be saved in the Judgment Day.[112]

This is consistent with Paul's comments on the Eucharist in I Cor. 11:27–32. If in fact those partaking of the body and blood unworthily are eating and drinking their own damnation, then it would be positively cruel to allow them to continue. Chrysostom admonishes his ministers to deny the Eucharist to notorious sinners, for the sake of the sinner himself. "Let no Judas receive, lest he suffer the fate of Judas"; to give such a one the consecrated bread and wine would be to "give a sword instead of food." "But I am saying these things, not that we may repel them only or cut them off, but so that we may correct them, and bring them back, that we may take care of them."[113]

The writings of the Fathers are full of warnings of the present dangers of unworthy communion to the unworthy themselves. Cyprian, for example, tells of a Christian baby girl whose nurse took her to the magistrate, where a piece of bread left as an offering to a pagan idol was placed in the baby's mouth. She was later returned to her mother, who knew nothing of the misdeed, and mother and child went together to celebrate the Eucharist with the Christian community. As the prayers were being offered, the baby began to convulse and cry, "confessing, as if under torture, in every way it could" what had happened at the magistrate's. At communion time the deacon was able to place a small amount of the consecrated wine in her mouth, but it provoked a terrible choking and vomiting.[114] Cyprian summons this and similar examples

[112] See Jerome Murphy-O'Connor, "The First Letter to the Corinthians," in *The New Jerome Biblical Commentary*, ed. Raymond Brown, Joseph Fitzmyer, and Roland Murphy (Englewood Cliffs, NJ: Prentice Hall, 1990), 803.
[113] St John Chrysostom, *Homily on Matthew* 82.6, in *The Eucharist*, ed. Sheerin, 292–3.
[114] St Cyprian of Carthage, *The Lapsed* 25, trans. Maurice Bévenot, Ancient Christian Writers, no. 25 (New York: Newman Press, n.d.), 32–3.

to support his contention that those who had apostatized during the persecution of Decius should not be readmitted to full communion with the church
without going through a proper cleansing through penitential discipline. Of
those who advocate readmittance to the Eucharist without a lengthy penance,
Cyprian says:

> Those men do as much harm to the lapsed as hail to the crops, as a wild tempest
> does to trees; they are like a ravening plague to cattle, like a fierce storm to ships
> at sea. They rob men of the comfort of hope, they tear them up by the roots,
> their poisonous words spread a deadly contagion, they dash the ship against the
> rocks to prevent its making port. Their indulgence *does not mean the granting of
> reconciliation but its frustration*, it does not restore men to communion but bars
> them from it and from salvation.[115]

We must resist the temptation to dismiss Cyprian's concerns as revolving
around quaint superstitions about the magical power of the Eucharist.
Cyprian's concern is the visible unity of the church, the sinner's true
reconciliation to the body of Christ. He insists on a long penance not as
punishment, but as a retraining of the habits of the apostate. The wounds
inflicted on the body of Christ will not heal with a simple verbal apology.
What is required for true reconciliation of the apostate is a renewed discipline
of body and soul, a discipline which wrests control of the whole person away
from the discipline of the Roman state, to which she had succumbed. Without
such retraining, the sinner may suffer on the Day of the Lord a fate far worse
than physical sickness.[116]
    The importance of the church's discipline for the sinner can be seen more
clearly if we take note of Paul's words to Titus regarding those who cause
divisions in the church. After two warnings, the community should have
nothing to do with such a person; the person is "self-condemned" (Titus
3:11). Although Paul mentions no provisions for the reconciliation of such a
person to the community, his language of *self*-condemnation indicates that
exclusion from the church occurs at the initiative of the sinner. The First
Letter of John likewise indicates that those who deny that Jesus is the Christ
have excluded themselves from the church (I John 2:18-19, 22). For this

---

[115] Ibid., 26 [16], emphasis added. Out of the same concern for the salvation of the
lost, Cyprian is equally opposed to the rigorists who would deny apostates any
possibility of reconciliation; James Dallen, *The Reconciling Community: The Rite of
Penance* (Collegeville, Minn.: The Liturgical Press, 1991), 37–42.
[116] Ibid., 34 [26].

reason, Origen remarks that formal excommunication is precisely that – a mere formality which the bishop undertakes only after the actual excommunication, which is caused by the sin itself.[117] Excommunication, therefore, is not the expulsion of the sinner from the church, but a recognition that the sinner has *already excluded himself* from communion in the body of Christ by his own actions. Excommunication by the community clarifies for the sinner the seriousness of the offense, and, if accompanied by a proper penitential discipline, shows the sinner the way to reconciliation with the body of Christ while shielding the sinner from the adverse effects of continued participation in the Eucharist in the absence of true reconciliation. As an invitation to reconciliation, then, excommunication done well is an act of *hospitality*, in which the church does not expel the sinner, but says to her, "You are already outside our communion. Here is what you need to do to come back in." Excommunication does not abandon the sinner to her fate; in fact, precisely the opposite is the case. It is *failure* to excommunicate the notorious sinner that leaves her to eat and drink her own condemnation.

Early church penitential disciplines are best understood in this light. The procedures for excommunication and reconciliation depended on the local bishop and local customs, varying from place to place, but by the third century a general pattern of penitential practices across many different churches had developed. Usually the procedure was based on exclusion from the Eucharist and a period of rehabituation. Known sinners who had confessed their sins to the bishop were given a regimen of fasting, praying, and good works usually oriented toward the poor. While completing these tasks, the penitents were, like catechumens, generally allowed to be present at the liturgy for the reading of scripture and the homily, but were dismissed before the Eucharist. The entire congregation in many instances actively participated in the offender's rehabilitation, thus showing that reconciliation was not only a matter between the individual and God, but was made actual primarily in the reconciliation of the individual to the body of Christ. It was common in many places to have the congregation pray over the penitents weekly, and penitents were often assigned sponsors to support them through the process. When rehabilitation was complete, after a period ranging from weeks to years, the bishop, in the presence of all, laid his hands on the penitents as a sign of their reconciliation to the Eucharistic community.[118]

[117] Hein, *Eucharist and Excommunication*, 317.

[118] Joseph Martos, *Doors to the Sacred: A Historical Introduction to Sacraments in the Catholic Church*, expanded edn (Liguori, Mo.: Triumph Books, 1991), 274–5.

The most notable instance of public penance in the ancient church is the excommunication of the Emperor Theodosius by Bishop Ambrose of Milan. In 389 a group of irate citizens in Thessalonika rebelled against the demands of the Roman army and killed the army commander stationed there. Theodosius gave the order for a general retaliation in which 7,000 Thessalonians were herded into the circus and slaughtered. Ambrose wrote a beautiful letter to Theodosius which placed his firm resolve to exclude Theodosius from the Eucharist in the context of a deep longing for the Emperor's reconciliation. Ambrose writes of his own fearful obligation to excommunicate Theodosius, for to allow him to attend Mass without reconciliation would be a sign of contempt for God.[119] As Theodoret tells it, Ambrose met Theodosius at the door of the church and forbade him to enter: "Submit to the exclusion to which God, the Lord of all, wills to sentence you. He will be your physician; he will give you health."[120] The Emperor did penance for eight months, then presented himself as a public penitent before the people during the Christmas celebration in 390, whereupon he was reconciled to the community.

Until this point we have been discussing excommunication from the point of view of the salvation of the individual Christian. The discipline of the individual body, however, always has reference to the discipline of the ecclesial body, and can only be understood in this light. The primary concern of the church in this regard is the visibility in history of the true body of Christ. The only point to disciplining the individual sinner is to reconcile her to the body of Christ, for without incorporation into Christ's body, salvation is jeopardized. Pastoral concern for the individual Christian, therefore, is not opposed to, but is inextricably bound up with, concern for the visibility of the church as it is enacted in the Eucharist. If the church is not itself visible, then it does not witness Christ to the world, and the very salvation of the world is not advanced.

For this reason, following on Jesus' words in Matthew 18, Paul and the patristic writers are often anxious to minimize contact between the church and the grave sinner. A line separating the church from the world is drawn, placing the notorious sinner outside the boundary. In this way it becomes apparent – at least temporarily and provisionally – what is and is not the body of Christ. The Christian practice of excommunication has certain affinities to Old Testament concepts of maintaining the identity and purity of God's people.

---

[119] Ambrose of Milan, "Letter to Emperor Theodosius," in Rahner, *Church and State in Early Christianity*, 114–19.
[120] Theodoret, *Ecclesiastical History*, excerpted in Rahner, *Church and State in Early Christianity*, 119–23.

The early church thought of itself as the eschatological gathering of Israel, a people set apart. This community must be recognizably holy in order to serve as a visible sign of salvation for the world.[121] Jesus, therefore, commands his disciples not to throw what is holy to dogs, or to cast their pearls before swine (Mt. 7:6).

Nevertheless, all of the sacrificial purifications demanded by the Old Covenant are no longer in force, for Jesus' one blood sacrifice on the cross suffices for the purification of humankind. Christians now drink blood – an abomination according to Jewish law – at the Eucharist, which is a sacramental participation in Christ's sacrifice. To be "unclean" is no longer a matter of racial identity or conformity to Jewish rites of purification. The "unclean" are instead those who reject Christ in word or action.[122] Thus the Letter to the Hebrews compares the sacrifices of the Israelites wandering in the desert with that of Christ:

> We have an altar from which those who officiate in the tent have no right to eat. For the bodies of those animals whose blood is brought into the sanctuary by the high priest as a sacrifice for sin are burned outside the camp. Therefore Jesus also suffered outside the city gate in order to sanctify the people by his own blood. Let us then go to him outside the camp and bear the abuse he endured. For here we have no lasting city, but we are looking for the city that is to come (Heb. 13:10–14).

Since the altar is the key to the identity of the community, exclusion from the altar is used to locate that identity. As Kenneth Hein argues, this text from Hebrews exemplifies the primitive church distinguishing itself from the Jewish community through the concept of sacrifice, and thus setting a "Eucharistic limit" to the church.[123] It is significant for the church, however, that this limit does not establish a "lasting city." The Eucharistic limit is meant to reveal the contours of the heavenly city on earth, not create an earthly city with permanent boundaries policed by a church analogous to the state. The limit is Eucharistic precisely because the church is on pilgrimage and must constantly receive itself anew from the Holy Spirit in the Eucharist. "Purity" and "identity" are not attributes the earthly church can claim for itself, but rather characterize the eternal church as God sees it.

---

[121] Gerhard Lohfink, *Jesus and Community: The Social Dimension of Christian Faith* (Philadelphia: Fortress Press, 1982), 7–73.
[122] Hein, *Eucharist and Excommunication*, 17–23.
[123] Ibid., 147–50.

The Eucharist gathers Christians into one body. As Paul says, those who eat the sacrifices become "partners in the altar" (I Cor. 10:18). For precisely this reason, Paul would exclude from the Eucharist those who partake of pagan sacrifices (10:20-1). "Partnership" with others in Christ is exclusive of other types of partnership. Paul applies this not only to explicit worship of other gods, but to other forms of "immorality" as well: he orders the community to avoid associating with those engaged in sexual immorality, greed, idolatry, drunkenness, theft (I Cor. 5:11). These types of conduct are also a denial that "your bodies are members of Christ" (6:15), and so they give the body over to the realm of the world. This endangers not just the individual sinner but the entire body of Christ on earth, for association with the unclean risks contamination; "a little yeast leavens the whole batch of dough" (5:6). What is at stake in excommunication is the visibility of the body of Christ, not simply the condemnation of individual wrongdoing. Therefore Paul orders the members of the community to drive the unrepentant from among them, but not to concern themselves with judging those outside the church, whom God alone will judge (5:12-13).

Paul would exclude from the Eucharist those who fail to "discern the body," meaning not only Christ's sacramental body but especially his ecclesial body (I Cor. 11:29).[124] The specific sin Paul addresses in this passage is the "humiliation" of the poor by the rich, who eat their fill when the community gathers while others go hungry (11:21-2). According to Paul this is not simply sin against individuals but "contempt for the church of God" (11:22). The rich bring divisions into the church, and thus threaten the visiblity of the body of Christ.[125] Exclusion of the offenders from the Eucharist is meant to restore the church as a sign of reconciliation by leading the offenders to change their conduct (11:31-2). If they do not repent, exclusion from the Eucharist also safeguards the witness of the church by anticipating the Lord's final judgment, when His own will be separated out from the world (11:32).

For the patristic writers also, the overriding concern in prescribing excommunication is the church's visibility in time. The *Didascalia* establishes excommunication for notorious sinners out of concern for the notorious sinner, but also out of concern that other Christians will be "defiled" by communication with that person.[126] Origen castigates those bishops who are

---

[124] It is unnecessary to exclude either interpretation, given the close relationship between the ecclesial and sacramental bodies in Paul's thought; see Wainwright, *Eucharist and Eschatology*, 81–2.

[125] Hein, *Eucharist and Excommunication*, 58–64.

[126] Ibid., 358–9.

overly indulgent with serious sinners: "What sort of kindness and mercy is that, to be sparing to one person and to lead everyone else into a crisis?"[127] Since the entire flock is in danger, Origen says the offender should be placed outside the church for the sake of the whole. For the early church the soteriological implications of excommunication cannot be separated from its ecclesiological implications because salvation was a matter of one's relationship to the body of Christ.[128] That the integrity of the church should be decided around the issue of participation in the Eucharist should be unsurprising, given the logic of the Eucharist as that which both produces and demands the church's unity.

Unity in the church is much more than agreement on doctrine or the general ability of the members of the church to get along, nor is it just participation in a common project or community. It is participation in Christ, and so requires a narrative display of the life, death, and resurrection of Jesus Christ. Unity is based on assimilation to Christ, and so the unity and the identity of the church are the same issue. Jesus was tortured to death. Tortured and torturers in the same church therefore threaten the transparency of the church as the body of Christ.

The gravity of an offense is often invoked in separating ordinary sins from sins meriting excommunication. I would argue that this not be understood as simply a matter of *degree* but of *kind*. In other words, excommunication is not reserved for those individuals who simply outdo the rest of the church's ordinary sinners in the number or degree of their sins. Excommunication is better understood as applicable to those kinds of sin which impugn the identity of the body of Christ. Excommunication, by definition, is for ecclesiological offenses. If, as I have already argued, the excommunicated person puts herself outside the church in the very act of her sin, then the sin itself must be construed as a sin against the body of Christ. I am arguing, then, that the use of excommunication should not be extended, but rather limited to those sins which threaten the very visibility of the body of Christ.

The 1983 Code of Canon Law would seem to support this interpretation. Of the particular offenses named as deserving excommunication, virtually all have to do with interference with the proper functioning of the church. The first section of such offenses (canons 1364-9) is entitled "Offenses against Religion and the Unity of the Church." The second is "Offenses against Church Authorities and the Freedom of the Church" (1370-7). The third is "Usurpation of Ecclesiastical Offices and Offenses Committed in their Exercise" (1378-89).

[127] Origen, cited in Hein, *Eucharist and Excommunication*, 330.
[128] Hein, *Eucharist and Excommunication*, 439–40.

The next two sections have to do with false accusations against clerics and abuses of the clerical state (1390-6). Finally, in the last section listing specific offenses, we find two canons under the title "Offenses against Human Life and Liberty" mandating excommunication for murder, abduction, confinement, wounding, and abortion (1397-8).[129] The Code of Canon Law envisions excommunication as applicable primarily to those who offend against the church itself, not just those individuals who exceed some arbitrary limit of sinfulness.

The difficulty is that "church" is often too narrowly defined as meaning those who hold ecclesiastical office. The danger is that excommunication – which is reserved to the bishops – can be seen primarily in terms of defending episcopal prerogatives instead of defending communion on behalf of the church as a whole. Some would therefore prefer to abandon any talk of excommunication at all, given the dangers of abuse of power in a hierarchical church structure. I take these concerns very seriously, and yet the church cannot simply deny the importance of judgment without denying the position of the Eucharist as the source of the church's unity. As Raymond Brown puts it,

> If one voices the objection that exclusion belongs to God alone, he must face the fact that from its earliest days and with the approval of its most notable spokesmen the Church has exercised the power of exclusion, especially in doctrinal and moral matters. And so a protest against all excommunication is not simply a protest against canon law but against the preachers of the Gospel.[130]

But why reserve the power of excommunication to the bishop? In Brown's judgment it has to do with the position of the bishop as presider at the Eucharist. At least by the year 100, two parallel developments in the early church are clearly discernible: first, the twelve apostles and the missionary apostles had disappeared, and many of their functions had been taken over by presbyter-bishops; second, the presbyter-bishops were identified as the sole celebrants of the Eucharist in their communities.[131] As Ignatius of Antioch expressed so emphatically, the role of the bishop was to produce and preserve unity: "How much more fortunate must I count you, who are as inseparably one with [your bishop] as the Church is with Jesus Christ, and Jesus Christ with the Father; so constituting one single harmonious unity throughout."[132]

---

[129] *The Code of Canon Law*, trans. The Canon Law Society of Great Britain and Ireland (Grand Rapids, Mich.: Wm. B. Eerdmans Publishing Company, 1983), 243–8.

[130] Raymond Brown, *Priest and Bishop: Biblical Reflections* (Paramus, NJ: Paulist Press, 1970), 33–4.

[131] Ibid., 40–3, 73–5.

[132] Ignatius of Antioch, *Epistle to the Ephesians*, 5, in *Early Christian Writings*, 77.

The Eucharist is the source of this unity with the bishop, since through the Eucharist the whole community is gathered into the eschatological body of Christ, which is one. As the presider of the Eucharist, the bishop is the one who offers the sacrifice in communion with the multitude of people gathered around the altar. The bishop therefore came to be seen as the one who brings the many, united into one body, before the throne of God. As head of the Eucharistic community, the bishop was to transcend divisions, even those divisions among different orders of clergy and laity.[133]

If the Eucharistic source of the episcopacy is understood, therefore, it should be plain that the bishop is not meant to stand above the people or the other bishops. The bishop presides at the Eucharist, but there is no Eucharist without the people gathered around the altar, precisely because of the eschatological nature of the Eucharist. The Eucharist *is* the eschatological gathering of the whole body of Christ, and not a sacrifice done by the bishop for the sake of the people. As *Lumen Gentium* (*LG* 10) makes clear, the laity participate in the offering of the Eucharist. Likewise, the Eucharist is only truly celebrated when the bishop stands in apostolic succession and is in communion with the other bishops (*LG* 22). This dependence on the laity and on the other bishops through the Eucharist should in practice serve as a check on the fallible judgment of any one bishop in matters of excommunication. Formal excommunication should only be undertaken rarely, and then with extensive consultation with laypeople and other bishops.

To base such safeguards in a merely formal and procedural account of "checks and balances," however, would be a profound mistake. Without question, where human beings wield authority, there is the potential for the abuse of that authority. But if we grant the necessity at times of peril for some kind of judgment within the church in order to resist the disciplines of the world, then the democratization and bureaucratization of that judgment in a purely procedural sense would only uproot judgement from its proper locus in the Eucharist and implant it in the human will. The only hope we have for a discipline which is not demonic is in the Eucharist. There, according to John's Revelation, the celebrant stands as the Lamb who was slain, still bearing the marks of his wounds, surrounded by the multitude in the heavenly liturgy. The bishop's position as the center of unity for the Eucharistic community is an imperative to the bishop not to accumulate power, but to "lay down his life for his sheep" (*LG* 27).

As successor to the apostles, the role of the bishop is to preserve continuity with Jesus, to "do this in memory of me." But this memory is, in Johannes

---

[133] Zizioulas, *Being as Communion*, 152-8; see also *Lumen Gentium*, 26.

Metz's celebrated phrase, a "dangerous memory;" the Eucharist is a memorial of Christ's death at the hands of the worldly authorities. Eucharistic discipline in the way I have described it fulfills the bishop's obligation to keep alive the dangerous memory of Jesus' conflict with the principalities and powers. At the same time as they are preservers of the past, however, bishops also exercise an eschatological function as they who gather the community around the altar to participate in the heavenly Eucharist. As Zizioulas points out, the keys given to Peter are the keys *of the Kingdom*. Binding and loosing is only properly understood in an eschatological context, as the anticipation of what will be bound and loosed in heaven.[134] As a consequence, all judgments must be seen in an eschatological context as ultimately subject to revision.

As the center of Christian unity and visibility, the Eucharist separates the church from the sinful "world," because in the Eucharist the church deconstructs the world and is caught up into the Kingdom. This does not mean that the pilgrim church on earth is not sinful, or that the Eucharist is reserved for an elite of people of surpassing personal holiness. The exclusion of those who fail to "discern the body" from participation in the Eucharist is used as a sign not of the church's present purity, but of its present participation in the future Kingdom. In the Eucharist, as we have seen, the church anticipates the Kingdom, and supplants the imagination of secular time with the eschatological imagination. The excommunication of one who sins against the body of Christ is both a sign that such a person has brought a foretaste of the future judgment upon himself, and an anticipation of the eternal church, with all the saints, standing unblemished before God.[135]

It should be clear that the eschatological imagination is, by definition, incomplete. We never know exactly what to anticipate; we learn to cultivate the expectation of the unexpectable. Even as we discern judgment, we do so provisionally, always in the hope of surprise, that the sinner will repent, that reconciliation will take place. More than this, we are never sure what form reconciliation will take, what the church that we long to see visible will look like, or who will be a member of the eternal church. The Eucharist itself is not guaranteed to the church; in the epiclesis we plead for the Spirit to come upon the gifts and make them holy.

> In an epicletical context, history ceases to be in itself a guarantee for security. The *epiclesis* means ecclesiologically that the church *asks to receive from God what*

---

[134] Zizioulas, *Being as Communion*, 183–4.
[135] See Hein, *Eucharist and Excommunication*, 55–7, 416–17.

she has already received historically in Christ as if she had not received it at all, i.e. as if history did not count in itself.[136]

The Holy Spirit does not simply reanimate a pre-existing structure given in the historical past, but brings the future into the present as something not wholly anticipatable.

The earthly church anticipates the Kingdom only by assimilation to the body of Christ of all times and places in the Eucharist. This is not a claim for the heroic holiness of the church. It is only because of Christ's self-gift, His assumption of our humanity, that we participate in the sacrifice. Not just our sins but even our *virtues* are burned away in the Eucharist: "it is no longer I who live, but it is Christ who lives in me" (Gal. 2:20). In the discipline of the Eucharist, the church does not discipline itself, but rather the whole church stands under the discipline of Christ in the Spirit. This is not the discipline of the world but the discipline of the cross. We are formed into a body which transfigures the world's violence through self-sacrifice and reconciliation.

If anyone is to "discern the body," then it must become visible in present time. As we saw in chapter 1, it is the effect of some state disciplines to render the church invisible, to "disappear" the body of Christ. The Eucharist, as the gift which effects the visibility of the true body of Christ, is therefore the church's counter-imagination to that of the state. Formal excommunication makes the church visible, if only temporarily, by bringing to light a boundary between church and world which those who attack the church have themselves drawn.

In this chapter I have tried to display how the Eucharist builds a visible social body capable of resisting the state's strategy of disappearance. The Eucharist anticipates the future Kingdom, re-members Jesus' conflict with the powers of this world, and brings both future and past dimensions of Christ into the present in the form of a visible body. The result is a "confusion" of the spiritual and the temporal, an invasion of worldly time and space by the heavenly, and thus the possibility of a different kind of social practice.

In the next chapter I will attempt to display this Eucharistic "politics" through three practices of the church in Chile under the military regime. The first such practice is excommunication, used as a tool of resistance against the Pinochet regime. As we will see, its use in Chile was not unambiguous, but it does suggest how the Eucharist is a resource for Christian social practice, for Christ is at work in the Eucharist even when the

---

[136] Zizioulas, *Being as Communion*, 185.

church has succumbed to its own faulty ecclesiology. In other words, the emergence of the practices I will describe, in spite of the church's ecclesiology, is only intelligible assuming the constant giving of the presence of Christ in the Eucharist.

Chapter Six

PERFORMING THE BODY OF CHRIST

If there is such a thing as a Eucharistic "counter-politics," what would it look like in the contemporary world? In this final chapter, I display three practices of the church under the Pinochet regime which at least suggest answers to this question. Under the military regime, the true body of Christ appeared; part of the church in Chile found a way to escape confinement to the soul and take body. Although the practices I will describe are not always explicitly Eucharistic, I hope to provide an adequate theological articulation of these practices based on my exposition of the logic of the Eucharist in chapter 5. With these practices the church in Chile showed that in the Eucharist Christ has a "politics" which ultimately cannot be defeated by bad ecclesiology.

This chapter has four sections. In sections 1–3, I display three practices of the church in Chile – excommunication, the Vicariate of Solidarity, and the Sebastián Acevedo Movement against Torture – which illustrate what a Eucharistic imagination of resistance to state discipline could look like. In the final section, I show why the Eucharist is the church's own response to torture.

1 "But Father, Look at this Body"

In December 1980 seven Chilean bishops excommunicated torturers in their respective dioceses.[1] The declaration of excommunication issued by the

---

[1] The bishops were Carlos González and Alejandro Jiménez (bishop and auxiliary bishop of Talca), Carlos Camus (Linares), José Manuel Santos (Valdivia), Juan Luis Ysern (Ancud), Sergio Contreras (Temuco), and Tomás González (Punta Arenas). In December of 1983, the plenary assembly of the bishops' conference incorporated a decree of excommunication for torturers into their document "Un Camino Cristiano." The relevant passage reads, "torturers, their accomplices, and those who are able to

bishops of Talca and Linares begins with a recognition that their hands were consecrated to pardon rather than condemn, "because these hands should be an extension of the hands of Jesus."[2] Nevertheless, the bishops also cite their power to bind and loose (Jn. 20:23), and the necessity since the time of Paul[3] to resort to disciplinary measures for especially serious sins: "These are the sins which affect the common good, the dignity of persons and the sense of unity which signifies communion."[4] Torture is identified as such a sin, and *latae sententiae*, or automatic, excommunication is declared for those who (a) participate in torture, (b) incite, solicit, or order it, or (c) are in a position to stop it and fail to do so. The bishops refer to the "medicinal character" of the sanction of excommunication, and explain that a person who falls under its terms can be absolved by a priest who judges that he has sincerely repented and changed his ways.

   The declaration was remarkable in many ways, but it was not the first time that excommunication had been used by the church hierarchy in Chile. In 1626 the Synod of Santiago, under the direction of Bishop Francisco Salcedo, excommunicated slave traders, provoking the age-old complaint from the King's representatives that the church was interfering in matters outside its competence.[5] Conflicts between the church and the state hit their highest pitch in 1873, when the Congress passed one law imposing harsh sanctions on any cleric who acted on Pontifical decrees deemed injurious to the security of the state, and another law punishing priests who encouraged disobedience to any of the state's laws. Archbishop Valdivieso responded by issuing a statement of excommunication applicable to all those who had voted for the new laws, including the President of the Republic. Reaction was furious. One government minister protested that there was no cause for excommunication, since they had simply held the position that "there is nothing above the sovereignty of the Nation."[6] President Errázuriz complained of the bishops'

---

stop torture and do not do it, cannot receive Holy Communion nor can they morally be godparents in the Sacraments of the Church, unless they sincerely repent"; *Documentos del episcopado: Chile 1981–1983* (Santiago: Ediciones Mundo, 1984), 147.
[2] Bishop Carlos González, Bishop Alejandro Jiménez, and Bishop Carlos Camus, "Excomunión a torturadores," *Mensaje* 30, no. 296 (Jan.–Feb. 1981), 68.
[3] They cite I Cor. 6:11–13, probably intending 5:11–13.
[4] González, et al., "Excomunión a torturadores."
[5] Pedro Azócar, "No hay límites en los temas que debe tocar la iglesia," *El Sur*, Concepción, April 22, 1977.
[6] Fidel Araneda Bravo, *Historia de la Iglesia en Chile* (Santiago: Ediciones Paulinas, 1986), 508.

interference in politics, and wished for bishops "who conserve the purity of the sanctuary of religion!"[7]

Although the most common uses of excommunication in twentieth-century Chile would be related to abortion and divorce,[8] excommunication would not cease to be involved in matters more directly ecclesio-political. In 1940, for example, Archbishop José María Caro threatened with excommunication any *patrón* who did not pay just wages to his workers.[9] From the other end of the political spectrum, excommunication was used to dissuade Catholics from participating in, or abetting in any way, the Communist Party, which had grown to be the largest of its kind in Latin America. In 1949, the official *Revista Católica* published the Vatican's decree of excommunication for anyone cooperating either directly or indirectly with the Communists. When the Christian Democratic Party in 1958 supported the repeal of the law banning the Communist Party in Chile, Conservatives suggested publicly that any Catholic favoring repeal should be deprived of the sacraments.[10]

As these examples show, the church in Chile has on occasion used excommunication not to address grave individual sins but to protect the ecclesial body itself from perceived threats. In 1970 ultraconservative Salvador Valdés Morandé was excommunicated after publishing his third book within four years accusing Cardinal Silva, the Jesuits, and the progressive wing of the church in Chile of being Marxists and apostates (sample title: *The Society of Jesus: Oh Jesus, What a Society!*).[11] In November 1975 Jaime Guzmán recanted after he was publicly threatened with excommunication for his comments on the Malloco affair. On national television Guzmán had suggested disobedience to the Archbishop's orientations concerning succor for fugitives from the

[7] Ibid. A fuller account of the affair is found in Agustin Edwards, *Cuatro Presidentes de Chile*, vol. 2 (Valparaiso: Sociedad Imprenta y Litografia Universo, 1932), 155–267.

[8] The first Plenary Council of the church in Chile in 1946 issued a decree of excommunication for those who, being married in the church and by the state, fraudulently annuled their civil marriage, and also for those who, having married in the church, were divorced and remarried by the state. With papal permission, the Chilean bishops nullified this ruling in 1984; Conferencia Episcopal de Chile, "Declaración sobre Pena de Excomunión para los Divorciados que Vuelven a Casarse," in *Documentos del Episcopado: Chile 1984–1987*, 26–7.

[9] Maximilano Salinas Campos, *Historia del pueblo de Dios en Chile: La evolución del christianismo desde la perspectiva de los pobres* (Santiago: Ediciones Rehue, 1987), 208.

[10] Brian Smith, *The church and Politics in Chile: Challenges to Modern Catholicism* (Princeton, NJ: Princeton University Press, 1982), 101–2.

[11] *La Compañía de Jesús, ¡Ay! Jesús, ¡Que Compañía!*. Valdés published his version of events under the title *La Excomunión de un Tradicionalista* (Santiago: 1970).

regime. In Cardinal Silva's eyes, Guzmán had threatened "the most precious thing that the church has: its unity."[12] Less than a year later, the episcopal conference made this purpose of excommunication explicit in disciplining the DINA agents who orchestrated the airport attack on the three bishops returning from Riobamba. The bishops acknowledged that the church normally puts its trust in dialogue, persuasion, patience, and "the fecundity of pain"; nevertheless the nature of the church's mission occasionally compels it to "resort to extreme measures, set forth in her juridical ordering, to *safeguard her identity* and efficaciously move the conscience of her children."[13]

As the above examples illustrate, the identity and unity of the church have been at issue in many cases of excommunication, but safeguarding the identity of the church has too often been narrowly understood as protecting the authority of the hierarchy. It was not until the excommunication of torturers that the broader ecclesiological implications of excommunication were more fully explored. The bishops responsible singled out torture among the available crimes for several related reasons. Bishop Carlos Camus recalls his focus on torture as a disciplining of society. "Not just any sin can be punished with excommunication. It has to be a sin which produces a significant social effect."[14] According to Camus, it is torture's nature as a "contagious defect" in the social body that caused him and the other bishops to apply excommunication to this particular problem.[15]

For Bishop Alejandro Jiménez, excommunication is the proper response to torture because torture attacks the unity of the body of Christ. According to Jiménez, the most acute tension in the "drama" that Chileans lived consisted in the brute fact that most of both tortured and torturers were Christians. "It was important that they saw that the bishops responsible for the magisterium of the church and the leaders of the People of God could not accept that Christians tortured brother Christians, or even when they weren't Christians who were tortured, they were still children of God."[16] The concern here is much broader than protecting the institutional interests of the hierarchical

---

[12] Departamento Opinión Pública del Arzobispado de Santiago, "Evangelio y misericordia: réplica a un comentarista de TV Nacional," *Mensaje* 24 (Jan.–Feb. 1976), 599. This incident is discussed above in chapter 2.

[13] "Declaración sobre la detención y ataque en Pudahuel a 3 obispos chilenos detenidos en Ecuador," *Documentos del Episcopado: Chile 1974–1980*, 160–1, emphasis added.

[14] Bishop Carlos Camus, interview by author, July 9, 1993.

[15] Ibid. ["lacra contagiosa"]

[16] Bishop Alejandro Jiménez, interview by author, July 30, 1993.

church. The concern is to sustain the integrity of the body of Christ. As theologian José Aldunate says, "Torture is the most vehement attack against the body of Christ"; according to Aldunate, it is Christ himself who is tortured.[17]

In Bishop Sergio Contreras's view, excommunication is the church's proper response to torture because of its revelatory nature. When asked why excommunication was applied to torture and not, for example, to political killings, Contreras replies, "The problem is that it was something very hidden and carried on with impunity, very difficult to punish. Killings in a way were a public action which permitted you to attempt some type of public action [in response]."[18] Bishop Jorge Hourton concurs: "When an entire society, because of the scandal given by the authorities who are justly in charge of the common good, has things so confused, so hidden, so distorted . . . we are enveloped in a social sin. Excommunication reveals it to us."[19]

Did the decree of excommunication against torturers actually work this way? Here we encounter some ambiguity in the bishops' practice. The decree was anonymous: no torturers were named, no clandestine torture centers were brought to light. As the decree stated, "It is a penalty which affects 'in conscience,' that is, which marks the interior of the persons who have committed this crime."[20] Several bishops and priests cited cases in which a torturer had come to confess his sins and be absolved, having been moved by the decree. Probably more common was the experience of Bishop Tomás González, who received a phone call from General Humberto Gordon, head of the CNI, asking about the decree. The two met soon afterward in Santiago. There Gordon told the bishop that the decree had stung him, and that subsequently he had not approached the altar at Mass. Happily, said the general, a military chaplain had extinguished any doubts gestating in his mind by assuring him that Bishop González was a "loco" and that he need not pay him heed. The general told the bishop that he proceeded to take the Eucharist with a tranquil conscience.[21]

If the decree of excommunication did bring some individuals to reconcile with the church, the revelatory nature of excommunication – the making visible of the body of Christ – was somewhat obscured by the anonymous

---

[17] Fr. José Aldunate, SJ, interview by author, July 1, 1993, Santiago, tape recording.
[18] Bishop Sergio Contreras, July 15, 1993, Temuco, tape recording.
[19] Bishop Jorge Hourton, "¡Si no dejan de torturar, dejen de comulgar!," chap. in *Combate Cristiano por la Democracia* (Santiago: CESOC, 1987), 90.
[20] González, et al., "Excomunión a torturadores."
[21] Bishop Tomás González, interview by author, July 26, 1993.

form in which the excommunication was given. The bishops faced a dilemma. On the one hand, they recognized that excommunication was an appropriate response to the disappearance of the body by the invisible system of torture established by the regime. On the other hand, the regime had been so successful in hiding its security apparatus that the bishops were simply unable to cite torturers by name.

Nevertheless, the regime did have a public face, and a self-proclaimed Christian one at that. The generals in charge of the secret police, and all the members of the Junta but one, were observant Catholics; some, such as General Pinochet, wore their Catholicism quite publicly. Should the bishops have excommunicated General Manuel Contreras, head of the DINA and architect of the system of torture and disappearance? Should they have excommunicated General Pinochet himself?

The question was discussed in church circles throughout General Pinochet's long reign. Several of the bishops I spoke with acknowledged that the topic had been debated among certain groups of bishops, but never in the bishops' plenary assemblies. Opinions fell into four categories. First, some bishops were against excommunication in principle, seeing it as a throwback to a church more inclined to anathematize than evangelize. Second, others felt that they lacked decisive proof that any particular person, even Generals Contreras and Pinochet, were responsible for torture. Third, some bishops worried that excommunicating a figure such as General Pinochet would invite increased persecution on the church, and the poor at the base of society would bear the brunt. Fourth, others said they would have excommunicated General Pinochet if it were up to them, but there was no unanimity among the bishops on this matter, and Cardinals Silva and later Fresno, to whose Archdiocese General Pinochet belonged, were not inclined to do it.[22] Silva was asked on several occasions to excommunicate General Pinochet; his standard reply was that the church is not called to break with the government.[23] Let us consider each of these four positions in turn.

[22] Under canon law, a bishop may only excommunicate within his own diocese. There is some question as to whether excommunicating a head of state requires the pope's approval. Several bishops are under the impression that such is the case. Canon lawyer Ricardo Tong, on the other hand, says that the language of canons 1401 and 1405 of the 1983 Code indicates that the pope's approval is only required when excommunicating a head of state for a matter considered "spiritual," as opposed to crimes such as torture and murder; Father Ricardo Tong, interview by author, June 25, 1993, Santiago, tape recording.

[23] Father José Aldunate, SJ, interview by author, July 1, 1993; Father Fermín Donoso, CSC, interview by author, June 20, 1993, Calle Larga, tape recording.

Some bishops opposed excommunicating General Pinochet not out of support for his authoritarian regime, but out of fear that the church would thereby come to imitate it. The church's response to torture is not to reproduce its own Inquisition; "the church is not an investigator," as Bishop Bernardino Piñera says.[24] Manuel Camilo Vial, bishop of San Felipe, echoes the same convictions about the kinder, gentler post-Vatican II church, and adds that it is not necessary for a bishop to excommunicate, since the notorious sinner has already put himself outside the church.[25] Liberation theologian Ronaldo Muñoz rightly emphasizes that Jesus' meals with tax collectors show the need to build, not burn, bridges between the oppressed and the oppressors. Curiously, though, Muñoz supports his position by citing I Cor. 11:29; formal excommunication is unnecessary because those who partake of the Eucharist unworthily eat and drink their *own condemnation*.[26]

If the argument I have made in chapter 5 about the nature of excommunication is correct, then a church which would reconcile rather than condemn has no choice but to excommunicate formally those it knows are outside, as an invitation to rejoin the flock. I asked Bishop Carlos González what General Pinochet would have to do to be excommunicated. "He *is* excommunicated!" the Bishop replies. He is? "Yes, yes. If he gave orders to torture, you saw the decree . . . If Pinochet is the intellectual author, he is excommunicated. If he is not, he is not excommunicated."[27] But if the church truly judges that General Pinochet is excommunicated, shouldn't someone tell him? Left to oneself, the human being has a great capacity for self-deception which can be self-damning; as Bishop González says, "Each person self-justifies everything that he does, including General Pinochet."[28] The General might not know for certain if the decree applies to him without a community to help him discern. And he will be unable to achieve true conversion and reconciliation without the support of the church community.

But how can the church judge the guilt or innocence of particular people

---

[24] Bishop Bernardino Piñera, interview by author, July 21, 1993, Santiago, tape recording.

[25] Bishop Manuel Camilo Vial, interview by author, July 22, 1993, San Felipe, tape recording.

[26] Father Ronaldo Muñoz, SS.CC., interview by author, June 30, 1993, Santiago, tape recording.

[27] Bishop Carlos González, interview by author, July 28, 1993.

[28] Ibid. González continues, "I have spoken with torturers. I was with a doctor . . . He said 'The life of my children or the life of my enemies. With those alternatives, I will torture.' "

in a matter as occult as torture? Lack of solid proof is the second of the concerns voiced by the bishops, a concern shared by many of them, even those sympathetic to excommunicating by name. The bishops I spoke with were not unaware that torture was taking place; several had seen tortured people in the flesh. Tomás González was moved to excommunicate after being shown a woman who had been burned in the local army base. "The doctors called me: 'But Father, look at this body . . .' "[29] Nor were the bishops unaware that torture was being done *systematically*. Indeed, that was the problem. It was difficult to pin it on any particular persons.

If the revelatory character of Eucharist and excommunication is taken seriously, however, it would seem that it could be used to bring the truth to light, to make it visible. For example, General Pinochet or General Contreras could have been confronted with the thousands of files in the church's Vicariate of Solidarity giving firsthand testimony of torture, including names of many places and some persons. Would it be unfair at that point to shift the burden of proof to the Commander in Chief? Could not the bishops demand that General Pinochet, under pain of excommunication, allow them access to Villa Grimaldi, Londres no. 38, or any of a number of known but invisible torture centers? General Pinochet had publicly boasted "In this country not a leaf moves without me knowing about it." If he did not order the systematic abuses – which he certainly did – at the very least he was in a position to stop the torture, and refused to do so.

Protecting the vulnerable from further persecution was the third serious reservation raised by some bishops about the possibility of excommunicating General Pinochet. "We bishops had a defense; our situation as bishops defended us. But who could insure the defense of priests, nuns, and laity?"[30] The irony here is that the poor and many of the priests and religious who worked with them supported the idea of excommunicating General Pinochet. Calls to do so came repeatedly from base communities of the church and their pastoral workers.[31] Brian Smith's 1975 survey showed priests, nuns, and

---

[29] Bishop Tomás González, interview by author, July 26, 1993. ("Los médicos me llamaron: pero Padre, mire este cuerpo . . . ") Mons. Carlos González recalls being in a meeting with three fellow bishops when a man arrived with his hands badly damaged. The next day the bishop met with a commander from the local base, who explained that the man's wounds must be "self-tortures"; Bishop Carlos González, interview by author, July 28, 1993.

[30] Bishop Sergio Contreras, interview by author, July 15, 1993.

[31] This was verified for me by Bishop Carlos Camus, Fr Ricardo Tong, Fr José Aldunate, SJ, and Fr Tony Mifsud, SJ.

laypeople favoring by a wide margin a more prophetic stance by the bishops.[32] My own conversations on the subject of excommunication with active church members in poor areas of Santiago affirm (in an unscientific way) that the great majority of those who see themselves as direct or indirect victims of the regime would approve of General Pinochet's excommunication. As lay catechist Hugo Valdivia puts it, "I don't feel in communion with him."[33] When asked if she favored excommunicating Pinochet despite the risk of increased suffering for the people, Rosa Gutiérrez of Peñalolén exclaims "The people *couldn't* have suffered more!"[34] Fr Roberto Bolton takes a slightly different angle, believing that the repression never would have taken on the proportions it did if the church had used excommunication and other decisive actions in the early days of the regime.[35]

Finally, Cardinal Silva was unwilling to excommunicate General Pinochet because of a fundamental conviction that to do so would be divisive instead of unifying. The ecclesiology discussed in chapters 2–4 above had led him to believe that church and state must stand together to ensure the unity of rich and poor in one organic entity called Chile. As we have seen, this is a faulty ecclesiology which posits unity only on the level of the "spiritual" and pluralism on the level of the "temporal." This false unity becomes a way of glossing over the real conflict between oppressors and oppressed. As Jon Sobrino says, "the appeal to pluralism . . . often becomes a weapon of ecclesial politics in defense of clearly conservative attitudes and interests."[36] Ronaldo Muñoz caricatures those attitudes in the anti-creed he dedicated to the parishoners of a wealthy parish who, after receiving communion at the Christmas Eve Mass, turned over to the police a group of religious peacefully protesting torture outside the church. The following is an excerpt:

> And by all means the public denunciation
> of social sin
> is *not* Christian nor evangelical,
> because the Christian is to be a sign
> of reconciliation

[32] Smith, *The Church and Politics in Chile*, 302–4.
[33] Hugo Valdivia, interview by author, August 1, 1993, Santiago, tape recording.
[34] Rosa Gutiérrez, interview by author, August 6, 1993, Santiago, tape recording.
[35] Fr Roberto Bolton, interview by author, August 4, 1993.
[36] Jon Sobrino, "Unity and Conflict in the Church," chap. in *The True Church and the Poor* (Maryknoll, NY: Orbis Books, 1984), 198.

and *not* of conflict,
and because consensus
and *not* the truth
will set us free.

And so,
Merry Christmas!
for oppressors and oppressed,
for torturers and tortured.
Because Christmas is a great mystery,
much above such material things
as economic oppression
and the torture of the body.[37]

If Eucharistic discipline is rightly understood, then excommunication does not rend the unity of the church, but makes visible the disunity and conflict, already so painfully present, between the body of Christ and those who would torture it. Only when this disunity becomes visible can real reconciliation and real unity be enacted. For this reason, in I Cor. 11:18-19 Paul both scolds the Corinthians for the divisions among them, and states that "there have to be factions among you, for only so will it become clear who among you are genuine."

At the end of 1987, a group of 150 priests, nuns, and lay missioners issued an open letter laying personal moral responsibility for the regime's atrocities on General Augusto Pinochet and calling for his exclusion from the sacraments of the church. The open letter was not well received by Cardinal Fresno, who felt that the group, in issuing the statement on their own account, had lacked a sense of communion with their bishops. Besides, according to Fresno, the letter had used language which was "trenchant and absolute," contradicting the bishops' Christmas address which asked that Christians who confront political matters do so "without offending or disqualifying others."

Fr Roberto Bolton, one of the authors of the open letter, wrote to Cardinal Fresno to explain why the group had judged Pinochet so personally.

---

[37] Fr Ronaldo Muñoz, SS.CC., "El antievangelio de algunos cristianos," in Hernán Vidal, *El movimiento contra la tortura "Sebastián Acevedo:" derechos humanos y la producción de símbolos nacionales bajo el fascismo chileno* (Minneapolis: Institute for the Study of Ideologies and Literature, 1986), 146–8, emphasis in original. One of the protesters reacted to the aggression of the wealthy parishioners in the following way: "How is it possible, you've just received the Eucharist!"; ibid., 238.

It is a matter of having pointed out as responsible a public figure – the one with the greatest responsibility in the country – whose atrocities are public and without precedent in the history of the nation; who has persecuted the Church, who has harassed and ridiculed even members of the hierarchy (you among them). The History of the Church is full of such cases and, always or almost always, such figures were publicly and boldly denounced and, at times, condemned by the hierarchical Church and by the faithful.[38]

This is not a matter of private sinfulness. We are confronted by "a working reality of the death of the people and of the church itself, of which he calls himself an observant son, practicing sacramental gestures scandalously publicized."[39] The language of the open letter is trenchant but not absolute, since it calls for Pinochet's conversion. He is not irredeemably condemned in the letter. He can be reconciled, provided that he "radically change."

Bolton concludes by giving the prime motivation for the group's action: "The poor cannot wait any longer."[40] He implicitly recognizes the eschatological character of the church. The Eucharist is the promise and demand that the church enact the true body of Christ now, in time. Worldly kingdoms have declared the Kingdom of God indefinitely deferred, and the poor are told to suffer their lot quietly and invisibly. In the Eucharist the poor are invited now to come and to feast in the Kingdom. The Eucharist must not be a scandal to the poor. It demands real reconciliation of oppressed and oppressor, tortured and torturer. Barring reconciliation, Eucharist demands judgment. "Let no inhuman person be present, no one who is cruel and merciless, no one at all who is unclean," Chrysostom tells those who minister the Eucharist. "Even though someone may be a general, or a prefect, or even the one who is invested with the diadem [i.e., the emperor], if he approaches unworthily, forbid him. Your authority is greater than his."[41]

Formal excommunication remembers the tortured body of Christ and anticipates judgment against the torturers, thus making visible in the present what is and is not the church. Excommunication is one of the clearest examples of how the Eucharist is a resource for the social practice of the church. It should be apparent that this social practice is not based on any

[38] Fr Roberto Bolton, letter to Cardinal Juan Francisco Fresno, January 17, 1988, typed manuscript.
[39] Ibid.
[40] Ibid.
[41] St John Chrysostom, *Homily on Matthew* 82.5-6 in *The Eucharist*, Message of the Fathers of the Church, no. 7, ed. Daniel J. Sheerin (Wilmington, Del.: Michael Glazier, 1986), 291–2.

perfectionist ethic for the church. My argument that torture, as an anti-liturgy of absolute power which attacks the body of Christ itself, should be met with excommunication is by no means an argument for the use of excommunication in general for other types of sin. This is *torture*, not theft or masturbation. If accepted, my argument would *limit* excommunication, to keep it from being used in the service of right-wing ecclesiastical politics. Furthermore, formal excommunication is not the only key to the church's visibility. It is not so much a solution as a recognition that something has gone terribly wrong. The church's own ecclesiology had contributed to making the Pinochet regime thinkable in the first place. The bishops who were trained in that ecclesiology for the most part reacted courageously to the situation in which they found themselves, but they lacked the independence necessary to recognize that General Pinochet had put himself outside the church. That recognition was more clear at the base of the church, the faithful poor and the priests and nuns who accompanied them.

2 Knitting the Social Fabric

Perhaps the most tangible way in which the church in Chile reappeared under the military regime was through the social programs of COPACHI and the Vicariate of Solidarity. Offering a wide range of programs covering legal and medical assistance, job training, soup kitchens, buying cooperatives, assistance to unions and more, these organizations became the focus of church resistance to the regime. "The Church was almost a parallel state. It had its own health clinics, it had its own systems of food distribution."[42] In a moment when the state had outlawed base-level organizations and was atomizing the body politic, the church provided a space in which organization could take place and social fragmentation could be resisted.

As described in chapter 2, the Committee of Cooperation for Peace in Chile, COPACHI, was born to respond to the immediate emergency of the coup in 1973, but soon became much more. Legal aid was provided to victims of the repression, to laborers who had lost their jobs, and to university students and professors expelled for political reasons. More importantly COPACHI established an entire network of parish-based social programs to counter the regime's political and economic strategy of individualization. With unemployment soaring due to the regime's neoliberal "shock treatment," COPACHI sponsored small groups in which the unemployed would pool resources,

---

[42] Eduardo Rojas, interview by author, August 2, 1993.

organize to meet their basic necessities, and work at alternative sources of income. The dismantling of the state health system was met by the establishment of health clinics. Cooperative soup kitchens were set up in the churches to give lunch to children. COPACHI also sponsored youth clubs, groups for relatives of political prisoners, cottage industries, counseling for alcoholics, and a range of other groups.[43]

Social organizations at the base of society were illegal in the early years of the regime. Since a regime claiming to be the savior of Christian civilization could not directly attack the church, the only alternative social space to remain open, precariously at that, was under the church's protection. When General Pinochet forced the closing of COPACHI, therefore, Cardinal Silva constructed its successor as a Vicariate of the Catholic church itself. After its founding in the beginning of 1976, the Vicaría quickly established offices in every diocese in the country. In the first five years of its existence, it provided services to 900,000 people. On average, each year one out of every sixty Chileans was directly involved with the Vicaría. In Santiago, it was one out of twenty-three.[44]

The Vicaría grew into a large network of organizations, whose functions can be categorized as legal, informational, and social. A battery of lawyers provided legal aid to victims of repression. Thousands of writs of habeas corpus were filed with the courts. All but a handful were rejected, but the Vicaría's files became an invaluable source of information on the abuses of the regime. This served the Vicaría's informational purpose by supplying data and stories for the organization's publications in Chile and abroad denouncing the regime's abuses. These publications, especially the biweekly *Solidaridad*, were often the only source of alternative information in a media landscape entirely dominated by regime functionaries and supporters.[45]

The largest part of the Vicaría's work was dedicated to the network of social

[43] *Vicaría de la Solidaridad: historia de su trabajo social* (Santiago: Ediciones Paulinas, 1991), 30–40; and Brian Smith, "Chile: Deepening the Allegiance of Working-Class Sectors to the Church in the 1970s," in *Religion and Political Conflict in Latin America*, ed. Daniel H. Levine (Chapel Hill, NC: University of North Carolina Press, 1986), 163–5.

[44] Smith, "Chile: Deepening the Allegiance of Working-Class Sectors to the Church in the 1970s," 165.

[45] Hugo Fruhling, "Resistance to Fear in Chile: The Experience of the Vicaría de la Solidaridad," in *Fear at the Edge: State Terror and Resistance in Latin America*, ed. Juan E. Corradi, Patricia Weiss Fagen, and Manuel Antonio Garretón (Berkeley: University of California Press, 1992), 126–7.

groups which it organized under the church's protection. Health clinics located in parishes employed doctors blacklisted from the health system for political reasons, and trained poor people as basic health workers. Nutritional needs were addressed by parish soup kitchens which, from 1982 onward, were located in people's homes, signifying a greater emphasis on self-help and cooperation.[46] Direct food aid was given to desperate families, but more emphasis was put on the vegetable garden project and *Comprando Juntos*, purchasing cooperatives to help the poor buy food more cheaply by buying in bulk as a community.[47] The Vicaría developed cooperative house-building projects.[48] Self-employment workshops continued under the Vicaría, and expanded in the early 1980s to include training in trades such as shoe repair and pipe fitting.[49] During this period women's groups under the auspices of the Vicaría took on a special significance. Women became aware of their own situation and began to take leadership roles in grassroots organizations. The Vicaría also sponsored sewing and handicraft workshops, and helped them sell their products. Through their famous *arpilleras*, scenes of life in the poor *poblaciones* sewn from odd bits of fabric, these groups of women became some of the most eloquent critics of the regime.[50]

The Vicaría sponsored many projects which were specifically educational: training for labor leaders, summer camps for youth, capacitation for leaders of neighborhood organizations and pastoral workers, and others. In fact, however, none of the Vicaría's programs was without an educational component. There people learned to name the abuses they suffered, and they learned that resistance meant "solidarity." The Vicaría provided education, technical assistance, and some funding for the projects, but the emphasis was always on creating dependence among the people, not on the Vicaría itself but on one another. *Solidaridad* was not only the name of the Vicariate: it was a key word among the poor and in church circles which captured the realization that the only way the regime's social control could be resisted was through cooperation and membership in one another. Asked to reflect on the word *solidaridad*, one participant in the Vicaría's programs says "That word before was unknown to me, besides being difficult to pronounce. . . . Thanks to the Church and due to the unjust system that we had to live

[46]   *Vicaría de la Solidaridad*, 87–8; and Isabel Donoso, interview by author, July 2, 1993.
[47]   Fruhling, "Resistance to Fear in Chile," 128; and Annual Report of the Vicaría de la Solidaridad, 1984.
[48]   *Vicaría de la Solidaridad*, 89.
[49]   Ibid., 111; and Isabel Donoso, interview by author, July 2, 1993.
[50]   *Vicaría de la Solidaridad*, 88.

through, many more of us learned to act with solidarity. The word became easier."[51]

An article entitled "Resistance to Fear in Chile: The Experience of the Vicaría de la Solidaridad" by Chilean social scientist Hugo Fruhling displays how the practices of solidarity were effective in combating the regime's machine of fear. Fruhling argues that the Vicaría resisted terror in Chile by opening social spaces where people could meet each other, learn the truth, and overcome the silence which engulfed them. In effect, these spaces were where the people replaced the voice of the regime with their own voice.[52] This analysis is echoed in the comments of the participants themselves: "Once we began to participate in the organizations, that immense fear and disorientation that we felt began to leave us."[53] Or again: "The space of the organization was like a second home that welcomed us with understanding and solidarity."[54]

The image of knitting recurs in literature on the Vicaría and interviews with its personnel. The church is said to have helped reknit the social fabric torn by the regime's strategy of atomization. The *arpilleras* of the women's groups are both products and reflections of the work of solidarity. The organizations help to "knit the people together."[55] As we saw in chapter 1, the strategy of torture and disappearance attacks all intermediary organizations between the individual and the state by isolating individuals from one another. The church in Chile resisted this strategy precisely by knitting people back together, connecting them as members of one another. The church thereby undertakes the fundamentally Eucharistic task described above as building up the true body of Christ, a counter-discipline to the discipline of the state. The practices of the Vicaría are best understood as based on an account of unity which is only found in the Eucharist.

The work of the Vicaría is Eucharistic because it is not just any body which the church realizes, but the body of Christ. Christ's true body is enacted here by the incarnation of the church in the bodies of the poor. The true body of Christ is the suffering body, the destitute body, the body which is tortured and sacrificed. The church is the body of Christ because it performs an *anamnesis* of Christ's sacrifice, suffering in its own flesh the afflictions taken on by Christ. In the church's communities of solidarity, the poor are fed by Christ but, insofar as they become Christ's body, they also become food for others. The

---

[51] Teresa Pavez, quoted in *Vicaría de la Solidaridad*, 124.
[52] Fruhling, "Resistance to Fear in Chile," 121–41.
[53] Aída, quoted in *Vicaría de la Solidaridad*, 39.
[54] Mónica Araya, quoted in *Vicaría de la Solidaridad*, 120.
[55] See *Vicaría de la Solidaridad*, 109–10, 120.

Eucharist reveals the true meaning of solidarity. It should come as no surprise that reception of the Eucharist increased dramatically among the poor during the military dictatorship.[56]

In the work of the Vicaría, we see the church breaking out of its confinement to an imagined realm of the purely "spiritual" and taking body in spaces from which it had been banished. The church becomes visible, obeying the Eucharistic demand that true unity be achieved, that people overcome alienation from each other and become reconciled, caring for each other, especially the weak, in community and solidarity. The church, as in the Eucharist, thus becomes a present foretaste of the future eschatological feast. The poor can wait no longer; the church must witness to the Kingdom in the present.

The church receives a foretaste of the fullness of the Kingdom in the Eucharist, but nevertheless, it remains a foretaste, and not the final fulfillment of the Kingdom. The Kingdom does not come in full, nor is the church meant simply to supplant earthly kingdoms and establish its own ecclesial state. Although some referred to the Vicaría as an "alternative state" or a "parallel state," the Vicaría was clearly never in a position actually to replace the bureaucratic organs of the state. This is true because of lack of resources, but more fundamentally because of the nature of the church as a body which exists liturgically, in its performance of the Eucharist. That is, the Eucharist enacts a different kind of "politics."

The church should not simply attempt to reassert dominance over the state as in Christendom, nor try to reoccupy political space currently under the state's control, nor attempt some "sectarian withdrawal" to a space physically separate from the world. To take body does not indicate that the church is called to emerge from its confinement to the "spiritual" only to fill in public "temporal" spaces without redrawing the lines which supposedly separate these "planes." Just as Jesus called a community which is neither Praetorium nor Temple,[57] the Eucharist calls into question the very categories of "politics" and "religion," or "temporal" and "spiritual," which have been imposed on the church in the modern world, and which Christian ecclesiology has accepted all too easily. I have written of an alternative Christian "politics" only in an analogous sense; it is better to speak of alternative disciplines, imagina-

---

[56] See Bishop Bernardino Piñera, "La iglesia en Chile hoy," in *Documentos del episcopado: Chile 1974–1980*, 215; and "Jesucristo ayer, hoy, y mañana," *Documentos del episcopado: Chile 1974–1980*, 470.
[57] See Oliver O'Donovan, *The Desire of the Nations: Rediscovering the Roots of Political Theology* (Cambridge: Cambridge University Press, 1996), 92–3, 136–41.

tions, or performances, because the church is not called to present itself as yet another type of *polis*. *Ecclesia* is neither *polis* nor *oikos*, but an alternative which radically reconfigures the dichotomy between public and private used to domesticate the Gospel.[58] The problem is manifested in the use of exclusively spatial metaphors to describe both the "temporal plane" and the church. The creation of the temporal as an autonomous space was accompanied by the bureaucratization of the church in the later Middle Ages. Henceforth, the church became a present space, an institution, rather than a performance enacted liturgically in time. In other words, the church lost much of its sense of homelessness in the world, its sense, in Augustinian terms, of being the heavenly city on pilgrimage in time, a stranger in a world of violence, keeping in correspondence with its eternal home by means of the Eucharist.[59] The church has tended to adopt the rhythm of secular history, become opaque, this-worldly, and either to compete with the state for political space, or retreat into the space of the "spiritual."

Part of the solution to this modern dilemma may be, as John Milbank suggests, to envisage the church in temporal rather than spatial terms, according to the mode of gift. Because it is enacted liturgically, the church is a series of dramatic performances, and not a state of being. The church is not a constant presence, an identifiable site firmly bounded and policed by law. This is so because in the Eucharist we are always being assimilated into something else, namely Christ. The point of saying that the Eucharist makes the church is that the body of Christ is not a perduring institution which moves linearly through time, but must be constantly received anew in the Eucharistic action. Christ is not the possession of the church, but is always being given to the church, which in turn gives Christ away by letting others feed on its own body.[60]

And yet, if body it be, we must not too hastily give up the metaphor of space. If the church is not a political space in the world's sense, neither is it defined by mere absence, a no-space, a utopia or otherworldly or purely interior space. To concede "space" entirely risks giving ontological status to the territorial hegemony of the nation-state. The church then becomes at best

---

[58] See Reinhard Hütter, "The Church as Public: Dogma, Practice, and the Holy Spirit," *Pro Ecclesia* 3, no. 3 (Summer 1994), 334–61.
[59] See Frederick C. Bauerschmidt, "Walking in the Pilgrim City," *New Blackfriars* 77, no. 909 (Nov. 1996), 504–17.
[60] John Milbank, "Enclaves, or Where is the Church?" *New Blackfriars* 73, no. 861 (June 1992), 341–52.

just a protest against reality, a mere howling at the moon. If the Eucharist defines what is truly real for the church, then the church is more than a spasmodic event, a lightning bolt from a God who visits but does not transform. To deconstruct this dilemma of institution versus event, Zizioulas argues that in the Eucharist the church is both institution and event, since Christ instituted the Eucharist at the Last Supper as "the structure of the Kingdom," which would continue to gather the church out of dispersion into one body and thereby provide a framework for the life of the church through history. There is no Kingdom without communion centered on Christ surrounded by the apostles; the Eucharist therefore assumes a community gathered around those who stand as successors to the apostles. At the same time, however, this gathering is eschatological. The body of Christ is never guaranteed by the past or by any formal institution, but only comes epicletically, in the constantly renewed pleading of the faithful that the Holy Spirit enact the Kingdom in their midst. Historical continuity never determines the presence of Christ; the eschaton rules history, but is also enacted *in* history.[61]

The Eucharist is therefore an "event" in the sense of an eschatological performance in time which is not institutionally guaranteed, but it is an event which is ontologically determinative; as Zizioulas says, the Eucharist is "*the reality which makes it possible for us to exist at all.*"[62] But the Christian in the world is never able to hold onto that reality as something which can be kept. It is not adequately characterized as a "deposit," nor does it produce virtue as a "sediment" in the human soul. Paradoxically, it must be given away in order to be realized. On the other hand, the church is not therefore a merely transient reality. Summarizing Zizioulas, Paul McPartlan speaks of the "rhythmic stability" of the church in the Eucharist; the Eucharist is the "*beating* heart" of the church.[63] Day by day, week by week, the church is gathered around the Eucharist, but then disperses, only to be gathered again at the next Eucharist.

This is an inadequate characterization of the church if it is viewed two-dimensionally. The ecclesiological temptation is to assume implicitly a "distinction of planes" paradigm, and then debate whether the church is an institution occupying some permanent space on the temporal plane, or an event of the spiritual order which periodically breaks onto the temporal plane. The church then either carves out a temporal space it must police, or lives

---

[61] John Zizioulas, *Being as Communion* (Crestwood, NY: St Vladimir's Seminary Press, 1985), 204–8.

[62] John Zizioulas, quoted in Paul McPartlan, *The Eucharist Makes the Church: Henri de Lubac and John Zizioulas in Dialogue* (Edinburgh: T. & T. Clark, 1993), 270.

[63] McPartlan, *The Eucharist Makes the Church*, 270, 274.

u-topically between events of divine vandalism. Both conceptions assume the solid reality of the temporal plane and the regular march of time. As we have seen, however, the body of Christ in the Eucharist is multi-dimensional. It gathers the church of all times and all places. The church is not *a* social body, on analogy with the state, political party, corporation, or labor union; it is the true body of Christ, which exists simultaneously in heaven and on earth. This is not to say that it straddles the spiritual and the temporal planes; it denies the imagination of the spiritual and the temporal as two separate planes or two separate places. The body of Christ engulfs creation, contains past, present, and future. In the Eucharist heaven and earth are intermingled, and we are made fellow-citizens with the marytrs and saints of all times in heaven. The invisible church is only that church of heaven which is made visible in the Eucharist on earth.

The church, therefore, is not *polis*, but neither is it merely *oikos*. It has a place, but that place has its center of gravity in the church's eternal home toward which it remains on pilgrimage. It is a gathering, but is not therefore marked by a "fascist" binding – a homogeneous exclusion of otherness – precisely because the church must constantly receive itself as a gift of God who is Other in the Eucharist. The church is a body, but not just *a* social body, one of a genus of other social bodies which can be described and plotted sociologically. The church is the true body of Christ, a *sui generis* gathering which deconstructs the necessity of divisions between public and private, body and soul.

The church is Christ's true body insofar as it is a discipline, that is, a way of inscribing bodies into certain practices. It is not relegated to some ghostly interior realm of the soul as separable from bodily practices – gathering, feeding, judging, reconciling – which modernity ascribes to the realm of "politics" and the "temporal." Christ's *corpus verum* is not simply another state however, because its discipline is a preparation not for surveillance and dominance over a particular earthly territory but for martyrdom. The true body of Christ is wounded, marked by the cross. As the body of Christ, the church participates in the sacrifice of Christ, his bloody confrontation with the powers of this world. The church's discipline then is only the discipline of martyrdom, for Christ's body is only itself in its self-emptying. The church does not exist for its own sake; it is not predicated on its own perpetuation, as is the state. Its discipline is a constant dying to itself for the sake of others.

Participation in the programs of the Vicaría was therefore never contingent on ecclesiastical affiliation narrowly defined. Participants included non-Catholics and non-Christians. Certainly a significant percentage of those who sought the church's aid in cases of permanent disappearance were Marxists with no religious affiliation. The church must not act for its own aggrandizement, but for the reconciliation of the whole world, even those who do not yet acknowledge the Lordship of Christ. The church therefore remembers not only its own martyrs but also the many other victims of the antievangelical powers of the world. As Mt. 25:31-46 startlingly reveals, victims are members or potential members of Christ's body, but this is revealed only on the Last Day. That the body of Christ be made *visible* in history is for the sake, not of itself, but of all people, whether they explicitly acknowledge Christ or not. The church is the sacrament of salvation, the visible sign of Christ's redemption; the church offers itself as the visible body of Christ for the feeding and reconciliation of the world.

Fr Cristián Precht, head of the Vicaría for much of its existence, struggles to express the recognition that the church is a different kind of "politics" in the following passage:

> *the Church enters into the broad field of the political, but it does not act as a political party nor does it allow itself to be used by any party*: she does not attempt to conquer power, nor to make prevail a concrete model of society; she does not have a political program, nor does she use political methods. The Church *does not fight for a political project* – since it would escape her direct competence – *but rather to reaffirm an historical option in favor of the weakest and most marginalized people of the society.*[64]

Precht still has not completely overcome the construal of "the political" as a given space beyond the church's direct competence. Nevertheless, he recognizes that the "broadly political" practice of the church is identified precisely by its operation in the margins of "society." The actual programs of the Vicaría moved beyond the New Christendom ecclesiology to transgress the boundaries between the "political" and the "spiritual." They refused to recognize and legitimize the omnicompetence of the state over matters bodily. The church creates spaces of resistance where the Kingdom of God challenges the reality and inevitability of secular imaginations of space and time. "God chose what is low and despised in the world, things that are not, to reduce to nothing things that are" (I Cor. 1:28).

Because the church lives from the future, it is a thing that is not. The church inhabits a space and time which is never guaranteed by coercion or institutional weight, but must be constantly asked for, as gift of the Holy Spirit. The Eucharist is the imagination of the church, but it is not our imagination in the sense that Christians build the church. The Eucharist is God's imagination of

---

[64] Cristián Precht Bañados, *El imperativo de la solidaridad: entre el dolor y la esperanza* (Santiago: Ediciones Paulinas, 1986), 40, italics in original.

the church; we participate in that imagination insofar as we are imagined by God, incorporated into the body of Christ through grace.

Those involved in COPACHI and the Vicaría often spoke of them as a "response to an emergency;"[65] we might consider this as a characterization of the church itself. This is perhaps what it means to say that the church does not occupy a fixed space; the church always has a responsive character. This is not to suggest that the Pinochet regime and the Vicaría were exceptions to the normal functioning of the state and church. If Walter Benjamin's thesis of history as "state of emergency" is correct, then the church is *always* located as a "response to an emergency" until the Lord comes again. Eschatology is always in tension with history. This is the church's story. It is not reactive in the sense that the church is defined and located by the state, or by other narratives external to its own. Opposition to the powers and principalities of the world is written into the very narrative of the death and resurrection of Jesus Christ which is commemorated in the Eucharist.

3 Mysterious Channels

On September 14, 1983, a group of seventy nuns, priests, and laypeople appeared suddenly in front of the CNI clandestine prison at 1470 Borgoño Street in Santiago and unfurled a banner: A MAN IS BEING TORTURED HERE. They blocked traffic, read a litany of regime abuses, handed out leaflets signed "Movement against Torture," and sang. It did not take long for the *Carabineros* to arrive; twenty-four of the group were arrested. They offered no resistance.[66] Less than two months later, two children of a construction worker named Sebastián Acevedo were taken by the CNI. After three days of desperately trying to learn their whereabouts, Sebastián Acevedo sat down at the foot of a cross in front of the Concepción cathedral, doused himself with gasoline, and set himself on fire. A passing priest gave him last rites and captured his words with a tape recorder: "I want the CNI to return my children. Lord, forgive them, and forgive me too for this sacrifice."[67] Upon hearing this account, the Movement against Torture took Sebastián Acevedo's name.[68]

---

[65] Ibid., 21–2, for example.
[66] Vidal, *El movimiento contra la tortura "Sebastián Acevedo"*, 1.
[67] Ibid., 160–7.
[68] There is some ambiguity in assigning Sebastián Acevedo's name to the movement, since Acevedo's death can be described as suicide, and there is a not inconsequential theological difference between suicide and participation in Christ's sacrifice. Acevedo

The Sebastián Acevedo Movement against Torture will be our third example of a practice of the church in Chile which displays what it means for the church to take body in opposition to the regime of torture. If it is true, as I argued in my first chapter, that torture is a kind of anti-liturgy in which the state manifests its power, then the Sebastián Acevedo Movement will help us to see what it means for the church to perform liturgically the body of Christ in opposition to the state's liturgy of torture. It will also help illustrate what it means for the church to create spaces of resistance that disrupt the regime's surveillance of the city.

Until the Movement began, public denunciation of torture had been carried on primarily at the level of words and in doomed judicial proceedings. What was so different and disruptive about the Sebastián Acevedo Movement was its sense of liturgy; Roberto Bolton and José Aldunate use the term *liturgias* to refer to these public ritual acts of solidarity and denunciation that members would perform with their bodies.[69] Locations were chosen for their symbolic importance: places of torture, the courts, government buildings, media headquarters. Exactly at a prearranged time, members of the Movement – sometimes as many as 150 – would appear out of the crowds, unfurl banners and pass out leaflets, often blocking traffic. The actions would include songs and reciting together a litany such as this one:

They arrest Juan Antonio Aguirre	– and the justice system is silent
They lock him up in Precinct 26	– and the justice system is silent
They torture him	– and the justice system is silent
They make him disappear	– and the justice system is silent
His mother requests habeas corpus	– and the justice system is silent
The Vicaría requests an investigator	– and the justice system is silent
Ten days pass	– and the justice system is silent
Twenty days pass	– and the justice system is silent
Thirty-five days pass	– and the justice system is silent
The *Carabineros* say "we don't have him"	– and the justice system is silent
The Minister denies his arrest	– and the justice system is silent

---

himself apparently understood his act as a Christ-like sacrifice on behalf of his children. Traditionally, however, Christian martyrs do not die at their own hands, believing that their lives are not theirs to take. It can also be argued, on the other hand, that Acevedo did not exactly die "at his own hands;" in other words, his death was no more a "free choice" on his part than is the tortured person's "confession."

[69] Fr Roberto Bolton, interview by Sr Gay Redmond, CSJ, May 6, 1991, Santiago, tape recording, and Fr José Aldunate, SJ, interview by Sr Gay Redmond, CSJ, March 22, 1991, Santiago, tape recording.

Mendoza says "forget about it"	– and the justice system is silent
Jarpa says "disappearances are normal"	– and the justice system is silent
Torture is generalized	– and the justice system is silent
They torture in police buses	– and the justice system is silent
They torture in the poor areas	– and the justice system is silent
They torture in the police stations	– and the justice system is silent
All Chile is a land of torture	– and the justice system is silent[70]

Most of these actions were planned to last no more than five or ten minutes. Most times the police would descend upon them almost immediately; other times the group was able to finish and disperse quickly into the crowds again.

This type of street liturgy precisely reverses the anti-liturgy of torture in that it irrupts into and radically reconfigures the public places of the city which the regime has so carefully policed. New spaces are opened which resist the strategy of place which the regime has imposed. What Fr José Aldunate, one of the group's main spokespersons, calls a "new conception of society" (*nuevo proyecto de sociedad*) is thereby affirmed, and "this affirmation is attested by our presence. They can beat us or attack with water and gases, but there we are to anticipate this new society."[71] The future Kingdom of God is brought into the present to bring the world's time under the rule of Divine Providence, and thus create spaces of resistance where bodies belong to God, not the state.

Suddenly the silence and invisibility under which the torture apparatus operates are shattered, interrupting its power. In an astonishing ritual transformation, clandestine torture centers are revealed to the passersby for what they are, as if a veil covering the building were abruptly taken away. The complicity of other sectors of the government and society is laid bare for all to see. The entire torture system suddenly appears on a city street. Techniques of torture are detailed, places of torture identified, names of victims and names of those responsible – including sometimes the names of the immediate torturers themselves – are made publicly known. Victims are thus transformed into martyrs, as their names are spoken as a public witness against the powers of death. The spell of fear cast by invisibility is broken, at least temporarily. As one of the participants put it, the dictatorship "maintains itself in power through fear. To have a group that's capable for a few minutes to stand out against it and be seen to be battered and bashed and still return next week is

---

[70] Ibid., 354–5. "Mendoza" refers to César Mendoza, head of the Carabineros and member of the Junta. "Jarpa" refers to Sergio Onofre Jarpa, Minister of the Interior.
[71] José Aldunate, SJ, "La acción que habla a las conciencias," in José Aldunate, SJ, et al., *La No Violencia Activa: presencia y desafíos* (Santiago: ILADES, 1988), 4.

a way of trying to diminish fear in other people."[72] The imagination of the state is supplanted by another imagination.

Most importantly, this dramatic visibility is not accomplished by mere denunciation in words and song. The repressive apparatus is made visible on the very bodies of the protesters as they are beaten, tear gassed, hosed down, and dragged away to prison. Members of the Sebastián Acevedo Movement use their bodies as ritual instruments. As in Paul and Cyprian, the body becomes the battleground between evangelical and antievangelical forces. As Hernán Vidal states, in the Movement "defenseless bodies use their weakness to punish and morally challenge those responsible for the terrorism of the State."[73] The ritual is designed to make the tortured body, which has been disappeared by the state, miraculously appear in the bodies of the protesters.

The Movement was born in the Vicariate of the Western Zone of the Santiago Archdiocese, but was not an officially Christian organization, and increasing numbers of nonbelievers joined after the first couple of years. The actions were open to anyone to participate, but for the Christian members of the group, the actions resonated with a certain Christian logic and symbolism.[74] In the literature and rituals of the Sebastián Acevedo Movement against Torture, there is a frequent identification of three terms: the redemptive suffering of Christ, the suffering of those being tortured, and the sufferings inflicted on members of the Movement. Members speak of the actions as "carrying Christ's cross";[75] Roberto Bolton says "for many of us, it was to do something for Jesus Christ who is tortured today in those who are tortured."[76] The Movement's "Act of Remembrance" for its second anniversary echoes these ideas:

> In the man humiliated and defeated by torture we discover the Servant of Yahweh, Jesus who is crucified today, the prophet who denounces the personal and social sin of his time and ours, the Son of God dead and resurrected, present in every action which transforms History.[77]

---

[72] Church worker, interview by Sr Gay Redmond, CSJ, May 2, 1991, Santiago, tape recording.

[73] Vidál, *El movimiento contra la tortura "Sebastián Acevedo*, 5.

[74] See ibid., 34, 51–52, 67, 337.

[75] Accountant, interview by Sr Gay Redmond, CSJ, March 7, 1991, Santiago, tape recording.

[76] Fr Roberto Bolton, interview by Sr Gay Redmond, CSJ, May 6, 1991, Santiago, tape recording.

[77] "Acto de recordación," in Vidál, *El movimiento contra la tortura "Sebastián Acevedo"*, 89.

Here we see clearly the simultaneity of past and future in the present which characterizes the Christian eschatological imagination of time. Jesus is as present in the tortured today as He was in Jerusalem 2000 years ago, and that presence effects the transformation of mere historical time into the Kingdom. This transformation is effected in the bodies of the members of the Movement during their actions. "And if to some extent we share the sufferings of the tortured, He who was tortured by Roman justice and nailed on the Cross accompanies us and we for our part accompany Him, because He identifies Himself with the tortured."[78] Torture plays on the incommunicability of pain to isolate the victim. Here, however, this isolation is overcome by the sharing of pain. "With symbolic gestures that expressed our desires, we were able to break the isolation of their incommunication, take their chained hands, embrace their broken bodies. We believe that there exist mysterious channels which can make the solidarity of friends reach those who languish in the deepest dungeons."[79] The strategy of isolation is resisted because members of Sebastián Acevedo and those who are being tortured are united in the tortured body of Christ. "Conditioned by the knowledge of those 'mysterious channels,' their bodies are transformed into powerful flesh for the sacrifice in which they lovingly commune [*comulgan*, receive the Eucharist] with those who suffer."[80] The members of Sebastián Acevedo become Eucharist by uniting their bodies in sacrifice with the body of Christ.

The Sebastián Acevedo Movement against Torture thus performs the three temporalizations of the Eucharist. The true body of Christ disrupts present historical time and opens a new space in opposition to the regime. The bodies of those disappeared reappear in the reappearance of the visible body of Christ. The performances of the Movement are both a remembering of the forsaken prisoners and a re-membering of them into Christ's body. Christ's body reappears precisely as a suffering body offered in sacrifice; Christ's body is made visible in its wounds. But this body is also marked with future glory, for Christ has suffered in order to triumph over suffering and defeat the powers of death. The space it creates is therefore a space crossed by the Kingdom of God. We witness a liturgical anticipation of the end of history and the resurrection of the body.

---

[78] Aldunate, "La acción que habla a las conciencias," 5.

[79] José Aldunate, SJ, "Por los cuerpos torturados . . . el movimiento 'Sebastián Acevedo'," cited in Vidal, *El movimiento contra la tortura "Sebastián Acevedo"*, 74.

[80] Vidal, *El movimiento contra la tortura "Sebastián Acevedo"*, 100.

4 Torture and Eucharist

Lawrence Thornton's novel *Imagining Argentina* centers around a man named Carlos Rueda, a director of children's theater, whose wife and daughter are disappeared under the military dictatorship. The regime could easily take him too, but his suffering is greater for his fruitless search for those he loves. In the course of sharing the anguish of other victims of the regime, Carlos is visited with a peculiar, miraculous gift. Carlos tells a boy whose father has been disappeared for several days that that very night a colonel will visit his father in his cell. The colonel will bring food and a carafe of wine, and tell his father, a university professor, that he must be more careful in what he says to his students. Two soldiers will come, allow him to shave, and release him. Even as Carlos tells the boy this story, he trembles at the fear that it is a cruel lie. But it isn't. It happens exactly as he says. And people begin to fill Carlos's garden every evening hoping to learn the fate of their husbands and daughters and grandchildren.

What is especially astonishing is that Carlos's gift is more than just the gift of seeing; his stories about people can actually alter reality. Men appear in the middle of the night to give back babies snatched with their mothers. Holes open in solid concrete walls, and tortured prisoners walk through to freedom. Carlos's imagination actually *finds* people who have been disappeared. He is only visited with visions as a gift, however, and sometimes what he sees is not good news. Sometimes his stories end in torture and death with no escape. He cannot control this imagination, for it is not his alone.

Confronted with evidence of the miraculous, Carlos's friends nevertheless remain skeptical, convinced that Carlos cannot confront tanks with stories, helicopters with mere imagination. They can only see the conflict in terms of fantasy versus reality. Carlos, on the other hand, rightly grasps that the contest is not between imagination and the real, but between two types of imagination, that of the generals and that of their opponents. The nightmare world of the torture and disappearance of bodies is inseparable from the generals' imagination of what Argentina and Argentines are. Carlos realizes that "he was being dreamed by [General] Guzmán and the others, that he had been living inside their imagination."[81]

A Ford Falcon driven by security agents drives slowly by. Carlos tells his friend Silvio what he thinks the men in the car see.

---

[81] Lawrence Thornton, *Imagining Argentina* (New York: Doubleday, 1987), 131.

They see sheep and terrorists because they imagine us that way. But look at the people, Silvio, that old woman, the man in shirt sleeves. They remember a time before the regime, but they do not take their imaginations beyond memory because hoping is too painful. So long as we accept what the men in the car imagine, we're finished. All I've been trying to tell you is that there are two Argentinas, Silvio, the regime's travesty of it, and the one we have in our hearts . . . We have to believe in the power of imagination because it is all we have, and ours is stronger than theirs.[82]

To refer to torture as the "imagination of the state" as I have done is obviously not to deny the reality of torture, but to call attention to the fact that torture is part of a drama of inscribing bodies to perform certain roles in the imaginative project which is the nation-state. Likewise, in *Imagining Argentina*, Carlos's imagination is manifested in real effects; escaping the imagination of the state means that bodies go free. The imagination is defined as nothing less than "the magnificent cause of being."[83]

Thornton's novel provides us with a glimpse of what it means to make the odd claim that the Eucharist is the key to Christian resistance to torture. To participate in the Eucharist is to live inside God's imagination. It is to be caught up into what is really real, the body of Christ. As human persons, body and soul, are incorporated into the performance of Christ's *corpus verum*, they resist the state's ability to define what is real through the mechanism of torture.

If torture is essentially an anti-liturgy, a drama in which the state realizes omnipotence on the bodies of others, then the Eucharist provides a direct and startling contrast, for in the Eucharist Christ sacrifices no other body but His own. Power is realized in self-sacrifice; Christians join in this sacrifice by uniting their own bodies to the sacrifice of Christ. Christians become a gift to be given away to others, as illustrated in the practices of the Vicaría and the Sebastián Acevedo Movement. In giving their bodies to Christ in the Eucharist, a confession is made, but it is not the voice of the state that is heard. The torturer extracts a confession of the unlimited power of the state. The Eucharist requires the confession that Jesus is Lord of all, and that the body belongs to Him.

The state counts on the inherent instability of the language of pain so that it may appropriate the suffering of those tortured for its own purposes, to lend legitimacy to its claims of power. Christian thought, too, implicitly recognizes the alienability of pain in theories of atonement, but here Jesus' pain is

---

[82] Ibid., 65.
[83] Ibid., 79.

appropriated by others to redeem, not increase, suffering. Jesus' suffering is redemptive for the entire world. His one unrepeatable sacrifice, His death by torture on the cross, serves to abolish other blood sacrifices once and for all. We do not find other bodies to torture and sacrifice, but only remember in the Eucharist the one sacrifice which takes away the world's pain.

The Christian economy of pain, therefore, overcomes the strict incommunicability of pain on which torture relies. Torture is so useful for isolating individuals in a society from one another in large part because of the inability of people to share pain. Pain is incommunicable beyond the limits of the body, and the sufferer must suffer alone. Christians, nevertheless, make the bizarre claim that pain *can* be shared, precisely because people can be knitted together into one body. The Sebastián Acevedo Movement relies on the "mysterious channels" of this body, its joints and ligaments, to assume the pain of the tortured. On a larger scale, the Vicaría frustrates the torture of the body politic by forming communities where sufferings and deprivations can be shared and overcome.

In constructing the body of Christ, the Eucharist overcomes not just spatial isolation but temporal isolation as well. Torture brings the victim's world down to the limits of the body, and also limits the victim's temporal horizons to the present. Past relationships and future hopes are eliminated from a sharply focused circle of fear and pain. This is true of both the individual victim and the tortured body politic. The world of the state expands to encompass and police reality itself, the space-time of the "temporal plane," while the "spiritual" is crowded into an interior space and a time absent from history. The eschatological dimension of the Eucharist, on the other hand, opens temporal horizons in both directions and connects them with the present. In the Eucharist the church keeps alive the subversive memory of Christ's past confrontation with, and triumph over, worldly power. At the same time, the Eucharist anticipates the future realization of a new society, the Kingdom of God, which will shatter the obdurate monuments of the mighty. Excommunication is a practice which anticipates this eschatological judgment by shedding light on the dark recesses of inhuman evil. The light of hope is thereby sustained in even the darkest hours of totalitarian power.

Above all, modern torture is predicated on invisibility, that is, the invisibility of the secret police apparatus and the disappearance of bodies such as the church which would counter the state's power. Excommunication and the street liturgies of the Sebastián Acevedo Movement expose the torture system to the light of day. These practices and those of the Vicaría help make the true body of Christ visible. They resist the disappearance of the church into the interior "soul" of the individual.

The disappearance of the church is the corrollary of the disappearance of individuals off the streets of the nation. The state's project is to create victims only and not martyrs, for power of this kind shrinks from the light. The state's sacrifices take place in the secret catacombs of the regime; torture is the state's *disciplina arcani*. The Eucharist, meanwhile, creates martyrs out of victims by calling the church to acts of self-sacrifice and remembrance, honoring in Jesus' sacrifice the countless witnesses to the conflict between the powers of life and the powers of death. The true "discipline of the secret" calls Christians to become the true body of Christ, and to bring to light the suffering of others by making that suffering visible in their own bodies.

Christianity itself is founded on a disappearance. The tomb is empty, the body is gone. At Emmaus (Lk. 24:13-35) Jesus blesses bread, breaks it, and gives it to His companions, but then vanishes from their sight. And yet the disappearance is not the last word. In the very act Jesus assures His followers that they will have His body, a body which the powers of death cannot bury or erase. When they hear the Emmaus story, the disciples cease to mourn, for they now recognize that they will always know Jesus in the breaking of the bread.

INDEX